FOUNDATIONS OF PHYSICALLY BASED MODELING AND ANIMATION

T0266621

FOUNDATIONS OF PHYSICALLY BASED MODELING AND ANIMATION

DONALD H. HOUSE

Clemson University
School of Computing
Clemson, South Carolina, U.S.A.

JOHN C. KEYSER

Texas A&M University
Department of Computer Science and Engineering
College Station, Texas, U.S.A.

CRC Press
Taylor & Francis Group
Boca Raton London New York

CRC Press is an imprint of the
Taylor & Francis Group, an **informa** business

The ball and blocks cover image is courtesy of Alex Beatty.

CRC Press
Taylor & Francis Group
6000 Broken Sound Parkway NW, Suite 300
Boca Raton, FL 33487-2742

First issued in paperback 2020

© 2017 by Taylor & Francis Group, LLC
CRC Press is an imprint of Taylor & Francis Group, an Informa business

No claim to original U.S. Government works

ISBN-13: 978-1-4822-3460-2 (hbk)
ISBN-13: 978-0-367-65820-5 (pbk)

Library of Congress Cataloging-in-Publication Data

Names: House, Donald, 1945- author. | Keyser, John C., 1972- author.
Title: Foundations of physically based modeling and animation / Donald H. House, and John C. Keyser.
Description: Boca Raton : Taylor & Francis, a CRC title, part of the Taylor & Francis imprint, a member of the Taylor & Francis Group, the academic division of T&F Informa, plc, [2017]
Identifiers: LCCN 2016039625 | ISBN 9781482234602 (acid-free paper)
Subjects: LCSH: Computer animation. | Physics in art.
Classification: LCC TR897.7 .H68 2017 | DDC 777/.7--dc23
LC record available at https://lccn.loc.gov/2016039625

Visit the Taylor & Francis Web site at
http://www.taylorandfrancis.com

and the CRC Press Web site at
http://www.crcpress.com

In memory of my father
Henry Allen House
—Donald H. House

For my family
—John C. Keyser

Contents

SECTION III **Rigid Bodies and Constrained Dynamics**

List of Figures

List of Tables

Preface

T HE IDEA FOR THIS BOOK WAS BORN BACK IN 1994, when Donald House began teaching a course in Physically Based Modeling within the Visualization MS Program at Texas A&M University. He has taught a version of this course every year since then, including after moving to Clemson University in 2008. When Don left A&M, John Keyser took over the course there and has continued to this day. Although we have been teaching the course for 22 years, we have never had a textbook to support it. All of the color illustrations in the book come from student projects undertaken in this course. The students are credited in the figure captions.

The book covers the material that we teach in the course and much more. It is conceived as a broad introduction to the field of Physically Based Modeling and Animation, suitable as either a textbook or a reference for researchers entering the field. Our idea in choosing topics for the book was to provide a foundation from which it would be possible to implement code to support animation projects and to dive into the expanding research literature in the field. For students planning to use existing physical simulation toolkits to implement their own code, or professional tools such as the physics engines in the major animation packages, it provides much of the background needed to understand what is going on "under the hood."

Because we wanted the book to be relatively timeless, it is not written with any programming language or graphics API in mind. Therefore, while the book uses pseudo-code to document algorithms, it does not include sample code. In our courses, students work in C++ and use *OpenGL* as the graphics API. The choice of C++ with *OpenGL* is determined by performance considerations. But, with a performance hit, reasonable projects could be developed in *Java*, *C#*, or *Python*, combined with any reasonable graphics API, or either *Processing* or D3, which have their own built-in graphics.

The students who take our class have a variety of motivations, from pursuing research in this or related fields, to using animation for artistic purposes. Many of our students are preparing for careers as VFX artists in the film, animation, and game industries, where literally hundreds of our former students are employed. A number of them have gone on to become FX leads on major films, and VES award winners and nominees. Thus, our students come from backgrounds ranging across the spectrum, from engineering to fine art. What they do not share in training, they do share in interests and proclivity. Because of this expected audience, the course is not pitched solely at computer science and engineering students. It is assumed that students will have had at least two semesters of calculus so that they are familiar with the concepts of differentiation and integration, and they must also be competent programmers and have mastered the basics of graphics display.

To accommodate this diverse range of students, we weave the necessary introductory mathematical principles into the curriculum, with an emphasis on linear algebra. For the book, we decided to separate this material out into a set of six appendices. We chose this organization, so that this background material does not interrupt the main flow of the book. Instructors can weave this material back into their courses as needed for their student population. Some review of basic concepts, and brief explanations of more advanced mathematical concepts, are included inline with the chapters.

While the course that we teach is meant to be introductory, the book is also designed as an invitation to the field for those with a research orientation. To meet this need, we have chosen a number of more advanced topics for inclusion. This material is located throughout the book. Additional detail is provided on a number of topics including advanced numerical integration methods, methods for speeding up simulations, stability analysis, fluid simulation techniques, handling multiple contacts in rigid body simulations, constraint systems, and articulated dynamics. This material could form the basis for a second course, or simply be used for additional study.

Every book has its limitations, and ours does too. Most notably, it does not cover several important topics in physically based animation, including finite element modeling, signed distance fields, fluid surface simulation, and character animation. Finite elements are increasingly used in the simulation of deformable materials, fracture, and fluids. Signed distance fields have numerous uses, from capturing the evolving shape of a fluid surface, to providing an efficient mechanism for predicting collisions. It is often the case that only the fluid surface is of interest for a water scene. This is best handled with approaches such as height fields and waves, rather than the Navier-Stokes equations. And, bringing characters to life has always been the ultimate goal of animation. This continues to be true today in both games and film, as physically based animation is increasingly integrated with motion capture to produce highly realistic character motion. It is our hope that, if the book proves successful, these topics can be added by experts in these areas in a second edition or as an additional volume.

It is our plan to maintain a website to provide ongoing support for readers of the book. Initially, it will contain suggested exercises to go along with each chapter, demonstration software to augment explanations in the book, and support libraries such as matrix and vector routines. As we learn of errors or shortcomings in the book we will also provide an errata list. The website is hosted at http://www.cs.clemson.edu/savage/pba

For instructors planning a course, we would like to suggest three sample curricula, depending on the target audience.

Curriculum for Undergraduate Mid-Level Computer Science Students

This 15-week curriculum focuses on particle-based simulation. Possible projects could include a 3D bouncing ball, a particle system simulation, a flocking system, and spring-based deformable objects. If there is time, it is very motivating for the students to design their own project and execute it as a final assignment. We have found that requiring a proposal that includes some visual reference is important for success. The visual reference can be anything that shows the look that they are trying to achieve. For example, it could be original sketches or photos, or images, or animation from the web. We formally review and approve the proposals, along with any necessary modifications, and grade based on how successful the students were in achieving the goals of their proposals.

Day	Readings	Topics
1	Chapter 1	Introduction to the course
2	Chapter 2.1–6	Foundations of physical simulation
3	Appendix A	Vector mathematics
4	Chapter 2.7–8	3D motion with air resistance
5	Chapter 3.1–3	Collisions with an infinite plane
6	Appendix B	Matrices
7	Appendix C	Affine transformations
8	Chapter 3.4–5	Collisions with polygons
9	Appendix F, Chapter 3.6–7	Barycentric coordinates and collisions with triangles
10–13	Chapter 4	Particle systems
14–17	Chapter 5	Particle system choreography
18	Chapter 6.1–2	State vector representation
19	Appendix D	Coordinate system transforms
20–21	Chapter 6.3	Spatial data structures
22	Chapter 6.4	Astronomical simulation
23–24	Chapter 6.5	Flocking systems
25–26	Chapter 7.1, 7.3–5	Numerical integration
27–28	Chapter 8.1–2	Springy objects
29	Chapter 8.5	Springy collision detection and response
30	Chapter 8.6–7	Lattice deformers and cloth

Curriculum for Upper-Level Undergraduate or First-Year Graduate Students

This 15-week curriculum covers particle simulation in more detail and provides an introduction to rigid body simulation and fluid dynamics. This is similar to the version of the course that we have been teaching. In addition to the above projects, students could implement either a rigid body simulation including collision with an infinite plane or a 2D SPH fluid simulation. In our experience, finishing the course with a project of the student's own devising is very popular and elicits the very best work. We recommend the same proposal and grading guidelines outlined in the previous curriculum.

Day	Readings	Topics
1	Chapter 1	Introduction to the course
2	Chapter 2.1–6	Foundations of physical simulation
3	Appendix A	Vector mathematics
4	Chapter 2.7–8	3D motion with air resistance
5	Chapter 3.1–3	Collisions with an infinite plane
6	Appendix B, C	Matrices and affine transformations
7	Chapter 3.4–5	Collisions with polygons
8	Appendix F, Chapter 3.6–7	Barycentric coordinates and collisions with triangles
9, 10	Chapter 4	Particle systems
11, 12	Chapter 5	Particle system choreography
13	Chapter 6.1–2	State vector representation
14	Chapter 6.3–4	Spatial data structures and astronomical simulation
15	Chapter 6.5	Flocking systems
16	Chapter 7.1, 7.3–5	Numerical integration
17	Chapter 8.1–2	Springy objects
18	Appendix D	Coordinate system transforms
19	Chapter 8.5	Springy collision detection and response
20	Chapter 8.6–7	Lattice deformers and cloth
21	Chapter 9.1	Rigid body state
22	Chapter 9.2	Moment of inertia
23	Appendix E	Quaternions
24	Chapter 9.3–4	Rigid body state update and implementation
25	Chapter 10.1–2	Rigid body collision response
26	Chapter 11.1–2	Rigid body collision detection
27	Chapter 13.1–3	Mathematical foundations for fluid simulation
28	Chapter 14	Smoothed particle hydrodynamics
29	Chapter 15.1	Finite difference methods
30	Chapter 15.2	Semi Lagrangian method

Curriculum for Graduate Students with Background in Computer Graphics, Linear Algebra, and Differential Equations

This curriculum could conceivably cover the entire book, with an emphasis on the more advanced topics, including multiple rigid body collisions and contacts with friction, constrained systems, articulated dynamics, and a full treatment of fluid simulation. Going beyond the material in the book, instructors might consider covering one or more of the following topics using papers from the literature: advanced cloth models including self-intersection detection, signed distance fields, finite element methods, and character animation. Instead of attempting to recommend a sequence for this level of course, we would encourage instructors to develop a focus for the course content, design a series of two or three homework projects to establish foundations, and then let the students develop their own project designs and work on their implementations.

I

Foundations

CHAPTER 1

Introduction

1.1 WHAT IS PHYSICALLY BASED ANIMATION?

T HE TERMS *Physically Based Animation* or *Physically Based Modeling* are used interchangeably. Both imply the use of the principles of physics, usually classical mechanics, to model dynamically evolving phenomena and to capture these models in the form of simulation algorithms run on a computer. The goal is to produce a sequence of states of the system as it evolves in time, and to capture this sequence as a set of images that are played sequentially to depict the motion. An example is shown in Figure 1.1, showing a ball being tossed into a net and bouncing away into a second net.

The original meaning of the term *animation* is the "action of imparting life" [Harper, 2016]. In this book, we are attempting to assist the reader to bring to life the objects and actors that make up the denizens of virtual worlds. The methods that we will be emphasizing are those of the computer simulation of phenomena described by the mechanical models of classical physics.

In computer games, computer animation, and visual effects, the term *animation* usually refers to the artistic discipline engaged in by highly trained, skilled artists, known as *animators*. Animators are the actors of animated films, in that they provide the motion, emotion, and human subtlety to the characters that they are animating. An animator's primary task is to generate what is known as *primary animation*; which is the body motion, facial expressions, and subtle gestures that make a character come alive and express its personality.

On the other hand, physically based animation is used mainly to generate *secondary animation*; which typically includes non-character motion in a scene, often driven by the primary animation. Examples of secondary animation include the response of a character's hair and clothing to its motion, or non-character motion like flags blowing in the wind, water splashing in a pool, exploding fireworks, bouncing balls, or falling objects. In addition, secondary animation can include the animation of characters that are extras in a scene, like warriors in a battle scene, or schooling fish.

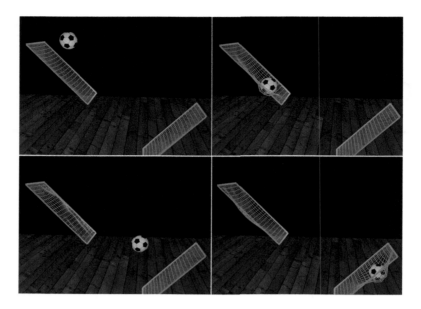

FIGURE 1.1 Four frames from a ball and net animation. (Courtesy of Himanshu Chaturvedi.)

1.2 DYNAMIC VERSUS DISCRETE EVENT SIMULATION

When we refer to *dynamic simulation* in this text, we are referring to the simulation of continuously evolving phenomena, as opposed to *discrete event simulation*. This latter form of simulation is often used in engineering or the business world to model events that happen in discrete units. Examples are physical inventories, the flow of work through an assembly line, or transactions in a financial system. In physically based animation, although we are capturing events in a scene in a set of discrete steps over time, we are always seeking to emulate the analog world, where these events actually evolve in a continuous fashion. An example might serve to delineate the differences. A simulation to analyze arrival times and departures of an elevator at the floors of a building would best be done as a discrete event simulation. There would be no need to incorporate any of the physical characteristics of the elevator. It would be sufficient to model its control mechanism, and to measure time between floors, door opening and closing times, and leveling time. On the other hand, if we wanted to follow the elevator in its travels, and monitor its motion and the movement of its parts this would best be done as a physically based dynamic simulation. This is the type of simulation that we are aiming at in this book, and would require knowing the elevator's mass, the torque produced by its motor, and many other physical characteristics governing its motion.

1.3 MATHEMATICAL NOTATION CONVENTIONS

The language of physics is mathematics, and physically based animation is no exception; the book uses mathematics as a primary language. Since we make extensive use of mathematical notation, we have adopted conventions that we have been careful to use throughout the book. These notational conventions are summarized by the examples shown here:

a lower case: scalar variables and parameters

ω greek letters: scalar variables and parameters

$\mathbf{v}$ bold lower case: vector variables

$\boldsymbol{\omega}$ bold greek letters: vector variables

$\hat{\mathbf{v}}$ bold lower case with hat: unit or direction vectors

M upper case: matrices

$\mathbf{J}$ bold upper case: Jacobian matrix

I or $\mathbf{1}$ upper case I or bold 1: identity matrix

All vectors are assumed to be column vectors. When a vector is expanded to show its terms, if presented as part of an equation on a separate line, we use the notation

$$\mathbf{v} = \begin{bmatrix} x \\ y \\ z \end{bmatrix}.$$

When an expanded vector is shown inline with the text, it will be written in transpose form as $\mathbf{v}^T = \begin{bmatrix} x & y & z \end{bmatrix}$.

1.4 TOOLKITS AND COMMERCIAL SOFTWARE

While the purpose of this book is to acquaint the reader with the underlying concepts of physical simulation as applied to animation, most production animation is done starting with software toolkits or commercial animation packages. The most popular APIs for use in computer games, at the writing of this book, are *Bullet, Havok,* and *PhysX.* The *Open Dynamics Engine (ODE)* is a highly accessible open-source toolkit that is used extensively in research and individual projects.

The animation package providing the most integrated and flexible support for physics simulation is *Houdini,* which has become the primary tool in the production of visual effects in animation and VFX houses. Besides this, all of the major animation packages have built-in physics support. These include the commercial packages *Maya* and *3D Studio Max,* as well as the popular open-source package *Blender.* Most of these also have available plug-ins to support all of the major physics APIs.

1.5 STRUCTURE OF THE BOOK

The book is divided into four main sections: Foundations, Particle-Based Models, Rigid Bodies and Constrained Dynamics, and Fluid Simulation. The chapters in each of these sections pertain closely to the section title, with the exception of Chapter 7, which covers numerical integration. There was no logical home for this chapter, so it is placed just after the study of large numbers of interacting objects, and the introduction of system state notation, and just before the study of deformable objects, which demands the use of accurate and stable integration techniques.

The book also includes appendices providing a foundation in the mathematical principles necessary to the study and understanding of physically based animation. These cover vectors, matrices, affine transformations, coordinate frames, quaternions, and barycentric coordinates.

CHAPTER 2

Simulation Foundations

2.1 MODELS AND SIMULATIONS

TWO KEY COMPONENTS ARE REQUIRED TO GENERATE a physically based animation: a *model* and a *simulation*. A model is a set of laws or rules governing how something behaves or operates, while a simulation is the encapsulation of the model in a framework allowing the prediction of the evolution of this behavior over time.

A physically based model is a model that defines the physics of how a system behaves: the rules governing motion of objects, behavior of the environment, interactions between objects, etc. Commonly, a physically based model is based on real-world behavior, the laws that govern how our world actually works. However, it is important to remember that even "real" models are almost always simplified. Effects that are considered minor are often ignored, and the model might describe large-scale behavior without every detail. For example, a car simulation does not need to track every atom, but instead will concentrate on describing the behavior of the large-scale components of the car.

Furthermore, for animation purposes, it is often desirable to define physics that do not necessarily conform to the physics of the real world. For example, *Wile E. Coyote* is famous for running off of a cliff, being suspended in the air for a moment until he realizes his situation, and then falling even faster than the real physics would dictate—he is kind of catching up with "lost" falling time! To capture behavior such as this, the animator has the opportunity to reinvent physical laws, building a cartoon physics to fit the effect that is desired [Hinckley, 1998].

A physically based simulation takes a physically based model and some initial conditions (such as a starting point and velocity), and tries to determine how the object being modeled behaves over time. There are a variety of simulation techniques, and choosing one involves examining trade-offs in accuracy, speed, robustness, and appropriateness to the particular model.

To illustrate the ideas of modeling and simulation, and the general simulation process, we will begin by walking through a simple example that everyone will be familiar with from real life: dropping a ball under the force of gravity. Later, we will extend that example to include the effects of air resistance and wind.

2.2   NEWTON'S LAWS OF MOTION

Before we actually define our physically based model for this example, let us first look at some fundamental laws that are the foundation for physically based simulation: Newton's Three Laws of Motion. Roughly stated, Newton's laws are as follows:

1. An object in motion will remain in motion, or an object at rest will remain at rest, unless acted upon by an outside force.

2. The force on an object is equal to its mass times its acceleration. This is often written $\mathbf{F} = m\mathbf{a}$.

3. When one object exerts a force on a second object, there is an equal and opposite force on the first object.

These three laws are critical to understanding how physically based simulations behave in practice. We will deal with the first two of these laws in this chapter, and we will see the third law in action later in the book.

The key concept embedded in the first law is that of *inertia*. Objects will continue to move at a fixed rate, and in a fixed direction, unless an external force is applied. How difficult it is to overcome the inertia of the object is determined by the object's mass. Related to inertia is *momentum*, which is the product of the object's mass and velocity, written $\mathbf{P} = m\mathbf{v}$.

The second law gives us the exact relationship between *force* and the rate of change of momentum, which we call *acceleration*. We will usually define a physically based model by determining a set of forces. From these forces we can determine acceleration by Newton's second law, written $\mathbf{a} = \frac{1}{m}\mathbf{F}$. From acceleration and an initial state, we can determine velocity and position.

Differentiation is the mathematical term defining the rate at which something is changing over time or space. In physically based animation, we are typically interested in the rate at which something is changing over time. Position $\mathbf{x}$, velocity $\mathbf{v}$, and acceleration $\mathbf{a}$ are all related to each other via differentiation, because velocity is defined to be the rate of change of position, and acceleration is defined to be the rate of change of velocity. Expressed mathematically, velocity is the time rate of change of position,

$$\mathbf{v} = \frac{d\mathbf{x}}{dt},$$

and acceleration is the time rate of change of velocity,

$$\mathbf{a} = \frac{d\mathbf{v}}{dt}.$$

Therefore, we see that acceleration is the second time derivative of position, which we write

$$\mathbf{a} = \frac{d(\frac{d\mathbf{x}}{dt})}{dt} = \frac{d^2\mathbf{x}}{dt^2}.$$

Throughout this book, a dot notation is used as a shorthand to indicate time derivatives. One dot over a variable indicates the first time derivative, and two dots indicates the second time derivative. Consequently, we would commonly write the derivative expressions relating position, velocity, and acceleration as

$$\mathbf{v} = \dot{\mathbf{x}}, \quad \mathbf{a} = \dot{\mathbf{v}}, \quad \text{and} \quad \mathbf{a} = \ddot{\mathbf{x}}.$$

Integration is the opposite of differentiation, in that an integral describes how small changes accumulate over time, resulting in a total change. Mathematically speaking, integration is the inverse of the differentiation operation. Looked at in this way, we see that if we begin with acceleration, we can integrate once to find the velocity, and then integrate velocity to find the position. This is one of the key ideas in the numerical simulation of physical systems—we start with accelerations, integrate these to find velocities, and integrate these to find positions.

Expressed mathematically, velocity is the time integral of acceleration,

$$\mathbf{v} = \int \mathbf{a} \, dt,$$

and position is the time integral of velocity,

$$\mathbf{x} = \int \mathbf{v} \, dt.$$

In a calculus course, you will have learned how to compute these integrals in a closed algebraic form if the expressions for $\mathbf{a}$ and $\mathbf{v}$ are simple. However, in the complex dynamic problems that we will encounter in simulation for animation, it will almost never be the case that we can solve these integrals using the principles of calculus. Instead, what we will do is to compute these integrals approximately, using numerical integration techniques. The approach will be to begin with a known position and velocity at a certain point in time, use these to compute the acceleration, and then numerically integrate to advance a short interval forward in time, giving a new position and velocity. This process is then repeated in a loop, advancing time from the start time to a desired ending time in a series of short timesteps.

To illustrate the process, let us look at the case when the acceleration $\mathbf{a}$ is constant. In this very simple case, we can actually find a closed algebraic solution to the problem, since the integration process is straightforward. We will assume that the initial position is $\mathbf{x}_0$ and initial velocity is $\mathbf{v}_0$. Then, integrating

$$\mathbf{v} = \int \mathbf{a} \, dt$$

once gives us

$$\mathbf{v} = \mathbf{a}t + \mathbf{v}_0. \tag{2.1}$$

Integrating this expression

$$\mathbf{x} = \int (\mathbf{a}t + \mathbf{v}_0) \, dt$$

gives us

$$\mathbf{x} = \frac{1}{2}\mathbf{a}t^2 + \mathbf{v}_0 t + \mathbf{x}_0. \tag{2.2}$$

Conceptually, if we are given the acceleration, a starting velocity $\mathbf{v}_0$, and starting position $\mathbf{x}_0$ we can find the velocity and the position at any future time t.

So, our general process will be as follows:

1. (Modeling) Define a model of the forces that govern behavior. By Newton's second law, these forces determine the accelerations.

2. (Provide Initial Conditions) Define initial starting positions and velocities.

3. (Simulation) Use integration to solve for positions and velocities over time.

The process can become much more complicated, with various twists to each of these steps. However, this basic outline can bring us a long way, including through most of what we will see in this book.

2.3   DROPPING A BALL IN 1D

We will now turn to the simple example we will use to illustrate this process: dropping a ball. To keep this example as simple as possible, we will assume that the only force we care about is gravity, so we will ignore air resistance. We will worry only about a single dimension (the height), and we will assume that the object is just a single point. Since we are working only in 1D, all of our values will be scalars, and we will take direction to be positive upward. Our first step is to define the model we will use.

We will assume we are dealing with an object near the ground. In this case gravity exerts an almost constant downward force, $F = -mg$, where g is the gravitational constant. In our simple example, this is the only force we care about. Since $F = ma$, we have $a = -g$, which we see is independent of the ball's mass.

The gravitational acceleration constant g is, of course, a well-studied "real-world" value known on Earth to be roughly 9.8 m/s^2 or 32 ft/s^2. The specific numerical value is not so important: we could be using a different distance measure than meters or feet, or be simulating gravity on another planet, or just wanting to describe an artificial simulation. For simulating a "real-world" situation, it is important to keep track of units correctly and use correct values for all constants. More than one expensive disaster has occurred when people have done this incorrectly!* However, for our illustration, and for many graphics animations, we are under no requirements to stick to "true" values for constants. To make things simple, then, we will let $g = 10$ units of distance per second squared.

Now that we have our (very simple) model $a = -10$, we need to define some initial conditions. Let us assume that we start at rest, so $v_0 = 0$, and at a height of 100 units, so $x_0 = 100$.

2.4   DIFFERENTIAL EQUATIONS OF MOTION

At this point, we have a model for the motion of our dropping ball along with initial conditions. Our goal is to find the position of the dropping ball at a series of time values, say $t = (0, 1, 2, 3, 4)$. You can think of these values as being the times when we want to know a position so that we can render a frame of an animation.

Because this is a really simple model, we can actually integrate using Equations 2.1 and 2.2 to get

$$\mathbf{v} = at + \mathbf{v}_0 = -10t + 0 = -10t, \quad \text{and}$$

$$\mathbf{x} = \frac{1}{2}at^2 + \mathbf{v}_0 t + \mathbf{x}_0 = \frac{1}{2}(-10)t^2 + 0t + 100 = 100 - 5t^2.$$

It is important to realize that *we do not normally have a nice closed-form algebraic solution like this!* Normally, we have expressions for multiple forces that are vector valued, and cannot be integrated to get closed-form expressions for $\mathbf{v}$ and $\mathbf{x}$ like we did here. In the next section we will learn how we integrate numerically when we do not have such a nice formulation.

In this case, though, we have an exact solution for our model, and can determine the velocity and position at each time value of interest. The table below gives these values at five timesteps, and the figure to the right shows how the ball's position changes from its starting position at the top to its position at 4 seconds, near the bottom.

	t	0	1	2	3	4
Exact	v	0	-10	-20	-30	-40
	x	100	95	80	55	20

Next, we will see how we can handle more general integration within the simulation loop.

---

*The most famous example is the 1999 Mars Climate Orbiter, which was destroyed when it came too close to the planet due to a mixup between metric units of force (Newtons) and English units of force (pounds).

2.5   A BASIC SIMULATION LOOP

In a more general problem, we will have an expression for forces that does not allow us to integrate to get closed-form solutions like those in Equations 2.1 and 2.2. Instead, we must integrate to find velocity and position using numerical techniques. There are a variety of numerical integration techniques, several of which we will encounter later, but for now we will introduce the most basic technique—*Euler integration.*

Numerical integration techniques all rely on the notion of a *timestep.* They work by starting with a given state at a particular time, and then computing the state one timestep into the future. Although the notation used in the physically based simulation literature can vary from publication to publication, the timestep is usually denoted by h, and we will follow that convention in this book.

First, we must understand what it is we are wanting to simulate. The *state* of a simulation refers to the values of the changing simulation parameters at an instant in time. In our simple example the state is just the velocity $\mathbf{v}$ and position $\mathbf{x}$ of the ball. We have an initial state ($\mathbf{v}_0$ and $\mathbf{x}_0$) at time $t = 0$, and we want to determine the state at the various time values $t = (1, 2, 3, 4)$.

Using this notion of state, the general simulation loop will take the following form:

> current-state = initial-state;
> $t = 0$;
> **while** $t < t_{max}$ **do**   // *note: here* current-state *is the state at time t*
>   Determine forces at current-state;
>   Determine accelerations by Newton's second law: $\mathbf{a} = \frac{1}{m}\mathbf{F}$;
>   new-state = Integration of accelerations over timestep h;
>   current-state = new-state;
> $t = t + h$;
> **end**

Notice that at the beginning of each loop iteration, the state and the current time t are in-sync.

For notation purposes, we will use a superscript in square brackets on a variable to indicate the loop iteration we are on, and we will use n to denote the "current" iteration. The value of a variable at the initial time will use a superscript [0], after one timestep it will be [1], etc. Notice that the superscript refers to the number of iterations, not the actual time. If the iteration number is n, the actual time is $t = nh$.

The simplest numerical integration technique is *Euler integration.* The basic assumption of Euler integration is that all values being integrated in the simulation stay constant during a timestep. Thus, if we know the acceleration at the beginning of a timestep, we can assume that it is constant throughout the timestep. Referring back to Equation 2.1, we can see that this means that the new velocity is just the old velocity increased by acceleration times time. Likewise, we assume velocity is constant over the course of the timestep, so the new position is found similarly. So, Euler integration to determine a velocity and position from the old velocity and position can be written

$$\mathbf{v}^{[n+1]} = \mathbf{v}^{[n]} + \mathbf{a}^{[n]}h,$$
$$\mathbf{x}^{[n+1]} = \mathbf{x}^{[n]} + \mathbf{v}^{[n]}h. \tag{2.3}$$

The simulation loop for Euler integration for our basic ball example will look as follows:

```
v[0] = 0; x[0] = 100;
t = 0; n = 0;
while t < t_max do
    a[n] = −10;
    if t is an output frame time then
        Output v[n], x[n];
    end
    v[n+1] = v[n] + a[n]h;
    x[n+1] = x[n] + v[n]h;
    n = n + 1; t = nh;
end
```

The **if** statement is used because it can be that not every simulation step needs to be output as an animation frame. Typically, a simulation will run for several iterations to cover the time taken by one frame. For example if we are producing 20 frames per second for display purposes, and our simulation timestep is $h = 0.005$ seconds, then we only want to output a frame every 10 iterations.

For this example, let us pick a timestep of $h = 1$, and output every new state. The resulting ball positions are shown in the figure, compared with those of the exact solution. The corresponding values are

		t	0	1	2	3	4
Exact	**v**		0	−10	−20	−30	−40
	x		100	95	80	55	20
Euler	**v**		0	−10	−20	−30	−40
$h=1$	**x**		100	100	90	70	40

Unfortunately, this is not giving us quite the correct solution. It is getting some of the general behavior—the velocity values match exactly, and the ball is dropping downward at an ever-increasing rate—but over the length of the simulation, the Euler solution is lagging behind the exact solution. The assumptions made in Euler integration give us a clue as to why this is happening. We are assuming that both acceleration and velocity remain constant over the timestep. While this is true for acceleration, it is not true for velocity, which is increasing continually as the ball falls. Thus, the integration of acceleration to determine velocity is exactly correct, but the integration of velocity to determine position always yields a result that is underestimated. In the next section, we will see some ways we might get better results.

2.6 NUMERICAL APPROXIMATION

Given that Euler integration was not as close to the correct answer as we would like, we want to think about some ways that we might get more accurate numerical approximations. We will briefly look at three possible options.

First, let us consider the step size. In our earlier example, we set $h = 1$—that is, that the step size was the same as the rate at which we wanted to know results. What if we took a smaller step size, say $h = 0.5$? In this case, we will take two simulation steps for every output value. The results are shown in the figure and in the table below.

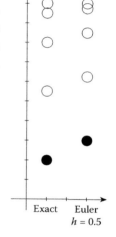

	t	0	0.5	1	1.5	2	2.5	3	3.5	4
Exact	v	0		−10		−20		−30		−40
	x	100		95		80		55		20
Euler	v	0		−10		−20		−30		−40
$h = 1$	x	100		100		90		70		40
Euler	v	0	−5	−10	−15	−20	−25	−30	−35	−40
$h = 0.5$	x	100	100	97.5	92.5	85	75	62.5	47.5	30

This approach has brought us quite a bit closer to the correct answer, however it also required twice as many simulation steps, and thus twice as much computation time. In fact, as we continue to shrink the step size (i.e., take more intermediate steps between each output time), we will get closer and closer to the correct solution. This approach works in general (the smaller the step size, the more accurate the integration) for any problem. If you recall from calculus the way derivatives and integrals are developed, they are usually expressed as a limit when some value goes to zero. By reducing the timestep to smaller and smaller values, we are in effect approaching that limit, making the integration more accurate. Reducing the timestep is usually the first approach to try when you are worried that your integration is not giving good enough results—shrink the step size and see if things improve. Reducing timesteps will get us closer and closer to the correct answer, but never quite there.

Besides decreasing the step size, we might consider whether a different integration scheme entirely could give better results. One thing that you might notice is that with Euler integration, no change in the position is seen until after a full timestep. This is because we are using the velocity value from the previous state, which will not change from 0 until after that full timestep. Instead, we could try using the value from the end of the timestep, so that we get a change immediately. Equations 2.3 become

$$\mathbf{v}^{[n+1]} = \mathbf{v}^{[n]} + \mathbf{a}^{[n]}h,$$
$$\mathbf{x}^{[n+1]} = \mathbf{x}^{[n]} + \mathbf{v}^{[n+1]}h.$$

(2.4)

Notice that we keep the same integration scheme for acceleration that we used previously to determine velocity. Trying to use
acceleration at the end of the time step would be more difficult
since that acceleration is not known until we first know the state
at the end of the timestep (a chicken-and-egg problem)! If we integrate using velocity at the end of the timestep, with the original
timestep $h = 1$, we get the following:

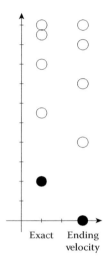

	t	0	1	2	3	4
Exact	v	0	−10	−20	−30	−40
	x	100	95	80	55	20
Euler	v	0	−10	−20	−30	−40
$h = 1$	x	100	100	90	70	40
Ending	v	0	−10	−20	−30	−40
velocity	x	100	90	70	40	0

Exact   Ending velocity

That gave us different results, but really no better than in our original Euler
example. Instead of undershooting on position we are now overshooting—moving
too far in one timestep.

As a third approach, let us try using the average of the Euler approach and the
ending value approach we just tried. Now, our equations are

$$\mathbf{v}^{[n+1]} = \mathbf{v}^{[n]} + \mathbf{a}^{[n]}h,$$
$$\mathbf{x}^{[n+1]} = \mathbf{x}^{[n]} + \frac{\mathbf{v}^{[n]} + \mathbf{v}^{[n+1]}}{2}h.$$

(2.5)

Using this average step approach gives us the following results
shown in the figure and table.

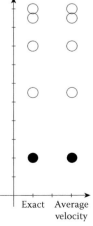

	t	0	1	2	3	4
Exact	v	0	−10	−20	−30	−40
	x	100	95	80	55	20
Euler	v	0	−10	−20	−30	−40
$h = 1$	x	100	100	90	70	40
Average	v	0	−10	−20	−30	−40
velocity	x	100	95	80	55	20

Exact   Average velocity

Now we are getting the same values as the exact calculation. In fact, this approach turns out to be an exact way to integrate a set of equations with constant acceleration. For a more general problem, it will give a better answer than simple Euler but it is also more complicated to compute. We will see more details and discuss why this is the case in Chapter 7. For now, though, the thing to notice is that by selecting a different integration technique, we actually achieved better results than we would have achieved with Euler, regardless of the step size.

2.7 3D MOTION IN AIR

For the example so far, we have illustrated a ball dropping under the force of gravity. Although all of this example and our illustrations were in just one dimension (height), the methods and equations used apply equally well when we extend our simulation to two or three dimensions. From this point forward, we will generally be describing our equations in 3D, recognizing that the simplification to 2D is usually straightforward.

2.7.1 Tracking Three Dimensions

We will still keep track of a position $\mathbf{x}$ and a velocity $\mathbf{v}$; however, each of these will be a 3D vector, rather than a single scalar value. Our gravity vector will be $\mathbf{g} = [0 \ -g \ 0]^T$ for some constant value g. Given this model, all of the equations described earlier apply exactly the same way. The height y of the ball will follow a path just as previously described. If the only force is from gravity, in the horizontal direction (x and z) there will be no change in velocity since the gravitational acceleration has no x or z component.

As a quick illustration, let us assume that the initial velocity is $\mathbf{v} = [10 \ 0 \ 30]^T$, the initial position is $\mathbf{x} = [0 \ 100 \ 0]^T$, and the gravitational constant $g = 10$. If we were to use simple Euler integration (with $h = 1$) as in Section 2.5, we would calculate the motion:

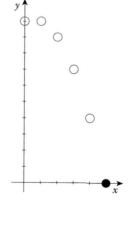

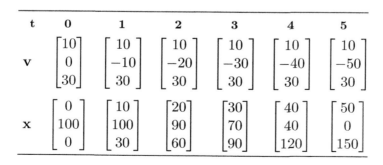

t	0	1	2	3	4	5
$\mathbf{v}$	$\begin{bmatrix} 10 \\ 0 \\ 30 \end{bmatrix}$	$\begin{bmatrix} 10 \\ -10 \\ 30 \end{bmatrix}$	$\begin{bmatrix} 10 \\ -20 \\ 30 \end{bmatrix}$	$\begin{bmatrix} 10 \\ -30 \\ 30 \end{bmatrix}$	$\begin{bmatrix} 10 \\ -40 \\ 30 \end{bmatrix}$	$\begin{bmatrix} 10 \\ -50 \\ 30 \end{bmatrix}$
$\mathbf{x}$	$\begin{bmatrix} 0 \\ 100 \\ 0 \end{bmatrix}$	$\begin{bmatrix} 10 \\ 100 \\ 30 \end{bmatrix}$	$\begin{bmatrix} 20 \\ 90 \\ 60 \end{bmatrix}$	$\begin{bmatrix} 30 \\ 70 \\ 90 \end{bmatrix}$	$\begin{bmatrix} 40 \\ 40 \\ 120 \end{bmatrix}$	$\begin{bmatrix} 50 \\ 0 \\ 150 \end{bmatrix}$

The figure, showing just the x and y components, illustrates the positions computed in the table. The motion of the ball follows a parabolic arc downward.

The object continues to move at a constant rate in the horizontal direction, while accelerating downward continuously.

Just like in Section 2.6, we could use different integration schemes and smaller timesteps to get more accurate results.

2.7.2   Air Resistance

We have a ball moving through the air under the force of gravity, however this is still not a very interesting simulation. Since gravitational force is proportional to mass, the acceleration is independent of mass, i.e. a feather will fall at the same rate as a bowling ball. To make our model more interesting, and to get the difference in behavior across different types of objects, we need to add another factor to our model: *air resistance.*

We will use a very simple model of air resistance here. Real air resistance is actually a very complicated physical effect, involving the linear and angular velocity of the object, the geometry and orientation of the object, and the properties of the fluid (i.e. air) that it is inside of. While an engineer designing an airplane needs to take all of this into account, for our purposes a very basic model will suffice and will help us illustrate how an animator might create forces to generate a desired effect.

Air resistance is a force that pushes against the ball opposite the direction of its motion. So, the direction of the force will be in the direction opposite current velocity, i.e., $-\hat{\mathbf{v}}$. Two factors contribute to its magnitude. First, the air resistance force will increase the faster we are going. So, as a first approximation, we will make it proportional to the magnitude of the velocity $\|\mathbf{v}\|$. As velocity doubles, the wind resistance will also double. We will also assume that there is a constant d that accounts for the overall factors (such as geometry) contributing to air resistance: for a sleek, slippery object, d would be small, while for a rough object that catches a lot of wind, d would be large. This user-tunable constant gives an animator more direct control over the amount of air resistance desired.

Our wind resistance force is thus $\mathbf{F}_{\text{air}} = -d\,\|\mathbf{v}\|\hat{\mathbf{v}} = -d\mathbf{v}$.[*] If we couple this with our gravitational force $\mathbf{F}_{\text{gravity}} = m\mathbf{g}$, we get:

$$\mathbf{F} = \mathbf{F}_{\text{gravity}} + \mathbf{F}_{\text{air}},$$
$$m\mathbf{a} = m\mathbf{g} - d\mathbf{v}, \quad \text{or}$$
$$\mathbf{a} = \mathbf{g} - \frac{d}{m}\mathbf{v}.$$

This acceleration accounts for both gravity and air resistance.

---

[*]Note that the notation here $d\mathbf{v}$, which is the product of constant d with the vector $\mathbf{v}$, should not be confused with the differential $d\mathbf{v}$.

Let us look at an example to see the effect. We will use the same conditions as the previous example, but now assuming that $d = 0.4$ and that $m = 1$. Thus, our equation for acceleration is $\mathbf{a} = [0\ -10\ 0]^T - 0.4\mathbf{v}$. Using a basic Euler simulation gives us the following results:

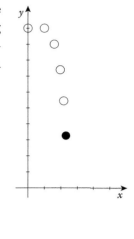

t	0	1	2	3	4	5
v	$\begin{bmatrix} 10 \\ 0 \\ 30 \end{bmatrix}$	$\begin{bmatrix} 6 \\ -10 \\ 18 \end{bmatrix}$	$\begin{bmatrix} 3.6 \\ -16 \\ 10.8 \end{bmatrix}$	$\begin{bmatrix} 2.2 \\ -19.6 \\ 6.5 \end{bmatrix}$	$\begin{bmatrix} 1.3 \\ -21.8 \\ 3.9 \end{bmatrix}$	$\begin{bmatrix} 0.8 \\ -23.1 \\ 2.3 \end{bmatrix}$
x	$\begin{bmatrix} 0 \\ 100 \\ 0 \end{bmatrix}$	$\begin{bmatrix} 10 \\ 100 \\ 30 \end{bmatrix}$	$\begin{bmatrix} 16 \\ 90 \\ 48 \end{bmatrix}$	$\begin{bmatrix} 19.6 \\ 74 \\ 58.8 \end{bmatrix}$	$\begin{bmatrix} 21.8 \\ 54.4 \\ 65.3 \end{bmatrix}$	$\begin{bmatrix} 23.1 \\ 32.6 \\ 69.2 \end{bmatrix}$

In this example, both the horizontal and the vertical motion are slowed considerably by the air resistance.

If the simulation were to continue, the x and z velocities would gradually approach 0, while the vertical velocity would approach a constant. Thus, accounting for air resistance has allowed us to simulate the idea of *terminal velocity*. Terminal velocity occurs when the force of air resistance exactly compensates for the force of gravity, meaning that an object no longer accelerates downward, but rather moves at a constant speed downward. Setting $\mathbf{a} = \mathbf{0}$ and solving for $\mathbf{v}$ in the equation above, it is easy to see that terminal velocity occurs when $\mathbf{v} = \frac{m}{d}\mathbf{g}$. In the above example, the terminal velocity in the y direction would be -25. We can see that even in the few timesteps we have in the table, we are getting close to that terminal velocity.

2.7.3 Wind

One final point should be noted about air resistance. In many animations, an animator is interested in applying forces to guide the simulation in a particular way, and one common way to do this is using "wind" forces. Figure 2.1 shows a frame from a falling leaves animation that was simulated using wind forces. The air resistance model we have described here does not distinguish what the source of the air pressing on the object is, and thus a wind force can be handled just like air resistance. In other words, wind blowing in some direction on a stationary object is the same as if the object were moving opposite that direction in still air. In either case, the force is acting to slow the object relative to that wind direction. The wind force, then, will be given by

$$\mathbf{F}_{\text{wind}} = d\,\mathbf{v}_{\text{wind}},$$

so the overall acceleration is

$$\mathbf{a} = \mathbf{g} + \frac{d}{m}(\mathbf{v}_{\text{wind}} - \mathbf{v}).$$

FIGURE 2.1   Falling leaves blown by the wind. (Courtesy of Lana Sun.)

The term $(\mathbf{v}_{\text{wind}} - \mathbf{v})$ in this equation is known as the relative velocity of the object with respect to the wind.

Building on the previous example, if we had a wind velocity of $[-12.5 \ 0 \ 0]^T$, our simulation would result in the following:

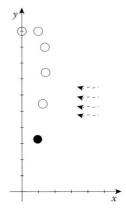

t	0	1	2	3	4	5
v	$\begin{bmatrix} 10 \\ 0 \\ 30 \end{bmatrix}$	$\begin{bmatrix} 1 \\ -10 \\ 18 \end{bmatrix}$	$\begin{bmatrix} -4.4 \\ -16 \\ 10.8 \end{bmatrix}$	$\begin{bmatrix} -7.6 \\ -19.6 \\ 6.5 \end{bmatrix}$	$\begin{bmatrix} -9.6 \\ -21.8 \\ 3.9 \end{bmatrix}$	$\begin{bmatrix} -10.8 \\ -23.1 \\ 2.3 \end{bmatrix}$
x	$\begin{bmatrix} 0 \\ 100 \\ 0 \end{bmatrix}$	$\begin{bmatrix} 10 \\ 100 \\ 30 \end{bmatrix}$	$\begin{bmatrix} 11 \\ 90 \\ 48 \end{bmatrix}$	$\begin{bmatrix} 6.6 \\ 74 \\ 58.8 \end{bmatrix}$	$\begin{bmatrix} -1.0 \\ 54.4 \\ 65.3 \end{bmatrix}$	$\begin{bmatrix} -10.6 \\ 32.6 \\ 69.2 \end{bmatrix}$

While the motion in y and z is the same as in the previous example, there is a wind force in the $-x$ direction, that overcomes the ball's original velocity in the $+x$ direction, and begins moving the ball backward.

Just as there was a vertical terminal velocity counteracting gravity, the constant wind force will cause there to be a horizontal terminal velocity, matching the horizontal wind speed of -12.5. Thus, if left to run indefinitely, the simulated ball would eventually approach a constant velocity of $[-12.5 \ -25 \ 0]^T$.

Figure 2.2 illustrates the three examples we have shown, side by side, so that it is easy to compare the effects.

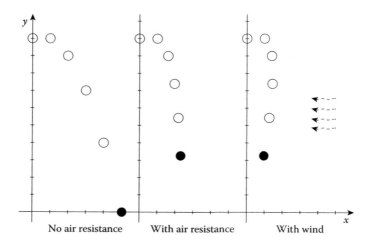

FIGURE 2.2 Ball drop showing the effects of air resistance and wind.

2.8 SUMMARY

Here is a brief review of some of the main concepts to take away from this chapter:

- The general process for simulation involves three stages: defining a model, establishing initial conditions, and simulating.

- Typical simulation involves computing forces based on the current state of the system.

- From these forces we obtain accelerations using Newton's second law written $\mathbf{a} = \frac{1}{m}\mathbf{F}$.

- We use these accelerations to project forward in time to update velocities and positions. This projection process is numerical integration.

- Euler integration (see Equation 2.3) provides a simple way to perform numerical integration.

- We can improve our integration results by reducing the timestep at the cost of increased simulation time, or by using a better integration technique.

- A simple gravitational model hides the effect of mass on acceleration, because the force due to gravity and the force needed to accelerate an object are both proportional to mass.

- Adding air resistance to the gravitational model brings the effect of mass back into play, and provides a convenient mechanism to build wind effects into a simulation.

CHAPTER 3

Follow the Bouncing Ball

I N CHAPTER 2 WE COVERED THE BASICS OF CREATING a model and a simulation based on that model. Specifically, we saw how a falling ball could be modeled and simulated, including the notions of gravity, 3D motion, and wind resistance. But, objects in the real world are not free to fall endlessly; at some point they end up colliding with other objects. A falling ball will eventually hit the ground, and bounce. Studying approaches to handling such collisions will bring us to the point where we are able to simulate a ball bouncing around in a box. We will then extend these ideas to handling the ball bouncing off of other objects in space.

3.1   COLLISIONS WITH PLANES

In order to improve our simulation of a ball moving in a real 3D environment, we first look at how to handle its collision with an infinite ground plane. Such a collision creates a "break" in the standard simulation process: when the ball collides with another object, it no longer follows a path governed by the general equations of motion as we described above. Rather, the simulation must account for the nearly instantaneous change in object motion due to the collision.

Real collisions involve very large forces that are applied over a very short period of time. Even when two "rigid" objects collide, they will deform slightly as they hit, before internal forces in the objects reverse this deformation to return them to their original shape. These restoration forces cause the objects to separate. The high-speed photo of a golf ball being hit is a good example of this. If we were to accurately model all of the internal forces involved and look at extremely small timesteps, we could potentially simulate the collision process in detail.

Image used by permission of
Acushnet Company, MA.

However, this process happens so quickly, relative to the time frame of the motion we are trying to capture in an animation, that the effect seems instantaneous: the object appears to hit and immediately "bounce" back without deforming. For this reason, in physically based animation, collisions between rigid objects are usually treated as instantaneous events, resulting in changes in velocities, rather than continuous processes involving deformation forces and accelerations.

Different models have been used for handling collisions, and the process becomes more involved once we are dealing with objects that can rotate. For our ball simulation example, though, we will keep things very simple. We will assume the ball does not rotate, so it is effectively just a point with a radius. A discussion of collisions involving rotation will be given in Section 10.1.

In terms of handling collisions, there are three distinct phases that we must deal with. While these phases are sometimes handled together, it is useful to realize that they are really distinct. Depending on the situation, different methods might be used for each phase, and they can occur at different points in the simulation. The phases are

1. *Collision Detection*: Did a collision occur or not?

2. *Collision Determination*: Exactly where and when did this collision occur?

3. *Collision Response*: What is the resulting effect of the collision?

We will describe initially how the first two phases, collision detection and collision determination, are handled when the collision is between the ball and an infinite plane. We will then describe how the simulation loop is affected by the need to deal with collisions. Later, in Section 3.2 we examine collision response, and in Section 3.3 we discuss implementation. Finally, in Section 3.5 we discuss how the handling of collisions differs if the collisions are with finite polygons, rather than infinite planes.

3.1.1 Collision Detection

Collision detection is the process of determining whether or not a collision occurs. In some situations, the detection process is the only thing one cares about, such as in a game where you want to determine if a shot hit a target or not. However, in most animation it is just the first phase of the collision process. If there is not a collision, then the later phases are not necessary.

We will begin with a simple 1D situation, and then extend it to an arbitrary infinite plane. Suppose that we have a moving ball whose center is at position y, and there is a barrier at position b. To begin with, let us not concern ourselves with the ball's radius, but just think of its center as a point moving in space. During our simulation process, we can determine easily which side of the barrier the center of the ball is on by examining the sign of $y - b$. If the sign is positive, then y is on one side, if it is negative it is on the other,

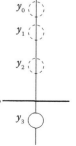

and if it is zero, it lies directly on the barrier. For now, let us assume that $y > b$, so the sign is positive, and that the rate of change of y is negative, so that the ball is moving toward the barrier. As we take each timestep, we can examine the sign of $y - b$. As long as the sign remains positive, there is not a collision. When the sign becomes negative it means that during the last timestep we moved from one side of the barrier to the other, and thus a collision occurred. In the figure, showing the position of the ball at several timesteps, we see it collided with the barrier sometime during the third timestep. In this case, we say that we have detected a collision, and the collision determination step will be used to determine exactly when and where the collision occurred.

Let us extend this to a 3D example, where we have an arbitrary plane serving as the barrier. Chances are that you first learned the plane equation as something like $Ax + By + Cz + D = 0$. When you plug a point $\mathbf{x} = (x, y, z)$ into the left side of this equation, if the value is 0 then the point lies on the plane. Otherwise, the sign of the 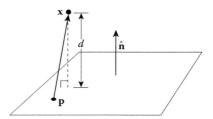 value will determine which side of the plane it lies on. However, it is more useful in collision detection and determination to represent the plane another way using a plane normal vector, and a point $\mathbf{p} = (p_x, p_y, p_z)$ that lies on the plane. The plane normal vector $\hat{\mathbf{n}} = [n_x \ n_y \ n_z]^T$ is a direction vector perpendicular to the plane and pointing away from the positive side of the plane. These can be used to construct a form of the plane equation as $n_x x + n_y y + n_z z - \hat{\mathbf{n}} \cdot \mathbf{p} = 0$, or more compactly

$$(\mathbf{x} - \mathbf{p}) \cdot \hat{\mathbf{n}} = 0.$$

The figure illustrates this idea graphically. Here $\mathbf{x}$ represents an arbitrary position in space that is to be tested. The difference $(\mathbf{x} - \mathbf{p})$ gives a vector from the given point on the plane to the test point. The dot product of this vector with the plane normal $\hat{\mathbf{n}}$ gives the length of its projection in the normal direction,

$$d = (\mathbf{x} - \mathbf{p}) \cdot \hat{\mathbf{n}}. \tag{3.1}$$

Thus, the magnitude of d is the distance of the point $\mathbf{x}$ away from the plane, and the sign of d is positive above the plane, zero on the plane, and negative below the plane. Our collision check for an arbitrary plane, then, becomes a matter of calculating d at each timestep, and determining whether the sign of d has changed since the previous timestep.

Now that we know how to detect the collision of the center of the ball with an arbitrary plane, we can extend our approach to handle a ball of non-zero radius r and determine the collision of the surface of the ball with the plane. Notice that if the surface of the ball is in contact with the plane, then the center of the ball is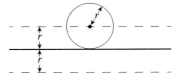

a distance r from the plane. Thus, we can check for a collision between a ball and a plane by checking for a collision between the center of the ball and a plane offset by r in the normal direction. To do this correctly, we need to know which side of the plane the ball is on. If the ball is on the positive side (i.e., the normal points toward the ball), then the check is $d = (\mathbf{x} - \mathbf{p}) \cdot \hat{\mathbf{n}} - r$, while if it is on the negative side of the plane, the check is $d = (\mathbf{x} - \mathbf{p}) \cdot \hat{\mathbf{n}} + r$.

3.1.2 Collision Determination

If we have detected that a collision occurs during a timestep, the next phase is to determine exactly when within the timestep and where in space that collision occurred. If we are using Euler integration in our simulation, we can do this by examining the position of the object before and after that timestep and linearly interpolating between those positions to find the collision point.

Recall that our calculation above gives us d, the distance from the surface. Let $d^{[n]}$ be the distance at the beginning of the timestep, and $d^{[n+1]}$ be the distance at the end. If we assume a constant velocity during the timestep (which is true for Euler integration), then time is directly proportional to the distance traveled, and

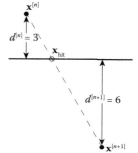

$$f = \frac{d^{[n]}}{d^{[n]} - d^{[n+1]}} \qquad (3.2)$$

will be the fraction of the timestep at which the collision occurred. Referring to the example in the figure, if we start out the timestep three units above the plane, and end six units below the plane, then $d^{[n]} = 3$, $d^{[n+1]} = -6$, and $f = \frac{1}{3}$, i.e., the collision will occur one third of the way through the timestep.

To find the exact point of collision, we must then reintegrate from the prior position, but by the fractional timestep fh instead of the full timestep h. When we do this, the position we find at the end should lie exactly on the plane. At this point, then, we have both the time $t_{\text{hit}} = t + fh$ and the position $\mathbf{x}_{\text{hit}}$ at which the collision occurred. From here, we should determine the collision response and then integrate for the remainder of the timestep.

3.1.3 Updating the Simulation Loop

Following collision determination, we must calculate the collision response. We will discuss that in more detail shortly, but for now we will just assume that we have some response, and describe how all of this affects the simulation loop.

In Section 2.5 we described the simulation loop that can be used to simulate an object undergoing continuous motion. Collisions, however, introduce discontinuities and thus "break" the standard simulation approach. To account for collisions, we must check for collisions, and if one has occurred, back up and take a fractional timestep to the collision time and position. We then handle the collision by making

h is the timestep, n is the step number, t is current time,
s *is the "working" state (position and velocity)*
s = **s**$_0$; *set initial position and velocity*
$n = 0$; $t = 0$;
while $t < t_{max}$ **do** *loop invariant:* **s** *is the state at time t*
    output state for step number n here

    TimestepRemaining = h;
    Timestep = TimestepRemaining; *try to simulate a full timestep*
    while TimestepRemaining > 0 **do**
        $\dot{\mathbf{s}}$ = GetDeriv(**s**); *determine accelerations*

        integrate from state **s** *using derivative* $\dot{\mathbf{s}}$ *for time* Timestep
        s$_{new}$ = Integrate(**s**, $\dot{\mathbf{s}}$, Timestep);

        if CollisionBetween(**s**, **s**$_{new}$) **then**
            calculate first collision and reintegrate
            Calculate f; *using Equation 3.2*
            Timestep = f Timestep;
            s$_{new}$ = Integrate(**s**, $\dot{\mathbf{s}}$, Timestep);

            s$_{new}$ = CollisionResponse(**s**$_{new}$);
        end
        TimestepRemaining = TimestepRemaining - Timestep;
        s = **s**$_{new}$;
    end
    $n = n + 1$; $t = nh$;
end

FIGURE 3.1 Simulation algorithm with collision handling.

any required changes to positions and velocities, and then continue the simulation for the remainder of the timestep. The updated simulation algorithm would be structured like that shown in Figure 3.1.

Let us look at what is going on in this algorithm. The key idea is that we have a timestep h that we would like to take, but because of collisions we might need to do this in pieces. The variable TimestepRemaining keeps track of how much time still needs to be simulated to get to the full timestep h. The variable Timestep determines how long we are going to simulate for when we perform integration. Initially, both TimestepRemaining and Timestep are set equal to h, and we integrate just as before. If there is no collision, then the overall process is just as in the earlier simulation loop. The **if** statement is skipped, and so the interior **while** loop is executed only once.

On the other hand, if there is a collision found, then we calculate at what point the collision occurred and re-integrate for that fraction of the timestep. That new integration puts our state at the point of collision. We can then apply collision response, which changes the new state. Since we have not simulated for the full timestep, we then update `TimestepRemaining` to determine how much longer we need to simulate to get a full timestep. Since it is possible that we may encounter a new collision in the remainder of the timestep, this process must be repeated until we have simulated the full original timestep h.

The figure shows one consideration that must be made in the collision detection process. It is quite possible that an object could pass through multiple planes in a single timestep. When this is the case, the collision detection algorithm must detect all possible collisions, and then select the one that occurs first. To do this, Equation 3.2 should be calculated for each potential collision. The collision with the smallest value of f is the one that would occur first and should be selected to be handled first.

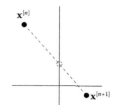

Since multiple collisions can occur within a single timestep, the interior **while** loop could be executed an arbitrary number of times. Although this will yield an accurate simulation, sometimes animators will prefer that a timestep take a fixed amount of time to compute. This is important for real-time graphics (such as games), or when synchronizing multiple simulation threads. In such cases, an animator will typically take some shortcuts to simulate key collision behavior, at the cost of accuracy. One approach for doing so will be discussed in Section 4.4.3.

One problem that will come up in a loop like this is when the `Timestep` is so small that its floating point representation rounds to 0. In that case the test `TimestepRemaining > 0` never becomes false, because `TimestepRemaining` does not decrease, leaving us stuck in an infinite loop. This can be solved by changing the test to `TimestepRemaining > ` ϵ, where ϵ is a small positive constant, typically several orders of magnitude smaller than the timestep. We discuss this and other numerical precision errors in more detail in Section 3.3.1.

3.2 COLLISION RESPONSE

Collision response is calculated once we have determined the time and location of the collision and is treated as an instantaneous change in the state of the particle. Keep in mind that our current motivating problem is a simple situation. We have a ball that does not rotate, and the infinite plane that it is colliding with is fixed. So, the only thing we need to determine in collision response is how the velocity of the ball changes as a result of the collision. The position of the ball is unchanged, and nothing else in the environment changes. Later, when we have two moving objects collide, we will need to consider momentum and how multiple objects respond.

We will break the collision response calculation into two parts: elasticity and friction. These will be calculated separately, and then combined in the end. We will designate our state just before the instantaneous collision with a superscript $-$, and the state just afterward with a superscript $+$. So, since the position of the ball does not change, $\mathbf{x}^- = \mathbf{x}^+$, and our goal is to find $\mathbf{v}^+$ given $\mathbf{v}^-$.

Elasticity will be an effect in the normal direction. Recall that $\hat{\mathbf{n}}$ is the normal of the plane the ball is colliding with. Because the ball is colliding with the plane, the velocity $\mathbf{v}^-$ of the ball must be moving toward the plane. The component of the velocity before the collision in the direction of the plane normal is

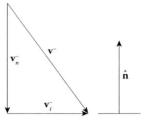

$$\mathbf{v}_n^- = (\mathbf{v}^- \cdot \hat{\mathbf{n}})\hat{\mathbf{n}}. \qquad (3.3)$$

Friction will be an effect in the tangential direction, with respect to the collision surface at the point of contact. If we remove the component of the velocity in the direction of the normal, we are left with the tangential velocity

$$\mathbf{v}_t^- = \mathbf{v}^- - \mathbf{v}_n^-. \qquad (3.4)$$

These two orthogonal velocity components are used separately to compute the elasticity and friction effects.

3.2.1 Elasticity

We will use the term elasticity to refer to the "bounce" of an object when it collides with another object. There is a more precise and formal definition of elasticity that describes how an object responds to strain when force is removed, but we will use a simpler model here that gives us the behavior we are looking for. Although we will use the term *elasticity*, our definition will be based on the idea of restitution, or how much of the energy is returned after the collision.

The elasticity calculation will assume that some fraction of this energy is returned as a part of the collision process, so that if the ball is moving toward the plane at some speed beforehand, it will move away from the plane with some fraction of that speed afterward. That fraction will be given by what is called the *coefficient of restitution* c_r. Thus, our new velocity in the plane normal direction after collision will simply be

$$\mathbf{v}_n^+ = -c_r \mathbf{v}_n^- = -c_r(\mathbf{v}^- \cdot \hat{\mathbf{n}})\hat{\mathbf{n}}. \qquad (3.5)$$

A c_r value of 1 represents a completely elastic collision where all of the energy of the ball in the normal direction is returned by sending the ball at the identical speed in the opposite direction. A ball dropped in the absence of air resistance would return to its same starting height. c_r values near 0 are highly inelastic collisions, where most of the momentum in the normal direction is lost in the collision, and a dropped ball will just barely move off of the floor. Values between 0 and 1 represent varying levels of inelasticity. Values below 0 would be completely unrealistic and would result in a collision response that moves the ball past the plane, instead of bouncing away. Those above 1 will result in more energy being added to the system via the collision. Though this is not at all realistic, it was the reason that "Flubber" was such a great invention in the 1961 movie *The Absent Minded Professor.*

In reality, c_r is a function of both of the objects involved in the collision, so a ball dropped on a rubber floor will behave differently than if dropped on a concrete floor. Further, factors such as temperature and humidity can affect its value. Values of c_r have been measured experimentally in a variety of circumstances. To give some examples, a baseball hitting a wood surface has a c_r value of a little over 0.5 [Kagan and Atkinson, 2004], a tennis ball dropped on a court should have a c_r between 0.73 and 0.76 [ITF Technical Centre, 2014], and a basketball dropped on a court is required to have a c_r between 0.82 and 0.88 [FIBA Central Board, 2014].

3.2.2   Friction

In addition to elasticity, the other factor to consider in collision response is friction. Friction is the resistance that occurs when objects rub against each other. For the ball collision response, friction should slow down the object's motion parallel to the plane. Again, a real model of this effect would be more complicated, and we would need to account for things like rotational motion of the ball, which we are ignoring in our simple example. We will instead describe two basic models for friction here.

Friction is a force that is applied in the tangential direction relative to the surface.

We will begin with a very simple model of friction. Assume that friction serves to slow the tangential motion of the object, proportional to its tangential velocity. The coefficient of proportionality, which we will call the *coefficient of friction* c_f, is a number from 0 to 1 giving the fraction of tangential speed lost during the collision. Therefore the relation between tangential velocity before and after collision is

$$\mathbf{v}_t^+ = (1 - c_f)\mathbf{v}_t^- = (1 - c_f)(\mathbf{v}^- - \mathbf{v}_n^-). \tag{3.6}$$

For a c_f value of 0, we have no friction, and thus the tangential velocity is unchanged. This can be thought of as a very slippery surface. For larger values of c_f, more and more tangential velocity is lost, corresponding to a rougher, surface. When c_f is 1, tangential velocity is completely wiped out.

Note that this is actually not a very realistic model of the physics involved in friction. However, it does capture the main idea of friction, i.e. slowing tangential motion, and is very simple to implement. Thus, it is a popular choice for providing friction during collision in animations, where true realism is less important. However, it is not that much more difficult to move to a more realistic friction model.

True friction is a function not just of the tangential velocity, but also of the force pressing the object into the surface. Imagine two objects with the same shape but different weights sliding along a rough surface. The heavier object will rather obviously encounter more frictional force. Since it also takes more force to slow a heavier object, the actual change in velocity due to friction might not vary between the two objects, but the amount of force will. This model is known as the *Coulomb model of friction*. The Coulomb friction model states that the frictional force in the tangential direction is proportional to the force in the normal direction, $\|\mathbf{F}_t\| = \mu\|\mathbf{F}_n\|$. The coefficient of friction μ is similar in effect to the c_f defined earlier, but since this is an actual measured quantity, we will use a different term.

Like the coefficient of restitution, the coefficient of friction is a function of both materials involved in the process. Values of μ can be looked up for various combinations of materials, and the value will vary depending on factors such as whether the material is wet. To give a sense of the range, something very smooth, such as teflon moving over teflon, will have a μ less than 0.05. Wood on wood will have a μ of between 0.25 and 0.5. Steel on steel will have a μ value between 0.5 and 0.8, and some combinations of metals, like silver on silver, will have μ values greater than 1.0 [The Engineering Toolbox, 2016].

During a collision, we assume that the force is applied for some (very very small) length of time. Integrating forces over time gives momentum, and thus we can model the frictional effect of a collision response by substituting momentum $m\mathbf{v}$ in place of force $m\mathbf{a}$. So, our change in tangential momentum is proportional to the momentum with which the object collides, in the normal direction of the surface. Since the momentum of the object prior to collision is $m\mathbf{v}_n^-$, that means that our frictional force should be proportional to $m\|\mathbf{v}_n^-\|$. Note that this frictional force, which is applied in the tangential direction, should never be higher than the force needed to halt tangential motion, though it can be just enough to halt tangential motion. To account for this, we will need to examine the change in tangential velocity due to the frictional force and ensure it is never greater in magnitude than the original tangential speed. Taking all this into account and dividing by mass to get the change in velocity, yields the new tangential velocity

$$\mathbf{v}_t^+ = \mathbf{v}_t^- - \min(\mu\|\mathbf{v}_n^-\|, \|\mathbf{v}_t^-\|)\hat{\mathbf{v}}_t^- . \tag{3.7}$$

Note that the min operation ensures that the tangential velocity is never reversed, but simply set to 0 if the friction is high enough. Although this model is clearly more realistic, in an animation context the difference in behavior between Equations 3.6 and 3.7 might not be noticeable, and an animator might choose to use the simpler model.

3.2.3 Putting It All Together

The figure shows the bounce velocity $\mathbf{v}^+$ after collision, that would result from our simple elasticity and friction models. This velocity is compared with the "mirror reflection" velocity $\mathbf{v}^m$, which would result without any energy loss due to elasticity or friction.

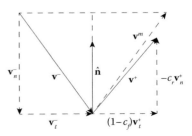

We can summarize the complete collision response process as follows:

1. Divide the velocity just before the collision $\mathbf{v}^-$ into normal and tangential components, $\mathbf{v}_n^-$ and $\mathbf{v}_t^-$, via Equations 3.3 and 3.4.

2. Compute the elasticity response $\mathbf{v}_n^+$ via Equation 3.5 and the friction response $\mathbf{v}_t^+$ via Equation 3.6 or 3.7.

3. Change the velocity of the object to the new velocity $\mathbf{v}^+ = \mathbf{v}_n^+ + \mathbf{v}_t^+$.

3.3   IMPLEMENTING A BOUNCING BALL

At this point, we have presented all the tools needed to implement a ball bouncing around inside of a box. We would strongly encourage the reader to try implementing such a simulation at this point. Once you have an implementation, it will quickly become apparent that there are some issues that make the simulation behave slightly differently than you might expect. There are two aspects of this that we will discuss in more detail here: numerical precision and resting conditions.

3.3.1   Numerical Precision

Most people are already familiar with the idea of floating-point round-off error. Round-off error comes from the fact that most numbers are represented in a binary floating point format, and thus cannot exactly represent most real numbers. Instead, the number we want to use is rounded off to the nearest number that the computer can represent. This is usually a very small change in the number but can play havoc with tests requiring exact precision. Round-off errors are one example from a class of issues known as numerical-precision problems or simply *numerical error*.

In simulations, numerical error can arise from a wide variety of sources. Round-off error occurs when we represent positions, vectors, matrices, etc., and the results of mathematical operations between them. Besides round-off error, there is integration error: the error that arises during integration. Integration error arises from the use of discrete timesteps instead of continuous time, coupled with an imprecise method of representing the motion within the timestep (e.g., assuming velocity is constant over a timestep). Yet another source of error is discretization of geometry, where a surface that is intended to be smooth is approximated closely by individual polygons, or a solid is approximated by voxels. Regardless of the source, the end result is that we should never assume that we have an "exact" numerical value within the simulation.

Even in the basic simulation we have already seen, there are several places where we may encounter numerical errors and associated problems:

- Calculating the distance from a plane (Equation 3.1) will have round-off error.

- This error can be further compounded when we calculate the fraction of a timestep f (Equation 3.2).

- The calculation of f also has numerical error from the assumption of the velocity being constant throughout the timestep. While this is true for Euler integration, it is not true for other integration techniques.

- Multiplying f times the timestep to get the time for simulation has two problems (see algorithm in Section 3.1.3):

  - The error from f further propagates to the timestep, making the estimate of the time of collision inaccurate.

  - The timestep could round to 0, or be so small that when subtracted from `TimestepRemaining`, there is no change. This effect, seen especially when the ball is nearly at rest, can potentially result in an infinite loop.

- Even if the timestep were represented exactly, integration error would mean that the position of the ball would not be calculated precisely.

- As a result, the position of the ball at the time of collision is very unlikely to be exactly on the surface. It could be a little bit above, or a little bit below.

Whether the ball is very slightly above, exactly on, or very slightly below the surface may seem like a minor issue, and often it will cause no problems. However, if the ball is miscalculated as being below the surface, this can cause significant problems at the next timestep, since any motion that would have occurred from the collision response will seem to be causing the ball to collide again with the plane from the "back" side. The result of this can be that the ball just passes through a wall of the box.

The above list illustrates how easily numerical error occurs and propagates in a very simple simulation. In a more complex simulation, the opportunities for and consequences of numerical error only grow. Dealing with the various issues of numerical precision is a full topic of study in its own right, with many papers and books on topics related to numerical analysis, robust computation, etc. As one deals with more complex issues in physically based simulation, the importance of dealing with numerical error issues grows, but for now we can describe a simple method for surviving most numerical errors: tolerances.

Tolerances: Tolerances are used to represent a "buffer" region for a numerical calculation. Anything within the buffer region is assumed to be identical to the thing the buffer is around. A typical tolerance will be a very small number, with the intention being that it is large enough to capture any numerical error, while being small enough that two things that are not the same will not be caught in the buffer region. Following convention, we will choose to represent tolerances with the designation ϵ (δ is another common choice). Anywhere that we want to use tolerances, instead of checking for equality, we will say that two numbers are equal if they are within ϵ of each other.

When implementing tolerances, it is often most efficient to compare two numbers by looking at the difference between them. Without tolerances, we might write a conditional check as $a = b$. Notice that this is equivalent to (and computer hardware often implements it as) $a - b = 0$. If we have tolerances, rather than writing $a > b - \epsilon$ AND $a < b + \epsilon$, we can just write $|a - b| < \epsilon$.

We must be careful in how we write our tolerance comparisons. For example, to check whether $a > b$, we must check whether $a - b > \epsilon$, and to check whether it $a < b$ we must check whether $a - b < -\epsilon$. The figure makes this visually apparent. Although this seems like a very simple idea, it is easy to make a sign error in tolerance comparisons, and we need to be careful to always account for equality whenever we compare two values.

Limitations with tolerances: Despite their usefulness, tolerances are not a universal solution, and it can be difficult to overcome all the numerical errors simply from the use of tolerances. There are two main ways that tolerances are limited.

First, it can be very difficult to set a "good" tolerance. As tolerances grow larger, more numerical errors are caught, but there is also the chance of incorrectly classifying things that should be different as the same. It can be impossible to find a tolerance value that catches all errors and causes no false equivalencies. Typically, when tolerances are implemented, there is some global constant tolerance defined, and this tolerance is used throughout the program to deal with all numerical errors. However, if it is even possible to get "good" tolerances, different tolerance values might be needed in different parts of the computation. While it is possible to do this, it can add significant complexity to the code that is developed.

A second problem with tolerances is what is called *incidence intransitivity*. Transitivity is the mathematical property of a relationship operator, demonstrated in the example that if $a = b$ and $b = c$, then $a = c$. It is easy to illustrate that transitivity does not necessarily hold when tolerances are being used. Imagine that we have three values, $A = 1.5$, $B = 1.7$, and $C = 2.0$, and a tolerance value of $\epsilon = 0.4$. We find that $A = B$ since $|1.5 - 1.7| < 0.4$, and likewise that $B = C$. But, it is not true that $A = C$, since $|1.5 - 2.0| > 0.4$, i.e., transitivity is violated. Often, algorithms are developed implicitly assuming transitivity, and as a result, tolerances can cause fundamental problems with algorithm behavior, leading to complete program failure. Avoiding this requires careful examination of all of the algorithms and assumptions in the program, to ensure that transitivity is not incorrectly assumed.

When numerical error becomes a big enough problem that tolerances are insufficient, a more systematic approach is needed. The first step is to closely examine all of the areas where numerical error is created and propagated in the simulation, and then identify which areas of the algorithm rely on numerical accuracy. Often

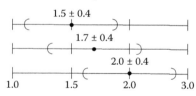

the conditionals in the algorithm (e.g., is the object above or below the plane?) are the most critical to get correct, since these are the points where a "wrong" decision has clear differing consequences. Once this is done, a developer can find ways to reduce or eliminate the numerical error in those critical locations. Better integration schemes, higher precision numbers, reformulation of equations or computations, exact computation predicates, different discretizations, and other techniques can all be useful alternatives for reducing the problems of numerical precision.

3.3.2 Resting Conditions

Assuming that collisions are not completely elastic, over the time of a simulation a bouncing ball should gradually bounce less and less. In reality, one would expect the ball to eventually come to a stop. However, if you examine our equations of motion, you will see that our model does not allow this to happen! Instead, the ball will keep bouncing with smaller and smaller velocity, losing energy with each bounce, but never actually coming to a stop. There are a few problems with this effect. First, we will run into numerical accuracy issues, as described above, as velocities become extremely small. Next, even if we manage to avoid numerical error problems, the ball will appear to jitter and vibrate as the simulation continues, rather than coming to rest, giving a very unrealistic look. Furthermore, we waste computing resources simulating these very small movements that are so small as to be inconsequential. While this might not matter for a single ball, when we want to simulate the behavior of large numbers of objects, this wasted computation can be a problem. Finally when we move to using a better integration technique than Euler integration, such as ones we will see in Chapter 7, the ball might repeatedly collide with the ground plane during a single timestep, making the timestep calculation last far too long.

For all these reasons, we would like to find a way to detect when the ball is very nearly at rest. If it is nearly at rest, we will just stop simulating it further and leave its position fixed until it encounters some new force. The question we face, then, is to detect when the ball is nearly at rest.

One obvious criterion for determining whether the ball is at rest is its velocity. If $\|\mathbf{v}\|$ is small enough, we can assume that the ball has "stopped" (at least temporarily), and this is clearly a necessary condition to be at rest. However, if the ball is at the top of a bounce, its instantaneous velocity at its maximum height will be zero, even though it is clearly not at rest. So, we must add another criterion: whether the ball is in contact with a plane. If we examine the collision distance d with a plane and find it is (nearly) zero, then it means that the ball not only has no velocity, but is also touching a plane. Again, while this is a necessary condition for our ball example, it is not sufficient. Imagine that the ball is bouncing right next to a vertical wall, or that it hits the high point of its bounce right as it comes into contact with the top of the box. In these cases, the ball has no velocity and is touching a wall, but the forces are going to move it away from the wall. So, we will need to consider the total force $\mathbf{F}$ acting on the object, and ensure that the force is toward the plane (i.e., that the dot product of acceleration $\mathbf{F}$ with the surface normal is negative).

While the above is usually sufficient for simulating a ball in a box, to get even more realistic results we would also have to ensure that the tangential forces on the object are insufficient to overcome static friction. That is, we need to make sure that we allow an object to slide down a slope if the force is sufficiently high, and do not consider an object at rest when it should be sliding. To do this, we would need to calculate the force on the object in the tangential direction, and compare that to the Coulomb friction discussed earlier. If we divide the force into normal and tangential components ($\mathbf{F}_n$ and $\mathbf{F}_t$), the frictional force $-\mu\|\mathbf{F}_n\|$ must be sufficient to overcome the tangential force $\mathbf{F}_t$ for the object to remain at rest.

The above conditions describe how to find that an object is totally at rest. Sometimes we want to determine when the object is not "bouncing" but may still be sliding, i.e., it is "resting" in the normal direction but might have tangential motion. In this case, we examine $\|\mathbf{v}_n\|$ rather than $\|\mathbf{v}\|$ as our first check, and ignore the friction check just described.

Note that for these comparisons, since we are very unlikely to have exact values, we will need to compare within tolerances, as we discussed in Section 3.3.1. Thus, our test for coming to rest is a four-part comparison:

1. is $\|\mathbf{v}\| < \epsilon_1$? If so, then

2. is $d < \epsilon_2$ for some plane? If so, then

3. is $\mathbf{F} \cdot \hat{\mathbf{n}} < \epsilon_3$? If so, then

4. is $\|\mathbf{F}_t\| < \mu\|\mathbf{F}_n\|$?

If so, then the object is at rest. Note that $\hat{\mathbf{n}}$ is the plane normal, we assume the object is on the positive side of the plane, and the total force on the object $\mathbf{F}$ is broken into a normal component $\mathbf{F}_n = (\hat{\mathbf{n}} \cdot \mathbf{F})\hat{\mathbf{n}}$ and a tangential component $\mathbf{F}_t = \mathbf{F} - \mathbf{F}_n$.

Even this computation is still quite simple: in complex simulations where multiple objects are stacked and piled on each other, computing whether or not an object is at rest involves analyzing all of the various forces to test for equilibrium. Doing this exactly for a large pile of objects has been shown to be computationally intractable (i.e., the problem is NP-complete). The various approximate methods used to handle this problem are beyond the scope of what we will discuss here, though we will discuss how forces can balance out for a rigid object in Chapter 9.

3.4 POLYGONAL GEOMETRY

Until this point, we have been considering just collisions with infinite planes. To make a more useful simulator, we will need to be able to detect collisions with finite geometric objects in a scene. In computer graphics systems, such geometric objects are typically represented by finite polygonal faces, and not infinite planes. Here we will first describe how geometry is commonly represented, and then (in Section 3.5) discuss how to perform collisions with this geometry.

A geometric object approximated by a set of polygons is called a *polygonal model.* The *polygons* in a polygonal model are specified by the 3D coordinates of their vertices, and a scheme for connecting these vertices to form edges and faces. For example, the cube to the right is specified by its eight vertices, $\mathbf{p}_0 \dots \mathbf{p}_7$, the 12 edges formed by adjacent vertices, and the six faces formed by the connected edges. With the vertex coordinates given, we see that the cube is centered at the origin, aligned so its sides are parallel to the x-y, y-z, and z-x planes, and each face is a 2×2 square.

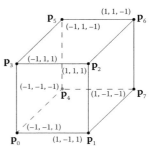

If we want to have a bouncing ball collide with and bounce off of a polygonal model, instead of an infinite plane, we need at least two things:

1. A way to detect the intersection of a moving point with the polygons of the geometry

2. A way to determine a surface normal at each intersection

We start the consideration of point-polygon intersection with the definition of a *simple polygon.* A simple polygon is an ordered set of vertices, all lying in a single plane, such that the edges connecting the vertices, taken in order, form a closed loop with no edges crossing. Some example simple polygons are shown to the right. These are all *convex polygons,* since the internal angles formed by connecting edges at each vertex are all less than $180°$.

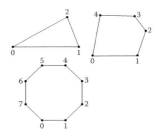

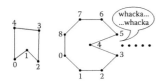

To the left are some more simple polygons. These are both *concave polygons,* since at least one pair of edges connect to form an internal angle greater than $180°$. Note, that even *Pac Man* is a polygon!

The star and diamond shown to the right are not simple polygons according to our definition. The star has crossing edges and the diamond consists of two disconnected loops, with one forming a hole in the other. We could expand our definition of a polygon to include these sorts of figures. In fact, they are often called *complex polygons.* We will not consider them further in this book, and from here will simply use the term *polygon* when referring to a *simple polygon.*

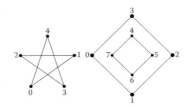

Finally, the quadrilateral to the right, formed from vertices 0–1–2–3, is not a polygon at all, since vertex 2 does not lie in the same plane as vertices 0, 1, and 3. This is a common occurrence when modeling complex shapes using quadrilaterals (or *quads* as modelers like to call them). Note that since triangles have only three vertices, they will always lie in a single plane, and thus a triangle will always be flat. For this reason, rendering systems will invariably preprocess the model by breaking each quad into two triangles. This is done by inserting an extra edge between diagonal corners, and is usually invisible to the user of the renderer. For example, in the figure, an edge could be inserted between vertex 0 and vertex 2 so that the quad is represented by two triangles: 0-1-2 and 0-2-3. The same trick should be used in physically based animation collision systems, to assure that point-plane collisions can be calculated easily.

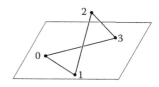

A plane is uniquely defined by a surface normal $\hat{\mathbf{n}}$ and a single point $\mathbf{p}$ lying in the plane. Because a polygon is planar by definition, we can determine the surface normal to its plane by taking the cross-product of any two nonparallel edges, and normalizing. For example,

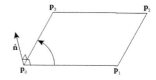

$$\hat{\mathbf{n}} = \frac{(\mathbf{p}_1 - \mathbf{p}_0) \times (\mathbf{p}_3 - \mathbf{p}_0)}{\|(\mathbf{p}_1 - \mathbf{p}_0) \times (\mathbf{p}_3 - \mathbf{p}_0)\|}.$$

And, we can choose any polygon vertex to complete the plane definition, e.g.,

$$\mathbf{p} = \mathbf{p}_0.$$

As we described in Section 3.1, the distance of any point $\mathbf{x}$ above the plane of the polygon is

$$d = (\mathbf{x} - \mathbf{p}) \cdot \hat{\mathbf{n}}, \tag{3.8}$$

and the set of all points lying on the plane must satisfy the plane equation

$$(\mathbf{x} - \mathbf{p}) \cdot \hat{\mathbf{n}} = 0. \tag{3.9}$$

3.5 POINT-POLYGON COLLISION

We can intersect a moving point with a polygon in three steps:

1. Find the plane equation for the polygon.

2. Perform collision detection and (if necessary) collision determination to find the intersection point $\mathbf{x}_{\text{hit}}$ between the particle and the plane.

3. Determine whether or not $\mathbf{x}_{\text{hit}}$ falls inside or outside of the polygon.

The first step was just described in Section 3.4. The process for collision detection and determination between a point (i.e., a particle) and a plane was discussed in Section 3.1. We will restate this in a slightly different form here, treating the motion of the particle during the timestep as a parametric equation based on time, t, and solving for the value of t where the particle hits the plane.

If we assume that the velocity of a particle remains constant during a timestep, to detect a particle-plane intersection, we replace $\mathbf{x}$ in the plane equation (Equation 3.9) by the current position of the particle $\mathbf{p}_i$, projected ahead in time t along the velocity vector $\mathbf{v}_i$, or $\mathbf{x} = \mathbf{p}_i + t\mathbf{v}_i$. We then solve for the time t_{hit} satisfying this equation:

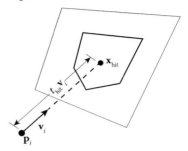

$$t_{\text{hit}} = \frac{(\mathbf{p} - \mathbf{p}_i) \cdot \hat{\mathbf{n}}}{\mathbf{v}_i \cdot \hat{\mathbf{n}}}.$$

If $0 \le t_{\text{hit}} < h$ then there is a collision at time t_{hit} during the timestep; otherwise the particle is either traveling away from the plane or will not collide until a time beyond the current timestep. Note that t_{hit} is exactly the same as f in Equation 3.2, just written in a different form.

If there is a collision during the timestep, it will occur at the position

$$\mathbf{x}_{\text{hit}} = \mathbf{p}_i + t_{\text{hit}}\mathbf{v}_i.$$

Determining if $\mathbf{x}_{\text{hit}}$ is inside or outside of the polygon will tell us if the collision is within the polygon.

Although the inside-outside test looks like a 3D problem, it is really planar, because all of the vertices of the polygon and $\mathbf{x}_{\text{hit}}$ lie in the same plane. Further, note that a simple orthographic projection onto one of the three 2D coordinate planes will not change the inside-outside relationship of $\mathbf{x}_{\text{hit}}$ to the polygon, unless the polygon is projected "edge on" into a single 2D line.

To avoid projecting the polygon into a line, we should choose to project the polygon onto the coordinate plane having the largest orthographic projection (image) of the polygon. The best coordinate plane can be determined by examining the surface normal $\hat{\mathbf{n}}$. The element of $\hat{\mathbf{n}}$ that has the largest magnitude determines the direction of the normal most perpendicular to the plane. Therefore, the projection should be as follows:

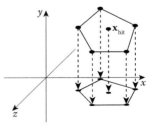

$|\hat{n}_x|$ **largest** project to y-z plane: $(x, y, z) \Longrightarrow (y, z)$.

$|\hat{n}_y|$ **largest** project to z-x plane: $(x, y, z) \Longrightarrow (z, x)$.

$|\hat{n}_z|$ **largest** project to x-y plane: $(x, y, z) \Longrightarrow (x, y)$.

Note that in all cases, after the projection, we relabel the coordinates (x, y), so that in 2D we are always working in the standard 2D (x, y) frame.

Here is an algorithm for making the inside-outside test that will work for any *convex* polygon.[*] The algorithm should be organized in a loop that can be exited as soon as a sign change is detected:

1. Make the problem 2D by projecting all points into a 2D coordinate plane.

2. Compute a 2D edge vector for each vertex, by subtracting this vertex from the next consecutive vertex.

3. Compute another 2D vector for each vertex by subtracting the vertex from $\mathbf{x}_{\text{hit}}$.

4. Form a 2×2 matrix for each vertex using its edge vector as the top row, and its vector toward $\mathbf{x}_{\text{hit}}$ as the bottom row.

5. Compute the determinant of the matrix for each vertex.

6. If the signs of all of the determinants are identical, then $\mathbf{x}_{\text{hit}}$ must lie inside the polygon.

This algorithm can be understood if we recognize that each of the determinants being calculated above are equivalent to the z components of the cross-product of the edge vectors (extended to 3D by setting $z = 0$) and the vectors toward $\mathbf{x}_{\text{hit}}$. For example, the edge from $\mathbf{p}_0$ to $\mathbf{p}_1$, together with $\mathbf{x}_{\text{hit}}$ gives the determinant

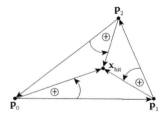

$$\begin{vmatrix} x_1 - x_0 & y_1 - y_0 \\ x_{\text{hit}} - x_0 & y_{\text{hit}} - y_0 \end{vmatrix} = (x_1 - x_0)(y_{\text{hit}} - y_0) - (y_1 - y_0)(x_{\text{hit}} - x_0).$$

Likewise, the cross-product between the vectors from $\mathbf{p}_0$ to $\mathbf{p}_1$, and from $\mathbf{p}_0$ to $\mathbf{x}_{\text{hit}}$, extended to 3D, gives the identical result:

$$\begin{bmatrix} x_1 - x_0 \\ y_1 - y_0 \\ 0 \end{bmatrix} \times \begin{bmatrix} x_{\text{hit}} - x_0 \\ y_{\text{hit}} - y_0 \\ 0 \end{bmatrix} = \begin{bmatrix} 0 \\ 0 \\ (x_1 - x_0)(y_{\text{hit}} - y_0) - (y_1 - y_0)(x_{\text{hit}} - x_0) \end{bmatrix}$$

As long as $\mathbf{x}_{\text{hit}}$ lies inside the triangle, these cross-products must all either point up out of the plane, or all point down into the plane.

---

[*]This algorithm will not work correctly for a concave polygon. This is rarely a problem, because in 3D graphics, geometry is almost always built from convex polygons.

Consider the triangle

$$\mathbf{p}_0 = (3,1,1), \quad \mathbf{p}_1 = (2,2,4), \quad \mathbf{p}_2 = (1,4,2), \quad \text{with } \mathbf{x}_{\text{hit}} = (1.9, 2.5, 2.3).$$

Without bothering to scale to a unit vector, the normal to the triangle is given by

$$\mathbf{n} = (\mathbf{p}_1 - \mathbf{p}_0) \times (\mathbf{p}_2 - \mathbf{p}_0) = (-8, -5, -1).$$

The largest component of $\mathbf{n}$ is the x component, so we project the y and z components to x and y in the 2D projective space, leaving

$$\mathbf{p}_0 = (1,1), \quad \mathbf{p}_1 = (2,4), \quad \mathbf{p}_2 = (4,2), \quad \text{with } \mathbf{x}_{\text{hit}} = (2.5, 2.3).$$

The edge vectors are

$$\mathbf{e}_0 = \begin{bmatrix} 1 \\ 3 \end{bmatrix}, \quad \mathbf{e}_1 = \begin{bmatrix} 2 \\ -2 \end{bmatrix}, \quad \mathbf{e}_2 = \begin{bmatrix} -3 \\ -1 \end{bmatrix}.$$

The vectors from the vertices to $\mathbf{x}_{\text{hit}}$ are

$$\mathbf{h}_0 = \begin{bmatrix} 1.5 \\ 1.3 \end{bmatrix}, \quad \mathbf{h}_1 = \begin{bmatrix} 0.5 \\ -1.7 \end{bmatrix}, \quad \mathbf{h}_2 = \begin{bmatrix} -1.5 \\ 0.3 \end{bmatrix}.$$

The matrices formed from the edge and hit vectors are

$$M_0 = \begin{bmatrix} 1 & 3 \\ 1.5 & 1.3 \end{bmatrix}, \quad M_1 = \begin{bmatrix} 2 & -2 \\ 0.5 & -1.7 \end{bmatrix}, \quad M_2 = \begin{bmatrix} -3 & -1 \\ -1.5 & 0.3 \end{bmatrix},$$

and the determinants of these matrices are

$$|M_0| = -3.2, \quad |M_1| = -2.4, \quad |M_2| = -2.4.$$

Since all of the determinants are negative, we conclude that $\mathbf{x}_{\text{hit}}$ is inside the triangle. This can be confirmed by a sketch.

FIGURE 3.2 Worked example of the particle polygon collision algorithm.

On the other hand, if the point lies outside of the triangle, it is impossible that all of the cross-products will point in the same direction, as illustrated in the above figure. Figure 3.2 shows a worked example of this method.

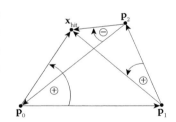

3.6 A SPECIAL CASE: TRIANGLE INTERSECTION

We noted earlier that a triangle is always planar. Further, it is true that a triangle is always a polygon, since its three ordered vertices always lie in a single plane, no edges can cross, and there can be no holes. This is why graphics systems will triangulate surface primitives, wherever possible, before doing rendering or other calculations requiring polygons.

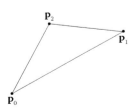

Triangles are especially handy for doing point-polygon collision tests, since we can compute the barycentric coordinates (u, v, w) of any point in the plane of a triangle using the algorithm described in Appendix F. Given a triangle, and the position $\mathbf{x}_{hit}$ in the plane of the triangle, we can use the barycentric coordinates u, v of $\mathbf{x}_{hit}$ to make the simple inside-outside test

$$u \geq 0, \quad v \geq 0, \quad u + v \leq 1.$$

If all three of these conditions hold, then $\mathbf{x}_{hit}$ is inside the triangle, otherwise it is outside.

3.7 SUMMARY

Here is a brief review of some of the main concepts to take away from this chapter:

- The process of handling collisions in a physically based system involves collision detection (Does a collision occur?), determination (When and where does it occur?), and response (How is velocity updated to account for the collision?).

- The simulation loop must be modified to account for collisions. The loop still iterates in discrete timesteps, but each timestep might be interrupted by a collision, and then continued. This can happen repeatedly, so the collision logic must account for the possibility that multiple collisions might occur during one timestep.

- The simplest collision detection task is checking for the collision of a moving point with an infinite plane, which requires checking which side of the plane a point is on at the beginning and end of a timestep.

- Collision determination between a moving point and an infinite plane is done by solving the implicit equation representing the plane, while representing the path of the moving point using time as a parameter.

- Collision response considers both restitution and friction between the colliding object and the plane. Restitution affects what fraction of the normal component of velocity is reflected, and friction affects how much the tangential component of velocity is reduced.

- The surfaces of geometric models are typically represented by finite polygons, and not infinite planes, so handling collisions with polygons is an important task.

- Collision handling of a moving point with a polygon, rather than an infinite plane, requires first performing detection and determination on the infinite plane that the polygon lies in, and then testing whether or not any potential collision point is actually inside the polygon.

II

Particle-Based Models

CHAPTER 4

Particle Systems

I N THE PREVIOUS CHAPTER we were concerned with the behavior of a single ball falling in gravity, being affected by wind, and bouncing off of planes. This allowed us to develop some key ideas related to physical simulation on a computer, including stepping forward through time in discrete timesteps, using numerical integration to convert accelerations to velocity updates and velocities to position updates, detecting and responding to sub-timestep phenomena like collisions, and visualizing an evolving simulation as a sequence of animation frames. In this chapter, we move on from the single ball problem to the problem of handling a *particle system*.

4.1 WHAT IS A PARTICLE SYSTEM?

A particle system typically consists of a massive collection of particles, generated from one or more locations in space, whose motion is determined by external forces. These forces can be environmental, like wind and gravity for realistic effects, or artificial, for more bizarre effects. Particles are usually able to detect and respond to collisions or otherwise interact with scene geometry. Particle systems are especially good for representing phenomena such as rain, snow, fire, smoke, dust, sandstorms, fireworks, splashes, and spray. Figure 4.1 shows a few examples. In his classic paper, *Particle systems—A technique for modeling a class of fuzzy objects*, Reeves [1983] refers to these as *amorphous phenomena*, because they lack a concrete geometric form and tend to spread over a region.

In the bouncing ball problem, we were dealing with a single ball of some radius, while in particle systems we attempt to deal with a very large number, typically hundreds of thousands or millions, of particles, but we allow the radii of these particles to go to 0, so that each one can be handled as a single point. We typically want these particles to interact with complex scene geometry, so instead of a single ball bouncing off of a few polygons, we might have millions of particles colliding with hundreds of thousands of polygons. Examples might be a waterfall cascading down over rocks, or snow falling over the roof of a house. Although we are dealing with a large number of particles, the particles do not interact with each other, so we can ignore such things as particle-particle collision. Simply creating particles and getting them to move is not interesting in itself, and would hardly lead to something

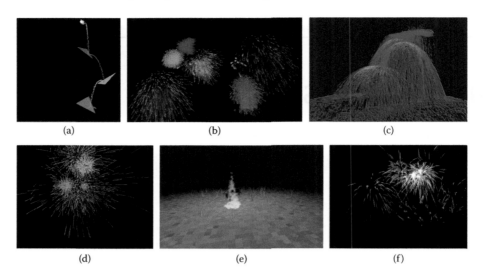

FIGURE 4.1 Example particle system effects. (a) Justin Kern, (b) Gowthaman Ilango, (c) Meng Zhu, (d) Heitan Yang, (e) Dan Lewis, and (f) Jon Barry.

that we would call a particle system. Particles become interesting when there is a coherence to their motion that gives the illusion that we are reproducing some type of point-sampled physical phenomenon.

The desired coherence of a particle system, and the ability to locate it in 3D space, is achieved by associating a *particle generator* with each particle system. This is a geometric object that can be placed in a scene, and is equipped with a procedure for creating and injecting particles into that scene. As each particle is generated, it receives an initial position and velocity from its particle generator, and is also given a set of parameters that affect its look, behavior, and duration. There are many options for the choice of particle generator, and these are normally adopted to match the desired particle effect. The examples shown in Figure 4.2

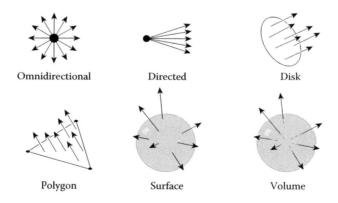

FIGURE 4.2 Some particle generator styles.

include a single point, from which particles are emitted in all directions; a point together with a direction vector that emits particles most strongly in one direction; a 2D surface, like a disk or a polygon, from which particles are emitted across the face of the surface with direction governed by the surface's normal; or a 3D volume that emits particles from its surface or from within the volume.

The data structure used to represent an individual particle needs to be tailored to suit the structure of the particular particle system. It will always contain the position and velocity of the particle. Besides position and velocity, a particle will also carry with it any number of other characteristics affecting its look and behavior. Examples of physical parameters that affect the particle's behavior are its mass, coefficient of restitution, coefficient of friction, and life span. Examples of parameters affecting its look are its color and opacity. In addition, when a particle is generated, it is normal to mark it with a time stamp, so that its age can be computed. Age is often used to vary the behavior of a particle or to update its parameters. An example of this might be a particle representing a spark from a fireworks explosion. When first created it is heavy and of a distinct bright color. As it ages, burning changes both its weight and its color, until it completely burns out, leaving just a light ash that floats to the ground. Finally, it is sometimes useful to store a particle history, which might contain the position of the particle over the past several timesteps, or the time of the most recent collision. Particle history is most often used during rendering to do things like provide information needed for motion blur, or adjust a particle's color based upon how long it has been since its last collision.

4.2   RANDOM NUMBERS, VECTORS, AND POINTS

When a particle generator creates a new particle, assigning its initial position, velocity, and parameters, it is usually necessary to provide some randomness. Although there are situations where it is desirable that all particles have the same characteristics, more typically each particle is given a unique signature by drawing its parameters from a random process. In generating random numbers to randomize particle parameters, one should resist the simple solution of calling the operating system's `rand()` function, because it is designed to produce only uniformly distributed random numbers. A *uniform distribution* is one in which any value within the range of the distribution is equally likely. Instead, one should ask what random characteristics do we want in a parameter? Consider the weight of a collection of apples. Let us say that the average weight is 80 grams, with a range from 50 to 110 grams. Is it reasonable to assume that there will be just as many apples weighing 55 grams as weighing 82 grams? Certainly not! It is much more likely that an apple will weigh near the average than an unusually low or high weight.

The solid curve to the right depicts a *Gaussian* or *normal* distribution, given by the probability density

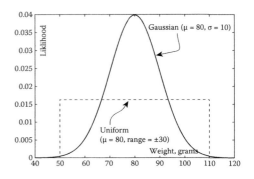

$$p(x) = \frac{1}{\sigma\sqrt{2\pi}}e^{\frac{(x-\mu)^2}{2\sigma^2}}.$$

The mean μ is the center of the distribution, around which most values cluster, and the standard deviation σ determines the spread of the distribution, or how widely values tend to deviate from the mean. The rule of thumb is that 68% of values fall within $\pm\sigma$ of the mean, 95% fall within $\pm2\sigma$, and 99.7% fall within $\pm3\sigma$. Note, that a true Gaussian distribution is not bounded, so it is possible, although highly unlikely, that values far outside of $\pm3\sigma$ may occur. The Gaussian curve in the figure has mean $\mu = 80$ g, and standard deviation $\sigma = 10$ g. The vertical axis is a measure of the likelihood that a value will fall within a small range of the value indicated on the horizontal axis. This distribution seems close to what we would expect for the distribution of weights in a collection of apples. Contrast this with the uniform distribution of mean $\mu = 80$ g and range ±30 g, indicated by the dashed curve. Here, all weights in the specified range are equally likely, and no weights can fall outside of this range. For most natural parameters, such as weight, a Gaussian distribution will give the best results. In designing a particle generator one should carefully choose what type of distribution to use for each randomly determined parameter.

In order to facilitate further discussion, let us define $U(u_{\min}, u_{\max})$ to be a function returning a uniformly distributed random scalar in the range $[u_{\min} \ldots u_{\max}]$, and $G(\mu, \sigma)$ be a function returning a normally distributed random scalar with mean μ and standard deviation σ. When implementing these, the C++11 standard library [cplusplus.com, 2014] provides implementations of both uniform and normally distributed random number generators, as well as generators for a number of other distributions.

What we will need to compute for each new particle is its initial position $\mathbf{x}_0$, and its initial velocity $\mathbf{v}_0$. In order to compute these, we will need to be able to compute not only random scalars but also random vectors and random points. The two types of random vector that we will need are a unit vector pointing in an arbitrary direction, and a unit vector that is angularly offset from the direction of another vector. Let us define the parameterless random vector generator $\mathbf{S}()$ that returns a unit vector uniformly distributed across the directions on the surface of a unit sphere. Let us also define two other random vector generators $\mathbf{D}_U(\mathbf{w}, \delta)$, and $\mathbf{D}_G(\mathbf{w}, \delta)$ that return unit vectors angularly displaced from the direction of vector $\mathbf{w}$ by an angle whose range is determined by δ. $\mathbf{D}_U$ returns a vector uniformly distributed about $\mathbf{w}$ with maximum deflection angle δ, and $\mathbf{D}_G$ returns a vector that is normally distributed about $\mathbf{w}$ with standard deviation of deflection angle $\sigma = \delta/3$. Finally, let

To demonstrate why the uniform random selection of θ and h achieves the goal of distributing directions uniformly across the surface of a sphere, let us look at the size of a differential area dA on a unit sphere. Distance s along the surface of a unit sphere in the longitudinal direction is parameterized by the elevation angle ϕ, as simply $s = \phi$. The relationship of h and ϕ is $h = \sin \phi$ or $\phi = \sin^{-1} h$. Therefore, s varies with height as

$$\frac{ds}{dh} = \frac{\partial s}{\partial \phi} \frac{\partial \phi}{\partial h} = \frac{\partial \sin^{-1} h}{\partial h} = \frac{1}{\sqrt{1 - h^2}},$$

or simply

$$\frac{ds}{dh} = \frac{1}{r}.$$

Distance t along the surface of the unit sphere in the latitudinal direction is parameterized by the azimuth angle θ, as $t = \theta \cos \phi$. Therefore, t varies with azimuth angle as

$$\frac{dt}{d\theta} = \cos \phi.$$

Now, the differential area on the surface of the sphere is given by

$$ds = \frac{1}{r} dh,$$

$$dt = \cos \phi \, d\theta,$$

$$dA = ds \, dt = \frac{1}{r} \cos \phi \, dh \, d\theta.$$

But, since $r = \cos \phi$,

$$dA = dh \, d\theta.$$

Since the integral of dA with respect to h yields $h \, d\theta$ and the integral with respect to θ yields $\theta \, dh$, we see that area varies linearly with both h and θ. Thus, it follows that if h and θ are chosen from a uniform distribution, we will have a uniform spread of particles on the surface.

us define two random position generators $\mathbf{C}_U(\mathbf{c}, \hat{\mathbf{n}}, R)$ and $\mathbf{C}_G(\mathbf{c}, \hat{\mathbf{n}}, R)$ that return random positions on a disk centered at the point $\mathbf{c}$, with surface normal $\hat{\mathbf{n}}$, and with radius R. $\mathbf{C}_U(\mathbf{c}, \hat{\mathbf{n}}, R)$ will return a point uniformly distributed across the face of the disk, and $\mathbf{C}_G(\mathbf{c}, \hat{\mathbf{n}}, R)$ will return a point that is normally distributed about the center of the disk, with the disk radius R corresponding with three standard deviations from the center.

We can compute the direction vector $\hat{\mathbf{v}} = \mathbf{S}()$, pointing in an arbitrary direction across a sphere, as follows. We first generate two uniformly distributed random variables, $\theta = U(-\pi, \pi)$ and $y = U(-1, 1)$. In spherical coordinates, θ is the azimuth angle, and y is height, which is used to determine the elevation angle $(\sin \phi = y)$. If we define $r = \sqrt{1 - y^2}$ (i.e., $r = \cos \phi$), then

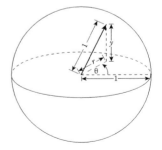

$$\hat{\mathbf{v}} = \begin{bmatrix} r \cos \theta \\ y \\ -r \sin \theta \end{bmatrix}.$$

Note that this approach uses spherical coordinates, but by letting the elevation angle be determined by height above the x-z plane, we adjust the distribution of directions so that those toward the poles are not favored, giving us a uniform distribution across the unit sphere.

The uniformly distributed unit vector $\hat{\mathbf{v}} = \mathbf{D}_U(\mathbf{w}, \delta)$, pointing in a direction angularly offset from a vector $\mathbf{w}$ given an angular range δ, can be computed as follows. The approach will be to first compute a vector that is angularly offset from the z axis, and then rotate this vector into a coordinate frame to align the z axis with the direction $\hat{\mathbf{w}} = \mathbf{w}/\|\mathbf{w}\|$. We define the vector's coordinate frame as follows. First choose $\mathbf{a}$ to be any vector not parallel to $\hat{\mathbf{w}}$. A good choice is

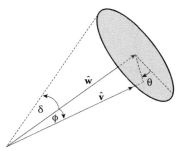

$\mathbf{a} = \begin{bmatrix} 1 & 0 & 0 \end{bmatrix}^T$. This will work except in the case where both w_y and w_z are 0, in which case we can use $\mathbf{a} = \begin{bmatrix} 0 & 1 & 0 \end{bmatrix}^T$. We want our original direction vector $\hat{\mathbf{w}}$ to be the z axis, so $\hat{\mathbf{u}}_z = \hat{\mathbf{w}}$, and we let the x axis be defined by $\hat{\mathbf{u}}_x = (\mathbf{a} \times \hat{\mathbf{u}}_z)/\|\mathbf{a} \times \hat{\mathbf{u}}_z\|$, so the y axis is $\hat{\mathbf{u}}_y = \hat{\mathbf{u}}_z \times \hat{\mathbf{u}}_x$. The matrix $M = \begin{bmatrix} \mathbf{u}_x & \mathbf{u}_y & \mathbf{u}_z \end{bmatrix}$ will rotate a vector into this new frame. We now find a unit vector $\hat{\mathbf{v}}'$ offset from the z-axis $\begin{bmatrix} 0 & 0 & 1 \end{bmatrix}^T$, and rotate it by M to obtain vector $\hat{\mathbf{v}}$ offset from $\hat{\mathbf{w}}$. Let the random fraction $f = U(0, 1)$, and let $\phi = \sqrt{f}\delta$, with $\theta = U(-\pi, \pi)$. Scaling δ by the square root of f provides for a uniform distribution of angular displacements ϕ, which would otherwise be more concentrated around small angles. Now, define

$$\hat{\mathbf{v}}' = \begin{bmatrix} \cos\theta \sin\phi \\ \sin\theta \sin\phi \\ \cos\phi \end{bmatrix}.$$

Finally, our offset vector is $\hat{\mathbf{v}} = M\hat{\mathbf{v}}'$. The normally distributed unit vector $\hat{\mathbf{v}} = \mathbf{D}_G(\mathbf{w}, \delta)$ is computed identically, except that we generate the random fraction f using a Gaussian distribution, $f = G(0, \delta/3)$.

The uniformly distributed position $\mathbf{p} = \mathbf{C}_U(\mathbf{c}, \hat{\mathbf{n}}, R)$ on a disk with center $\mathbf{c}$, surface normal $\hat{\mathbf{n}}$, and radius R can be computed as follows. We will use essentially the same approach as used for $\mathbf{D}_U$. We can let the surface normal play the role of the preferred direction $\mathbf{w}$, calculate the matrix M as above, but this time use radial coordinates to position our point on a disk in the x-y plane, instead of on the surface of a sphere. To generate this point, let a random fraction $f = U(0, 1)$, and its radius $r = \sqrt{f}R$, and let $\theta = U(-\pi, \pi)$. Our 3D point on the x-y plane is given by

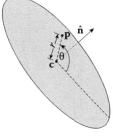

$$\mathbf{p}' = \begin{bmatrix} r\cos\theta \\ r\sin\theta \\ 0 \end{bmatrix},$$

To demonstrate why using the square root of a uniformly distributed random number between 0 and 1 to multiply the radius achieves the goal of distributing directions uniformly across the face of a disk, examine the size of a differential area dA on a unit disk. Distance s across the face of a disk in the radial direction is parameterized $s = r$. Distance t in the angular direction is parameterized $t = r\theta$. Therefore, the differential area on the surface of the disk is given by

$$ds = dr,$$
$$dt = r\, d\theta,$$
$$dA = ds\, dt = r\, dr\, d\theta.$$

Because the integral of dA with respect to r yields $\frac{1}{2}r^2\, d\theta$ and the integral with respect to θ yields $r\theta\, dr$, we see that area varies with the square of the radius r but linearly with θ. Thus, it follows that if θ is chosen from a uniform distribution, but r is chosen from a distribution for which r^2 is uniform, we will have a uniform spread of particles on the disk. Similar logic applies to using the square root in the choice of deflection angle ϕ when computing random vectors angularly offset from a particular direction.

which can be rotated into the plane of the disk and translated by the disk's center to yield our desired point $\mathbf{p} = \mathbf{c} + M\mathbf{p}'$. The normally distributed position $\mathbf{p} = \mathbf{C}_G(\mathbf{c}, \hat{\mathbf{n}}, R)$ is computed identically, except that we generate the random fraction f using a Gaussian distribution, $f = G(0, R/3)$.

4.3 PARTICLE GENERATORS

A particle generator may use any one of a number of strategies for injecting new particles into the system, depending on the desired effect. It is sometimes appropriate to generate all of the particles in a very short time interval (e.g., the flash for a gun shot), to generate a continuous stream of particles over a long period of time (e.g., water from a hose), or to generate discrete bursts of particles at regular intervals (e.g., a roman candle). What will usually work is to provide a time when the generator turns on, a time when it turns off, and a particle generation rate. If bursts are desired, the start and end times can be reset after each burst. The particle generation rate should be specified in particles per second. At each timestep, the generator tests its start and end times against the current time t to see if it should be generating particles. If it should, the product of the generation rate r and the timestep h will give the number of particles n to generate at this particular time, $n = rh$. In this way, even if the simulation timestep is changed during development, the number of particles generated per second will stay constant.

$$n = \lfloor rh \rfloor;$$
$$f = f + (rh - n);$$
$$\textbf{if } f > 1 \textbf{ then}$$
$$\quad n = n + 1;$$
$$\quad f = f - 1;$$
$$\textbf{end}$$

The desired number of particles are then turned on, with each assigned an initial position and velocity, along with settings for any other required parameters.

One caveat here is that rh is not necessarily integer, so in order to maintain the desired rate it is best to keep an accumulated fraction f of a particle at each step, and when this reaches 1, add 1 to the number of particles to emit this time step and reset the fraction.

How the initial position and velocity are chosen for each particle will depend on the type of particle generator being used. These fall generally into the strategies indicated in Figure 4.2: omnidirectional from a point, directed from a point, emanating from part of a disk or polygonal region on a plane, or emanating from the surface or interior of a 3D solid. For any particle generator, we can define the following parameters: let μ_s be the mean speed of a particle, and δ_s determine the range of speeds. We will call the initial position of a particle $\mathbf{x}_0$ and its initial velocity $\mathbf{v}_0$. Note that in computing velocity, it is usually most convenient to compute the initial speed s_0, and initial direction $\hat{\mathbf{v}}_0$ separately, so that $\mathbf{v}_0 = s_0 \hat{\mathbf{v}}_0$. The particle's initial speed is a scalar, which we will usually assume to be normally distributed about the mean with a standard deviation one third of the expected speed range,[*] so $s_0 = G(\mu_s, \delta_s/3)$. We often want the initial direction to be a random angular offset from a preferred direction, so most random number generators will have a parameter δ that is used to limit the range of these angular offsets. Once a particle generator determines a preferred direction $\hat{\mathbf{d}}$ for each particle, the particle's direction is randomized about $\hat{\mathbf{d}}$ using either $\hat{\mathbf{v}}_0 = \mathbf{D}_G(\hat{\mathbf{d}}, \delta/3)$ or $\hat{\mathbf{v}}_0 = \mathbf{D}_U(\hat{\mathbf{d}}, \delta)$.

Given these conventions, from the infinitely many possible configurations, let us consider the following most frequently used particle generators, chosen from the possibilities presented in Figure 4.2:

- **Omnidirectional:** This particle generator is located geometrically by a single emission point $\mathbf{p}$. Particles are emitted with equal likelihood in all directions. Therefore, $\mathbf{x}_0 = \mathbf{p}$, and $\hat{\mathbf{v}}_0 = \mathbf{S}()$.

- **Directed:** This particle generator is also located by a single emission point $\mathbf{p}$, but includes a fixed preferred direction $\hat{\mathbf{d}}$. Therefore, $\mathbf{x}_0 = \mathbf{p}$, and particle emission directions are determined as angular offsets from $\hat{\mathbf{d}}$.

- **From a disk:** This particle generator is a flat circular region, with equal likelihood that a particle will be emitted from any point in the region. Its center $\mathbf{c}$ and radius R must be specified, as well as its surface normal $\hat{\mathbf{n}}$. To generate a random position on a disk, we simply use our random position generator, so $\mathbf{x}_0 = \mathbf{C}_U(\mathbf{c}, \hat{\mathbf{n}}, R)$. Particle emission directions are determined as angular offsets from the surface normal $\hat{\mathbf{n}}$.

- **From a triangle:** There are a number of ways to generate a random particle position on a general polygon, but let us consider only the triangle case since it will usually be easy to convert our geometry into triangles. For a triangle, the vertices $\mathbf{p}_0, \mathbf{p}_1, \mathbf{p}_2$ must be specified, from which the surface normal $\hat{\mathbf{n}}$ can be calculated by taking the cross-product of any two nonparallel edges. We can

---

[*]Here we are making the choice that the maximum occurs at three standard deviations. This encompasses 99.7% of the possible values of the Gaussian distribution.

use our uniform random number generator to generate candidate barycentric coordinates $u = U(0, 1)$ and $v = U(0, 1)$ (see Appendix F). If these coordinates pass the inside-triangle test $(u + v \leq 1)$, then we use them, otherwise we iterate until we get a good candidate pair. Given the good (u, v) pair, $\mathbf{x}_0 = u\mathbf{p}_0 + v\mathbf{p}_1 + (1 - u - v)\mathbf{p}_2$. Particle emission directions are determined as angular offsets from the surface normal $\hat{\mathbf{n}}$.

- **From a sphere:** This particle generator is a sphere with center $\mathbf{c}$ and radius R. We can first use our spherical random vector generator to generate a random direction, $\hat{\mathbf{u}} = \mathbf{S}()$. If we want the particle to start from the surface of the sphere, we let $\mathbf{x}_0 = \mathbf{c} + R\hat{\mathbf{u}}$. If we want the particle to start from within the sphere, we generate the random fraction $f = U(0, 1)$, let radius $r = \sqrt[3]{f}R$, and then $\mathbf{x}_0 = \mathbf{c} + r\hat{\mathbf{u}}$. Particle emission directions are determined as angular offsets from the random direction $\hat{\mathbf{u}}$.

One consideration for all particle generators is that we usually want to simulate a process in which particles are generated continuously over time, not at discrete timesteps. Let us say that we are generating particles from a planar surface. If all of the particles start on the surface, then what we will

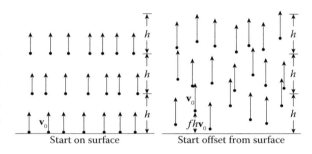

Start on surface   Start offset from surface

see in our simulation is a sequence of bursts of particles coming off of the surface, one burst for each timestep, rather than a continuous stream. An easy way to avoid this problem is to compute an offset for each particle along its velocity vector. Let $f = U(0, 1)$ be a uniformly distributed positive random fraction. If the particle's initial velocity is given by $\mathbf{v}_0$, and its position on the surface by $\mathbf{x}_0$, then $\mathbf{x}_0' = \mathbf{x}_0 + fh\mathbf{v}_0$ is the offset position, simulating a particle generated fh seconds into the timestep.

4.4 PARTICLE SIMULATION

4.4.1 Organization of the Computation

In dealing with particle systems we want to be able to handle a very large number of particles, so time and space efficiency will be of great concern. Our particle creation and destruction processes must be efficient, since in a typical particle system we will be creating and destroying many hundreds or thousands of particles every timestep. A problem is that memory allocation and deallocation via operating system calls (**new** and **delete** in C++-like languages, or automatically in Java-like languages) are highly generalized and thus tend to be slow. Therefore, we want to avoid their use as much as possible within the simulation loop. Fortunately, in the case of a particle system, every particle object is fundamentally identical in structure to every other particle, so we have a highly uniform problem, and it is relatively easy to develop an efficient allocation scheme. A second consideration is that we will be iterating over all of our particles one or more times every timestep, so iteration should be highly efficient. Both of these concerns, taken together, argue that all particles be maintained in a preallocated (or bulk allocated) array-like data structure contained within an object that we will call a `ParticleList`. A `ParticleList` needs to be equipped with an efficient way of activating and deactivating particles, and a way to test whether or not a given particle is active.

Reduced to its essentials, simulating a particle system can be as simple as the following algorithm:

$t = 0$; $n = 0$;
`ParticleList.Clear()`;
while $t < t_{max}$ **do**
    for *each particle generator* k **do**
        Generator$[k]$.`Generateparticles`(`ParticleList`, t, h);
    end
    `ParticleList.TestAndDeactivate`(t);
    `ParticleList.ComputeAccelerations`(t);
    if `OutputTime`(t) **then**
        `ParticleList.Display`();
    end
    `ParticleList.Integrate`(t, h);
    $n = n + 1$;
    $t = nh$;
end

The algorithm assumes that we have a data structure allowing us to iterate over all particle generators. Each particle generator has a `Generateparticles()` method that tells the `ParticleList` to activate and initialize an inactive particle for each new particle it generates. A `ParticleList` has the following methods: `Clear()` that makes all particles inactive; `TestAndDeactivate()` that asks each active particle if it should be killed, and if so, makes it inactive; `ComputeAccelerations()` that asks each active particle to compute and store its acceleration due to any forces acting on it; `Display()` that asks each active particle to render itself; and `Integrate()` that performs numerical integration to update each particle's position and velocity based on its acceleration.

The data organization shown to the right is one simple way to organize the internal storage and bookkeeping necessary to maintain a `ParticleList`. It shows the structure when

only three particles are active, and all of the others are inactive. The particles and all information associated with them is stored in the *particles* array. This array is N particles long, where N is chosen to be large enough to hold the maximum number of particles we expect to be active at any point in time. In the figure, each cell of this array is marked with a T (true) if the associated particle is active, or an F (false) if it is inactive. The *inactivestack* is an N-long array of indices into the *particles* array, used to maintain a stack of all cells that are currently inactive. The variable *inactivecount* holds the number of particles currently inactive, and serves as an index to the top of the stack. With this structure, whenever a particle is to be made active by a particle generator, we just pop the top index off of the stack, mark that cell active in the *particles* array, and decrement *inactivecount*. Whenever a particle goes from being active to inactive, we mark its cell inactive in the *particles* array, push its index onto the stack, and increment *inactivecount*. This data structure has no way to examine only active particles, so at every step in the simulation, every particle in the list must be visited.

Visiting every particle, even if it is inactive, may seem like a slow, expensive process, but in today's computing architectures it is actually quite efficient. Memory fetch lookahead and caching make looping through consecutive cells in memory much more efficient than accessing cells out of sequence. The message here is that any scheme looking to achieve maximum particle throughput must take the processing architecture into account.

One very obvious efficiency gain would be through the use of parallel processing. Since particles all run independently from each other, if we had enough processors it would be possible to assign one processor to each particle, theoretically allowing an entire particle system to run as fast as a single particle. Even if we cannot reach this limit, use of multiple cores within the CPU or, better, moving the entire particle simulation process to the GPU will achieve a considerable speedup, and is well worth the effort if high performance is a goal.

4.4.2 Deactivating Particles

If a simulation keeps activating new particles and never deactivating them it will quickly reach a point where the `ParticleList` data structure is full and no more particles can be generated. Even if a flexible data structure that can grow with the number of particles is used, the simulation will tend to slow excessively as the number of particles continues to grow. Therefore, it is necessary that particles deactivate themselves when they are no longer contributing to the scene. The strategy to be used to decide on particle deactivation should reside within each individual particle, as established when it is activated by a particle generator.

There are a number of deactivation strategies that can be used, with the choice dependent on the purpose of the particle system. The most frequently used criteria are particle age, particle velocity, particle position, and particle collision. Some examples will serve to illustrate how this decision could be made. A particle being used to represent a fireworks spark should be deactivated when it has burned out (based on age) or when it reaches the ground (based on height). A particle being used to represent spray from a breaking wave should be deactivated when it reenters the water (based on collision). A particle being used to represent smoke should be deactivated when it leaves the viewable region of the scene (based on position). A particle being used to represent snow in an avalanche should be deactivated when it comes to rest (based on velocity). In any case, every particle should implement some deactivation strategy.

4.4.3   Collisions

When simulating a single bouncing ball in Chapter 3, we handled collisions by testing to see if a collision would occur during the timestep, and if so, advancing the ball to the exact time of the collision, computing the reflection velocity, and then continuing the simulation to the end of the timestep. What this process allows us to do is to use the exact velocity at the time of collision to compute the reflected velocity, and to account for any change in accelerations that might occur at the time of collision, incorporating them into the remainder of the timestep. If we followed this procedure for a particle system our simulation would quickly grind to a halt, since it is highly likely that multiple collisions will occur in every timestep. Stopping the clock and restarting it for every collision would be cumbersome, error prone, and slow. Instead, we can take advantage of the fact that in a particle system simulation there is so much detail that small errors in collision calculations will not be noticed.

For a particle system, it will usually be sufficient to guarantee that particles bounce off of a surface in the correct direction, never appearing to penetrate the surface. To do this, after numerical integration we examine the particle's position $\mathbf{x}^{[n]}$ before the timestep, and $\mathbf{x}^{[n+1]}$ after the timestep. The particle's path defines a line segment $(\mathbf{x}^{[n]}\ \mathbf{x}^{[n+1]})$. Referring to the diagram to the right, we let $\mathbf{p}$ be a known point on the 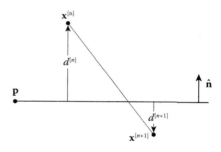 surface, and let $\hat{\mathbf{n}}$ be the normal to this surface. We can detect if the line segment passes through the surface by comparing the signed distance of the starting position above the surface, $d^{[n]} = (\mathbf{x}^{[n]} - \mathbf{p}) \cdot \hat{\mathbf{n}}$, with the signed distance of the ending position above the surface, $d^{[n+1]} = (\mathbf{x}^{[n+1]} - \mathbf{p}) \cdot \hat{\mathbf{n}}$. If their signs differ then $\mathbf{x}^{[n]}$ lies on one side of the surface and $\mathbf{x}^{[n+1]}$ on the other, so a collision must occur during the timestep.

Now, if we move the particle's ending position $\mathbf{x}^{[n+1]}$ the distance $|d^{[n+1]}|$ in the direction of the surface normal, the particle will be back on the surface. Remembering that c_r is the coefficient of restitution, if we move the particle an additional $c_r|d^{[n+1]}|$ in the direction of the normal, the particle will be near to where it would have been had it reflected off of the surface and had its speed reduced by ρ. Using this approach, the particle's updated position after collision response will be

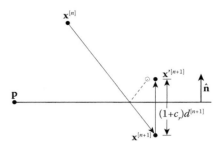

$$\mathbf{x}'^{[n+1]} = \mathbf{x}^{[n+1]} - (1 + c_r)d^{[n+1]}\hat{\mathbf{n}}.$$

The subtraction in this calculation assures that the displacement is in the direction of the normal. The diagram shows the final position $\mathbf{x}'^{[n+1]}$ compared to the dashed circle showing where the particle would have ended up if we had done the more accurate reflection calculation.

As in the bouncing ball problem, the particle's velocity will also have to be updated to account for the reflection, the coefficient of restitution, and any surface friction, but using the velocity $\mathbf{v}^{[n+1]}$ at the end of the timestep, rather than the collision velocity. Thus, the updated velocity is given by

$$\mathbf{v}_n = (\mathbf{v}^{[n+1]} \cdot \hat{\mathbf{n}})\hat{\mathbf{n}},$$
$$\mathbf{v}_t = \mathbf{v}^{[n+1]} - \mathbf{v}_n,$$
$$\mathbf{v}'^{[n+1]} = -c_r\mathbf{v}_n + (1 - c_f)\mathbf{v}_t,$$

where $\mathbf{v}_n$ and $\mathbf{v}_t$ are the normal and tangential components of the velocity, and c_f is the coefficient of friction for collision.

4.4.4 Geometry

We now know how to detect and respond to collisions of a particle with a particular surface, but how do we do this efficiently if our scene is made up of complex geometric models composed of thousands of polygonal faces? Clearly, we do not want to test every particle against every polygon for every timestep. Fortunately, there are several ways that the number of polygon tests can be significantly reduced. Any computer graphics book with a chapter on raytracing will enumerate a number of these methods, including organizing the scene polygons into some form of tree structure such as a kd-tree, Octree, or BVH-tree. Here, we will content ourselves with discussing a simpler approach, a spatial-hash based on a fixed spatial partition. We will see more sophisticated methods when we look at rigid body simulation in Chapter 9.

The idea here is that we divide space into a 3D grid of small cubes, usually referred to as voxels, aligned with the coordinate axes. Then we allocate a 3D array, each cell of which corresponds with one of the voxels, and will be used to store a list of those polygons that could cross that voxel. The array is usually arranged in depth-plane p, row r, and column c order. The lists

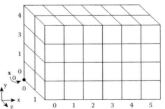

The 2D example shown in the figure to the right demonstrates how the spatial hash for a polygon is computed. Our grid is 8×8, with a cell width $\delta = 2.0$. The bottom left-hand corner of the grid is located at $(6.0, -4.0)$. The hash of this triangle is shown by the gray rectangle within the grid. The triangle's bounding rectangle, indicated with dashed lines, has bounds

$$x_{min} = 8.4, \qquad x_{max} = 16.8,$$
$$y_{min} = 0.2, \qquad y_{max} = 8.2.$$

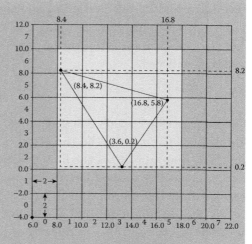

The array row indices r_{min} and r_{max}, and the array column indices c_{min} and c_{max} covering the extent of the bounding rectangle are

$$c_{min} = \lfloor (0.2 - (-4.0))/2.0 \rfloor = 2, \qquad r_{max} = \lfloor (8.2 - (-4.0))/2.0 \rfloor = 6,$$
$$r_{min} = \lfloor (8.4 - 6.0)/2.0 \rfloor \quad = 1, \qquad c_{max} = \lfloor (16.8 - 6.0)/2.0 \rfloor \quad = 5.$$

The hash is completed by adding the index of this triangle to the list of triangles maintained in each grid cell within this range:

```
for i in r_min to r_max do
    for j in c_min to c_max do
        grid[i][j].AddTriangleToList(triangle_index);
    end
end
```

of polygons are built as follows. For each polygon, construct its 3D bounding box, giving us minimum and maximum x, y, and z extents for each polygon. Let $\mathbf{x}_0 = (x_0, y_0, z_0)$ be the scene point with minimum x-y-z coordinates, covered by the grid. This point should correspond to the outside corner of array cell $[0, 0, 0]$. If the width of each cube is δ, then the spatial hash of point $\mathbf{x}$, with elements (x, y, z), is given by

$$\mathbf{h}(\mathbf{x}) = (\lfloor (z - z_0)/\delta \rfloor, \lfloor (y - y_0)/\delta \rfloor, \lfloor (x - x_0)/\delta \rfloor),$$

which provides the 3D array indices (p, r, c) of the cell that contains the point $\mathbf{x}$. Now, for each polygon, we find the spatial hash indices of the corners of the polygon's bounding volume, and add the polygon to each voxel contained in this range. Note that this may hash the polygon to some cells that it does not overlap, but the method is guaranteed to never miss a polygon.

To test for the collision of a particle with the geometric model, we find each voxel lying along the path of the particle during the timestep and test for a collision with the polygons hashed to these voxels. The details for efficiently finding the specific voxels crossed by a line segment are a little more involved than we will describe here; please see a raytracing book for a more detailed and optimized approach for the most general case [Watt and Watt, 1992]. We will instead describe a simplified version of this that works correctly but is not optimized.

First we find the voxels that the starting and ending points $\mathbf{x}^{[n]}$ and $\mathbf{x}^{[n+1]}$ hash to. All voxels encountered by the particle path in the timestep are included in an axis-aligned bounding box encompassing these voxels. So, next we find all of the cells within that bounding box. We check for collisions with the triangles hashing to all of those cells to find the first point of collision (if any) with a triangle.

Typically, voxel sizes are much larger than the distance a particle travels in a single timestep, so a particle usually remains in a single voxel during a timestep, occasionally crossing into an adjacent voxel in some direction. Thus, the bounding box will usually cover just one voxel, occasionally will cover two voxels, rarely will cover four voxels, and in a very few cases will cover eight voxels. In the four voxel and eight voxel cases, we are doing some additional checks, since the actual particle path would only cross three or four voxels, respectively. However, since these cases are rare, the overall extra work being done from checking the extra cells is minimal.

4.4.5 Efficient Random Numbers

A final efficiency issue is with the use of random numbers within a particle simulation. Random number generators utilize relatively slow numerical processes. In addition, the initialization step in the activation of every particle typically requires the generation of at least four random numbers to randomize position and velocity, and often requires many more to randomize particle parameters. Therefore, the time spent in generating random numbers is a real efficiency consideration when the particle generation rate is high.

The simplest way to reduce the time cost of generating random numbers during a particle simulation is to generate a large array of random numbers at the start of the simulation, and then every time a random number is needed simply index into the array to get the next number, incrementing the index at each fetch. When the end of the array is reached, the index is reset to 0. It might be convenient to create two such arrays, U and G, with the former generated with the uniform random number generator $U(0,1)$, and the latter with the Gaussian random number generator $G(0,1)$. Then, when a uniform random number u between $u_{\min}$ and $u_{\max}$ is required, the uniform array is indexed and the retrieved value is scaled and translated as follows:

$$u = (u_{\max} - u_{\min})\mathrm{U}[i] + u_{\min}.$$

When a normally distributed random number g with mean μ and standard deviation σ is required, the Gaussian array is indexed and the retrieved value is scaled and translated as follows:

$$g = \sigma\mathrm{G}[j] + \mu.$$

4.5 PARTICLE RENDERING

The fact that particles have no geometry, except a spatial position, means that approaches to rendering a particle system are limited only by your imagination and the available computing time. If your particle system is part of an interactive experience, like a video game, then time resources will be in the millisecond range per frame, but if it is to be used as part of a visual effect for a motion picture, then the time resources might be measured in hours per frame.

We want to start by saying that the first idea that probably comes to mind is to represent each particle by a sphere, and use our favorite renderer to create an image. Figure 4.3 shows a particle system rendered in this way. Although this can look all right, there are several reasons why this approach should usually be avoided. First, to make a sphere of reasonable resolution requires at least 96 triangles.[*] Thus, for every particle we will have to render nearly 100 triangles. Since most particles render to a very small screen area, we will be making a number of calculations far in excess of what is necessary for a good quality image. Second, for a typical particle system, we are making these unnecessary calculations for every one of hundreds of thousands of particles, and will pay an enormous performance price, even with a powerful graphics card. And third, a display of thousands of tiny spheres is going to look pretty boring. We can do much better, at much less computational cost.

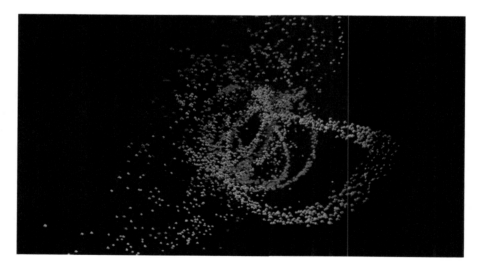

FIGURE 4.3 A particle system rendered as a collection of colored spheres. (Courtesy of Thomas Grindinger.)

---

[*]This assumes eight longitudinal steps and seven latitudinal steps, giving 8×5 quads $= 80$ triangles, and $2 \times 8 = 16$ triangles at the poles.

4.5.1 Points and Streaks

By far the simplest approach to rendering a particle system is to render each particle directly into the image as a single point. Using this approach assumes that you are able to compute the projection of each particle onto the virtual camera's image plane. In a raytracing environment you can do this by constructing a ray from the camera viewpoint to the particle and noting where the ray crosses the image plane. In a 3D graphics API, like *OpenGL* or *Direct3D*, you can use the API's call for drawing a single point based on its 3D position. Since a particle has no surface and no surface normal, it is not straightforward to render the particle using a standard lighting algorithm. Instead, what is normally done is to bypass the scene's lighting, and to specify the rendered color of the particle directly. This approach is natural for self-illuminating particles, representing things like sparks, but can actually work well in any case if careful attention is paid to coordinating particle color with the lit colors in the scene. If use of the scene's lighting is required, then some way will have to be devised to create a direction vector to be used as a stand-in for the surface normal for each particle.

One problem with rendering particles as points is that there are no inherent size cues to distance. Particles near to the camera and particles far away will render at the same size, thus losing perceptual depth cues due to perspective foreshortening. One approach to dealing with this problem is to composite particles into the image based on an opacity that is a function of distance from the screen. If this is done, nearby particles will be rendered at full brightness and with high contrast to the background, while particles that are far away will have their colors shifted toward the background color, reducing their brightness and contrast. The overall effect will be that of *atmospheric perspective*, giving the illusion of distance even though the rendered particle sizes remain the same. The illusion of distance can be further enhanced by *splatting* particles into the image, with a splat radius that is a function of distance from the camera. A splat is made by rendering the point into the image as a circle, with a given radius, with the opacity of pixels in the circle decreasing with distance from the circle's center [Zwicker et al., 2001]. Figure 4.4 takes advantage of splats to display a particle system representing a star field, whose stars range from near to far from the camera.

Another problem with rendering particles as points is that moving particles will appear to make discrete jumps across the screen at each frame change, disturbing the illusion of smooth animated motion. The usual way of overcoming this problem in animation is the use of motion blur. Motion blur is expensive to compute in a raytracing renderer, and is complex to compute using a 3D graphics API. Fortunately, in rendering particles, the illusion of motion blur is easy to achieve. Instead of rendering a particle directly into the image as a point, it can be rendered as a line or streak. The simplest approach to doing this is to have each particle save its position at the previous timestep, and then draw a line from this previous position to the particle's current position. This can be improved on by determining what

FIGURE 4.4 A particle system rendered using splats. (Courtesy of Christian Weeks.)

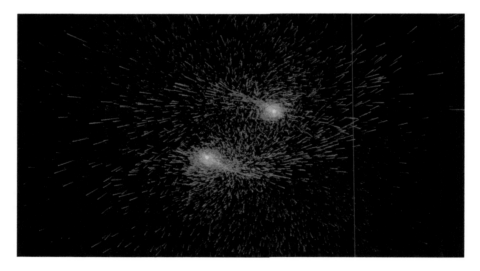

FIGURE 4.5 A particle system rendered as a set of streaks. (Courtesy of Sam Casacio.)

the time duration of a motion blur streak should be and saving as many previous particle positions as necessary to draw a streak of that length in time. The same ideas supporting foreshortening can be used for rendering streaks as for rendering points—adjusting streak opacity and width with distance from the camera. A further improvement is to give each streak a starting and ending opacity, making it most opaque at the beginning of the streak and least opaque at the end, which gives it the illusion of fading with time. Figure 4.5 shows a set of particles rendered as streaks, using this idea.

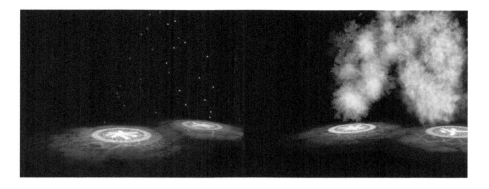

FIGURE 4.6 Left—a particle system rendered as points. Right—using sprites. (Courtesy of Cory Buckley.)

4.5.2 Sprites

If a more sophisticated look is required for rendering the particles, a common approach is the use of *sprites*. A sprite consists of a rectangle and an associated texture map. At each frame, the rectangle is centered on a particle and oriented so that its surface normal faces the camera's viewpoint. To do this, the vector between the particle position and the camera viewpoint is used as the direction of the normal. The texture map typically includes opaque and transparent regions, so that the shape projected by the particle, with attached sprite, does not have to be rectangular. The sprite is then rendered as normal texture mapped geometry using whatever renderer and lighting system is in use. Figure 4.6 demonstrates how the use of sprites can greatly enhance the look of even a simple particle system. Sprites have the advantage of providing a complex look at the very low computational expense of rendering only two triangles per particle.

4.5.3 Geometry

We said earlier that attaching a sphere to a particle is a poor idea, but there are situations where compute time is not a problem, and we would like to represent each particle by its own geometry. For example, we might want each particle to represent a falling leaf in an Autumn scene, or a cruiser in a space armada. In this case, providing geometry for each particle can make sense, but more is needed than just the particle's position. We will need to be able to orient the geometry as well as position it. A usual approach to building a rotation matrix to orient the geometry is to use the particle's velocity vector to determine one direction in a local coordinate frame for the particle. If we pick a second direction to be the world's vertical axis, we can use cross-products to complete the particle's coordinate frame, and a rotation matrix to rotate the geometry so it is aligned with this frame. Another option is to use the particle's acceleration as a second vector to cross with the velocity vector.

FIGURE 4.7 Left—a particle system rendered as points. Right—rendered volumetrically together with additional elements. (Courtesy of Hugh Kinsey.)

4.5.4 Volume Rendering

Volume rendering has become the primary way that particles are rendered in visual effects work for film. The idea here is that the 3D volume representing the space in which the particle system resides is divided into a 3D grid of voxels. As particles move through space, they deposit density in the voxels through which they pass. This density usually either fades or is dispersed in the volume with time, with the net effect being a streak of density in the volume that tends to be most dense in the current region of the particle, and less dense along its position history. The density trails can be further perturbed by various processes, like Perlin noise, or flow simulations to create interesting detail. Finally, a *direct volume renderer* can be used to render the density pattern in the volume. This approach has been used to model a great variety of effects. Some examples are explosions, volcano eruptions, water spray, avalanches, vapor trails, rocket exhaust, and falling snow. A nice example, showing a mothership landing, is in Figure 4.7.

4.6 SUMMARY

Here is a brief review of some of the main concepts to take away from this chapter:

- Particle systems, consisting of large numbers of discrete point masses, can be used to simulate a wide variety of phenomena that do not exhibit a coherent organized structure.

- The particles in a particle system interact with the scene but not with each other.

- The particles in a particle system originate from particle generators. These particle generators are typically geometric objects that can be manipulated and moved about within a scene.

- The characteristics of particles within a particle system and the initial locations and velocities of particles coming from particle generators are typically drawn from random distributions. Gaussian distributions are often the most realistic.

- Since the number of particles in a system is usually quite large, efficient methods need to be used. Most importantly, the use of the operating system memory management should be avoided by preallocating and maintaining a list of particles that can be activated and deactivated.

- Again, to improve efficiency, shortcuts in collision detection and response can be made to avoid timestep subdivision.

- Spatial subdivision is a simple but highly effective way to reduce the number of particle-polygon collision detection tests that need to be made in a timestep.

- There are numerous ways to render particles into a scene, including points, streaks, sprites, and volumetric methods.

CHAPTER 5

Particle Choreography

I N BUILDING A PARTICLE SYSTEM simulation the primary intent is always to create an interesting visual effect, treating the system as a whole to achieve a coordinated bulk motion. To do this, we will need to think like animators, as well as engineers, since our desired goal goes beyond the technical problems of creating, simulating, and rendering particles. We need to also be able to choreograph the particles to create the motion we want. Figure 5.1 shows a frame from a highly choreographed sequence, where the particles are always under the control of the animator.

In his seminal paper *Particle Animation and Rendering Using Data Parallel Computation*, Sims [1990] laid the foundations of high-performance particle system simulation in a parallel computing environment, but the main emphasis of his paper is on the aesthetics of a particle simulation—he has a lot to say about choreography. A key idea that he introduced, informing work with particles to this day, is that we can think of the choreography of particles in terms of a set of operators affecting their motion. These fall into the categories of *initialization operators*, *acceleration operators*, and *velocity operators*. And, he adds to these the idea of *bounce*, i.e., particle collision response.

In Chapter 4, we covered the mechanics of creating and running a particle system, including initialization and bounce. In this chapter, we focus on the aspects of the choreography of particles involving the use of acceleration and velocity operators. We also look at methods for steering particles around objects to avoid collisions, and for creating wind fields.

5.1   ACCELERATION OPERATORS

An acceleration operator implements a choreography method that causes a change in the particle's velocity. Velocity changes can be created by summing forces, which when divided by mass yield acceleration, together with directly applied accelerations to yield a net acceleration. We will call the additive acceleration operators $\mathbf{a}^{+\text{op}}$. These include the gravitational acceleration and air-resistance forces we studied in Chapter 3. Another possibility is to apply an operator to modify the velocity

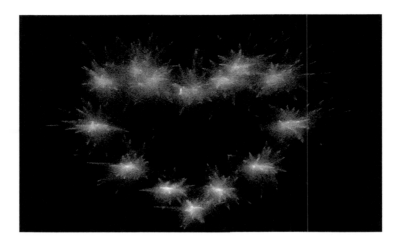

FIGURE 5.1 Fireworks particle system choreographed to create a valentine. (Courtesy of Chen-Jui Fang.)

obtained from numerical integration. These operators will typically take the velocity before and after integration as parameters and return an updated velocity. An example of this type of operator is the velocity update after collision as described in Section 4.4.3. We will call these operators $\mathbf{A}^{\mathrm{op}}()$, to indicate that they are functions. In the simulation loop, the effects of all active additive acceleration operators $\mathbf{a}_k^{+\mathrm{op}}$ on a particle i are summed, and the net acceleration is applied in the integration step to update particle i's velocity. Then, any functional acceleration operators are applied consecutively to the resulting velocity to yield a final modified velocity:

$$\mathbf{a}_i^{\mathrm{net}} = \sum_k \mathbf{a}_{ki}^{+\mathrm{op}},$$

$$\mathbf{v}_{\mathrm{new}} = \mathbf{v}_i^{[n]} + \mathbf{a}_i^{\mathrm{net}} h,$$

$$\mathbf{v}_{\mathrm{new}} = \mathbf{A}_1^{\mathrm{op}}(\mathbf{v}_{\mathrm{new}}, \mathbf{v}_i^{[n]}), \quad \mathbf{v}_{\mathrm{new}} = \mathbf{A}_2^{\mathrm{op}}(\mathbf{v}_{\mathrm{new}}, \mathbf{v}_i^{[n]}), \quad \cdots$$

$$\mathbf{v}_i^{[n+1]} = \mathbf{v}_{\mathrm{new}}$$

Below, we introduce several examples of acceleration operators. Readers are encouraged to be inventive, taking these examples as a starting place for their own designs.

5.1.1 Gravitational Attractors

We have already seen one type of gravitational attractor. That is the attraction of a very large object on a very small object over a very constrained range of separations of the two objects, like the gravitational effect of the earth on a ball. In this case, we have the simplest form of additive acceleration operator, a constant vector,

$$\mathbf{a}^{+\mathrm{op}} = \mathbf{g}.$$

The large object does not move, but the small object moves toward the large object in the direction of the vector $\mathbf{g}$ and with its speed growing at the rate $\|\mathbf{g}\|$.

Gravity gets more interesting when the two objects are at a distance from each other, so that change of distance affects the gravitational attraction. This is the type of force that produces the choreography of the heavens. Planets orbit the sun, comets follow highly elliptical paths with orbits that take them near and then very far from the sun, and interstellar objects follow parabolic paths as they swoop into our solar system and then are thrown back out by the gravitational "slingshot" effect.

In a particle system, one of the objects will be a geometric object in a fixed position, and the other will be a moving particle. Let us call the fixed object the attractor a, give it mass m_a, and label its position $\mathbf{x}_a$. Now, consider this attractor's 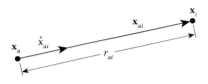 effect on particle i with position $\mathbf{x}_i$. We will call the vector from the attractor to the particle $\mathbf{x}_{ai} = \mathbf{x}_i - \mathbf{x}_a$, with magnitude $r_{ai} = \|\mathbf{x}_{ai}\|$ and direction $\hat{\mathbf{x}}_{ai} = \mathbf{x}_{ai}/r_{ai}$. According to Newtonian physical law, the force of attraction on particle i due to the attractor will be

$$\mathbf{f}_{ai} = -G\frac{m_a m_i}{r_{ai}^2}\hat{\mathbf{x}}_{ai},$$

where G is known as the universal gravitational constant. To arrive at the acceleration, not the force, on particle i, we divide by the particle's mass m_i. It is also convenient to multiply together Gm_a to yield a single constant G_a. This gives us the final additive acceleration operator

$$\mathbf{a}_{ai}^{+\mathrm{op}} = -G_a\frac{1}{r_{ai}^2}\hat{\mathbf{x}}_{ai}.$$

The effect of this operator is to accelerate particle i toward the position of the attractor a with an acceleration that is independent of the particle's mass and inversely proportional to the square of the distance between the particle and the attractor. The constant G_a can now be thought of as a "strength" constant that is freely tunable by the animator to adjust the gravitational effect.

We can move away from Newtonian physics a bit and give even more control to the animator by replacing the power 2 in the denominator with a constant p, yielding the additive acceleration operator

$$\mathbf{a}_{ai}^{+\mathrm{op}} = -G_a\frac{1}{r_{ai}^p}\hat{\mathbf{x}}_{ai}.$$

Setting $p = 2$ will give us the usual gravitational effect, resulting in particle i taking a parabolic or elliptical orbital path around attractor a, depending on particle i's velocity. Setting $p = -1$ will cause the operator to act like a spring, producing an acceleration on particle i that is proportional to its distance from the attractor.

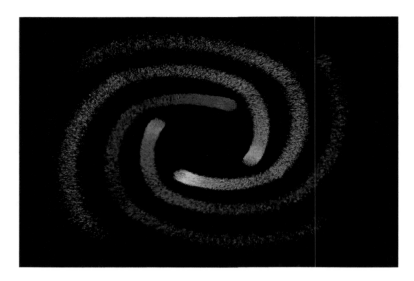

FIGURE 5.2 Spiraling particles choreographed using an attractor. (Courtesy of Kevin Smith and Adam Volin.)

This will cause the particle to be pulled toward the attractor, but it will "bounce" about the attractor like a ball on a rubber band. Other settings of p will produce different effects that are best explored by experimentation. Figure 5.2 shows an example of particle spiraling, created using a gravitational attractor.

If gravity can pull a particle toward a point, we could also define an attractor that pulls a particle toward a line with force affected by distance from the line. This could be an infinite line or a line segment of finite length. Let us see how this would be done for a line segment. We specify the line segment by a starting point $\mathbf{x}_a$, a unit vector $\hat{\mathbf{a}}$ in the direction of the line, and length L. Referring to the diagram to the right, consider this attractor's effect on particle i with position $\mathbf{x}_i$. The vector from the starting point of the line segment to particle i is $\mathbf{x}_{ai} = \mathbf{x}_i - \mathbf{x}_a$. The length 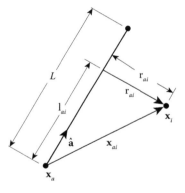 of the projection of this vector onto the line segment's direction is $l_{ai} = \mathbf{x}_{ai} \cdot \hat{\mathbf{a}}$. At this point, we can test l_{ai} to see if the particle lies within the extent of the line segment. If $0 \leq l_{ai} \leq L$ then particle i lies within the line segment's extent, otherwise it does not. If, instead of a line segment, we want to use an infinite line attractor, all that needs to be done is to ignore this test, and its ramifications below. If the particle lies within the line segment's extent then the vector orthogonal to the line segment out to point $\mathbf{x}_i$ is $\mathbf{r}_{ai} = \mathbf{x}_{ai} - l_{ai}\hat{\mathbf{a}}$, and the distance from the particle to the line is $r_{ai} = \|\mathbf{r}_{ai}\|$. If the particle lies outside of the line segment's extent, we have two choices: we can ignore the line segment's gravitational effect entirely, or we can compute the distance of the particle from the nearest end point of the line segment, yielding

$$\mathbf{r}_{ai} = \begin{cases} \mathbf{x}_i - (\mathbf{x}_a + L\hat{\mathbf{a}}) & \text{if } l_{ai} > L, \\ \mathbf{r}_{ai} & \text{if } 0 \leq l_{ai} \leq L, \\ \mathbf{x}_{ai} & \text{if } l_{ai} < 0, \end{cases}$$

$$r_{ai} = \|\mathbf{r}_{ai}\|,$$

$$\hat{\mathbf{r}}_{ai} = \mathbf{r}_{ai}/r_{ai}.$$

Now, we can define the additive acceleration operator like we did between two points

$$\mathbf{a}_{ai}^{+\mathrm{op}} = -G_a \frac{1}{r_{ai}^p} \hat{\mathbf{r}}_{ai}.$$

Although the final equation looks quite similar to that of the point attractor, the effect will be quite different. As long as the particle is within the line segment's extent, there will be no acceleration parallel to the line, so any motion of the particle in the parallel direction will be unaffected by the line. If the particle would normally go into an elliptical orbit about a point, it will go into an elliptical spiral around the line segment. If we ignore the effect of the line attractor for particles beyond the line's extent, the particle will spiral around the line and then get thrown out when it moves beyond the end of the attractor.

5.1.2 Random Accelerations

A way to introduce interesting motion to particles is to apply additive accelerations that act randomly. This can be used to simulate any turbulent process, like snowflakes falling subject to slight breezes, or atoms undergoing Brownian motion.

To achieve this type of motion, the random vector generator $\mathbf{S}()$ from Section 4.2 can be scaled by a scale factor S_i and used to produce a small perturbation in particle i's velocity at each timestep. This has the problems that the magnitude of the perturbation will be scaled by the timestep during integration, and the rate at which perturbations occur will be governed by the timestep of the simulation. To produce random perturbations that occur independently from the time step, S_i can be scaled by the timestep

$$\mathbf{a}_{si}^{+\mathrm{op}} = \frac{S_i}{h} \mathbf{S}(),$$

and random perturbations can be issued on a schedule independent of timestep. For example, we might want one random acceleration per frame of the animation, so if the animation proceeds at 30 frames per second, we would only create a random acceleration when the time passes an integer multiple of $1/30$ of a second.

5.1.3 Drag and Undrag

Additive acceleration operators do not have to be position based. In the bouncing
ball problem of Chapter 3 we looked at the effect of air resistance and wind on the
ball. The same sort of effect can be used as an acceleration operator for particles. We
will call these operators "drag" operators. Letting $\mathbf{v}_i$ be the velocity of particle i, m_i
its mass, and $\mathbf{w}$ a constant wind velocity vector, the simplest drag operator would be

$$\mathbf{a}_{wi}^{+\text{op}} = \frac{D}{m_i}(\mathbf{w} - \mathbf{v}_i),$$

where D is a drag "strength" constant that is adjustable by the animator to produce
the desired effect.

By changing the sign of D, we create "undrag"—that is, a force tending to
increase the speed of the particle. As long as "undrag" is applied, the particle will
increase in speed, so this acceleration operator is typically only applied for a short
period of time, or until the particle achieves a desired velocity. Used in this way, it
is a good way to smoothly increase a particle's speed.

5.1.4 Velocity Limiters

Often we want to assure that a particle maintains at least a minimum speed, or that
it is limited to some maximum speed. Sims presents a method to ensure a particle's
speed rises to a minimum speed, V_τ, and then remains above that speed. This
operator is applied after numerical integration, so it is not an additive acceleration,
but operates on the new and previous velocities to produce an updated new velocity:

$$\mathbf{A}^{\text{op}}(\mathbf{v}_i^{[n+1]}, \mathbf{v}_i^{[n]}) = \mathbf{max}[\mathbf{v}_i^{[n+1]}, \mathbf{min}(\mathbf{v}_i^{[n]}, V_\tau\hat{\mathbf{v}}_i^{[n]})].$$

In this operator, the **max** and **min** functions select the vector with the largest
or smallest magnitude from their two-vector arguments. As long as a particle's
new speed $\|\mathbf{v}_i^{[n+1]}\|$ is above V_τ the new velocity will be selected unchanged, since
the second parameter's magnitude can never exceed V_τ. Likewise, if the new speed
is above the previous speed $\|\mathbf{v}_i^{[n]}\|$, the new velocity will be selected. Otherwise,
the speed will be set to V_τ with direction the same as the previous velocity if the
previous speed is greater than V_τ, or will be set to the previous velocity if it is less
than V_τ. A similar approach can be used to assure that a particle never exceeds a
given maximum speed.

5.2 VELOCITY OPERATORS

In contrast to the acceleration operators, velocity operators work outside of physical
law, providing velocity updates for a single timestep, without changing the momentum of a particle. The effect is to reposition the particle, as if there were a velocity,
but the velocity itself is not modified. In this way, both acceleration operators and
velocity operators can act on the same particle without any interference. This is

implemented by modifying the velocity that is used in the numerical integration to compute the new position. Sims uses a modified integrator to compute the new position by the update

$$\mathbf{x}_i^{[n+1]} = \mathbf{x}_i^{[n]} + \frac{\mathbf{v}_i^{[n+1]} + \mathbf{v}_i^{[n]}}{2} h.$$

We think of a velocity operator $\mathbf{V}^{\mathrm{op}}$ as a function applied to a velocity to return a new velocity. Applying a velocity operator during the integration process, the position update is modified to be

$$\mathbf{x}_i^{[n+1]} = \mathbf{x}_i^{[n]} + \mathbf{V}^{\mathrm{op}} \left(\frac{\mathbf{v}_i^{[n+1]} + \mathbf{v}_i^{[n]}}{2} \right) h.$$

If multiple velocity operators are applied in one timestep we understand $\mathbf{V}^{\mathrm{op}}$ to be the repetitive application of all of the velocity operators taken in order.

5.2.1   Affine Velocity Operators

All of the affine transformations can be used as velocity operators, with the most useful being translation by offset $\triangle\mathbf{v}$:

$$\mathbf{V}^{\mathrm{op}}(\mathbf{v}) = \mathbf{v} + \triangle\mathbf{v},$$

rotation by angle θ about axis $\hat{\mathbf{u}}^*$:

$$\mathbf{V}^{\mathrm{op}}(\mathbf{v}) = R(\mathbf{v} : \theta, \hat{\mathbf{u}}),$$

and scale by scale factor s:

$$\mathbf{V}^{\mathrm{op}}(\mathbf{v}) = s\mathbf{v}.$$

All of these operators can be given interesting variation by applying a small amount of randomness to the operator's parameter at each step. Figure 5.3 shows a sequence with a helicopter formed from particles, and then destroyed by a projectile. The formation motion is guided by velocity operators attracting the particles to an underlying, invisible geometric model.

In using velocity operators it is important to remember that their effect is scaled by the step size h to update position at each timestep. For example, the translation operator will cause the position of the particle to be moved by $\triangle\mathbf{v}h$ at each timestep. If a total translation of $\triangle\mathbf{v}$ is desired, then the velocity operator will have to stay in effect for $1/h$ timesteps (i.e., if $h = 1/30$ then the operator will have to be applied for 30 timesteps). This will result in a smooth translation over the required time. If a sudden jump is desired, then instead of the translation $\triangle\mathbf{v}$, the translation $\triangle\mathbf{v}/h$ may be used for a single timestep.

---

*This can be implemented using Rodrigues' formula, see Appendix D.6.

FIGURE 5.3 Particles choreographed to form a helicopter, which is later destroyed. (Courtesy of Hongyuan Johnny Jia.)

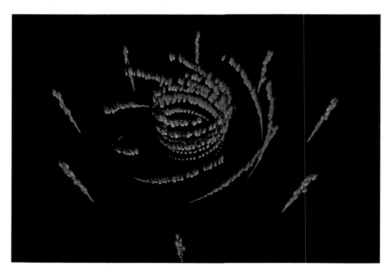

FIGURE 5.4 Spiraling particles choreographed using a vortex. (Courtesy of Ashwin Bangalore.)

5.2.2 Vortices

One of the most interesting velocity operators is the vortex operator. A physical vortex, like a tornado or the water draining in a sink, is a fluid phenomenon characterized by the fluid rotating around an axis, with angular velocity that is very high, at the physical limit, near the rotational axis but that decreases with distance from the axis. The decrease with radial distance r from the axis is usually characterized by the scale factor $1/r^2$. Figure 5.4 shows a vortex in action, with particles rendered in a flame-like style.

We can create a vortex effect in our particle system using a velocity operator. If we attempted to create a vortex effect using an acceleration operator, the momentum caused by the high angular velocity near the axis would cause the particles to be flung out of the vortex, rather than being captured by it. By using a velocity operator, we can avoid this problem.

A vortex operator is specified by a cylindrical region in space with base center location $\mathbf{x}_v$, axis oriented along the direction $\hat{\mathbf{v}}$, length L, and radius R, as indicated in the figure to the right. We can think of this as the vortex volume. A particle i, with position $\mathbf{x}_i$ located inside this volume is affected by the vortex, but if it is outside it is unaffected. The vector from the vortex base center to particle i is

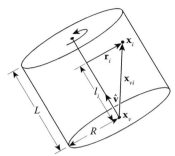

$$\mathbf{x}_{vi} = \mathbf{x}_i - \mathbf{x}_v.$$

The length of the projection of this vector onto the vortex' direction is

$$l_i = \hat{\mathbf{v}} \cdot \mathbf{x}_{vi}.$$

If $0 \le l_i \le L$ then particle i lies within the vortex' axial extent, otherwise it does not. The orthogonal vector from the axis to particle i is

$$\mathbf{r}_i = \mathbf{x}_{vi} - l_i \hat{\mathbf{v}},$$

so the distance from the particle to the axis is

$$r_i = \|\mathbf{r}_i\|.$$

If $r_i > R$ then the particle lies outside of the vortex's radial extent, otherwise it is inside the vortex. Now, let f_R be the rotational frequency of the vortex at radius R, measured in cycles per second (Hz). The rotational frequency at the particle's distance r_i is then

$$f_i = \left(\frac{R}{r_i} \right)^{\tau} f_R.$$

The exponent τ can be thought of as a "tightness" parameter that governs how quickly the vortex decays with distance from its axis. For a physical vortex $\tau = 2$. To avoid numerical problems very near the axis, we can apply a frequency limit $f_{\max}$, giving $f_i = \min(f_{\max}, (\frac{R}{r_i})^{\tau} f_R)$. Now, we need to rotate the particle's velocity vector through an angle that will achieve the rotational frequency f_i. If we set the particle's angular velocity to

$$\omega = 2\pi f_i,$$

then the actual rotation achieved in one timestep will be ωh, or exactly $2\pi f_i$ radians in 1 second of simulation time.

5.3 COLLISION AVOIDANCE

In Chapter 3 we covered the handling of collisions between a ball and a geometric object, but often the effect that we desire is to avoid collisions, directing particles around environmental objects so that they never collide. Imagine a stream of air blowing across a pole. Due to the pressure of the air, the flow will be directed around the pole, with very few air molecules actually colliding with the pole. Collision avoidance in a particle system is a way to have a stream of particles mimic this sort of behavior. We will see this topic again in Chapter 6, when we look at the simulation of the behavior of a flock of birds or school of fish.

5.3.1 Potential Fields

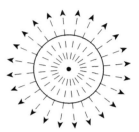

The simplest way to implement collision avoidance is to build a potential field around each environmental obstacle that provides an acceleration away from the obstacle. The point or line gravity acceleration operators described in Section 5.1.1 will work very well for this purpose. By removing the minus sign from these operators, they will act to repel objects rather than attracting them, making them anti-gravity operators.

If the object to be avoided is regular in shape, similar to a sphere or a cube, placing a single anti-gravity point at its center may be sufficient. If the object is elongated, like a pole or skyscraper, then an anti-gravity line can be used. For complex shapes, a collection of points and lines might be needed.

A useful idea here is to provide an extent for each of the operators, so that it exerts no acceleration beyond a maximum distance. In this way, we avoid the problem of having to compute and add the effect of multiple operators at every timestep. Only operators near to a particle will affect it.

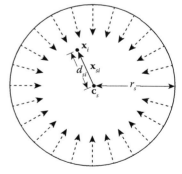

Sometimes it is desired to constrain a particle system to remain inside a geometric object. In this case, we can make the entire surface of the containing object be the field generator, so that particles are always pushed away from the surface of the object. A simple example would be a sphere s with center $\mathbf{c}_s$, and radius r_s acting as a container. The acceleration operator would be computed as follows:

$$\mathbf{x}_{si} = \mathbf{x}_i - \mathbf{c}_s,$$
$$d_{si} = \|\mathbf{x}_{si}\|,$$
$$\mathbf{a}_{si}^{+\mathrm{op}} = -G_s \frac{1}{(r_s - d_{si})^{p_s}} \hat{\mathbf{x}}_{si}.$$

Here, G_s is a tunable strength constant, and p_s governs how quickly the force of the anti-gravity falls off with distance from the sphere surface.

Although potential fields are easy to implement and can be effective in preventing collisions, they often produce effects that are not physically realistic. A particle headed directly toward an anti-gravity point will be slowed down and pushed backward but will not turn away. Another problem is that a particle near an anti-gravity point will be pushed away by it whether or not there is any danger of a collision. The net effect will be that particles are prevented by the net force field from colliding with protected objects but in a way that can look physically nonrealistic. However, it can look remarkably like "Shields up Captain!"

5.3.2 Steering

A more complex but more interesting approach to collision avoidance is particle *steering*. Here we think of the particle as an intelligent actor, imagining that it has eyes looking ahead, and the ability to steer itself by planning a route around impending obstacles. The approach is to locate a viewing coordinate frame at the position of the particle, with its z axis aligned with the velocity vector. We associate with this an angular field of view, which can be tuned by the animator to achieve the desired behavior. Finally, we set a maximum viewing distance, which should be determined by the particle's speed and the estimated time required to take evasive action. The faster the particle is traveling, the farther this distance should be. Now, we imagine that each object within the particle's view cone can be seen by the particle, and its image used by the particle to plan any required evasive action. If the particle's current velocity will bring it into collision with an object, the particle estimates the time to collision and checks the angular distance to the nearest silhouette edge of the obstacle. It then computes an acceleration that will cause it to turn enough to avoid the obstacle within the allotted time. An example will serve to illustrate the process.

The simplest nontrivial example is that of a single fixed sphere obstacle. In practice, this example is actually very useful, as it is often expedient to represent geometry, for collision avoidance purposes, by a simple convex bounding object. For the following analysis, let the sphere center be located at the point $\mathbf{c}_s$ in world coordinates, and its radius be r_s. Let the position of particle i be $\mathbf{x}_i$, and its velocity be $\mathbf{v}_i$. Since we want the particle to pass by the sphere without con-

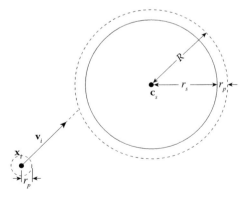

tacting it, we also define the distance r_p to be a "safe" distance from the collision sphere, and imagine that the particle is protected within a sphere of this radius. The resulting path is identical to steering the particle so it grazes a sphere of radius $R = r_s + r_p$.

We only have to worry about the sphere if the particle is on a collision path with it, and if the collision is scheduled to occur soon. To begin, we compute the particle's closest predicted approach to the sphere's center, assuming that the particle continues to travel at its current velocity. Normalizing the velocity, we create the direction vector $\hat{\mathbf{v}}_i = \mathbf{v}_i / \|\mathbf{v}_i\|$, and we let the vector defined by the sphere center and the particle's position be

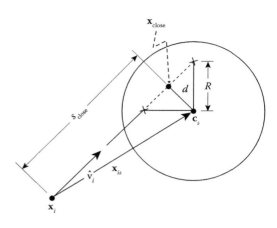

$$\mathbf{x}_{is} = \mathbf{c}_s - \mathbf{x}_i.$$

We can treat the particle position together with its velocity direction vector as a ray extending out from the particle along its current direction of travel. The distance along this ray, at the ray's closest approach to the sphere center, is given by

$$s_{\text{close}} = \mathbf{x}_{is} \cdot \hat{\mathbf{v}}_i.$$

If $s_{\text{close}} < 0$ then the sphere is behind the particle and we can ignore it. Also, if the sphere is far in front of the particle we can ignore it until we get closer, so we compute a distance of concern

$$d_c = \|\mathbf{v}_i\| t_c,$$

where t_c is a threshold time to collision that can be set by the animator. If $s_{\text{close}} > d_c$, we can ignore the sphere. If we are still concerned with the sphere, we compute the point of closest approach

$$\mathbf{x}_{\text{close}} = \mathbf{x}_i + s_{\text{close}} \hat{\mathbf{v}}_i.$$

The distance of this point to the sphere center is

$$d = \|\mathbf{x}_{\text{close}} - \mathbf{c}_s\|.$$

If $d > R$ then the closest the ray comes to the sphere center is greater than the expanded sphere radius, so there is no predicted collision and we can ignore the sphere. Otherwise, we are scheduled for an imminent collision with the sphere, and we need to take corrective action.

The corrective action will be to apply an acceleration that will adjust the particle's path so that it curves around the sphere. In order to provide the required steering, we first find a spatial target to direct the particle toward. The vector from the sphere center to the closest point of approach is orthogonal to the velocity vector and lies in the plane formed by the velocity vector and $\mathbf{x}_{is}$. This is denoted

$$\mathbf{v}_\perp = \mathbf{x}_{\text{close}} - \mathbf{c}_s.$$

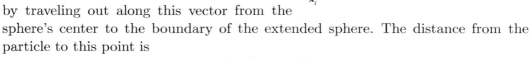

So, the direction from the sphere's center orthogonal to the velocity is $\hat{\mathbf{v}}_\perp = \mathbf{v}_\perp / \|\mathbf{v}_\perp\|$. We determine the turning target

$$\mathbf{x}_t = \mathbf{c}_s + R\hat{\mathbf{v}}_\perp$$

by traveling out along this vector from the sphere's center to the boundary of the extended sphere. The distance from the particle to this point is

$$d_t = \|\mathbf{x}_t - \mathbf{x}_i\|,$$

the speed at which this point is being approached is

$$v_t = \mathbf{v}_i \cdot (\mathbf{x}_t - \mathbf{x}_i)/d_t,$$

and the time to reach this point will be

$$t_t = d_t/v_t.$$

The increased average speed in the direction orthogonal to the current velocity that will be needed to reach this point in the allotted time is

$$\Delta v_s = \|\hat{\mathbf{v}}_i \times (\mathbf{x}_t - \mathbf{x}_i)\|/t_t.$$

To maintain an average speed increase in that direction of v_s, during the elapsed time, the required magnitude of the acceleration is

$$a_s = 2\Delta v_s/t_t.$$

Finally, the required acceleration is

$$\mathbf{a}^{\text{top}} = a_s \hat{\mathbf{v}}_\perp.$$

One note of caution about this approach to steering around a sphere is that it is still possible for a collision to occur. If other sources of acceleration act to cancel the steering acceleration, its effect can be negated. The solution to this is that the steering operator should override any acceleration opposite to it. If we let $\mathbf{a}_{\text{total}}$ be the sum of all of the other acceleration operators, we can compute its component

$$e = \hat{\mathbf{v}}_\perp \cdot \mathbf{a}_{\text{total}}$$

in the direction of the steering acceleration. If e is negative, then it is opposing the steering acceleration, so we need to strengthen the steering to cancel its effect.

If e is positive, then there is already some turning in the direction of steering and we can reduce the steering acceleration by this amount. In either case, this leaves us with the corrected acceleration

$$\mathbf{a}^{+\mathrm{op}} = \max(a_s - e, 0)\hat{\mathbf{v}}_\perp.$$

The other way in which steering can fail to prevent collision can be seen by examining the figure above. The vector between $\mathbf{x}_t$ and $\mathbf{x}_i$ actually passes through the expanded sphere, so if the correction $\mathbf{a}^{+\mathrm{op}}$ is applied just once, a collision may occur (depending on the safety factor r_p). In a simulation, this will normally not be a problem, since a corrective acceleration will be recomputed at each timestep, iteratively refining the solution. However, if the speed of the particle is so large that it can reach the sphere in just one or two timesteps, a collision may occur. A more perfect solution is to compute a tangent to the sphere that passes through the particle's position, lies in the plane defined by the particle's velocity and the vector to the sphere's center, and is nearest to the closest point of approach $\mathbf{x}_{\mathrm{close}}$. We leave the details as an exercise for the student.

5.4 SUMMARY

Here is a brief review of some of the main concepts to take away from this chapter:

- While a lot can be done with a particle system simply by making particle generator choices, gaining control over interesting motion requires the ability to choreograph particles to achieve a desired look or effect.

- One way to organize thinking about particle choreography is to think in terms of operators, operating on the position and velocity of the particles.

- Acceleration operators affect a particle's velocity by applying accelerations. These are equivalent to applying forces. These can be used to produce effects such as gravitational attraction, random perturbations, and drag.

- Velocity operators affect a particle's position by applying velocity increments. Unlike forces, these do not result in a change in particle momentum, but simply affect a particle's position. These can be used to produce effects such as vortices and affine transformations of the particles.

- Potential fields can be used to prevent particle collisions with an object by applying forces pushing away from the object.

- A more sophisticated approach to collision avoidance involves computing steering forces that tend to steer particles around an object.

CHAPTER 6

Interacting Particle Systems

BUILDING AND CHOREOGRAPHING PARTICLE SYSTEMS, consisting of noninteracting particles allowed us to produce many striking visual effects, but there are many systems that can only be simulated realistically if the particles are treated as interacting with each other. The most obvious example is the universe itself. At astronomical distances, all of the asteroids, moons, planets, stars, and indeed the galaxies, can be thought of as parti-

M81 Galaxy (source NASA)

cles. Their massive sizes are negligible, compared with the scale of the universe. But, their behavior, like that exhibited by the galaxy in the figure above, could never be modeled by a standard particle system. This is simply because the behaviors arise from the complex gravitational interactions that the heavenly bodies all exert on each other. Because of these attractions, moons orbit planets, planets orbit their suns, and suns group together to form spiral or globular galaxies. In turn, the gravity of these galaxies affects all of the other galaxies. The resulting complex patterns of motion, across many orders of magnitude of scale, could not possibly arise without the forces of interaction.

One of the first things to recognize when working with interacting particles is that it will be important to maintain a coherent notion and record of the entire system's state, and to update that state only once per simulation timestep. This is true since particles can no longer be treated as independent individuals. If we update the state of one particle, we are changing its position and velocity, which in turn will affect the forces acting on all of the other particles in the system. We need all of the particles' positions and velocities to remain frozen in time while we compute all of the forces acting on all of the particles. Only after all of the forces are computed can we use numerical integration to update the individual particle states. In a noninteracting particle system we could write a loop like this:

foreach *particle i* **do**
 | Determine total force on *i* due to environment;
 | *i*'s new-state = Integration of forces over timestep *h*;
end

But, for an interacting particle system the code needs to look more like this:

foreach *particle i* **do**
 | Determine and save total force on *i* due to environment;
 | **foreach** *particle j* **do**
 | | Add contribution of particle *j* to *i*'s total force;
 | **end**
end
foreach *particle i* **do**
 | *i*'s new-state = Integration of *i*'s total force over timestep *h*;
end

Another critical issue when working with interacting particles is that the complexity of the computation of forces goes up with the square of the number of particles. For a noninteracting particle system, the computational complexity is $O(N)$ in the number of particles. Since each particle is treated separately, all of the loops in the computation simply iterate over the number of particles. On the other hand, in an interacting system, to compute the forces on each of N particles we must consider all of the $N-1$ other particles, so the total number of interactions is $N(N-1) = N^2 - N$. We can invoke Newton's third law, that every action has an equal and opposite reaction, to save half of these calculations, since the force of particle i on particle j must be equal and opposite to the force of particle j on particle i. But, this still leaves us with $\frac{1}{2}(N^2 - N)$ interactions to compute. Therefore, the computational complexity of the interacting particle problem is $O(N^2)$. This is

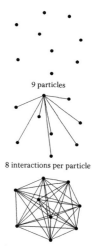

9 particles

8 interactions per particle

(9×8)/2 = 36 computations

not such a big problem if we are dealing with small numbers, but the nature of a particle system simulation is that we usually want to treat a very large number of particles, so the cost can be very high.

In Chapters 4 and 5, we explained how to create and choreograph simple noninteracting particle systems. In this chapter, we will lay the foundations for dealing with large systems of particles that do interact with each other. The two main conceptual and technical issues will be maintaining a coherent notion of the entire system's state, since particles can no longer be treated as independent individuals, and managing the computational complexity of our simulations to achieve reasonable performance. Our primary examples will be astronomical simulation and flocking systems.

6.1 STATE VECTORS

The problem of maintaining a coherent notion of the entire system's state can be conveniently addressed using the idea of a *state vector*. In the mathematical sense, a state vector is a vector whose elements record all information necessary to keep track of the state of a system. For a particle system, this will be the positions and velocities of all of the particles in the system. On the software side, a state vector is typically maintained as an object containing an array of particle positions and velocities, together with a set of methods for doing mathematical and maintenance operations over this array. We will start by building up the conceptual basis for state vectors, and then describe how they can be integrated into the simulation loop to support efficient interacting particle simulations.

6.1.1 State Vectors for Single Particles

When computing the motion of a particle in a noninteracting particle system, the particle's state consisted of its current position and velocity. We could abstract this using vector notation to describe the state of particle i by the *state vector*:

$$\mathbf{s}_i = \begin{bmatrix} \mathbf{x}_i \\ \mathbf{v}_i \end{bmatrix}. \tag{6.1}$$

This may appear to be a strange mathematical object, since we have been thinking of vectors as having scalar components, but the algebra of vectors will support elements that are themselves vectors. The additive, scaling, and dot product vector operations still apply:

$$\mathbf{s}_i + \mathbf{s}_j = \begin{bmatrix} \mathbf{x}_i + \mathbf{x}_j \\ \mathbf{v}_i + \mathbf{v}_j \end{bmatrix},$$

$$\mathbf{s}_i - \mathbf{s}_j = \begin{bmatrix} \mathbf{x}_i - \mathbf{x}_j \\ \mathbf{v}_i - \mathbf{v}_j \end{bmatrix},$$

$$a\mathbf{s}_i = \begin{bmatrix} a\mathbf{x}_i \\ a\mathbf{v}_i \end{bmatrix},$$

$$\mathbf{s}_i \cdot \mathbf{s}_j = \mathbf{x}_i \cdot \mathbf{x}_j + \mathbf{v}_i \cdot \mathbf{v}_j.$$

Because of this, vector notation can be highly effective in simplifying the notation needed to describe operations on particles, and can be used to develop data types and methods for operating on particles in a compact way. To see this, let us first examine the ramifications of this notation on how we might describe a noninteracting particle simulation.

At each step of the simulation, we compute the rate of change of the particle's position and velocity. To compute the rate of change of particle i's velocity, we sum the m individual forces on the particle, to obtain the total force

$$\mathbf{f}_i = \sum_{j=0}^{m-1} \mathbf{f}_i^j,$$

where the notation $\mathbf{f}_i^j$ indicates the jth force acting on particle i. Dividing by the particle's mass m_i we obtain the particle's acceleration,

$$\mathbf{a}_i = \frac{1}{m_i} \mathbf{f}_i.$$

The rate of change of the particle's position is simply its velocity, which we can use without any calculation. Thus, in our state notation, the rate of change of the state of the particle is

$$\dot{\mathbf{s}}_i = \begin{bmatrix} \dot{\mathbf{x}}_i \\ \dot{\mathbf{v}}_i \end{bmatrix} = \begin{bmatrix} \mathbf{v}_i \\ \mathbf{a}_i \end{bmatrix}. \tag{6.2}$$

An important point to note about the force calculation is that each of the individual forces $\mathbf{f}_i^j$ acting on the particle can be thought of as a function of the state of the particle and time. To see this, review the acceleration operators discussed in Section 5.1. You will find that each of them is affected by a set of parameters for the particle and the scene, and may have forces based on the particle's current position, current velocity, or both. If all of the parameters are fixed, the forces vary only with the particle's state. If any of the parameters is animated, so that it varies with time, then the force function will vary with time. Thus, each of the forces $\mathbf{f}_i^j$ acting on particle i can be expressed as a function $\mathbf{f}_i^j(\mathbf{s}_i, t)$; therefore, the acceleration on the particle is also a function of its state and time:

$$\mathbf{a}_i = \mathbf{a}_i(\mathbf{s}_i, t) = \frac{1}{m_i} \mathbf{f}_i(\mathbf{s}_i, t) = \frac{1}{m_i} \sum_j \mathbf{f}_i^j(\mathbf{s}_i, t). \tag{6.3}$$

6.1.2 State Vectors for Interacting Particles

Having established this, it can now be easily demonstrated that the entire rate of change of the particle's state is a function of its current state and time. Examining Equation 6.2, we see that the first term in the time derivative of the state vector is the particle's velocity, which is an element of its state, and the second term is its acceleration, which by Equation 6.3 is also a function of the particle's state and time. We summarize this insight by adopting the notation

$$\dot{\mathbf{s}}_i = \mathbf{F}_i(\mathbf{s}_i, t), \tag{6.4}$$

where

$$\mathbf{F}_i(\mathbf{s}_i, t) = \begin{bmatrix} \mathbf{v}_i \\ \mathbf{a}_i(\mathbf{s}_i, t) \end{bmatrix}. \tag{6.5}$$

We call the function $\mathbf{F}_i$ particle i's *particle dynamics function*, because it accounts for everything in the system acting to change the state of particle i.

After computing accelerations, the next simulation step is numerical integration. Using our notions of particle state, integration no longer needs to be separated into velocity and position updates. For example, Euler integration from timestep n to timestep $n+1$ could now be written

$$\mathbf{s}_i^{[n+1]} = \mathbf{s}_i^{[n]} + \dot{\mathbf{s}}_i^{[n]} h.$$

Using the particle dynamics function, Euler integration can also be written

$$\mathbf{s}_i^{[n+1]} = \mathbf{s}_i^{[n]} + \mathbf{F}_i(\mathbf{s}_i^{[n]}, t) h.$$

This way of describing integration will provide important insights when developing improved numerical integration methods in Chapter 7.

Having built a new conceptual structure around the concept of state, with respect to a noninteracting particle system, let us see how this conceptual structure needs to be updated when considering an interacting particle system. The most significant changes will be to Equations 6.3 through 6.5. In an interacting particle system, the forces on an individual particle need to also include the effects of all of the other particles. Thus, the forces and accelerations on a particle now need to be expressed as functions of the states of all of the particles in the system. If there are m forces on the particle not coming from the other particles, and there are n particles, the expression for total force on particle i will have to be rewritten

$$\mathbf{f}_i(\mathbf{s}_0, \cdots, \mathbf{s}_{n-1}, t) = \sum_{j=0}^{m-1} \mathbf{f}_i^j(\mathbf{s}_i, t) + \sum_{k=0}^{n-1} \mathbf{g}_i^k(\mathbf{s}_i, \mathbf{s}_k, t).$$

The terms $\mathbf{g}_i^k$ are the new interparticle forces, giving the force on particle i due to particle k. Note that each of these is a function of both particle i's state and particle k's state, so that the total force is now a function of the states of all of the particles. This results in a rather clumsy notation, which we can correct by making another notational and conceptual leap.

Instead of the state of an individual particle, we could construct a *system state vector* $(\mathbf{S})^*$ that holds the state of the entire particle system:

$$\mathbf{S} = \begin{bmatrix} \mathbf{s}_0 \\ \mathbf{s}_1 \\ \vdots \\ \mathbf{s}_{n-1} \end{bmatrix}.$$

Although we could work with this description of system state, more commonly the position elements of the particle states are grouped together at the top of the

---

*We adopt the notation that a *system state vector* is represented by a boldface capital letter.

state vector, and the velocity elements are grouped at the bottom. Thus, for n particles, the system state vector will have $2n$ elements, each of which is a 3D vector. This scheme has advantages for advanced applications, when it is desired to use different processing strategies for positions versus velocities. Written this way, the system state vector for n particles would be

$$\mathbf{S} = \begin{bmatrix} \mathbf{x}_0 \\ \mathbf{x}_1 \\ \vdots \\ \mathbf{x}_{n-1} \\ \mathbf{v}_0 \\ \mathbf{v}_1 \\ \vdots \\ \mathbf{v}_{n-1} \end{bmatrix}. \tag{6.6}$$

Now, the total force on an individual particle can be written

$$\mathbf{f}_i(\mathbf{S}, t) = \sum_{j=0}^{m-1} \mathbf{f}_i^j(\mathbf{s}_i, t) + \sum_{k=0}^{n-1} \mathbf{g}_i^k(\mathbf{s}_i, \mathbf{s}_k, t),$$

so the acceleration can be written

$$\mathbf{a}_i = \frac{1}{m_i} \mathbf{f}_i(\mathbf{S}, t).$$

Finally, the rate of change of the state of the system can be expressed as the vector

$$\dot{\mathbf{S}} = \begin{bmatrix} \mathbf{v}_0 \\ \mathbf{v}_1 \\ \vdots \\ \mathbf{v}_{n-1} \\ \mathbf{a}_0 \\ \mathbf{a}_1 \\ \vdots \\ \mathbf{a}_{n-1} \end{bmatrix}.$$

With all of this notational structure, we can construct the *system dynamics function*

$$\dot{\mathbf{S}} = \mathbf{F}(\mathbf{S}, t). \tag{6.7}$$

The system dynamics function returns the sum of all of the forces acting on the particle system, from the environment and between particles. We will see below how this is integrated into the simulation code.

6.1.3 Implementation

We can now develop an implementation of an interacting particle system simulation, where the main simulation loop looks almost identical in structure to the code for a single particle, as described in Chapter 2.

In the code below, assume that we have defined a type Vector3D, consisting of an array of three floating point numbers, for which all of the standard vector operations are defined. Also assume that we have defined a type StateVector, for which the operations of multiplication by a scalar and addition between StateVector's have been defined. For N particles, the internal representation of the StateVector is a $2N$ array of elements of type Vector3D. The first N elements, $0 \cdots (N-1)$, are the positions of the particles, arranged in order by particle index. The next N elements, $N \cdots (2N-1)$, are the velocities of the particles, arranged in the same order. A StateVector must also record the number of particles N that it holds.

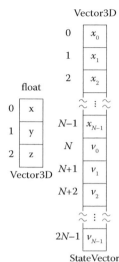

Given these data structures, the main simulation algorithm would look like this:

StateVector $\mathbf{S}, \dot{\mathbf{S}}$;

$n = 0;\ t = 0;$
$\mathbf{S} = \mathbf{S}_0;$
while $t < t_{max}$ **do**
$\quad$ $\dot{\mathbf{S}} = \mathbf{F}(\mathbf{S},\mathrm{t});$

$\quad$ *State and accelerations are all known.*
$\quad$ *Auxiliary variable computations and display go here.*

$\quad$ $\mathbf{S}^{\mathrm{new}} = \mathtt{NumInt}(\mathbf{S}, \dot{\mathbf{S}}, h);$

$\quad$ *The new and old states are known. Collision detection,*
$\quad$ *and other post integration steps go here.*

$\quad$ $\mathbf{S} = \mathbf{S}^{\mathrm{new}};$
$\quad$ $n = n + 1;\ t = nh;$
end

Integration of the entire interacting particle system, via Euler integration, can be expressed in one line within the numerical integration function:

StateVector $\mathtt{NumInt}$(StateVector $\mathbf{S}$, StateVector $\dot{\mathbf{S}}$, float h)
begin
$\quad$ StateVector $\mathbf{S}^{\mathrm{new}}$;

$\quad$ $\mathbf{S}^{\mathrm{new}} = \mathbf{S} + \dot{\mathbf{S}}h;$

$\quad$ **return** $\mathbf{S}^{\mathrm{new}}$
end

The system dynamics function can have the simple structure:

StateVector F(StateVector **S**, float t)
begin
$\quad$ StateVector $\dot{\mathbf{S}}$;

$\quad$ **for** $i = 0$ **to** $N\text{-}1$ **do**
$\qquad$ *Copy velocities from the state vector*
$\qquad$ $\dot{\mathbf{S}}[i] = \mathbf{S}[i+N]$;
$\qquad$ *Compute accelerations*
$\qquad$ $\dot{\mathbf{S}}[i+N] = \frac{1}{m_i}\mathbf{f}_i(\mathbf{S},t)$;
$\quad$ **end**

$\quad$ **return** $\dot{\mathbf{S}}$
end

In this function, each one of the individual particle force functions $\mathbf{f}_i$ can be implemented independently, or can take advantage of any common structure. A general particle force function can be implemented that takes the particle number as an additional parameter and returns the total force on that particle.

If we are working with a system where Newton's third law applies, then a more efficient organization would be to build one function to compute all of the accelerations from the forces, that works like this:

StateVector Accelerations(StateVector **S**, float t)
begin
$\quad$ StateVector $\dot{\mathbf{S}}$;
$\quad$ Vector3D $\mathbf{f}_i^j$;

$\quad$ *Compute environmental accelerations on all particles.*
$\quad$ **for** $i = 0$ **to** $N\text{-}1$ **do**
$\qquad$ $\dot{\mathbf{S}}[i+N] = \frac{1}{m_i}\mathbf{f}_f(\mathbf{S},i,t)$;
$\quad$ **end**

$\quad$ *Add interparticle accelerations to all particles.*
$\quad$ **for** $i = 0$ **to** $N\text{-}2$ **do**
$\qquad$ **for** $j = i\text{+}1$ **to** $N\text{-}1$ **do**
$\qquad\quad$ $\mathbf{f}_i^j = \mathbf{f}_g(\mathbf{S},i,j,t)$;
$\qquad\quad$ $\dot{\mathbf{S}}[i+N] = \dot{\mathbf{S}}[i+N] + \frac{1}{m_i}\mathbf{f}_i^j$;
$\qquad\quad$ $\dot{\mathbf{S}}[j+N] = \dot{\mathbf{S}}[j+N] - \frac{1}{m_j}\mathbf{f}_i^j$;
$\qquad$ **end**
$\quad$ **end**

$\quad$ **return** $\dot{\mathbf{S}}$
end

Here, the function $\mathbf{f}_f(\mathbf{S}, i, t)$ returns the sum of all of the environmental forces on particle i, while $\mathbf{f}_g(\mathbf{S}, i, j, t)$ returns the force on particle i induced by particle j. Because of Newton's third law, the force on particle j induced by particle i is equal and opposite. The procedure uses these functions to accumulate the sum of the accelerations on each particle in the $\dot{\mathbf{S}}$ vector, which is returned as the value of the function. Using this approach to the acceleration calculations, the system dynamics function would be reorganized as follows:

```
StateVector F(StateVector S, float t)
begin
    StateVector Ṡ;

    Ṡ = Accelerations(S, t);
    for i = 0 to N-1 do
        Ṡ[i] = S[i + N];
    end

    return Ṡ
end
```

6.2 EXPANDING THE CONCEPT OF STATE

So far, in this chapter, we have been confining our notion of state to recording only the position and velocity of particles, both of which are expressed as 3D vectors. In certain applications, it will be convenient to include other quantities as well. For example, we might want to record the color of a particle, if it is changing with time, or we might want to maintain a list of surfaces a particle is in resting contact with. When we study rigid body dynamics, we will see that the state of a rigid body must also include its current orientation and angular momentum. Some of these quantities are 3D vectors, but others may not be. Some consist of continuous quantities that can have a derivative, and others are discrete.

The primary purpose of a state vector is to allow the definition of a system dynamics function $\dot{\mathbf{S}} = \mathbf{F}(\mathbf{S}, t)$, and the primary purpose of $\dot{\mathbf{S}}$ is in numerical integration to update the system's state. Therefore, it only makes sense to include a quantity in the state vector if it has a derivative that is a function of only system state and time, and that should be integrated over time to update that quantity. So, the color of a particle could logically be included in the state vector, but a list of resting contacts must be handled in another way.

If the state vector is to include quantities that are not 3D vectors, we need an alternate type definition for StateVector. The implementation that provides maximum flexibility is to represent a StateVector as an array of floating point numbers, along with a cataloging scheme that provides a correspondence between index into the array and the quantities corresponding to a simulation object. This catalog can simply be hard-coded into the system dynamics function, or more general support can be provided by including an N element array, where N is the number of objects in the system, with each element providing an object identifier and an integer denoting how many floats are in this object's state.

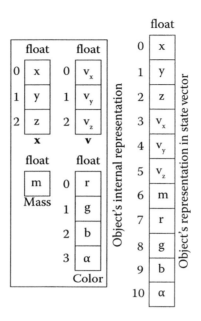

For example, the state of some object might include its position and velocity, both 3D vectors, as well as a variable mass, which is a scalar, and a translucent color, which is described by four floats: red, green, blue, and opacity α. So, this object would be represented by 11 floats in the state vector, with an ordering as chosen by the designer of the system dynamics function. The above figure shows one possible ordering, contrasting the object's internal variables with their representation in the state vector.

There is a trade-off between representation of the entire system state via a state vector, which simplifies system integration, and the convenience of having an object-oriented design, with each simulated object having its own local structure, and methods for manipulation. One solution to this design dilemma is to copy each object's variables to the state vector to begin the simulation calculation, and then copy them back to the objects after integration is complete. This may sound inefficient, but in an interacting particle system the computation is dominated by computation of the interparticle forces, so the addition of two $O(N)$ copying loops will have an insignificant effect on computation time. To facilitate the state copying approach, it will be useful to provide each dynamic object with two methods related to the state vector: one to store values from the object into the state vector, and another to retrieve the object's values from the state vector. Using this approach, we would rewrite our main simulation algorithm as follows:

StateVector $\mathbf{S}, \dot{\mathbf{S}}$;

$n = 0$; $t = 0$;
initialize all particles to their initial state;
while $t < t_{max}$ **do**

> *Computations based on the particle objects, including some auxiliary variable computations and possibly display, go here.*
>
> copy particle state from the particles to the state vector $\mathbf{S}$;
>
> $\dot{\mathbf{S}} = \mathtt{F}(\mathbf{S}, t)$;
>
> *State and accelerations are all known. Any computations or display requiring accelerations go here.*
>
> $\mathbf{S}^{\text{new}} = \mathtt{NumInt}(\mathbf{S}, \dot{\mathbf{S}}, h)$;
>
> *The new and old states are known. Collision detection, and other post integration steps go here.*
>
> copy particle state to the particles from the state vector $\mathbf{S}^{\text{new}}$;
> $n = n + 1$; $t = nh$;

end

Note that the ordering of variables within the state vector will affect only the system dynamics function, and the methods in the object's class used to retrieve and store state vector values. The main simulation loop and the numerical integration algorithm do not need any knowledge of the state vector's internal ordering.

6.3 SPATIAL DATA STRUCTURES

The problem of addressing the inherent $O(N^2)$ computational complexity of interacting particle systems almost always exploits the notion that the effect of one particle on another becomes weaker with physical distance. This is true for many real-world systems. For example, magnetic, electrical, and gravitational field strengths fall off according to an inverse-square law with distance. A nonphysical example would be people trying to walk in a crowd. In planning their movements, the members of a crowd will be much more concerned with negotiating a path through their immediate neighbors, than with more distant crowd members. This notion of decreasing effect with distance leads to two different strategies for reducing

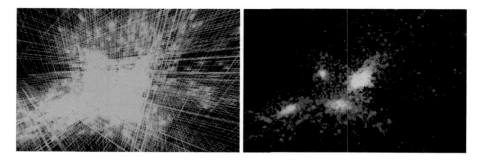

FIGURE 6.1 Octree used to support a colliding galaxy simulation. (Courtesy of Shengying Liu.)

computational complexity. The first is to specify one or more spatial regions about each particle, ignoring the interaction effects of any particles outside of nearby regions. The second would be to always consider all particles, but to provide a way of approximating the net effect of clusters of particles, far from a given particle, via a single calculation per cluster. Both of these strategies require the use of spatial data structures that provide the ability to quickly find particles in a spatial neighborhood, and that support such operations as clustering within spatial regions. In this section, we look at three different approaches to organizing the space containing the particles: uniform spatial grids, octrees, and kd-trees. The left side of Figure 6.1 shows an octree data structure being used to support the colliding galaxy simulation shown on the right side.

6.3.1 Uniform Spatial Grids

A uniform spatial grid is the simplest spatial data structure for organizing a set of particles. We have already described this data structure in Section 4.4.4, for speeding up particle-polygon collision tests. For completeness, we will expand on and briefly describe the structure again here, referring to the figure to the right. Starting with a bounding box of width W, height H, and depth D around all of the particles, we construct a 3D grid of uniformly sized, axis-aligned voxels. If the grid has L depth

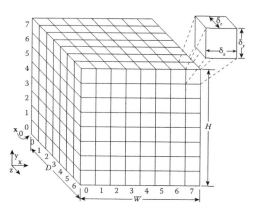

layers, M rows, and N columns, then the dimensions of a single voxel in the x, y, and z directions are $\delta_x = W/N$, $\delta_y = H/M$, and $\delta_z = D/L$. Each voxel corresponds to an element of a 3D array, in which we maintain a list of the particles residing in that voxel, along with any other information needed by the algorithm we are implementing. We define the location $\mathbf{x}_0 = (x_0, y_0, z_0)$ to be the grid corner with minimum x-y-z coordinates, which corresponds to the outside corner of array cell $[0,0,0]$. If the array indices are arranged in depth-plane, row, column order, then the index of the cell containing the point $\mathbf{x} = (x, y, z)$ is given by the spatial hash function

$$h(\mathbf{x}) = (\lfloor (z - z_0)/\delta_z \rfloor, \lfloor (y - y_0)/\delta_y \rfloor, \lfloor (x - x_0)/\delta_x \rfloor). \tag{6.8}$$

Any interacting particle algorithm using this uniform grid data structure will perform an initialization at the beginning of each timestep. The initialization will begin by looping through each of the particles in the system, hashing each particle's position to a grid cell, and placing that particle in the list for that voxel. After this particle mapping process is complete, the next step will be to loop through each voxel in the grid to compute any auxiliary information that may be needed by the algorithm making use of the data structure. For a large interacting particle system this initialization step will take negligible time compared with the time to compute particle interactions.

Neighbor finding in a uniform grid is as easy as computing offsets from a cell's array indices. If a particle is in plane p, row r, and column c its cell index is (p, r, c). Then, all "neighbor" particles, which are no more than two cell widths away from this particle, are contained in the 27-cell volume interval

$$I = (p - 1 \cdots p + 1, r - 1 \cdots r + 1, c - 1 \cdots c + 1).$$

Any particle in a cell outside of interval I is guaranteed to be more than one cell width away.

In some programming languages, allocation of a multidimensional array is not well supported. In this case, a uniform grid of L depth layers, M rows, and N columns can be allocated as a one-dimensional array of L x M x N cells. If the uniform grid is allocated in this way, the index for cell (p, r, c) will be

$$i = (pM + r)N + c.$$

In this case, it will be useful for the programmer to create a function returning the index value so it can be conveniently retrieved whenever it is needed.

6.3.2 Octrees

An octree is a spatial data structure that provides the ability to adaptively sample space at whatever resolution is required for a given particle distribution or a given algorithm. If all particles are distributed reasonably uniformly in the space of a problem, then a uniform grid will have about the same number of particles in each voxel. However, if the particle distribution contains dense and sparse regions, some of the uniform grid cells will be heavily populated, while others may have no particles or a very small number of particles. Algorithms exploiting a uniform spatial subdivision to gain speed-ups will lose efficiency under these conditions, and in fact can become slower than directly computing all interactions. An octree

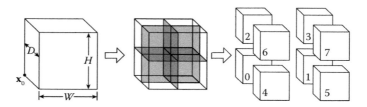

FIGURE 6.2 Subdivision of the root node of an octree into eight child octants.

provides spatial subdivisions simultaneously at a number of scales, so algorithms examining a region of space can work at whatever resolution is required, given the number of particles in the region and its spatial position.

Construction of an octree begins as demonstrated in Figure 6.2. Just as for the uniform grid, we start with a bounding box around the entire space of the problem. This becomes the single root node of the octree, residing at tree Level 0. The children of this cell are constructed by subdividing the cell into eight equal-sized child nodes, via axis-aligned cutting planes passing through the cell center. These child cells are the eight nodes residing at Level 1 of the tree. This subdivision process may be continued for as many levels as desired, so that for each level L, there are 8^L nodes. If the volume of the root cell is $V = DWH$, the volume represented by a cell at level L will be $V/8^L$, and the dimensions of the cell will be $D/2^L$, $W/2^L$, and $H/2^L$. This describes a full octree, where every node, not at the bottom level of the tree, has exactly eight children. However, subdivision of a node can be adaptive, leaving nodes farther up in the tree unsubdivided. One way that this might occur is if a node is selected for subdivision only if the number of particles residing in the node's cell is above some threshold.

As we did for the uniform spatial grid, we can make all spatial locations relative to the minimum x, y, and z coordinate $\mathbf{x}_0$ of the bounding box. We number the eight child octants of a cell $0 \cdots 7$ as shown in Figure 6.2. Now, if we know the spatial location $\mathbf{x}_i$ of a particle within a parent cell at tree level L, whose minimum x, y, z corner is $\mathbf{x}_p$, we can quickly compute the octant that the particle resides in, using the following logic. Compute the center of the parent cell $\mathbf{x}_c = \mathbf{x}_p + [W/2^{(L+1)}, H/2^{(L+1)}, D/2^{(L+1)}]^T$, and let $\mathbf{Dx} = \mathbf{x}_i - \mathbf{x}_c$, whose components are $(\Delta x, \Delta y, \Delta z)$. Now, construct a 3-bit binary index such that if $\Delta x > 0$, bit 0 is 1, if $\Delta y > 0$, bit 1 is 1, and if $\Delta z > 0$ bit 2 is 1. Converting this binary number to decimal gives the octant indices as shown in Figure 6.2.

There are various ways to allocate the cells of an octree. For a full octree, the most efficient approach is to allocate space for the full tree all at once, and then build an indexing structure into each of the nodes. For an octree that is not full, the usual approach is to allocate each tree node individually, and have each node store pointers to its parent and child nodes.

Here we summarize the indexing scheme for a full octree allocated as one array containing all of the nodes for all of the levels. At level L, a full octree will have $M_L = 2^L$ divisions along each axis and $N_L = 8^L$ nodes. Thus, an octree whose maximum level is $L_{\max}$ will have a total of $T = \sum_{p=0}^{L_{\max}} 8^p = \frac{8^{L_{\max}+1}-1}{7}$ nodes. The cells for level $L > 0$ will start at index $I_L = \sum_{p=0}^{L-1} 8^p = \frac{8^L-1}{7}$. Given the index i of a cell within the octree, its index within this cell's level is $i_l = i - I_L$. The depth-plane corresponding to this index will be $d_i = \lfloor i_l/M_L^2 \rfloor$, the row will be $r_i = \lfloor (i_l \mod M_L^2)/M_L \rfloor$, and the column will be $c_i = (i_l \mod M_L^2) \mod M_L = i_l \mod M_L$. The parent of this cell will be in level $L - 1$. The depth-plane, row, and column of the parent of cell i will be $d_p = \lfloor d_i/2 \rfloor$, $r_p = \lfloor r_i/2 \rfloor$, and $c_p = \lfloor c_i/2 \rfloor$, and its index will be $i_p = I_{L-1} + (d_p M_{L-1} + r_p)M_{L-1} + c_p$. The children of this cell will be in level $L + 1$. The depth-plane, row, and column of the first child of cell i will be $d_c^0 = 2d_i$, $r_c^0 = 2r_i$, and $c_c^0 = 2c_i$, and the index of the first child will be $i_c^0 = I_{L+1} + (d_c^0 M_{L+1} + r_c^0)M_{L+1} + c_c^0$. The indices of all eight child cells of cell i, in order by child number will be i_c^0, $i_c^1 = i_c^0 + 1$, $i_c^2 = i_c^0 + M_{L+1}$, $i_c^3 = i_c^2 + 1$, $i_c^4 = i_c^0 + M_{L+1}^2$, $i_c^5 = i_c^4 + 1$, $i_c^6 = i_c^4 + M_{L+1}$, and $i_c^7 = i_c^6 + 1$.

Most octree-based particle algorithms store the particles only in the leaves. If a full octree is used, a maximum tree level will have to be decided ahead of time. After space is allocated to handle this number of tree levels, each level will be a uniform spatial grid at a resolution dependent on its depth in the tree. In this case, particles can be assigned to the nodes at the lowest level of the tree, just as if they were being assigned to a uniform grid of that resolution. If the octree is not full, the tree will have to be built from the top down, assigning each particle to the root node, and then pushing it down into the tree, creating children as needed to maintain a maximum number of particles per leaf node. In other words, the tree is built by creating its structure in response to the particles being assigned.

6.3.3 kd-Trees

Another spatial subdivision structure that is commonly used to accelerate computations between interacting particles is the *kd-tree*.* A kd-tree is a binary tree. Each node of the tree corresponds to an interval in the x, y, and z dimensions. The children of a node represent a partitioning of all the points from the parent into two equal groups, around some point chosen on one of the axes. Generally, the point chosen is the median from all the points in the parent node. So, each division occurs directly on one point, and there are an equal number of points above and below that value. The tree thus remains balanced. For n points, there will be n nodes in the tree, and the tree will be of height $log_2 n$.

To build a kd-tree, first a bounding box is formed around the entire set of particles. Then, one axis is picked, and a median value of all points is found for that axis, choosing the larger value if there is an even number of points. Thus, the

---

*There are several variations for how this name is written, including kD-tree and k-d tree. These all refer to the same structure, which is a specialized form of a binary space partition.

splitting value is always exactly the coordinate of one of the points, and that point is stored at that node. This value is used to partition the points into two children nodes. If there are n points at the parent, the left (smaller valued) node will have $\lceil \frac{n-1}{2} \rceil$ points and the right node will have $\lfloor \frac{n-1}{2} \rfloor$ points in it. The axis chosen for division will usually rotate through a fixed pattern $(x, y, z, x, y, \ldots)$.

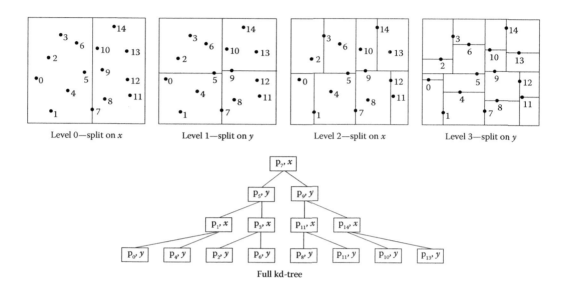

Consider the figure, in which there are 15 points (numbered 0 through 14) to be entered into a kd-tree. We will split first along the x axis, and point 7 has the median x value. Therefore, point 7 becomes the root node of the tree, and half the nodes (nodes 0 through 6 in the example) are in the left child, and half (nodes 8 through 14) in the right branch. The next split will be along the y axis. For the left branch, node 5 has the median y value, and thus is used for the next node. Half of those points (numbers 0, 1, and 4) are placed in the left child, and the other half (numbers 2, 3, and 6) in the right child. The process repeats for the other branch and on through subsequent levels until all nodes are placed in the tree. Although this example is in 2D, the process extends directly to 3D.

If we assume the number of particles is fixed, we can allocate all space for a kd-tree at once. Since the tree is a balanced binary tree, the structure of the tree will be known, although the particular values for the partitions (i.e., which point is stored in which node) at each level will not be. If we assume that the nodes are stored as an array from 0 to $n-1$, then the children of node i will be at index $2i+1$ and $2i+2$. Though you rarely need the parent, it will be at value $\lfloor \frac{i-1}{2} \rfloor$. If we assume we know the pattern of axes to use for partitioning, then the only thing we need to know at any one level is the point number to be stored. Thus, for a kd-tree such as the one in the figure, an array of indices $[7, 5, 9, 1, 3, 11, 14, 0, 4, 2, 6, 8, 11, 10, 13]$ will completely specify the kd-tree.

A common use for kd-trees is to find particles within a certain distance of a given point (which might be another particle location). This can be treated as a range-search problem, where we want to find all nodes that overlap a given range in x, y, and z. We can do a range search for a kd-tree via a recursive process that checks whether the partition point is within, above, or below the range for the given axis. If it is within the range, then that node is reported, and both children are checked. If it is above or below the range, then the left or right child (respectively) is checked. By continuing this process to the leaf nodes, we can report all points that overlap a given interval.

Note that there are variations on the default kd-tree. One approach is to choose an axis at each level, rather than following a set pattern. This potentially allows one to choose a better division (e.g., partitioning along the longest axis), but requires extra data storage and checks at each level. Another variation is to have a fixed number of levels in the tree. In this case the leaf nodes store several points, rather than just one. This can speed up some computations by limiting how many levels of the tree are traversed, at the cost of additional work when more points are found to overlap. The kd-trees can be constructed so that points are not evenly partitioned. This can lead to the intervals having better shapes, but causes an unbalanced tree, and often makes traversing the tree less efficient. Finally, kd-trees can be constructed such that internal nodes partition based on a given value, rather than a particular point. Points, then, are stored only at leaves. This approach requires extra storage, maintaining separate internal (partitioning) and leaf (point-storing) nodes, and the tree is generally one level deeper. However, it can potentially lead to better-shaped intervals at any one level.

6.4 ASTRONOMICAL SIMULATION

In an astronomical simulation, like that of the colliding galaxies in Figure 6.3, the goal is to reproduce the behavior of a large collection of objects distributed in space, given their initial configuration, and the gravitational attractions between them. Therefore, this is  a canonical example of an interacting particle system. In such a system, the force of one particle on another is inversely proportional to the square of the distance between them, and directly proportional to the product of their masses. In the real world, the constant of proportionality is known as the Universal Gravitational Constant, $G = 6.67384 \times 10^{-11}$ m^3/kg-s^2. Referring to the diagram to the right, particle j, with mass m_j, at location $\mathbf{x}_j$ exerts the force

$$\mathbf{f}_i^j = G \frac{m_i m_j}{r_{ij}^2} \hat{\mathbf{x}}_{ij}$$

FIGURE 6.3 Two galaxies colliding. (Courtesy of Christian Weeks.)

on particle i, with mass m_i, at location $\mathbf{x}_i$. This force is subject to Newton's third law, so the force of particle i on particle j is

$$\mathbf{f}_j^i = -\mathbf{f}_i^j.$$

This reciprocal relationship is particularly important, since the gravitational force between two particles will induce the two accelerations

$$\mathbf{a}_i^j = G\frac{m_j}{r_{ij}^2}\hat{\mathbf{x}}_{ij}, \text{ and}$$

$$\mathbf{a}_j^i = -G\frac{m_i}{r_{ij}^2}\hat{\mathbf{x}}_{ij}. \tag{6.9}$$

If we take an extreme case, where the mass of particle i is very large and the mass of particle j is very small, there will be no discernible acceleration of particle i, but a significant acceleration of particle j. This is identical with the effect that we saw with a point-based gravitational acceleration operator in Chapter 5. If, however, the particle's masses are of similar orders of magnitude, both particles will receive significant acceleration. This mutual attraction creates the intricate and fascinating behavior resulting in the complex dynamic organization of the universe.

Equation 6.9, and the simulation algorithms given in Section 6.1 give us everything we need to build an astronomical simulation. The problem is, the simulation will be intolerably slow for anything beyond a few hundred particles. This is due to the $O(N^2)$ time complexity of the interacting particle problem, as mentioned in the introduction to this chapter. This problem has been known to Astrophysicists for a long time. The first serious algorithm to address this issue was developed by Appel [1985], as his undergraduate thesis in Computer Science. He turned the $O(N^2)$ problem into a vastly faster $O(N \log N)$ algorithm, by hierarchically clustering the distant gravitational effect of particles using a modified kd-tree structure. Soon after, Carrier et al. [1988] developed the approach known as the Adaptive Fast Multipole Method, which offers an even faster $O(N)$ solution, and that simultaneously provides controlled numerical precision. To begin with, we will present a simple algorithm based on a fixed spatial subdivision. This will allow us to achieve $O(N^{\frac{3}{2}})$ computational complexity, which for systems of 10,000 particles is a 100 times speed-up. We will then show how to make a significant further improvement using a hierarchical octree-based spatial subdivision, providing $O(N \log N)$ computational complexity, and approximate numerical precision. Both of these algorithms borrow underlying structure from the seminal work cited above. After studying these algorithms, the reader wishing to go farther is encouraged to explore the Adaptive Fast Multipole Method, which is the state-of-the-art approach to the problem.

6.4.1 Clustering

All of the algorithms for speeding up gravitational interaction calculations capitalize on the fact that gravitational attraction falls off with the square of the distance between objects. Thus, if particles are far from each other the force of attraction becomes very weak. This might suggest that we simply discount the accelerations due to distant particles, by setting a maximum distance beyond which interactions are ignored. Although there are systems where this idea will work well, it does not provide a reasonable approximation to gravitational attractions, since it does not account for the bulk effect of a large number of far away particles exerting a strong attraction over a large distance. For example, a galaxy with 10 billion stars that is 100,000 light years away, will exert the same gravitational effect as a single star, of average size, that is only a single light year away. However, we can exploit clustering far away particles together to achieve big computational savings.

The figure shows how clustering might work for particles i and j, at positions $\mathbf{x}_i$ and $\mathbf{x}_j$, that are near to each other but 0 relatively far from a particle at position $\mathbf{x}$. Define R_i and R_j to be the distances of particles i and j from $\mathbf{x}$, and let $\hat{\mathbf{u}}_i$ and $\hat{\mathbf{u}}_j$ be the corresponding direction vectors from $\mathbf{x}$. Then, the net acceleration on $\mathbf{x}$ due to particles i and j will be

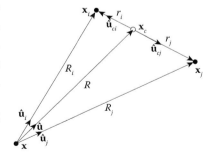

$$\mathbf{a} = G \left[\frac{m_i \hat{\mathbf{u}}_i}{R_i^2} + \frac{m_j \hat{\mathbf{u}}_j}{R_j^2} \right]. \qquad (6.10)$$

Now, let us try clustering i and j at their center of mass and compute the acceleration due to this cluster. The total mass of the cluster will be $M = m_i + m_j$. The center of mass of a collection of particles is defined to be the sum of the particles'

Here we show mathematically how the approximate and exact acceleration calculations differ. Expanding M and $\mathbf{x}_c$ into their components via Equation 6.11, and rearranging, this acceleration can be written

$$\mathbf{a}^c = G\left[\frac{m_i(\mathbf{x}_i - \mathbf{x})/R}{R^2} + \frac{m_j(\mathbf{x}_j - \mathbf{x})/R}{R^2}\right].$$

Replacing R by $\frac{R}{R_i}R_i$ and $\frac{R}{R_j}R_j$, and noting that $\hat{\mathbf{u}}_i = \frac{(\mathbf{x}_i - \mathbf{x})}{R_i}$, and $\hat{\mathbf{u}}_j = \frac{(\mathbf{x}_j - \mathbf{x})}{R_j}$, allows us to convert this acceleration to the form

$$\mathbf{a}^c = G\left[\left(\frac{R_i}{R}\right)^3\frac{m_i\hat{\mathbf{u}}_i}{R_i^2} + \left(\frac{R_j}{R}\right)^3\frac{m_j\hat{\mathbf{u}}_j}{R_j^2}\right]. \tag{6.12}$$

Comparing the acceleration due to the cluster given by Equation 6.12, with the exact acceleration given by Equation 6.10, we see that they are identical except for the scale factors $(\frac{R_i}{R})^3$ and $(\frac{R_j}{R})^3$. These scale factors can be shown to be 1.0 plus an offset dominated by the ratios $\frac{r_i}{R}$ and $\frac{r_j}{R}$. Thus, if the ratio $\frac{r_i}{R}$ is small, the exact and approximate accelerations will be nearly identical.

positions weighted by their fraction of the total mass. Thus, the center of mass of particles i and j is

$$\mathbf{x}_c = \frac{m_i\mathbf{x}_i + m_j\mathbf{x}_j}{M}. \tag{6.11}$$

Now, let r_i and r_j be the distances of particles i and j from their center of mass, let R be the distance from $\mathbf{x}$ to the center of mass, and let $\hat{\mathbf{u}}$ be the direction vector toward the center of mass. If we create a virtual particle with mass M and position $\mathbf{x}_c$, as shown in the figure, the acceleration of the particle at $\mathbf{x}$ due to this virtual particle would be

$$\mathbf{a}^c = G\frac{M\hat{\mathbf{u}}}{R^2}.$$

It is apparent from the diagram that in the original acceleration calculation, the component of the acceleration along the line between particles i and j will cancel each other, so that the only component of difference between the exact and approximate acceleration calculations will be along the direction $\hat{\mathbf{u}}$ to the center of mass. The error in acceleration, then, will come only from the differences between R_i and R and between R_j and R. These differences will be small if the ratios $\frac{r_i}{R}$ and $\frac{r_j}{R}$ are small. Thus, the accuracy of the approximate acceleration due to clustering particle masses at the center of mass can be minimized by making sure that the distance from the particle to the cluster is large compared with the radius of a sphere containing all of the particles in the cluster.

To summarize, we have demonstrated that if we represent a number of particles in a closed region by a single massive particle at their center of mass, this massive particle will have almost the same effect on the acceleration of a distant particle as all of the original particles considered separately. The error incurred by making this approximation is governed by the ratio $\frac{r}{R}$, where r is the maximum distance of a particle in the cluster from the cluster's center of mass, and R is the distance of the affected particle from the center of mass. Since this ratio approaches 0 quickly with distance, the error due to clustering approaches 0 with increasing distance from the cluster.

This idea leads directly to an algorithm, using fixed-size clusters, that exploits this approximation to achieve a considerable speed-up over computing all interparticle interactions directly. Further, because error is governed by this ratio, cluster size can be increased proportional to an increase in distance without incurring any additional penalty in accuracy. This idea leads to a second more sophisticated algorithm, using variable size clusters.

6.4.2   A Simple Algorithm Using a Uniform Grid

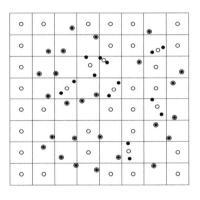

The simple algorithm is based on a uniform spatial partition. Starting with a bounding box around all of the particles, construct a 3D uniform spatial grid of voxels, as described in Section 6.3.1. To initialize the algorithm, each particle is placed in a list of member particles maintained in the voxel that the particle hashes to. After particles are mapped to voxels, the total mass, and center of mass in each voxel is calculated and saved. Any voxel with no particles is given a total mass of 0, and a center of mass at the center of the voxel. The figure shows an example of this in 2D. Each solid dot is a single particle, and each open circle marks the center of mass of its containing grid cell. For cells with only a single particle, the particle and the center of mass are in the same location.

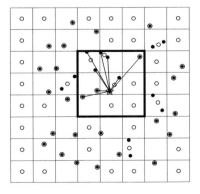

The total acceleration on each particle is initially set to the sum of the accelerations on the particle due to all of the particles in the 27 cells in the particle's immediate 3D neighborhood. Since these particles are nearby, their effects must be calculated directly. In the figure, the particle marked with a star is the particle whose acceleration we are computing. The dark square outline contains the cells in the neighborhood of this particle (in 2D there are 9 cells in the neighborhood, but in 3D there will be 27). The lines from the starred particle indicate the particles whose direct accelerations are being calculated. Note, that there are no connections to the center of mass of any of these cells, only to the individual particles.

Next, for each particle, the accelerations due to all of the other particles are computed by looping over all cells not in the neighborhood of the particle, adding the approximate acceleration that would be due to a virtual particle having the cell's total mass and positioned at the cell's center of mass. In the figure, we are showing the interactions being calculated for the top three rows of the grid. Connections to the other rows are not shown, to avoid clutter. All computations are done on the center of mass of each non-neighbor cell.

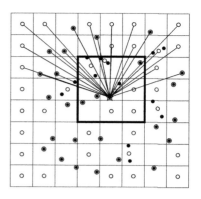

To understand the computational complexity of the improved algorithm, let N be the number of particles and M be the number of voxels. If we assume that the particles are distributed uniformly in the space, the average number of particles per cell will be N/M. The number of acceleration calculations per particle will be $T = (27N/M) + (M - 27)$, since for each of the 27 neighborhood cells we make a direct calculation, and for each of the remaining cells we make one calculation. Since compute time varies with the number of voxels, we need to make a good choice for M. The derivative of compute time with respect to the number of voxels is $\frac{dT}{dM} = \frac{M^2 - 27N}{M^2}$, so the optimal choice is $M = \sqrt{27N}$. Using this choice of M, the number of acceleration calculations will be $T = 2\sqrt{27N} - 27$. Since this number of calculations must be done for every particle, the computational complexity of the algorithm is $O(N\sqrt{N}) = O(N^{\frac{3}{2}})$. Of course, if the grid of voxels is cubic, the actual number of cells in the grid must be a perfect cube, so a good way to pick the number of cells is to set the number of divisions per axis to $D = \lfloor \sqrt[6]{27N} \rfloor$, and then $M = D^3$. Table 6.1 displays how the number of grid divisions D and the number of voxels M vary with the number of particles N, and shows the ratio $r = T/T_d$ of the corresponding number of acceleration calculations T for the voxel-based algorithm versus the number of calculations T_d for direct computation. We see from the table that the algorithm begins to result in an improvement when the number of particles approaches 1,000, and achieves a run time of only 2% of the direct run time when the number of particles reaches 1,000,000.

TABLE 6.1   Optimal Voxel Grid versus Direct Interparticle Computation

N	D	M	T	T_d	r
10	2	8	1.48×10^2	4.50×10^1	3.28
100	3	27	1.00×10^4	4.95×10^3	2.02
1,000	5	125	3.14×10^5	5.00×10^5	0.63
10,000	8	512	1.01×10^7	5.00×10^7	0.20
100,000	11	1,331	3.33×10^8	5.00×10^9	0.07
1,000,000	17	4,913	1.04×10^{10}	5.00×10^{11}	0.02

6.4.3 An Adaptive Algorithm Using an Octree

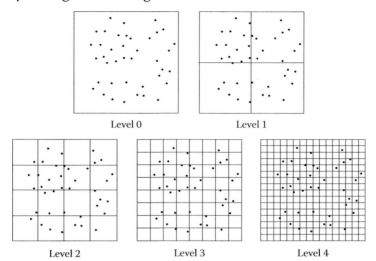

The second algorithm exploits the fact that if we keep the ratio of cluster size to distance constant, we can increase cluster size without incurring a decrease in accuracy. The method starts, like the previous algorithm, by building a bounding box around all of the particles under simulation. This is used to construct an octree covering all of the particles. One approach to deciding on the depth of the octree is to specify a maximum number of particles $n_{\max}$ that can reside in a leaf node, and continue subdivision until that limit is achieved. For clarity of presentation, the figure above shows construction of a 2D quadtree instead of a 3D octree. In this example, we have chosen $n_{\max} = 1$, but this is by no means necessary.

After the construction of the tree, an acceleration function using clustering is determined within each cell. This function gives the approximate gravitational acceleration that is exerted by all of the particles within the cell on a particle located far from the cell. It is parameterized by the sum of the masses of all the particles in the cell, and the cell's center of mass. If $\mathbf{x}_i$ is the location of particle i within cell k at the bottom level of the tree structure, and m_i is its mass, the total mass in the cell is

$$M_k = \sum_{\mathbf{x}_i \in k} m_i, \text{ and its center of mass is } \mathbf{c}_k = \frac{\sum_{\mathbf{x}_i \in k} m_i \mathbf{x}_i}{M_k}.$$

If the cell has no particles, the total mass M_k is set to 0, and the center of mass is set to the center of the cell. The acceleration function of the cell is

$$\mathbf{a}_k(\mathbf{x}) = GM_k \frac{\mathbf{x} - \mathbf{c}_k}{\|\mathbf{x} - \mathbf{c}_k\|^3}.$$

Note, that this function is identical in structure to the interparticle gravity functions of Equation 6.9, but with the calculation of the unit vector from the cell's center of mass to the point composed into the equation. Once the center of mass and total mass are known in each of the cells at the lowest level in the tree, the acceleration function of each of the parent cells p at the next highest level is parameterized by

$$M_p = \sum_{i=0}^{7} M_i, \text{ and } \mathbf{c}_p = \frac{\sum_{i=0}^{7} M_i \mathbf{x}_i}{M_p}.$$

Using the tree structure, we approximate accelerations due to particles far from the particle, but do a direct calculation of accelerations due to particles nearby. The process is illustrated in 2D in the figure to the right. The interparticle accelerations acting on each of the particles in the system are computed by working from the top of the tree down to its base. For each particle i at position $\mathbf{x}_i$, we initialize the particle's acceleration to 0, and then descend the tree level by level. At each level, we accumulate acceleration on this particle from cells that have not been accounted for at higher levels in the

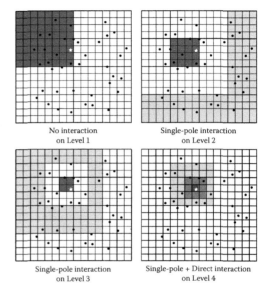

tree, using these cells' acceleration functions. Only cells that are not adjacent to the cell of the particle are used, assuring that they are at a good distance from the particle. When the bottom level of the tree is reached, accelerations are accumulated directly from other particles in particle i's cell, and all of the immediate neighbor cells. In a 3D octree, there will be a maximum of 27 cells in this neighborhood, and thus at most 27 $n_{\max}$ computations. In the figure, the particle marked by a star is the one whose acceleration we are computing, and at each level the cell that this particle resides in is marked in dark gray. The cells for which the clustered acceleration function will be used are marked in light gray, and the cells that are to be ignored are marked in white. At the lowest level, the immediate neighbor cells, surrounding the particle's cell, are marked in mid gray.

We can make a reasonable estimate that the time required to run the algorithm will be on the order $O(N \log N)$ in the number of particles. To simplify the argument, assume that we are building a full octree. The tree depth will depend on the maximum number of particles allowed per leaf cell, but in any case will not exceed $\log_8 N$. Assigning all of the particles to the leaf nodes will require $O(N)$ time, since it simply involves hashing each particle to a cell at the bottom level of the octree. Building the clusters of particles at the bottom level will again take $O(N)$ time, and passing them up through the tree to build clusters at each level will require looping over $\log_8 N$ levels, and doing a number of calculations at each level that will diminish geometrically, i.e., $N/8$, $N/64$, ..., as we move up the tree, resulting in a bound of $O(N)$. Finally, computing the acceleration of each particle will take $O(\log N)$ time (i.e., approximately a fixed amount of time at each level). But, this acceleration computation needs to be done for every particle, making it the dominating factor in the complexity, yielding a time complexity of $O(N \log N)$.

6.5 FLOCKING SYSTEMS

When viewing a large bird flock, like the simulated one shown in Figure 6.4, the impression is of a large many-bodied organism that has a mind of its own, exhibiting complex and intricate behaviors as it wheels and swirls through the sky. This fascinating group behavior is a wonderful example of what is known as an *emergent phenomenon*. Emergent phenomena occur when rules for interaction, followed at a small scale by many "actors," aggregate to produce a group behavior at a larger scale. Galaxy formation from billions of individual stars is one example of such an emergent phenomenon. The behavior of flocks of birds or schools of fish is another, quite different, emergent phenomenon. The difference is that galaxies are formed by mindless actors, all following identical interaction rules (i.e., gravitational attraction), while a flock of birds is made up of a collection of individuals, each with its own unique mind, physiology, and anatomy. We can think of the birds as individual decision makers, functioning within a system of guiding rules of behavior.

In his classic paper *Flocks, Herds, and Schools: A Distributed Behavioral Model*, Reynolds [1987] put his research in agent-based programming together with studies

FIGURE 6.4 Flock of birds. (Courtesy of Liang Dong.)

in behavioral biology to describe the first computer graphics algorithm capturing animal group behavior. Since his algorithm is general enough to apply across species, he calls the actors in his model "boids," short for "birdoid objects." His approach is completely agent based—there is no global control for the flock as a whole—the behavior of a flock is entirely emergent. Each boid follows a set of three simple rules guiding how it accelerates in response to the positions and velocities of its nearby neighbor boids.

The algorithm works as follows. At each timestep, each boid compiles a list of other boids in its neighborhood. For each of these neighbors, it computes three accelerations: collision avoidance, velocity matching, and centering. Collision avoidance provides an acceleration that prevents the boid from colliding with its neighbor. If it is too near to its neighbor, it accelerates away. Velocity matching is what makes the motion of the flock coherent. The boid will attempt to match its neighbor's velocity by applying an acceleration to correct the speed and direction of its own velocity. Centering attempts to keep the flock together by applying an acceleration that causes the boid to move toward its neighbor. The accelerations from all of the boids in a boid's neighbor list are then summed to produce the total flocking acceleration on the boid. Other accelerations, such as those due to gravity, wind, and the need to steer around environmental objects, can also be applied to fit the goals of the animation.

6.5.1 Core Algorithm

The figure to the right provides a vector diagram for computing the accelerations. Let us assume that we are dealing with boid i at position $\mathbf{x}_i$, and flying with velocity $\mathbf{v}_i$. It is near boid j whose position is $\mathbf{x}_j$ and has velocity $\mathbf{v}_j$. The vector from boid i to boid j is $\mathbf{x}_{ij} = \mathbf{x}_j - \mathbf{x}_i$, the distance from i to j is $d_{ij} = \|\mathbf{x}_{ij}\|$, and the direction vector from i to j is $\hat{\mathbf{x}}_{ij} = \mathbf{x}_{ij}/d_{ij}$. The three accelerations on boid i due to the presence of boid j are

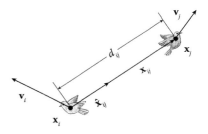

Collision avoidance: $\mathbf{a}^a_{ij} = -\frac{k_a}{d_{ij}}\hat{\mathbf{x}}_{ij}$, pushes boid i away from boid j,

Velocity matching: $\mathbf{a}^v_{ij} = k_v(\mathbf{v}_j - \mathbf{v}_i)$, adjusts boid i's velocity to match j's,

Centering: $\mathbf{a}^c_{ij} = k_c\mathbf{x}_{ij}$, pulls boid i toward boid j.

In these equations, k_a, k_v, and k_c are tunable scale factors governing the strength of each of the accelerations. Note that these accelerations are coming from the internal decision processes of boid i and not directly from boid j. Therefore, Newton's third law does not necessarily hold—i.e., there is no requirement that boid j's accelerations in response to boid i be equal and opposite.

Looking at each of these accelerations in turn, we can make the following observations. The collision avoidance strength drops off as the inverse of distance, so the effect will be strong only when the boids are quite near to each other. This makes sense, since the objective is to keep the boids from crashing into each other, not to keep them far from each other. Since the effect is inversely proportional to distance, it becomes unboundedly large as the boids get very near to each other. Therefore, in an implementation it will be a good idea to place a limit on the strength of this acceleration. It should be allowed to become quite large, but bounded to maintain the stability of the simulation. The velocity matching acceleration is not governed by distance, but goes to 0 if the two velocities match exactly. Thus, the effect of this acceleration will be to cause the neighbors to turn and either speed up or slow down until they are traveling in the same direction with the same speed. The centering acceleration strength increases with distance (note the use of $\mathbf{x}_{ij}$ not $\hat{\mathbf{x}}_{ij}$), so the farther the neighbors are from each other, the more they will tend to move toward each other. The constants k_a, k_v, and k_c should be adjusted to maintain flock coherence but not to pull all of the boids into a tight ball. Therefore, it is best to start by making k_v and k_c small and adjusting k_a to keep the boids from colliding. Then, k_v should be adjusted so that the motion becomes somewhat coherent, but not so tightly coupled that the boids all seem to move identically. Finally, k_c can be adjusted to keep the boids from drifting apart, but not so strongly pulled that they fly in too tight a group.

Surprisingly, this simple algorithm can be used to support a wide variety of behaviors. Figure 6.5 shows two examples. Both the animation of schooling fish shown on the left and the runners shown on the right were coordinated by the same basic algorithm. The fish are following the algorithm in 3D, while, to manage the positions of the runners, the algorithm was constrained to operate on the 2D road surface. The animation of the runners' body motions was provided by a commercial software package.

FIGURE 6.5 From left to right, fish schooling and runners racing. (Courtesy of Ashwin Bangalore, Sam Bryfczynski.)

6.5.2 Distance and Field-of-View

There are still two issues that need to be addressed to make the algorithm more true to the behavior of real animals. Remembering that the boids' actions are not physically based, but actually part of a decision-making process, there must be some prioritization scheme that causes the boids to pay more attention to their nearby neighbors and less to those far away. In addition, since a boid is a physical creature, it can exert only a limited amount of force at any instant in time, so it may have to prioritize the three types of acceleration to devote its strength to what is most important at the time. For example, it makes no sense for the boid to devote any of its energy to centering with its neighbors when it is about to collide with another boid. It needs to devote all of its resources to avoiding the collision.

One approach to prioritization with distance from neighbors is to apply an additional weighting factor to each of the individual accelerations that is a function of distance. The figure to the right shows one suggestion for how this might work. Choose two threshold distances r_1 and r_2, with $r_1 < r_2$. If d is distance from the boid then we can define the weighting factor

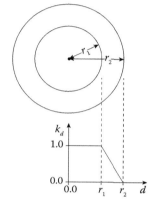

$$k_d(d) = \begin{cases} 1.0 & \text{if } d < r_1, \\ \frac{r_2 - d}{r_2 - r_1} & \text{if } r_1 \leq d \leq r_2, \\ 0.0 & \text{if } d > r_2. \end{cases}$$

If k_d, calculated with $d = d_{ij}$, is multiplied by each one of the accelerations before it is applied, then boid i will pay full attention to all of the other boids within distance r_1, will pay no attention to boids farther than r_2, and will pay attention that decreases with distance to boids between r_1 and r_2. This could be done with just a single threshold radius, but having the zone of gradually decreasing attention prevents the situation where a boid is alternately ignoring and paying full attention to another boid whose distance is near to the threshold. Such a situation can create jumpy behavior, very unlike the smooth motion exhibited by real birds.

All animals have a limited field of view. The Eastern Phoebe, shown to the near right, is a good example of a typical nonpredator bird. Note that its eyes are located on the side of its head, not in front, which gives the Phoebe a kind of "wrap-around" field of view. It is able to see above, below, and behind, as well as directly in front—just what is needed to keep watch for predators. There will be a "blind" area directly behind the bird, and a region of binocular acuity directly in front of the bird, where both the left and right eyes have overlapping visual fields. On the other hand, a predator like an owl, shown to the far

Eastern Phoebe

Great Horned Owl

right, has eyes in the front of its head, giving it very high binocular acuity looking straight ahead, but a much narrower field of view overall—just what is needed to seek out and catch its prey.

The diagram to the right gives an indication of what a typical bird's viewing environment is like, looked at from top down. In the darker gray frontal area the bird's vision will be binocular (seen with both eyes), while in the lighter gray peripheral area it will be monocular. The angle θ_1 measures the range of the binocular area, while θ_2 measures the full range of vision, including the monocular area. For example, in a pigeon θ_1 can be as small as $30°$, while θ_2 can be as large as $340°$. On the other hand, in an owl θ_1 can be $70°$ or larger, while θ_2 may be as little as $110°$. The visual systems of fish have similar characteristics.

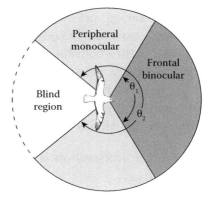

Comparable to the constant k_d that weights influence with distance, we could define the factor weighting influence by region of the visual field to be

$$
k_\theta(\theta) = \begin{cases} 1.0 & \text{if } -\theta_1/2 \le |\theta| \le \theta_1/2, \\ \frac{\theta_2/2 - |\theta|}{\theta_2/2 - \theta_1/2} & \text{if } \theta_1/2 \le |\theta| \le \theta_2/2, \\ 0.0 & \text{if } |\theta| > \theta_2/2, \end{cases}
$$

where θ is the angle formed between the boid's velocity vector and the other boid.

When accumulating the list of neighboring boids to interact with, a two-step approach can be used that is sensitive to both distance and angle. If we assume that the flocking algorithm is being run within a uniform spatial grid, then all boids within a fixed number of grid cells from a boid's cell are added to its interaction list. Then, this list is pruned by eliminating all boids that are not within distance r_2 or are in the boid's blind region, i.e., the magnitude of the angle from the boid's direction of flight exceeds $\theta_2/2$. Finally, the collision avoidance, velocity matching, and centering accelerations for boid i are summed over all of the boids j in its interaction list, taking into account the distance d_{ij} from boid i to boid j, and the angle θ_{ij} between boid i's velocity vector and the direction vector between boids i and j. These accelerations are given by

$$
\mathbf{a}_i^a = \sum k_\theta(\theta_{ij}) k_d(d_{ij}) \mathbf{a}_{ij}^a,
$$
$$
\mathbf{a}_i^v = \sum k_\theta(\theta_{ij}) k_d(d_{ij}) \mathbf{a}_{ij}^v,
$$
$$
\mathbf{a}_i^c = \sum k_\theta(\theta_{ij}) k_d(d_{ij}) \mathbf{a}_{ij}^c.
$$

6.5.3 Acceleration Prioritization

In Reynold's original paper on flocking, he suggests that the limited ability of an animal to exert force could be represented by specifying a limit on the magnitude of the acceleration, prioritized by urgency. Of the three acceleration sources, collision avoidance obviously needs to receive highest priority, matching velocities aids in avoiding future collisions, so it should receive next priority, while centering is of lowest urgency. One possible way to implement a prioritized acceleration limit is based on prioritized acceleration magnitudes. Each of the three accelerations is summed, in turn, but only up to an allowed acceleration limit. An algorithm for implementing this is as follows:

residual acceleration is the entire acceleration budget a_{max}
$a_{\mathrm{r}} = a_{\max}$;
collision avoidance gets top priority
$\mathbf{a}_i = \min(a_{\mathrm{r}}, \|\mathbf{a}_i^a\|)\hat{\mathbf{a}}_i^a$;
set residual to the unused acceleration budget
$a_{\mathrm{r}} = a_{\max} - \|\mathbf{a}_i\|$;
velocity matching gets next priority
$\mathbf{a}_i = \mathbf{a}_i + \min(a_{\mathrm{r}}, \|\mathbf{a}_i^v\|)\hat{\mathbf{a}}_i^v$;
set residual to the unused acceleration budget
$a_{\mathrm{r}} = a_{\max} - \|\mathbf{a}_i\|$;
centering gets lowest priority
$\mathbf{a}_i = \mathbf{a}_i + \min(a_{\mathrm{r}}, \|\mathbf{a}_i^c\|)\hat{\mathbf{a}}_i^c$;

6.5.4 Steering around Obstacles

In Section 5.3.2 we outlined an algorithm for steering particles around environmental obstacles. This algorithm can be directly applied to the acceleration calculations for the boids in a flocking system, inserting the calculated steering acceleration into the acceleration prioritization algorithm. It should probably be given top priority, since it is more important for a boid to avoid flying into a wall than to avoid bumping into its neighbor.

6.5.5 Turning and Banking

If a flocking algorithm is going to be used to choreograph birds or other flying creatures, it will be important to capture not only the position and velocity of each boid but also the rotation required for banking during turns. Consider an airplane. Were an airplane to attempt a turn without banking, there would be no significant force to counteract the centrifugal force induced by the turn, causing the plane to skid sideways. Because of this, the pilot banks the plane into a turn enough so that the radial component of the lift of the wings produces a centripetal force to balance the centrifugal force. Birds and all flying creatures utilize this same mechanism. Therefore, for an animation to look realistic, the model being used to represent a boid must not only be oriented in the direction of the velocity vector, but also banked appropriately during each turn. To do this efficiently, we need an appropriate coordinate frame for orienting the boid, and a mechanism for computing the banking rotation angle.

If the boid's acceleration $\mathbf{a}$ is not exactly aligned with its velocity $\mathbf{v}$ the boid will not only change speed, but will also change its direction of flight. This change in direction will manifest itself in a rotation of the boid's velocity vector about an axis perpendicular to both the velocity and the acceleration directions. Let

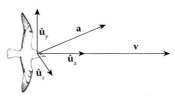

us define an orientation coordinate frame using this fact. First, let the x direction be parallel to the current velocity, and let the y direction be the turning axis, which is parallel to the cross-product of the velocity and acceleration. Finally, the z direction will be perpendicular to both the x and y directions. Summarizing, the three unit vectors forming the boid's coordinate frame are

$$\hat{\mathbf{u}}_x = \hat{\mathbf{v}},$$
$$\hat{\mathbf{u}}_y = \frac{\mathbf{v} \times \mathbf{a}}{\|\mathbf{v} \times \mathbf{a}\|},$$
$$\hat{\mathbf{u}}_z = \hat{\mathbf{u}}_x \times \hat{\mathbf{u}}_y.$$

As described in Appendix D, the rotation matrix to align the boid with this coordinate frame is

$$R = \begin{bmatrix} \hat{\mathbf{u}}_x & \hat{\mathbf{u}}_y & \hat{\mathbf{u}}_z \end{bmatrix}.$$

The total acceleration $\mathbf{a}$ on a boid can be thought of as having two components: a component $\mathbf{a}_v$ parallel to the boid's current velocity vector, which simply changes the boid's speed, and a component $\mathbf{a}_T$ orthogonal to the boid's velocity, which induces turning. These vectors are given by

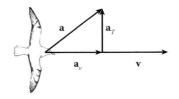

$$\mathbf{a}_v = (\mathbf{a} \cdot \hat{\mathbf{u}}_x)\hat{\mathbf{u}}_x,$$
$$\mathbf{a}_T = \mathbf{a} - \mathbf{a}_v.$$

Let us use an airplane analogy to determine how the banking angle should be computed. Assume that the airplane is in level flight, and begins to initiate a turn. In order to produce the turning acceleration $\mathbf{a}_T$, the airplane must be able to produce a force orthogonal to its direction of flight. Banking the airplane, by lowering the wing on the inside of the turn, will achieve this

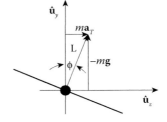

because the lift force produced by the wings will now have a component in the direction of the turn. Let the total lift force of the wings be $\mathbf{L}$, and the airplane's banking angle be ϕ. Since the airplane is in level flight, its y axis will align with the global vertical direction, and its x and z axes will be parallel to the ground. Therefore, to maintain a constant altitude, the component of the lift opposing the gravitational force $\mathbf{g}$ must be $\mathbf{L} \cdot \hat{\mathbf{u}}_y = -m\mathbf{g} \cdot \hat{\mathbf{u}}_y$, while the component of the lift producing the turning acceleration must be $\mathbf{L} \cdot \hat{\mathbf{u}}_z = m\mathbf{a}_T \cdot \hat{\mathbf{u}}_z$. We can take the ratio of these two expressions to obtain

$$\tan\phi = -\frac{\mathbf{a}_T \cdot \hat{\mathbf{u}}_z}{\mathbf{g} \cdot \hat{\mathbf{u}}_y},$$

or

$$\phi = -\tan^{-1}\frac{\mathbf{a}_T \cdot \hat{\mathbf{u}}_z}{\mathbf{g} \cdot \hat{\mathbf{u}}_y}.$$

The flocking algorithm ignores gravity, and boids can be oriented in any direction, making the level flight assumption a poor one. Nevertheless, this result can be generalized to handle nonlevel flight by noting that the term $\mathbf{g} \cdot \hat{\mathbf{u}}_y$ in the above expression will always be negative, and by replacing the denominator by a constant multiplier k_ϕ, which can be tuned by the animator to obtain the desired banking effect. Making these substitutions, the banking angle will be given by

$$\phi = \tan^{-1} k_\phi \mathbf{a}_T \cdot \hat{\mathbf{u}}_z.$$

A final note here is that the resulting banking angle will change instantaneously with changes in the turning acceleration. If the turning acceleration changes suddenly, the boid's banking behavior can appear to be erratic. Therefore, it may be useful to smooth the angle ϕ by maintaining a running average $\phi_{\mathrm{avg}}^{[n]}$, updated at each timestep as follows:

$$\phi_{\mathrm{avg}}^{[n]} = (1-\alpha)\phi_{\mathrm{avg}}^{[n-1]} + \alpha\phi.$$

Here, $0 < \alpha \leq 1$ is a smoothing constant determining what fraction of the new angle ϕ is added into the running average, and can be tuned by the animator to achieve the desired smoothness of banking action.

Now, to rotate the boid into a banking turn, we need only first rotate the boid by angle $\phi_{\mathrm{avg}}^{[n]}$ about its own x axis, before transforming the boid into world space via the matrix R.

6.6 SUMMARY

Here are some of the main points to take away from this chapter:

- The complexity of calculations involving interacting particles can grow far more quickly than when the particles are independent of each other. Thus, interacting particle systems tend to be significantly smaller in scope than other particle systems.

- By representing the entire system by a state vector that describes the state of all objects (particles) at one point in time, the simulation can be described more simply.

- Spatial data structures such as uniform spatial grids, octrees, and kd-trees can help to limit the number of particles examined for interaction. As one example, we see the benefit of such an effect in an astronomical simulation.

- By applying a few simple rules regarding particle-particle interactions, more complex behavior can result. These behaviors are known as emergent phenomena.

- To simulate flocking, particles can obey three simple rules relative to other particles, specifically collision avoidance, velocity matching, and centering.

- Flocking simulations can be made more realistic by incorporating models of behavior, including vision, obstacle avoidance, and banking.

CHAPTER 7

Numerical Integration

W E SAW BACK IN SECTION 2.6 that the method we use for integrating can play a significant role in the accuracy of the simulations we produce. It will be useful to review that section before proceeding forward. Up until this point, we have used the simplest integration scheme, Euler integration, to illustrate our simulations. However, we will quickly encounter a need for alternative integration techniques, either because we want something more accurate, more stable, or more efficient. In this chapter, we discuss several important ideas in integration, and present in detail a few of the most common integration methods used in physically based animation.

Numerical integration techniques have a long history, and while we will give a summary of key ideas and useful techniques here, there are many alternative sources that can provide a much more in-depth and rigorous treatment of the subject. A very useful practical reference source is the *Numerical Recipes* series [Press et al., 2007]. If the material in this chapter is intriguing, we would encourage the reader to pursue some of the more detailed discussion in those sources.

7.1 SERIES EXPANSION AND INTEGRATION

To understand the various methods of integration, it is very helpful to first understand what they are accomplishing. To do this, we must understand the functions we want to integrate.

Many of the problems we face can be described as an ordinary differential equation in the form

$$\dot{\mathbf{s}}(t) = \frac{d\mathbf{s}(t)}{dt} = \mathbf{f}(\mathbf{s}, t). \tag{7.1}$$

That is, we have a function $\mathbf{f}$, describing how the state $\mathbf{s}$ is changing at a particular point in time. In the examples we have seen to this point, and as in Section 6.1, for a state consisting of only position and velocity, the function $\mathbf{f}$ gives the velocity and acceleration.

Our goal in integration is to go from the current time t to some time in the future, $t + h$. In other words, given $\mathbf{s}(t)$, we want to find $\mathbf{s}(t + h)$. What we would like to compute is

$$\mathbf{s}(t + h) = \mathbf{s}(t) + \int_t^{t+h} \dot{\mathbf{s}}(\tau) d\tau$$

$$= \mathbf{s}(t) + \int_t^{t+h} \mathbf{f}(\mathbf{s}, \tau) d\tau.$$

Although we know $\mathbf{s}(t)$, unfortunately we do not usually have an analytic form for $\mathbf{f}(\mathbf{s}, \tau)$; rather we just have some way of evaluating it for a particular $\mathbf{s}$. So, we are faced with having to approximate the integral. The various numerical integration techniques we use are all ways of approximating this integral.

To understand the nature of this approximation, we need to introduce the notion of Taylor series. A Taylor series is an expansion of a function $f(x)$ around a particular value $x = a$, written

$$f(x) = \sum_{n=0}^{\infty} \frac{f^{(n)}(a)}{n!} (x - a)^n, \text{ or alternatively}$$

$$f(x + \Delta x) = \sum_{n=0}^{\infty} \frac{f^{(n)}(x)}{n!} \Delta x^n,$$

where $f^{(n)}$ refers to the nth derivative of f. Expanding the summation, we have

$$f(x + \Delta x) = f(x) + f'(x)\Delta x + \frac{1}{2}f''(x)\Delta x^2 + \frac{1}{6}f'''(x)\Delta x^3 + \dots .$$

This expansion only holds if all of the infinite derivatives of f exist in the neighborhood of the particular value of x for which we are evaluating the series. This means that it is required that the function be locally smooth, with no discontinuities in any derivative. If we let $f = \mathbf{s}$, $x = t$, and $\Delta x = h$, we can use a Taylor expansion to write

$$\mathbf{s}(t + h) = \mathbf{s}(t) + \dot{\mathbf{s}}(t)h + \frac{1}{2}\ddot{\mathbf{s}}(t)h^2 + \dots, \tag{7.2}$$

which gives how the state $\mathbf{s}$ advances with one timestep h.

For practical simulation, we cannot use the infinite terms in the Taylor series, so our integration methods are essentially ways of approximating truncated forms of the series. The more robust integration methods are usually the ones approximating a larger number of terms. The Euler integration that we have used to this point takes just the first two terms: $\mathbf{s}(t + h) \approx \mathbf{s}(t) + \dot{\mathbf{s}}(t)h$. This means that all the later terms in the Taylor series are ignored, and thus that this method has some error.

If we assume that h is a very small number, then the later terms of this series expansion will tend to get smaller and smaller since the factorial denominator will grow, the h^n factor will get smaller and smaller, and in physical systems the higher-order derivatives will not tend to grow in magnitude to compensate. A typical way of expressing this error is as $O(h^n)$, stating that as h is changed, the error will change proportional to h^n. For a small h value, the bigger n is the better. Euler integration would have error $O(h^2)$, for example, so that as the step size h is halved, error goes down roughly by a factor of 4. This is actually not very good compared with some of the other methods we will see.

We can classify many integration schemes by *order*, which refers to how many levels of derivatives are represented in the Taylor series expansion. Euler integration is a first-order method, since it is correct up through the first derivative. In general, an order n method will have $O(h^{n+1})$ error.

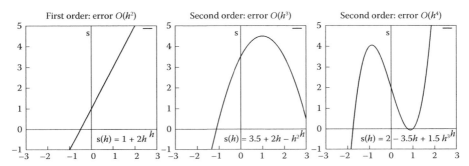

Another way of thinking about order is to understand the shape of the function that it can reconstruct, or the degree of the function that can be fit to the known data. So, a first-order function can reconstruct something that varies by a first-order (i.e., linear) polynomial. The leftmost figure, above, is an example. If you recall the falling ball example in Chapter 2, you will notice that Euler integration perfectly reproduced the velocity, which was changing linearly. However, it could not reproduce the position, which was following a parabolic path. A second-order method (such as the one in Equation 2.5) was able to reproduce the position exactly. The middle figure, above, provides an example of the path a second-order method could reproduce. At right is an example of a third-order result, where we begin having inflection points, i.e., the second derivative can change signs and thus the curve can "wiggle."

Although we speak about them in different ways when using them in simulation, the integration techniques we have are similar to those you may have learned when first learning integration in calculus. You may recall that one way of estimating the area under a curve is to put a large number of rectangular boxes under the curve and add up the area of those boxes. If we imagine the x axis is time, and the y axis is our function $\mathbf{f}$, the process of simulating over time is equivalent to finding this area (and the "gaps" are the error we were discussing). The width of each box is our timestep, h, and as we decrease h, we get closer and closer to the actual area.

If we form the rectangular boxes by setting the height equal to the value of $\mathbf{f}$ at the beginning t value, as in the figure below, this is identical to Euler integration. That is, we are taking the value of the derivative at the beginning of the timestep,

and assuming it is constant throughout the timestep. Notice that if the function we are integrating is constant (as acceleration was constant in our Chapter 2 examples), then this will exactly integrate the area under the curve.

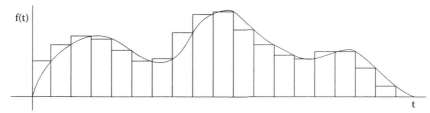

Consider now the other methods we looked at in Section 2.6. In Equation 2.4, we used the value of the function from the end of the timestep for our integration. We could rewrite these functions in terms of state as $\mathbf{s}(t+h) = \mathbf{s}(t) + \dot{\mathbf{s}}(t+h)h$. This is equivalent to using a box, but setting the height equal to the value of $\mathbf{f}$ at the *end* of each interval, as in the figure above. As should be clear from looking at this figure, there is still as much error as in Euler integration.

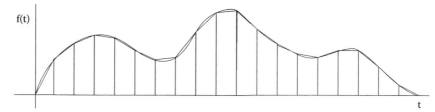

Now consider the method in Equation 2.5, which we could rewrite as $\mathbf{s}(t+h) = \mathbf{s}(t) + \frac{\dot{\mathbf{s}}(t)+\dot{\mathbf{s}}(t+h)}{2}h$. This method integrates by taking the value of $\mathbf{f}$ at the beginning of the interval and the value at the end of the interval, and averaging them. The shape formed is a trapezoid, which is why this is known as the *trapezoidal method*. From looking at the figure above, it seems as though the trapezoid can approximate the shape much more closely (i.e., with less error), and this is in fact true—it is a second-order method. The trapezoidal method also makes it possible to integrate functions that are linear in shape (thus are quadratic when integrated) exactly. From our examples in Chapter 2, velocity was varying linearly. Thus, the trapezoidal method was able to integrate the velocity to find position perfectly.

There are a variety of other integration techniques. Another second-order method is the Midpoint method, which can be written

$$\mathbf{s}(t+h) = \mathbf{s}(t) + \dot{\mathbf{s}}(t+0.5h)h. \qquad (7.3)$$

Simpson's method is an example of a third-order method, formed from a weighted combination of the trapezoidal (with weight $\frac{1}{3}$) and midpoint (with weight $\frac{2}{3}$). It is written

$$\mathbf{s}(t+h) = \frac{1}{3}\left(\mathbf{s}(t) + \frac{\dot{\mathbf{s}}(t) + \dot{\mathbf{s}}(t+h)}{2}h\right) + \frac{2}{3}\left(\mathbf{s}(t) + \dot{\mathbf{s}}(t+0.5h)h\right)$$

$$= \mathbf{s}(t) + \frac{h}{6}(\dot{\mathbf{s}}(t) + 4\dot{\mathbf{s}}(t+0.5h) + \dot{\mathbf{s}}(t+h)). \tag{7.4}$$

The problem with these methods is that the derivatives are generally not known for times in the future. For our simple gravity example from Chapter 2, we always knew the acceleration since it was constant. In general, though, the only thing we know reliably is the value of the derivative when we are given a specific state. For these reasons, we must look to other integration methods that provide ways of estimating these states in the future. We discuss some of the most common ones in the next few sections.

7.2 VERLET AND LEAPFROG INTEGRATION

As mentioned above, for the problems we face, in order to calculate the acceleration at some future time we need to know the state at that time. However, many of the most straightforward integration techniques require us to know the acceleration at that time in order to compute the state at that time. This can lead to a chicken-and-egg situation, which we can only resolve by using different integration techniques.

Verlet integration (and the similar leapfrog method) are one such class of integration methods. These methods assume that the acceleration is determined by position (not velocity). That is, we assume the forces are a function of position, $\mathbf{f}(\mathbf{x})$, and thus we can get the accelerations by just dividing by the respective masses: $\mathbf{a} = \frac{1}{\mathbf{m}}\mathbf{f}(\mathbf{x})$. Thus, a system of gravitational or spring forces works very well, while incorporating aspects such as air resistance, damping, or velocity matching in flocking is problematic.

The basic idea of Verlet integration is to try to compute the velocity separately from the position, and use the fact that accelerations are independent of velocity to be able to take more accurate steps.

7.2.1 Basic Verlet Integration

For Verlet integration, we must assume that position and velocity are treated differently in the computation, rather than treating the entire state as a whole. Basic Verlet integration describes only the position calculation. We will see below how we can also incorporate the velocity calculation.

For Verlet integration, we assume that we know *two* existing values of the position, as well as the acceleration (we do not use velocity explicitly). That is, we assume we know $\mathbf{x}^{[i]}$, $\mathbf{x}^{[i+1]}$, and $\mathbf{a}^{[i+1]}$, and we want to compute $\mathbf{x}^{[i+2]}$. Having two prior positions allows us to estimate the velocity $\mathbf{v} \approx \frac{\mathbf{x}^{[i+1]} - \mathbf{x}^{[i]}}{h}$.

We can understand how the Verlet integration method is derived by considering how we might represent acceleration if we only know positions. Assume for a moment that we know the positions $\mathbf{x}(t)$, $\mathbf{x}(t+h)$, and $\mathbf{x}(t+2h)$. We could estimate the velocity between the first two positions as $\mathbf{v}(t+0.5h) = \frac{\mathbf{x}(t+h)-\mathbf{x}(t)}{h}$, and between the second two positions as $\mathbf{v}(t+1.5h) = \frac{\mathbf{x}(t+2h)-\mathbf{x}(t+h)}{h}$. We could then estimate acceleration between those two velocity values as

$$\mathbf{a}(t+h) = \frac{\mathbf{v}(t+1.5h) - \mathbf{v}(t+0.5h)}{h}$$
$$= \frac{\frac{\mathbf{x}(t+2h)-\mathbf{x}(t+h)}{h} - \frac{\mathbf{x}(t+h)-\mathbf{x}(t)}{h}}{h}$$
$$= \frac{\mathbf{x}(t+2h) - 2\mathbf{x}(t+h) + \mathbf{x}(t)}{h^2}.$$

This can be solved for the position in two timesteps:

$$\mathbf{x}(t+2h) = \mathbf{a}(t+h)h^2 + 2\mathbf{x}(t+h) - \mathbf{x}(t).$$

You might have already been familiar with that derivation for acceleration, commonly called a second-order central difference. The key point for Verlet integration is that it allows us to write the position at $t+2h$ as a function of positions at t and $t+h$, and acceleration at $t+h$. This leads directly to the basic algorithm for Verlet integration:

$$\mathbf{x}^{[i+2]} = -\mathbf{x}^{[i]} + 2\mathbf{x}^{[i+1]} + \mathbf{a}^{[i+1]}h^2. \tag{7.5}$$

This method is derived from a second-order differentiation, and as a result, it is a second-order method.

There are a few challenges in using this method of Verlet integration. First, like all Verlet methods, the acceleration is only calculated based on position. While you could use some velocity estimates in this acceleration calculation, doing so is only approximate, and loses the theoretical higher-order guarantees that we would otherwise have. Second, it is not sufficient to just have starting conditions of $\mathbf{x}(0)$ and $\mathbf{a}(0)$. We must have two positions to begin the process, so a variety of methods are used to estimate a second initial position, after which Verlet integration can run as normal. A common way of doing so if we know the initial velocity is to estimate $\mathbf{x}(h) = \mathbf{x}(0) + \mathbf{v}(0)h + \frac{1}{2}\mathbf{a}(0)h^2$. Another challenge is that velocity is not explicitly calculated in this method. We can estimate velocities using another difference, i.e., $\mathbf{v}(t+h) = \frac{\mathbf{x}(t+2h)-\mathbf{x}(t)}{2h}$. However, this causes the velocity at $t+h$ to be computed only after the postion at $t+2h$ is computed. In many cases, that is too late to be useful. A better way of computing velocities is the Velocity Verlet method.

7.2.2 Velocity Verlet Integration

In most cases, we will want to know the velocity, also, so we will describe a version of Verlet Integration called Velocity Verlet. The Velocity Verlet method also has the advantage that by incorporating velocity, we can simplify some of the equations.

We assume that we know the position $\mathbf{x}^{[i]}$ and velocity $\mathbf{v}^{[i]}$ at one time, and we want to find the position $\mathbf{x}^{[i+1]}$ and velocity $\mathbf{v}^{[i+1]}$ after a timestep h. If we imagine taking a standard Euler step to compute velocity, we get $\mathbf{v}^{[i+1]} = \mathbf{v}^{[i]} + \mathbf{a}^{[i]}h$. We can then use this in the trapezoidal method to compute $\mathbf{x}^{[i+1]}$ as follows:

$$\mathbf{x}^{[i+1]} = \mathbf{x}^{[i]} + \frac{\mathbf{v}^{[i]} + \mathbf{v}^{[i+1]}}{2}h \tag{7.6}$$

$$= \mathbf{x}^{[i]} + \frac{\mathbf{v}^{[i]} + \mathbf{v}^{[i]} + \mathbf{a}^{[i]}h}{2}h \tag{7.7}$$

$$= \mathbf{x}^{[i]} + \mathbf{v}^{[i]}h + \frac{1}{2}\mathbf{a}^{[i]}h^2 \tag{7.8}$$

This is the same as we saw from integrating with constant acceleration in Equation 2.2.

We can use this approach to get a higher-order estimate of position. Once we know that position, we can compute the new acceleration at that point in the future, since we have an acceleration that is a function of just position. Finally, to find a higher-order estimate of velocity, we can use the trapezoidal method to take this new acceleration and compute the velocity. The method is summarized as follows:

$$\begin{aligned}
\mathbf{x}^{[i+1]} &= \mathbf{x}^{[i]} + \mathbf{v}^{[i]}h + \frac{1}{2}\mathbf{a}^{[i]}h^2, \\
\mathbf{a}^{[i+1]} &= \frac{1}{\mathbf{m}}\mathbf{f}(\mathbf{x}^{[i+1]}), \\
\mathbf{v}^{[i+1]} &= \mathbf{v}^{[i]} + \frac{\mathbf{a}^{[i]} + \mathbf{a}^{[i+1]}}{2}h.
\end{aligned} \tag{7.9}$$

You can see that the position is calculated using the second-order approach derived above, and the velocity is calculated using the trapezoidal method. Overall, then, this Velocity Verlet integration is a second-order method. However, it is important to realize that the second-order nature of the approach depends on being able to compute the acceleration from just the position. As can be seen in Equation 7.9, in order to compute $\mathbf{v}^{[i+1]}$ you must know $\mathbf{a}^{[i+1]}$, which is computed based only on the position.

7.2.3 Leapfrog Integration

The leapfrog method is a slight variation on the Velocity Verlet method. With leapfrog integration, the idea is to compute velocity values at a half-timestep different from the position and acceleration values. Thus, if we calculate position at times t, $t+h$, $t+2h$, $t+3h$, etc., we will calculate velocities at times $t+0.5h$, $t+1.5h$, $t+2.5h$, etc. The name "leapfrog" refers to the way that position and velocity calculations "hop" over each other in time.

To run the leapfrog method, we must know the initial positions $\mathbf{x}^{[0]} = \mathbf{x}(t)$, the "initial" velocities $\mathbf{v}^{[0.5]} = \mathbf{v}(t+0.5h)$, and a way to compute acceleration based on positions, i.e., $\mathbf{a}^{[i]} = \frac{1}{\mathbf{m}}\mathbf{f}(\mathbf{x}^{[i]})$. So, at any point in time, we can assume we know $\mathbf{x}^{[i]}$, $\mathbf{a}^{[i]}$, and $\mathbf{v}^{[i+0.5]}$, and we need to compute $\mathbf{x}^{[i+1]}$ and $\mathbf{v}^{[i+1.5]}$. The equations for doing so are as follows:

$$\mathbf{x}^{[i+1]} = \mathbf{x}^{[i]} + \mathbf{v}^{[i+0.5]}h,$$
$$\mathbf{a}^{[i+1]} = \frac{1}{\mathbf{m}}\mathbf{f}(\mathbf{x}^{[i+1]}), \tag{7.10}$$
$$\mathbf{v}^{[i+1.5]} = \mathbf{v}^{[i+0.5]} + \mathbf{a}^{[i+1]}h.$$

If you do not know $\mathbf{v}^{[0.5]}$, but do know $\mathbf{v}^{[0]}$ and $\mathbf{x}^{[0]}$ (and thus $\mathbf{a}^{[0]}$), you can get an initial estimate by taking a half-Euler step of velocity. Notice that both the velocity and the position are computed by formulas that are essentially equivalent to the midpoint method described above (Equation 7.3). This means that the leapfrog method is a second-order method.

7.3   RUNGE-KUTTA INTEGRATION

While Verlet integration can be very useful in many situations, it is not designed to handle cases where the acceleration is dependent on velocity. In practice, we often see velocity-related accelerations, and so Verlet integration can be inappropriate. Already, we have seen such models when dealing with air resistance (see Section 2.7.2) and with velocity matching in flocking (see Section 6.5.1), and it will come up again in future topics.

Another family of integration approaches is the *Runge-Kutta* family, which we will abbreviate RK. RK integration is useful since it operates on an entire state at once. This means that accelerations can be determined from any values in the current state, including velocity. Recall that the state of a system can be abbreviated as $\mathbf{S}$. Then, we assume that we have some function that can return the derivative of the state given a current state, i.e., $\dot{\mathbf{S}} = \mathbf{F}(\mathbf{S}, t)$ (Equation 6.7).

Also, we will see that RK methods can be of any order we want. In particular, we will use the term RKn, where n is some integer, to refer to the order of the RK method we are considering. So, RK2 is a second-order Runge-Kutta integration method, and RK4 is a fourth-order Runge-Kutta integration method.

RK integration is a powerful technique that has many variations and extensions. We will not provide a full derivation of the method or analysis of its error here, but rather give some basic definitions and *intuitive* insight into how these methods work.

7.3.1   First- and Second-Order Runge-Kutta

To give a sense for how Runge-Kutta methods work, we will start by describing the simplest RK methods.

In first-order Runge-Kutta integration we assume we have an initial state $\mathbf{S}^{[0]}$ and want to compute future states. We can perform iterations as follows:

$$\mathbf{K}_1 = \mathbf{F}(\mathbf{S}^{[i]}),$$
$$\mathbf{S}^{[i+1]} = \mathbf{S}^{[i]} + h\mathbf{K}_1.$$

Note that $\mathbf{F}(\mathbf{S}) = \dot{\mathbf{S}}$, so RK1 is equivalent to the Euler integration we have seen repeatedly. We will extend this now to get a second-order method.

We have already seen the midpoint method for integration (Equation 7.3), which relies on knowing the derivative halfway through the timestep. That is, we would need to know $\dot{\mathbf{S}}(t+0.5h) = \mathbf{F}(\mathbf{S}(t+0.5h))$. Unfortunately, since we do not know the state halfway through the timestep, we cannot compute the derivative of the state at that point, either. However, we can get an estimate of the state at that point, by just performing a half-Euler step. That is, we can assume that

$$\mathbf{S}(t+0.5h) \approx \mathbf{S}(t) + 0.5h\dot{\mathbf{S}}(t).$$

This is the fundamental idea behind the higher-order RK methods: that we can approximate higher-order derivatives using previously computed derivatives. Using the above approximation of the derivative at the midpoint, we can write an approach for RK2 as follows:

$$\mathbf{K}_1 = \mathbf{F}(\mathbf{S}^{[i]}),$$
$$\mathbf{K}_2 = \mathbf{F}(\mathbf{S}^{[i]} + 0.5h\mathbf{K}_1),$$
$$\mathbf{S}^{[i+1]} = \mathbf{S}^{[i]} + h\mathbf{K}_2.$$

In other words, $\mathbf{K}_1$ is just the original derivative, and we use that to get an estimate of the state at the halfway point of the timestep, $\mathbf{S}^{[i]} + 0.5h\mathbf{K}_1$. Then, $\mathbf{K}_2$ is the estimated derivative at that midpoint state. We use $\mathbf{K}_2$ to take our full step forward.

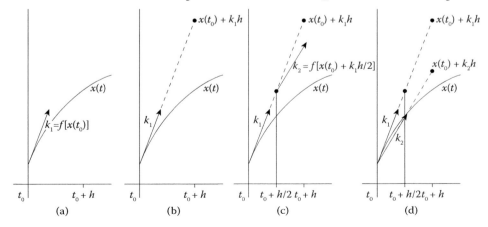

The figure above illustrates this idea. Assume that we have a one-dimensional function of time $x(t)$, which is shown exactly in the figures. We are currently at time t_0 and happen to know the value of the function $x(t_0)$ exactly. We also know the derivative function $\dot{x} = f(x)$. Now, we want to use RK2 integration to estimate the function at the next timestep $t_0 + h$. (a) The first step is to find the derivative of x at the current time, $k_1 = f[x(t_0)]$. (b) Using Euler integration, we would advance one timestep to $x(t_0) + k_1 h$. Note, that this results in a large deviation from the exact curve we are trying to approximate. (c) In RK2, we advance a half timestep to $x(t_0) + k_1 h/2$, and using this as the state, compute the derivative again, giving us $k_2 = f[x(t_0) + k_1 h/2]$. (d) Finally, we start back at t_0, but use k_2 to advance the full timestep, resulting in a final function estimate $x(t_0) + k_2 h$ that is considerably better than the estimate we would have obtained using only Euler integration.

RK2 is a second-order method. Notice that unlike Verlet integration, we are always directly computing derivatives of the entire state, so that the accelerations can be based on not just position, but also velocity. However, note also that RK2 requires us to compute that derivative $\mathbf{F}$ twice during each timestep, whereas Verlet integration required only one calculation of the derivative per timestep.

7.3.2 Fourth-Order Runge-Kutta

The family of RK methods is very extensible. RK techniques are capable of integrating at any order, and there can be multiple ways of computing an nth-order approximation. As should be obvious from the RK2 example, higher-order integration does take more time per step. In the RK2 algorithm, one timestep required evaluating the derivative function $\mathbf{F}$ twice, and as we use higher-order RK methods, we will have to compute $\mathbf{F}$ more often per timestep. Since computing $\mathbf{F}$ is typically the most expensive part of integration, there is thus a trade-off: we can get a more accurate estimate, but only if we spend more time per timestep.

Recall that we can also get more accurate estimates by taking smaller timesteps. That is, we could take two timesteps of half the length. As a result, we are faced with a challenge: if we need more accurate results, is it better to use a higher-order method, or to take smaller timesteps? This is discussed in more detail in Section 7.4.

There is actually an infinite number of variations on how RK4 can be computed, but there is one approach that is very commonly used, and when we say RK4, we usually refer to this method. Some people do not even make that much distinction: sometimes you will just see this approach called the Runge-Kutta approach. This commonly used RK4 approach is as follows:

$$
\begin{aligned}
\mathbf{K}_1 &= \mathbf{F}(\mathbf{S}^{[i]}), \\
\mathbf{K}_2 &= \mathbf{F}(\mathbf{S}^{[i]} + 0.5h\mathbf{K}_1), \\
\mathbf{K}_3 &= \mathbf{F}(\mathbf{S}^{[i]} + 0.5h\mathbf{K}_2), \\
\mathbf{K}_4 &= \mathbf{F}(\mathbf{S}^{[i]} + h\mathbf{K}_3), \\
\mathbf{S}^{[i+1]} &= \mathbf{S}^{[i]} + \frac{h}{6}(\mathbf{K}_1 + 2\mathbf{K}_2 + 2\mathbf{K}_3 + \mathbf{K}_4).
\end{aligned}
$$

Notice that we are computing $\mathbf{F}$ four times in each timestep. That is, we are having to evaluate the derivative of a state four different times. Only the first of these states (the $\mathbf{S}^{[i]}$ used to compute $\mathbf{K}_1$) is one we actually keep. The other states (such as $\mathbf{S}^{[i]} + 0.5h\mathbf{K}_1$) are used only in the intermediate computation, and then are discarded.

When faced with an unknown simulation, RK4 is a good, "safe" choice to use as a first attempt at integration.

7.4   IMPLEMENTATION OF HIGHER-ORDER INTEGRATORS

The introduction of integrators that are of higher order than Euler opens several design issues for the programming of simulations. The two of most immediate concern are how to handle the need to compute the system dynamics multiple times in one timestep, and how to correctly handle collisions.

7.4.1   State Vector Algorithm

The implementation of the higher-order integrators, like RK2 and RK4, follows exactly the implementation described in Section 6.1.3, except that the NumInt() function needs to be given access to the current time t and the system dynamics function F() so that the system dynamics can be calculated multiple times during the timestep. For example, the NumInt function implementation for RK4 might be written:

StateVector NumInt(StateVector $\mathbf{S}$, StateVector $\dot{\mathbf{S}}$, float h, float t,
StateVector F())
begin
    StateVector $\mathbf{K}_1$, $\mathbf{K}_2$, $\mathbf{K}_3$, $\mathbf{K}_4$;
    StateVector $\mathbf{S}^{new}$;

    $\mathbf{K}_1 = \dot{\mathbf{S}}$;
    $\mathbf{K}_2 = \text{F}(\mathbf{S} + \frac{h}{2}\mathbf{K}_1, t + \frac{h}{2})$;
    $\mathbf{K}_3 = \text{F}(\mathbf{S} + \frac{h}{2}\mathbf{K}_2, t + \frac{h}{2})$;
    $\mathbf{K}_4 = \text{F}(\mathbf{S} + h\mathbf{K}_3, t + h)$;

    $\mathbf{S}^{new} = \mathbf{S} + \frac{h}{6}(\mathbf{K}_1 + 2\mathbf{K}_2 + 2\mathbf{K}_3 + \mathbf{K}_4)$;

    return $\mathbf{S}^{new}$
end

7.4.2   Collision Detection with Higher-Order Integrators

Choosing an integration method for a particular problem involves a number of trade-offs. Besides the speed, stability, and accuracy of a particular integration method, there are software engineering issues. The most important of these is a consideration of how an integration scheme fits into the computational framework of the particular problem being worked on.

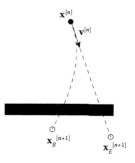

A classical example of a situation where software engineering concerns may outweigh other concerns is in problems involving collision detection. Euler integration has the very nice characteristic that it linearly extrapolates state over each timestep. The figure to the right shows a particle at timestep n, with position $\mathbf{x}^{[n]}$ and velocity $\mathbf{v}^{[n]}$. Euler integration will move the particle along the velocity vector, leaving it at a position we will call $\mathbf{x}_E^{[n]}$ at the next timestep. Any of the higher-order integration methods, like RK4 for example, will simulate the particle moving along a polynomial curve, leaving it at a position we will call $\mathbf{x}_R^{[n]}$. In the example shown, the exact collision position and time using Euler are easily determined from a ray-plane intersection calculation. With RK4, on the other hand, we would need to find the geometry-curve intersection point. It is quite possible that using RK4 there is no intersection, even though there is one with Euler, or that there is an RK4 collision but no Euler collision.

There are several ways to get around the problem with collision detection using a higher-order integrator. The simplest is to recognize that the first step of all of the RK integrators is to compute the derivative used in Euler integration. Thus, with minimal extra cost, it is possible to take a tentative Euler step, check to see if there would be a collision during that step, and if not, continue with the full integration calculation. However, if there would be a collision during the Euler step, it can be handled as if Euler integration were being used for the entire timestep. In this way, only timesteps involving a collision are handled using Euler integration, while most timesteps are handled using the higher-order method. This gives the advantages of both approaches: simplicity in dealing with collisions, and improved accuracy and stability between collisions.

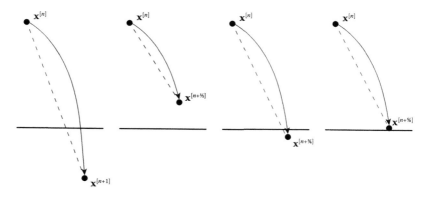

Another approach is demonstrated in the figure above. It is to always use the full higher-order integrator, and then test for a collision by building a line segment connecting the starting and ending positions of a particle, and looking for inter-sections of this line segment with the geometry. This is not a perfect test, but will catch most potential collisions. If, from this test, a collision is suspected, do a binary search within the timestep for the exact collision time, by first trying a step of $h/2$. Then if there is a collision try $h/4$ or if no collision try $3h/4$, repeating this timestep subdivision process until either it is confirmed that there is no col-lision or a collision is detected within an allowable tolerance. This will give the correct collision position and time, within a chosen tolerance, at the cost of some computational overhead.

7.5 STABILITY AND ACCURACY OF THE INTEGRATORS

In deciding on an integration scheme and an appropriate timestep, there are two primary considerations: *stability* and *accuracy*. For an integration scheme to be stable means that for a particular size timestep, iteratively performing the integra-tion on the system always yields a result that stays within reasonable bounds. If the integration is unstable, the result will be that the solution will diverge, usu-ally exhibiting an unbounded exponential growth. In plain language, "The solution blows up!" For an integration scheme to be accurate means that iteratively per-forming the integration always yields a result that is within some desired error bound from the exact solution. It can be the case that a stable integration scheme is grossly inaccurate, and it can also be the case that an unstable integration scheme produces quite accurate results up until just before it "blows up." To help us to know how to choose an integrator, appropriate to a particular problem, we will start by examining two classical linear differential equations: exponential decay and sinusoidal oscillation.

A spring is a common element of many physical systems. The behavior of a spring, that is compressed and then let go, is to bounce back and forth quite strongly initially, but with a motion that dies out over time. Exponential decay is a good model for processes, like springy motion, that die out over time. Sinusoidal oscillation is likewise a good model for processes, like springy motion, that repeat regularly over time. Therefore, studying the equations for exponential decay and sinusoidal oscillation is a good first step in understanding the behavior of integration schemes being used for physical simulation.

7.5.1 Exponential Decay and Sinusoidal Oscillation

The differential equation describing exponential decay can be written

$$\dot{x} = -\frac{1}{T}x.$$

The solution to this equation is

$$x(t) = x_0 e^{-\frac{t}{T}},$$

where x_0 is the initial condition $x(0)$. Differentiating this equation once yields $\dot{x} = -\frac{1}{T}x_0 e^{-\frac{t}{T}} = -\frac{1}{T}x$, demonstrating that the solution does indeed match the original differential equation.

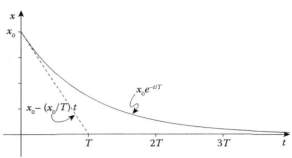

The graph of this function is shown to the right. The function starts out at height x_0, and gradually decays according to an exponential curve, approaching $x = 0$ as an asymptote. The constant T in the equation of the function is known as the *time constant* of the decay, because it determines how rapidly the decay proceeds. The larger the value of T, the longer the decay takes to die out. One way to think about this time constant is that it determines the initial slope of the curve, which is $-x_0/T$. If the curve followed a straight line with this slope, it would reach 0 exactly at $t = T$, as shown by the dashed line in the figure. Since it follows an exponential curve, after one time constant the curve reaches $x_0 e^{-1} \approx 0.37 x_0$ so 73% of the decay has occurred, after two time constants 86% has occurred, and after three time constants 95% has occurred. A glance at the curve will confirm this progression.

The differential equation describing sinusoidal oscillation, with a frequency of ω radians per second, is

$$\ddot{x} = -\omega^2 x.$$

When simulating for animation, it is often much more convenient to know the period P of oscillation, measured in seconds per cycle. This tells the animator directly how many frames it will take for a full oscillation to occur. The relationship between frequency and period is $\omega = 2\pi/P$, so the differential equation can be rewritten

$$\ddot{x} = -\left(\frac{2\pi}{P}\right)^2 x.$$

The solution to this equation is

$$x(t) = C\cos(\omega t - \phi), \quad \text{or} \quad x(t) = C\cos\left(2\pi\frac{t}{P} - \phi\right),$$

where C is the magnitude of the oscillation, whose envelope goes from $-C$ to C, and ϕ is a phase angle whose role is to position the curve along the t axis. Differentiating this equation once yields $\dot{x} = -\frac{2\pi}{P}C\sin(2\pi\frac{t}{P} - \phi)$, and differentiating this a second time gives $\ddot{x} = -\left(\frac{2\pi}{P}\right)^2 C\cos(2\pi\frac{t}{P} - \phi) = -\left(\frac{2\pi}{P}\right)^2 x$, demonstrating that the solution does indeed match the original differential equation.

The graph of this function, with the phase angle ϕ set to 0, is shown to the right. The function starts out at height C, reaching $-C$ at time $P/2$ and arriving back at C at time P, completing one full cycle. The oscillation continues forever.

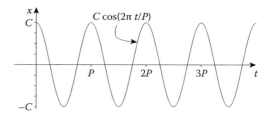

7.5.2 Integration of Exponential Decay

Let us first look at the behavior of the Euler, RK2, and RK4 methods in integrating exponential decay. The system dynamics function for exponential decay is

$$f(x) = \dot{x} = -\frac{1}{T}x.$$

The Euler integration process is

$$x^{[n+1]} = x^{[n]} + f(x)h.$$

For exponential decay, this becomes

$$x^{[n+1]} = x^{[n]} - \frac{1}{T}x^{[n]}h, \quad \text{or}$$
$$x^{[n+1]} = \left(1 - \frac{h}{T}\right)x^{[n]}.$$

Finally, we can divide both sides by $x^{[n]}$ to give the ratio of successive values of x as we integrate forward in time:

$$\frac{x^{[n+1]}}{x^{[n]}} = 1 - \frac{h}{T}.$$

For the system to converge over repeated iterations it must be true that $|1 - \frac{h}{T}| \le 1$, otherwise each successive value of x will be larger than its previous value, and the integration will "blow up." This leads us to the conclusion that for Euler integration of exponential decay to be stable, it is required that $h \le 2T$, i.e., that the integration timestep be less than twice the time constant of the decay.

The RK2 integration process is

$$k_1 = f(x),$$
$$k_2 = f\left(x + k_1\frac{h}{2}\right),$$
$$x^{[n+1]} = x^{[n]} + k_2 h.$$

For exponential decay, this becomes

$$k_1 = -\frac{1}{T}x^{[n]},$$

$$k_2 = -\frac{1}{T}\left(x^{[n]} - \frac{1}{T}x^{[n]}\frac{h}{2}\right),$$

$$x^{[n+1]} = x^{[n]} - \frac{h}{T}x^{[n]} + \frac{h^2}{2T^2}x^{[n]}, \quad \text{or}$$

$$x^{[n+1]} = \left(\frac{h^2}{2T^2} - \frac{h}{T} + 1\right)x^{[n]}.$$

Again, dividing both sides by $x^{[n]}$ gives the ratio of successive values of x:

$$\frac{x^{[n+1]}}{x^{[n]}} = \frac{h^2}{2T^2} - \frac{h}{T} + 1.$$

For the system to converge the right-hand side must be less than or equal to 1. Therefore, for RK2 integration of exponential decay to be stable it is required that

$$h \le 2T,$$

which is the same stability criterion as for Euler integration.

Carrying out a similar analysis for RK4 will show that for RK4 integration of exponential decay to be stable, it is required that, to two decimal places,

$$h < 2.78T.$$

A formal study of the accuracy of the integrators is more difficult to carry out. However, an informal study running simulations and graphing the resulting curves is easily performed. The results of such a study, showing the integration of exponential decay using Euler, RK2, and RK4 integrators, are depicted in Figure 7.1. While all integrators are stable for timestep $h = 2T$, only the RK4 integrator produces a curve that has the correct overall decay characteristic. Moving to a timestep of $h = T$, all three integrators have the correct overall shape, with RK4 producing nearly exact values at each timestep. Euler, however, is still highly inaccurate, in that it goes to 0 in only one timestep and then stays there. At a timestep $h = T/2$, both RK2 and RK4 resemble the exact curve very well, while Euler is starting to produce a shape similar to the exponential curve. At a timestep of $h = T/4$ both RK2 and RK4 are visually indistinguishable from the exact solution, while Euler is producing a curve that appears to be a reasonable approximation to the exponential.

7.5.3 Integration of Sinusoidal Oscillation

The differential equation describing sinusoidal oscillation is

$$\ddot{x} = -\omega^2 x.$$

As a notational convenience we use the frequency notation, converting to period only at the end. If we define a second variable $v = \dot{x}$, then the system dynamics

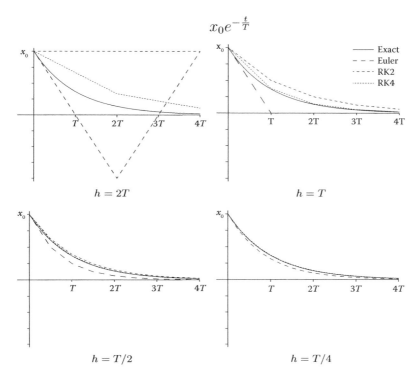

FIGURE 7.1 Exponential decay for four different-sized timesteps.

can be rewritten as the two equations

$$\dot{v} = -\omega^2 x, \quad \text{and}$$
$$\dot{x} = v.$$

We can use state notation, defining $\mathbf{s} = \begin{bmatrix} x \\ v \end{bmatrix}$, and the system dynamics function

$$f(\mathbf{s}) = \dot{\mathbf{s}} = \begin{bmatrix} \dot{x} \\ \dot{v} \end{bmatrix} = \begin{bmatrix} v \\ -\omega^2 x \end{bmatrix}.$$

Euler integration to advance the current state to the new state would be

$$\mathbf{s}^{[n+1]} = \mathbf{s}^{[n]} + f(\mathbf{s})h,$$

which in expanded form is

$$\begin{bmatrix} x^{[n+1]} \\ v^{[n+1]} \end{bmatrix} = \begin{bmatrix} x^{[n]} \\ v^{[n]} \end{bmatrix} + \begin{bmatrix} v \\ -\omega^2 x^{[n]} \end{bmatrix} h.$$

This equation can be rearranged into matrix-vector form to yield

$$\mathbf{s}^{[n+1]} = \begin{bmatrix} 1 & h \\ -\omega^2 h & 1 \end{bmatrix} \mathbf{s}^{[n]} = M\mathbf{s}^{[n]}.$$

Iteration of this equation will converge only if the determinant

$$|M| = 1 + (\omega h)^2, \quad \text{or} \quad |M| = 1 + 4\left(\frac{\pi h}{P}\right)^2$$

is less than 1. Since this determinant can never be less than 1, it is clear that Euler integration of a sinusoidal oscillation will always be unstable, even for a very small timestep h.

The analysis for RK2 follows a similar set of steps:

$$\mathbf{K}_1 = f(\mathbf{s}^{[n]}) = \begin{bmatrix} v^{[n]} \\ -\omega^2 x^{[n]} \end{bmatrix},$$

$$\mathbf{K}_2 = f\left(\mathbf{s}^{[n]} + \mathbf{K}_1\frac{h}{2}\right) = \begin{bmatrix} v^{[n]} - \omega^2 x^{[n]}\frac{h}{2} \\ -\omega^2(x^{[n]} + v^{[n]}\frac{h}{2}) \end{bmatrix},$$

$$\mathbf{s}^{[n+1]} = \mathbf{s}^{[n]} + \mathbf{K}_2 h = \begin{bmatrix} x^{[n]} \\ v^{[n]} \end{bmatrix} + \begin{bmatrix} v^{[n]} - \omega^2 x^{[n]}\frac{h}{2} \\ -\omega^2(x^{[n]} + v^{[n]}\frac{h}{2}) \end{bmatrix} h,$$

$$\mathbf{s}^{[n+1]} = \begin{bmatrix} 1 - \frac{(\omega h)^2}{2} & h \\ -\omega^2 h & 1 - \frac{(\omega h)^2}{2} \end{bmatrix} \mathbf{s}^{[n]} = M\mathbf{s}^{[n]}.$$

The determinant of the matrix M is

$$|M| = 1 + \frac{1}{4}(\omega h)^4, \quad \text{or} \quad |M| = 1 + 4\left(\frac{\pi h}{P}\right)^4$$

which can never be less than 1, so using RK2 to integrate a sinusoidal oscillation is also always unstable.

Carrying out a similar analysis for RK4 will show that it actually reaches stability for $h < P/2.3$, so when integrating an oscillating system using RK4 integration a good rule-of-thumb to assure stability would be to choose the timestep h to be smaller than one third of the period of the highest frequency oscillation.

Again, we can graph curves from simulations of a sinusoidal oscillation, and compare the curves to gain an understanding of the relative accuracy of the three integration schemes. Results are shown in Figure 7.2. With the timestep set to $h = P/2$ it is clear that all three integrators produce results that wildly deviate from the correct curve. When $h = P/4$, Euler and RK2 remain unstable, while RK4 is stable but inaccurate—instead of oscillating at a fixed amplitude, the oscillation decays asymptotically to 0. When $h = P/16$, Euler remains wildly unstable, RK2 is unstable but beginning to conform to the correct curve. RK4, however, matches the exact curve with high precision. When $h = P/128$, Euler is somewhat more controlled but still rapidly becoming unbounded. RK2 now looks highly accurate, even though our analysis has demonstrated that it is unconditionally unstable.

Looking at the equations for the determinants found for Euler and RK2 integration reveals why this is so. Iterating the Euler equation for n timesteps yields a

$$x_0 \cos 2\pi \frac{t}{P}$$

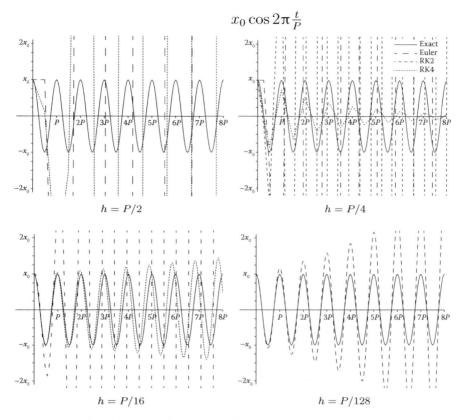

FIGURE 7.2 Sinusoid for four different-sized timesteps.

net *gain* (i.e., a multiplier on the original value) of

$$g = \left(1 + 4\left(\frac{\pi h}{P}\right)^2\right)^n,$$

while iterating RK2 n times yields the net gain

$$g = \left(1 + 4\left(\frac{\pi h}{P}\right)^4\right)^n.$$

Setting $g = 1.01$ in these equations, for a 1% total increase, and solving for the number of iterations required to produce this gain yields

$$n = \left\lceil \log 1.01 / \log \left(1 + 4\left(\frac{\pi h}{P}\right)^2\right) \right\rceil, \quad \text{for Euler, and}$$

$$n = \left\lceil \log 1.01 / \log \left(1 + 4\left(\frac{\pi h}{P}\right)^4\right) \right\rceil, \quad \text{for RK2.}$$

These relations can be used to build the following table of the number of timesteps before the oscillation amplitude increases by 1%:

h	P/8	P/16	P/32	P/64	P/128	P/256
Euler	1	1	1	2	5	17
RK2	1	2	27	429	6,856	109,683

We see that, for $h = P/128$, even after nearly 7,000 timesteps, RK2 remains highly accurate, while Euler almost immediately becomes inaccurate. A caution though, is that RK2 is ultimately unstable, and will eventually produce unbounded oscillations no matter how small the timestep.

7.5.4 Performance of the RK Methods

These stability and accuracy results are summarized in Table 7.1, along with the computational cost in number of evaluations of the system dynamics function, both at the stability limit and at the timestep required for high-fidelity simulation. For simple exponential decay, Euler is the least expensive at the stability limit, but if reasonable fidelity is desired then all three integration schemes have similar computational cost. The situation for sinusoidal oscillation is quite different. Neither Euler nor RK2 have a stability limit, since they are unconditionally unstable, making RK4 the clear preference. For high-fidelity simulation, RK4 is also the clear winner, requiring one quarter the computational cost of RK2, since a timestep eight times longer than for RK2 can be used.

7.5.5 Damping to Avoid Instability

If Euler or any low-order integration method is chosen, there will be the problem of instability if any part of the system acts like a sinusoidal oscillator. The usual method to circumvent this problem is to apply *damping*. What this means is that we apply forces that tend to dissipate the kinetic energy of the system. The kinetic energy of a mass m is given by $K = \frac{1}{2}m\mathbf{v}^2$, i.e., it is proportional to the square

TABLE 7.1 Comparison of Integration Methods

$e^{\frac{-t}{T}}$	h for stability	Evaluations per T	h for fidelity	Evaluations per T
Euler	$2T$	0.5	$T/4$	4
RK2	$2T$	1	$T/2$	4
RK4	$2.78T$	1.44	T	4

$\cos 2\pi \frac{t}{P}$	h for stability	Evaluations per P	h for fidelity	Evaluations per P
Euler	—	∞	—	∞
RK2	—	∞	$P/128$	256
RK4	$P/2.3$	9.2	$P/16$	64

of the velocity. Therefore, any force that tends to reduce velocity will reduce the kinetic energy. The most obvious physical analogy is air resistance. For example, if the sinusoidal oscillator equations are rewritten

$$f(\mathbf{s}) = \dot{\mathbf{s}} = \begin{bmatrix} \dot{x} \\ \dot{v} \end{bmatrix} = \begin{bmatrix} v \\ -\omega^2 x - dv \end{bmatrix},$$

where d is a damping constant, the resultant Euler and RK2 matrices will have determinants with negative terms, so for a correctly chosen damping constant d the integrators will be stable. The price that is paid is that enough undesired damping may be introduced into the system that performance will appear artificially smooth or sluggish. In a real physical system, damping will always be present—no physical oscillator can oscillate forever without an energy input—but the damping introduced to maintain integrator numerical stability may appear nonphysical. Another warning is that too much damping can also result in numerical instability, since it is equivalent to adding an exponential decay time constant that becomes shorter as damping is increased. The trick is to find the "sweet spot", where enough damping is added to prevent oscillations from becoming unstable, but not so much that the system becomes "slugish" or unstable due to excessively short time constants. Finding this spot is typically done experimentally.

7.6 ADAPTIVE TIMESTEPS

For interesting problems, the functions that we are integrating can vary over time. Although linear functions are smooth everywhere and thus easy to integrate, more interesting nonlinear functions can vary over time. At some times they might be "nicely" behaved, and thus easy to integrate with low-order integrators and large timesteps, while at other times they might be complex, requiring higher-order integration and small timesteps.

When we discuss integration, we usually do so assuming we have some fixed timestep h. However, there is nothing stopping us from taking different timesteps for each iteration of the simulation. Doing so makes our code somewhat more complicated, since we do not always move forward by a fixed amount of time. However, it also allows us the opportunity to adjust our step size so that we are taking bigger timesteps when it does not cause a problem, and smaller ones when we need more accuracy, thus being more efficient overall.

Adaptive timestep approaches attempt to adjust the size of the timestep to meet some specified level of accuracy. Conceptually, the process for setting a step size follows the process:

1. Assume we take the same step size h as in the previous iteration, and first integrate with that step size.

2. Using a smaller step size, integrate again to get a better estimate with less error. Typically you would use $\frac{h}{2}$ and integrate twice.

3. By comparing these two estimates, you have an approximate measure of how much the error was reduced by using the smaller step size. Knowing the order of the method, you can use this to estimate how error will be related to the step size, in general.

4. From this knowledge, you can estimate the step size needed to achieve a desired error bound.

   a. If the estimated step size is less than the smaller step size you used, then you can reintegrate yet again with that smaller step size.

   b. If the estimated step size is between the smaller and the larger step size you computed with, then you already have an accurate answer (from the smaller step size you used in the computation). You can use that estimate, and then use the new step size for the next iteration.

   c. If a larger step size is allowable, you can keep the estimate already computed, and then use the larger step size in the next iteration.

To provide a brief illustration, consider fourth-order Runge-Kutta integration. Because this is a fourth-order method you know the error is of order h^5. Thus, the real value $\mathbf{x}(t_0 + h)$ is approximately our computed value $\tilde{\mathbf{x}}(t + h)$ plus some error ch^5, i.e., $\mathbf{x}(t + h) \approx \tilde{\mathbf{x}}(t + h) + ch^5$, where c is some constant to be determined. Notice that if you integrate with a full timestep h you have an error of ch^5, and if you use two half timesteps $\frac{h}{2}$ you have a total error of $2c(\frac{h}{2})^5 = \frac{1}{64}ch^5$. We can estimate c from these two approximations, and thus we can determine the step size needed.

Here is a concrete example showing how adaptive timestepping works. Assume that you integrate with a full timestep $h = 0.1$ and get a value of 100, and then you integrate twice with a timestep of $h/2 = 0.05$ and get a value of 99. Thus, the reduction in error is

$$100 - 99 = (c(0.1)^5) - (2c(0.05)^5)$$
$$1 = 0.00001c - 0.000000625c$$
$$1 = 0.000009375c,$$

so

$$c = 106667.$$

So, if we wanted an error that should be less than 0.1, we could calculate the required timestep to be $0.1 = 106667h^5$, or $h = 0.0622$. In this case, we already have an estimate computed with $h = 0.05$, which is more accurate, so we do not actually need to recompute anything! However, in the next timestep $h = 0.0622$ would be used.

There are several issues worth noting:

• First, there have been methods developed that avoid the explicit calculation of error based on step size, instead embedding the adaptive step sizes within the integration process itself. We will not outline these methods here (see, e.g., Press et al. [2007] for more discussion), but they are more efficient overall and are used in practice.

- Second, the errors are only estimates of the true error: we are eliminating the higher-order terms, and there can be numerical error. Thus, there is usually an additional "fudge factor" incorporated to make sure the step size is small enough. For instance, we might multiply the computed step size h by a factor of 0.9 to be on the safe side.

- Finally, one must keep in mind that this error computation is local, i.e., just for one step. If you care about *global* error e over a time length T, then if you have $n = T/h$ timesteps, your error per step must be within $e/n = eh/T$. That is, the error you want is itself proportional to the step size! To account for this when computing an adaptive step size, you generally will need to reduce the order of the error by one—e.g., for RK4 you would assume error on the order of h^4 instead of h^5.

7.7 IMPLICIT INTEGRATION

We have seen an analysis of how methods such as RK can run into stability problems. When an oscillator has a small period or a decay has a very short time constant, the methods we have seen can run into serious stability problems. Often, the step size needed to ensure stability, if it even exists, is so small that the simulation takes unacceptably long to run. It would be acceptable to spend more time on any one timestep if it meant we could take significantly larger step sizes and maintain stability. Implicit integration methods provide a way of doing exactly this.

All of the integration methods we are describing attempt to determine a new state $\mathbf{S}^{[n+1]}$. When this is done based on the knowledge of the current state $\mathbf{S}^{[n]}$, we say this is an *explicit* integration approach. When we have a method where some knowledge of the next state is needed to determine that next state, we call that an *implicit* method.

One of the most basic implicit integration methods is *Implicit Euler* or *backward Euler* integration, which we compare to "standard" explicit Euler integration:

$$\mathbf{S}^{[n+1]} = \mathbf{S}^{[n]} + \mathbf{F}(\mathbf{S}^{[n]})h \quad \text{(Explicit Euler)}$$
$$\mathbf{S}^{[n+1]} = \mathbf{S}^{[n]} + \mathbf{F}(\mathbf{S}^{[n+1]})h \quad \text{(Implicit Euler)}$$

We have seen this idea previously in the position integration of Equation 2.4, and in the discussion near the beginning of this chapter. In these cases, acceleration is determined based on evaluating $\mathbf{F}(\mathbf{S}^{[n+1]})$, and thus we must solve

$$\mathbf{S}^{[n+1]} - \mathbf{S}^{[n]} - \mathbf{F}(\mathbf{S}^{[n+1]})h = 0 \quad (7.11)$$

for $\mathbf{S}^{[n+1]}$. More generally, implicit integration can be based on determining some combination of current and future states, such as the trapezoidal method of

Equation 2.5. We can write such equations, generally, as $\mathbf{G}(\mathbf{S}^{[n]}, \mathbf{S}^{[n+1]}) = 0$, where we want to solve for $\mathbf{S}^{[n+1]}$. Equation 7.11 is an example, where $\mathbf{G}(\mathbf{S}^{[n]}, \mathbf{S}^{[n+1]}) = \mathbf{S}^{[n+1]} - \mathbf{S}^{[n]} - \mathbf{F}(\mathbf{S}^{[n+1]})h$.

At first glance, implicit integration might seem nearly impossible: it seems as though we must already know the answer in order to determine the answer! Actually, though, it turns out that the equation $\mathbf{G} = 0$ is relatively straightforward to solve in some specific instances, and some more general approaches can be used when there is not a specific direct solution method.

7.7.1 Direct Solutions of Implicit Formulations

Certain specific problems will have a structure that allows for a direct solution to the implicit formulation. As an example, consider an implicit Euler formulation, where the derivative $\mathbf{F}$ is a linear function of the state variables. In this case, for an $n \times 1$ state vector $\mathbf{S}$, we can write $\mathbf{F}(\mathbf{S}) = \mathbf{M}\mathbf{S}$, where M is an $n \times n$ matrix. Then, we can rewrite Equation 7.11 as

$$\mathbf{S}^{[n+1]} - \mathbf{S}^{[n]} - \mathbf{F}(\mathbf{S}^{[n+1]})h = 0$$
$$\mathbf{S}^{[n+1]} - h\mathbf{F}(\mathbf{S}^{[n+1]}) = \mathbf{S}^{[n]}$$
$$\mathbf{S}^{[n+1]} - h\mathbf{M}\mathbf{S}^{[n+1]} = \mathbf{S}^{[n]}$$
$$(I - h\mathbf{M})\mathbf{S}^{[n+1]} = \mathbf{S}^{[n]}$$

where I is the identity matrix. Notice that the final equation is of the form $\mathbf{A}\mathbf{x} = \mathbf{b}$, which is the linear system formulation commonly seen in linear algebra (see Appendix B.2). The solution to this equation would be $\mathbf{x} = \mathbf{A}^{-1}\mathbf{b}$, but usually such systems are solved numerically. The matrix $\mathbf{A}$ often gets very large and is very sparse (most of the terms in $\mathbf{A}$ are 0). There are a wide variety of linear system solvers (Press et al. [2007]; Inria [2015]), and the solver chosen can play an important role in efficiency and accuracy of the solution. For sparse systems, it is particularly important to choose a solver optimized for sparse solutions. *Conjugate gradient* solvers are one commonly used approach.

Fortunately, some of the useful derivatives we will want to use have this linear property. As we see below in Section 7.7.4, we can solve the exponential decay and the oscillating function directly and easily. The Laplacian derivative ∇^2 also has this linear property, making it possible to write the "Laplacian matrix" and solve for implicit solutions to equations involving the Laplacian. We encounter the Laplacian in places such as the heat equation or viscosity in fluid simulation, as we will see in Section 13.2.

7.7.2 Jacobians and Linearizing Functions

Unfortunately, not all problems have a nice linear formulation that allows us to achieve a direct solution. For example, consider the gravitational force between two

Here is one quick example. The formulation of a damped oscillator, as will be seen in the next chapter, is $\dot{x} = -kx - dv$, so that $f(\mathbf{s}) = \begin{bmatrix} v & -kx - dv \end{bmatrix}^T$. We can write the implicit Euler formulation as

$$\begin{bmatrix} x^{[n+1]} \\ v^{[n+1]} \end{bmatrix} = \begin{bmatrix} x^{[n]} \\ v^{[n]} \end{bmatrix} + \begin{bmatrix} v^{[n+1]} \\ -kx^{[n+1]} - dv^{[n+1]} \end{bmatrix} h$$

$$\begin{bmatrix} x^{[n+1]} \\ v^{[n+1]} \end{bmatrix} = \begin{bmatrix} x^{[n]} \\ v^{[n]} \end{bmatrix} + \begin{bmatrix} 0 & 1 \\ -k & -d \end{bmatrix} \begin{bmatrix} x^{[n+1]} \\ v^{[n+1]} \end{bmatrix} h$$

$$\mathbf{s}^{[n+1]} = \mathbf{s}^{[n]} + \begin{bmatrix} 0 & h \\ -kh & -dh \end{bmatrix} \mathbf{s}^{[n+1]}$$

$$I\mathbf{s}^{[n+1]} - \begin{bmatrix} 0 & h \\ -kh & -dh \end{bmatrix} \mathbf{s}^{[n+1]} = \mathbf{s}^{[n]}$$

$$\begin{bmatrix} 1 & -h \\ kh & 1+dh \end{bmatrix} \mathbf{s}^{[n+1]} = \mathbf{s}^{[n]}$$

If we have values such as $k = 10$, $d = 2$, $h = 0.1$, and starting conditions $\mathbf{s}^{[n]} = \begin{bmatrix} 2 \\ -1 \end{bmatrix}$, then we have

$$\begin{bmatrix} 1 & -0.1 \\ 1 & 1.2 \end{bmatrix} \begin{bmatrix} x^{[n+1]} \\ v^{[n+1]} \end{bmatrix} = \begin{bmatrix} 2 \\ -1 \end{bmatrix},$$

which we can solve to get

$$\begin{bmatrix} x^{[n+1]} \\ v^{[n+1]} \end{bmatrix} = \begin{bmatrix} 1.77 \\ -2.31 \end{bmatrix}.$$

objects, where the force $\mathbf{F}$ is proportional to the inverse square of the distance between the objects. There is no way to write $\mathbf{F}(\mathbf{S}) = \mathbf{MS}$, and thus we cannot use a linear system solver to solve for the implicit formulation directly. However, at any point in state space there is a way that we can get a linear approximation to a nonlinear system, the *Jacobian*.

Assume we have the implicit Euler formulation $\mathbf{S}^{[n+1]} = \mathbf{S}^{[n]} + \mathbf{F}(\mathbf{S}^{[n+1]})h$, but we cannot express $\mathbf{F}(\mathbf{S})$ as a linear system. The Jacobian gives us a linear approximation of the derivative of $\mathbf{F}$ at one particular state. For the state $\mathbf{S}^{[n]}$, we can approximate the next state $\mathbf{F}(\mathbf{S}^{[n+1]})$ as follows:

$$\mathbf{F}(\mathbf{S}^{[n+1]}) = \mathbf{F}(\mathbf{S}^{[n]} + \Delta \mathbf{S}),$$

$$\approx \mathbf{F}(\mathbf{S}^{[n]}) + \frac{d\mathbf{F}}{d\mathbf{S}} \Delta \mathbf{S},$$

$$= \mathbf{F}(\mathbf{S}^{[n]}) + \mathbf{J} \Delta \mathbf{S}.$$

where $\mathbf{J}$ is the Jacobian matrix. The Jacobian is the first-order, linear, approximation to the change in $\mathbf{F}$ at the particular state $\mathbf{S}$, similar to the way the tangent gives the linear approximation to a curve at a particular point.

The Jacobian, then, is a matrix that approximates how the function $\mathbf{F}$ varies as the elements of $\mathbf{S}$ vary.

Let us first describe how this Jacobian matrix is structured in general, and then we will look at how it is used for this problem. Assume that $\mathbf{S}$ consists of m different variables s_j (for $0 \le j \le m-1$). The function $\mathbf{F}$ produces l different values from these m values of s_j. That is, we have $f_i(\mathbf{S})$ defined (for $0 \le i \le l-1$).

$\mathbf{J}$ will then be an $l \times m$ matrix. $\mathbf{J}$ is formed by taking partial derivatives of the function $\mathbf{F}$, so each row of $\mathbf{J}$ gives the linear approximation to the change in one of the f_i. The entries $J_{i,j}$ of the Jacobian matrix are defined as

$$J_{i,j} = \frac{\partial f_i}{\partial s_j}. \tag{7.12}$$

and this yields the Jacobian matrix:

$$\mathbf{J} = \begin{bmatrix} \frac{\partial f_0}{\partial s_0} & \frac{\partial f_0}{\partial s_1} & \cdots & \frac{\partial f_0}{\partial s_{m-1}} \\ \frac{\partial f_1}{\partial s_0} & \frac{\partial f_1}{\partial s_1} & \cdots & \frac{\partial f_1}{\partial s_{m-1}} \\ \vdots & \vdots & \ddots & \vdots \\ \frac{\partial f_{l-1}}{\partial s_0} & \frac{\partial f_{l-1}}{\partial s_1} & \cdots & \frac{\partial f_{l-1}}{\partial s_{m-1}} \end{bmatrix}. \tag{7.13}$$

We will see other uses for the Jacobian in the future, but for our implicit integration case f_i always gives the rate of change of an element of the state vector $\mathbf{S}$. Each row of $\mathbf{J}$, when multiplied by the vector $\mathbf{S}$, will give the (linear) change in one of the elements of $\mathbf{S}$, at that point in time. Thus, $l = m$, and the Jacobian matrix is square. It is important to emphasize that the Jacobian $\mathbf{J}$ is a function of the state $\mathbf{S}$, and must be recomputed at every timestep.

The advantage of using the Jacobian is that we can then formulate an implicit problem and solve it as was described in Section 7.7.1. That is, if we know $\mathbf{J}$, we can solve the implicit Euler formulation for $\Delta \mathbf{S}$ as follows:

$$\mathbf{S}^{[n+1]} = \mathbf{S}^{[n]} + h\mathbf{F}(\mathbf{S}^{[n+1]}),$$
$$\mathbf{S}^{[n]} + \Delta \mathbf{S} = \mathbf{S}^{[n]} + h(\mathbf{F}(\mathbf{S}^{[n]}) + \mathbf{J}\Delta \mathbf{S}),$$
$$\Delta \mathbf{S} = h\mathbf{F}(\mathbf{S}^{[n]}) + h\mathbf{J}\Delta \mathbf{S},$$
$$(I - h\mathbf{J})\Delta \mathbf{S} = h\mathbf{F}(\mathbf{S}^{[n]}).$$

Notice that $(I - h\mathbf{J})$ is a known square matrix, $\Delta \mathbf{S}$ is an unknown vector, and $h\mathbf{F}(\mathbf{S}^{[n]})$ is a known vector. So, this is a linear system of the form $\mathbf{Ax} = \mathbf{b}$ which can be solved with a good linear system solver. Once we know $\Delta \mathbf{S}$, we just add it to $\mathbf{S}^{[n]}$ to get $\mathbf{S}^{[n+1]}$.

Here we provide a relatively simple example of how to use the Jacobian in implicit integration. Assume we have the one-dimensional problem posed in the figure to the right. There are three points p_0, p_1, and p_2 connected to each other by springs. The position of point i is x_i and its velocity is v_i. The first point has a fixed position $x_0 = 0$, and therefore its velocity is $v_0 = 0$. The other points are

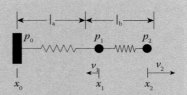

free to move. The springs exert force on the two points they connect, with one component of force proportional to how far apart the points are (i.e., how much the springs are compressed or stretched), and the other proportional to the cube of their relative velocities. Newton's third law applies, so the net force exerted by the spring on its left end will be equal and opposite to the force it exerts on the right end.

Therefore, if all springs are identical, the force acting on point p_i due to its spring connection to point p_{i+1} will be

$$f_{i,i+1} = k((x_{i+1} - x_i) - l) + d(v_{i+1} - v_i)^3,$$

and there will be similar forces acting between all other connected pairs. In this equation, k, l, and d are the spring constant, rest length, and damping coefficient, respectively, for the springs.

Based on this, we have the following state:

$$\mathbf{S} = \begin{bmatrix} x_1 \\ x_2 \\ v_1 \\ v_2 \end{bmatrix}.$$

If all particles have mass 1, the derivative function is

$$\mathbf{F} = \begin{bmatrix} v_1 \\ v_2 \\ -f_{0,1} + f_{1,2} \\ -f_{1,2} \end{bmatrix}$$

$$= \begin{bmatrix} v_1 \\ v_2 \\ -k[(x_1 - x_0) - l] - d(v_1 - v_0)^3 + k[(x_2 - x_1) - l_b] + d(v_2 - v_1)^3 \\ -k[(x_2 - x_1) - l_b] - d(v_2 - v_1)^3 \end{bmatrix}.$$

The resulting Jacobian matrix, is

$$\mathbf{J} = \begin{bmatrix} 0 & 0 & 1 & 0 \\ 0 & 0 & 0 & 1 \\ -2k & k & -3d[(v_1 - v_0)^2 + (v_2 - v_1)^2] & 3d(v_2 - v_1)^2 \\ k & -k & 3d(v_2 - v_1)^2 & -3d(v_2 - v_1)^2 \end{bmatrix}.$$

Let us look at a specific case. Let the spring constant be $k = 2$, the rest length $l = 10$, and the damping coefficient $d = 1$. Then, (remembering that $x_0 = v_0 = 0$) we have

$$\mathbf{F} = \begin{bmatrix} v_1 \\ v_2 \\ -2(x_1 - 10) - v_1^3 + 2((x_2 - x_1) - 10) + (v_2 - v_1)^3 \\ -2((x_2 - x_1) - 10) - (v_2 - v_1)^3 \end{bmatrix}$$

$$
\mathbf{J} = \begin{bmatrix} 0 & 0 & 1 & 0 \\ 0 & 0 & 0 & 1 \\ -4 & 2 & -3(v_1^2 + (v_2 - v_1)^2) & 3(v_2 - v_1)^2 \\ 2 & -2 & 3(v_2 - v_1)^2 & -3(v_2 - v_1)^2 \end{bmatrix}.
$$

So, if the first point is currently at $x_1 = 12$ with velocity $v_1 = -1$, and the second point is at $x_2 = 19$ with velocity $v_2 = 2$, we would have the following values:

$$
\mathbf{S}^{[n]} = \begin{bmatrix} 12 \\ 19 \\ -1 \\ 2 \end{bmatrix}, \quad \mathbf{F}(\mathbf{S}^{[n]}) = \begin{bmatrix} -1 \\ 2 \\ 0 \\ -3 \end{bmatrix}, \quad \mathbf{J} = \begin{bmatrix} 0 & 0 & 1 & 0 \\ 0 & 0 & 0 & 1 \\ -4 & 2 & -30 & 27 \\ 2 & -2 & 27 & -27 \end{bmatrix}.
$$

So, an implicit integration step would mean solving $(I - h\mathbf{J})\Delta\mathbf{S} = h\mathbf{F}(\mathbf{S}^{[n]})$ to find $\Delta\mathbf{S}$:

$$
\begin{bmatrix} 1 & 0 & -h & 0 \\ 0 & 1 & 0 & -h \\ 4h & -2h & 1+30h & -27h \\ -2h & 2h & -27h & 1+27h \end{bmatrix} \Delta\mathbf{S} = \begin{bmatrix} -h \\ 2h \\ 0 \\ -3h \end{bmatrix}.
$$

If we choose a step size $h = 0.1$,

$$
\begin{bmatrix} 1 & 0 & -0.1 & 0 \\ 0 & 1 & 0 & -0.1 \\ 0.4 & -0.2 & 4.0 & -2.7 \\ -0.2 & 0.2 & -2.7 & 3.7 \end{bmatrix} \Delta\mathbf{S} = \begin{bmatrix} -0.1 \\ 0.2 \\ 0 \\ -0.3 \end{bmatrix},
$$

and solving this, we get

$$
\Delta\mathbf{S} = \begin{bmatrix} -0.109 \\ 0.184 \\ -0.089 \\ -0.162 \end{bmatrix},
$$

so that the new state is

$$
\mathbf{S}^{[n+1]} = \mathbf{S}^{[n]} + \Delta\mathbf{S} = \begin{bmatrix} 12 \\ 19 \\ -1 \\ 2 \end{bmatrix} + \begin{bmatrix} -0.109 \\ 0.184 \\ -0.089 \\ -0.162 \end{bmatrix} = \begin{bmatrix} 11.891 \\ 19.184 \\ -1.089 \\ 1.838 \end{bmatrix}.
$$

At each timestep, we would repeat this process, computing a new derivative vector $\mathbf{F}$ and a new Jacobian matrix $\mathbf{J}$ from the new state vector $\mathbf{S}$.

Note that solving the Jacobian can be simplified in cases where the state consists of positions and velocities. As you can see from the examples, integrating position is relatively simple, given that it is based solely on the velocity; the integration of acceleration to obtain velocity is much more challenging. As such, we can eliminate the position portion of the state. This will require substituting $x^{[n+1]} = x^{[n]} + v^{[n+1]}h$ in the force term. By eliminating position, we have a state vector half the size, and thus a Jacobian one quarter the size, while the solution is identical.

Consider the example we just used. We now want to have a state

$$\mathbf{S} = \begin{bmatrix} v_1 \\ v_2 \end{bmatrix}.$$

And, following the prior derivation we have a derivative function for which we make the substitution $x_1 = 12 + v_1 h$ and $x_2 = 19 + v_2 h$:

$$\mathbf{F} = \begin{bmatrix} -2(x_1 - 10) - v_1^3 + 2((x_2 - x_1) - 10) + (v_2 - v_1)^3 \\ -2((x_2 - x_1) - 10) - (v_2 - v_1)^3 \end{bmatrix}$$

$$\mathbf{F} = \begin{bmatrix} -2((12 + v_1 h) - 10) - v_1^3 + 2(((19 + v_2 h) - (12 + v_1 h)) - 10) + (v_2 - v_1)^3 \\ -2(((19 + v_2 h) - (12 + v_1 h)) - 10) - (v_2 - v_1)^3 \end{bmatrix}$$

$$= \begin{bmatrix} -2(2 + v_1 h) - v_1^3 + 2(-3 + v_2 h - v_1 h) + (v_2 - v_1)^3 \\ -2(-3 + v_2 h - v_1 h) - (v_2 - v_1)^3 \end{bmatrix}.$$

The resulting Jacobian is

$$\mathbf{J} = \begin{bmatrix} -4h - 3(v_1^2 + (v_2 - v_1)^2) & 2h + 3(v_2 - v_1)^2 \\ 2h + 3(v_2 - v_1)^2 & -2h - 3(v_2 - v_1)^2 \end{bmatrix}.$$

Using the values $v_1 = -1$, $v_2 = 2$, and $h = 0.1$, we have

$$\mathbf{S}^{[n]} = \begin{bmatrix} -1 \\ 2 \end{bmatrix}, \quad \mathbf{F}(\mathbf{S}^{[n]}) = \begin{bmatrix} 0.8 \\ -3.6 \end{bmatrix}, \quad \mathbf{J} = \begin{bmatrix} -30.4 & 27.2 \\ 27.2 & -27.2 \end{bmatrix}.$$

So, an implicit integration step would mean solving $(\mathbf{I} - h\mathbf{J})\Delta\mathbf{S} = h\mathbf{F}(\mathbf{S}^{[n]})$ to find $\Delta\mathbf{S}$:

$$\begin{bmatrix} 4.04 & -2.72 \\ -2.72 & 3.72 \end{bmatrix} \Delta\mathbf{S} = \begin{bmatrix} 0.08 \\ -0.36 \end{bmatrix}.$$

Solving this we get

$$\Delta\mathbf{S} = \begin{bmatrix} -0.089 \\ -0.162 \end{bmatrix},$$

which is the same as we found in the earlier example. We can use this to calculate the velocity and position, e.g., $v_1^{[n+1]} = -1 + (-0.089) = -1.09$ and thus $x_1^{[n+1]} = x_1^{[n]} + v_1^{[n+1]} h = 12 + (-1.09)(0.1) = 11.891$, which again is exactly what we computed before.

7.7.3 Root-Finding Solutions of Implicit Formulations

The methods outlined above describe how we can perform implicit integration by using a linear system formulation. However, most systems will not allow a direct linear solution (as in Section 7.7.1), and formulating as a Jacobian (as in Section 7.7.2) can be difficult. When the other methods are not appropriate, a third approach is to use a root-finding method to find solutions to the implicit formulation.

Consider again Equation 7.11. For a particular problem, once $\mathbf{F}$ is expanded, you will have a (possibly quite complex) equation where the only unknown is the new state $\mathbf{S}^{[n+1]}$. The roots of this equation will be the possible values for $\mathbf{S}^{[n+1]}$, so solving the implicit formulation is equivalent to finding roots of a system of equations.

There are a wide variety of root-finding techniques, ranging from *Newton's method* to much more sophisticated approaches. Several of these are described in Press et al. [2007]. These approaches will usually be iterative, first finding an approximate solution (or set of solutions) and gradually refining the solution(s) to get more and more accuracy. The process itself can be time consuming, but in cases where explicit formulations are very unstable, there is still a net improvement.

Here is one example. Assume we are solving for a single variable x and our derivative function is $f(x) = x^2 - 10^{-x}$. This does not have a direct linear solution, and the Jacobian is difficult to define. In this specific case, our general model

$$\mathbf{S}^{[n+1]} = \mathbf{S}^{[n]} + \mathbf{F}(\mathbf{S}^{[n+1]})h$$

becomes

$$x^{[n+1]} = x^{[n]} + f(x^{[n+1]})h, \text{ or}$$
$$x^{[n+1]} = x^{[n]} + (x^{[n+1]})^2 h - 10^{-x^{[n+1]}}h.$$

So, we have

$$-(x^{[n+1]})^2 h + x^{[n+1]} + 10^{-x^{[n+1]}}h - x^{[n]} = 0.$$

Now, if we let $x^{[n]} = 1$ and $h = 0.1$, this equation becomes

$$-0.1(x^{[n+1]})^2 + x^{[n+1]} + 0.1(10)^{-x^{[n+1]}} - 1 = 0,$$

which can be solved numerically. A numerical solution would typically involve starting with a nearby solution (in this case the previous solution, $x^{[n]} = 1.0$) and using Newton's method or a similar approach to hone in on the root. Applying this method, we get a solution $x^{[n+1]} \approx 1.117$.

7.7.4 Accuracy and Stability of Implicit Formulations

To understand how implicit methods provide additional stability, let us analyze the stability of an implicit Euler integration on the same examples as we used in Section 7.5.

Assume our derivative function is the exponential decay function: $f(x) = -\frac{1}{T}x$. Thus, the implicit Euler formulation is

$$x^{[n+1]} = x^{[n]} - \frac{1}{T}x^{[n+1]}h, \text{ or}$$
$$\left(1 + \frac{1}{T}h\right)x^{[n+1]} = x^{[n]}.$$

So, the ratio of successive steps is

$$\frac{x^{[n+1]}}{x^{[n]}} = \frac{1}{1 + \frac{1}{T}h}.$$

Since $1 + \frac{1}{T}h$ must be greater than 1, the ratio of successive steps is always less than 1. Thus, the simulation will always converge to 0, and no matter what timestep size h we choose the implicit Euler formulation will be stable. This is in contrast to the explicit Euler formulation, where obtaining stability requires $h \leq 2T$.

Next, assume we are dealing with a sinusoidal oscillator $\ddot{x} = -\omega^2 x$, with $\mathbf{s} = \begin{bmatrix} x \\ v \end{bmatrix}$.

Therefore, $f(\mathbf{s}) = \begin{bmatrix} v & -\omega^2 x \end{bmatrix}^T$. We can write the implicit Euler formulation as

$$\begin{bmatrix} x^{[n+1]} \\ v^{[n+1]} \end{bmatrix} = \begin{bmatrix} x^{[n]} \\ v^{[n]} \end{bmatrix} + \begin{bmatrix} v^{[n+1]} \\ -\omega^2 x^{[n+1]} \end{bmatrix} h, \text{ or}$$

$$\begin{bmatrix} x^{[n+1]} \\ v^{[n+1]} \end{bmatrix} = \begin{bmatrix} x^{[n]} \\ v^{[n]} \end{bmatrix} + \begin{bmatrix} 0 & 1 \\ -\omega^2 & 0 \end{bmatrix} \begin{bmatrix} x^{[n+1]} \\ v^{[n+1]} \end{bmatrix} h,$$

so,

$$\mathbf{s}^{[n+1]} = \mathbf{s}^{[n]} + \begin{bmatrix} 0 & h \\ -\omega^2 h & 0 \end{bmatrix} \mathbf{s}^{[n+1]}.$$

This can be rearranged to the form

$$I\mathbf{s}^{[n+1]} - \begin{bmatrix} 0 & h \\ -\omega^2 h & 0 \end{bmatrix} \mathbf{s}^{[n+1]} = \mathbf{s}^{[n]},$$

to yield the linear system

$$\begin{bmatrix} 1 & -h \\ \omega^2 h & 1 \end{bmatrix} \mathbf{s}^{[n+1]} = \mathbf{s}^{[n]}, \text{ or}$$

$$M\mathbf{s}^{[n+1]} = \mathbf{s}^{[n]}.$$

Thus, we have $\mathbf{s}^{[n+1]} = M^{-1}\mathbf{s}^{[n]}$. The determinant of M is $1 + \omega^2 h^2$, and thus the determinant of M^{-1} is $\frac{1}{1+\omega^2 h^2}$. Since $\omega^2 h^2 > 0$, the determinant will be less than 1 regardless of step size h, and so the ratio of successive steps will always be less than 1, and the implicit Euler integration is stable for all values of h. Again, this is in contrast to the explicit Euler formulation, which is never stable!

So, as we can see, the implicit integration approaches give significantly greater stability guarantees; implicit Euler integration is *unconditionally stable*, i.e., stable for any step size h, for oscillation and exponential decay. We can confidently take any step size we wish, and know that the solution will not "blow up." However, this does come at a cost: in addition to the more complicated solution process, we encounter numerical dissipation.

Whereas explicit methods have the tendency to cause magnitudes to grow without bounds if the step size is too large, implicit methods will tend to decrease magnitudes with large step sizes. Over time, implicit methods can tend to push solutions toward 0, rather than toward the true answer. This effect is called *numerical dissipation*. To understand this dissipation, we will consider fidelity of an oscillator, similar to our analysis for explicit methods in Section 7.5.

As we just saw, for an oscillator, the matrix M^{-1} had a determinant of $\frac{1}{1+\omega^2 h^2} = \frac{1}{1+(\frac{\pi h}{P})^2} = \frac{P^2}{P^2+\pi^2 h^2}$. Thus, integrating n timesteps yields a net *loss* of

$$g = \left(\frac{P^2}{P^2 + \pi^2 h^2} \right)^n.$$

Therefore, the number of iterations before a 1% loss is

$$n = \left\lceil \log 0.99 / \log \left(\frac{P^2}{P^2 + \pi^2 h^2} \right) \right\rceil.$$

These relations can be used to build the following table of the number of timesteps needed for the oscillation amplitude to decrease by 1%. For reference, we will include the number of steps needed for an explicit method to increase by 1%:

h	P/8	P/16	P/32	P/64	P/128	P/256
Explicit Euler	1	1	1	2	5	17
Explicit RK2	1	2	27	429	6,856	109,683
Implicit Euler	1	1	2	5	17	67

Notice that the implicit Euler approach has a fidelity similar to that of the explicit Euler formulation, but significantly below RK2. That is, while implicit methods provide a more stable formulation, they do not provide a more accurate one.

7.8 SUMMARY

Here are the key ideas to take away related to integration:

- Order of integration methods refers to how closely the integration method can represent the function being integrated. This can be thought of as how many terms (i.e., how many derivatives) of a Taylor expansion are matched.

- The Verlet and Leapfrog methods provide second-order integration techniques, but assume that acceleration is a function of position only (i.e., not of velocity).

- Runge-Kutta methods can achieve much higher-order integration. They can also handle derivatives based on all aspects of the state.

- Choosing an integration scheme involves trade-offs in time, accuracy, and complexity of calculations. For most problems discussed in this book, RK4 is a good choice.

- Collision detection is more complex with higher-order integration. Finding a precise point of collision can involve a binary search in time to find the position within a fixed distance from the surface.

- Different integration methods can be analyzed for their stability and accuracy on different classes of problems. Some will be stable only with sufficiently small step sizes, and some will never be stable.

- To achieve a desired level of accuracy, step sizes can be adjusted by estimating the error from the current step size, and either increasing or decreasing the step size for the next step.

- Implicit integration offers a way of guaranteeing stability in the integration, though the solution process is more complex than for explicit integration, involving solution of a linear system at each step.

CHAPTER 8

Deformable Springy Meshes

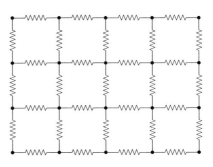

N THIS CHAPTER, we examine the idea of meshes of particles connected together with spring-like connections, allowing the whole mesh structure to be flexible, deformable, and springy. In this way, we will be able to model a variety of objects, like rubber sheets, cloth, jello cubes, teddy bears, and virtually any other deformable object describable by a polygonal geometric model. The diagram to the right shows one way that particles might be interconnected with springs, and Figure 8.1 is a nice example of how this approach can be used to create interesting shapes and behaviors. The ideas in this chapter received their original impetus from the influential early paper *The behavioral testbed: obtaining complex behavior from simple rules*, by Haumann and Parent [1988]. As a graduate student at Ohio State, Chris Wedge, who went on to found *Blue Sky Animation*, made the innovative animated short *Balloon Guy* [Wedge, 1987] using Haumann and Parent's software. Instead of groups of particles that interact based on proximity, their idea was to use springy meshes of particles, whose connections remain fixed. Since the connections match the connectivity of the mesh, there is no problem with establishing the set of particles interacting with each other. As long as the number of connections for any one particle is independent of the total number of particles, the basic springy mesh problem has complexity $O(N)$ in the number of particles.

The issues that we will deal with in this chapter include the representation of the springy connections, how these can be combined to make a springy mesh, and how the structural stability of the resulting mesh can be assured. Then, we will look at how collision detection has to be modified to handle objects that are changing in shape. We will see that highly complex geometry can result in too many tiny connections, making their deformations expensive to compute. In this case, we can build simplified flexible deformers that allow us to compute approximate but believable deformations of these complex objects. Finally, we look at the special case of cloth simulation.

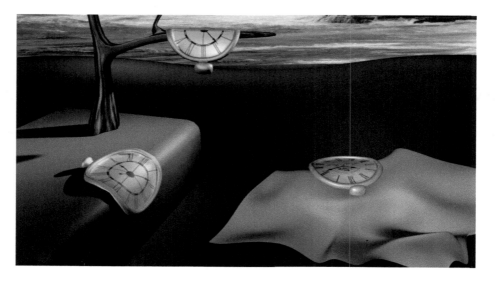

FIGURE 8.1 A frame from a Salvador Dali mimic animation, made using springy meshes. (Courtesy of Yujie Shu.)

8.1 DAMPED SPRINGY CONNECTORS

Before moving to springy meshes, we first need a good model for the connections of the mesh. These should produce forces that tend to keep the model in its undeformed rest state, while also providing a mechanism for controlling the persistence of oscillatory springy behavior. For example, we might want a jello cube to jiggle and bounce for a second or two, but a rubber ball should deform and bounce back into shape without any discernible oscillation. To give us this desired level of control we will use connectors modeled on a storm door closer.

A storm door closer consists of a metal tube, containing a spring and a piston, that connects by a movable rod at one end to the door frame, and at the other end by a fixed rod to the door. The job of the door closer is to pull the door shut after the person opening the door lets go of the door handle. The force pulling the door shut is produced by the spring in the door closer. If that were all

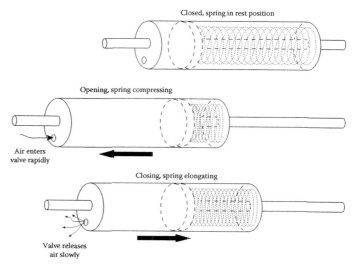

there were in the door closer, the door would be pulled back rapidly and slam shut. The figure shows how the closer is built to prevent this. The closer's piston compresses the spring when the rod connected to the door frame is pulled out to open the door. Also, as the piston slides inside the tube, it pulls air into the tube as the rod is extended and pushes air back out of the tube as the rod is retracted. A valve at the end of the tube lets air in rapidly as the rod is pulled out, but only lets air out slowly as the rod moves in. The spring force not only pulls on the door to close it, but must push against the air as it escapes the tube. The force of the spring is proportional to how much the spring is compressed, the force caused by the air is proportional to how fast the piston is moving in the tube.

8.1.1 Mathematics of a Damped Spring

The diagram on the right is a simplified one-dimensional model of the elements that produce forces within the door closer. A spring connects a mass m to an immovable wall. In parallel with the spring, a damper also connects the mass to the wall. The spring has a strength constant k, and the damper a damping constant d, which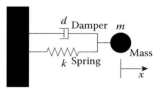
govern the strength of the forces they can exert. Let x be the position of the mass, where $x = 0$ when the spring is in its relaxed position and thus exerting no force on the mass. We assume linear spring and damping models. The spring exerts a force back on the mass proportional to how far the spring is compressed or extended from its rest position. The damping force does not depend on position, rather the damper exerts a force opposing the velocity of the mass. Mathematically, the force exerted by the spring is

$$f_k = -kx,$$

and the force exerted by the damper is

$$f_d = -dv.$$

If the mass is also being pushed or pulled with an external force f_e, by Newton's second law,

$$m\ddot{x} = f_e + f_k + f_d, \quad \text{or}$$
$$m\ddot{x} = f_e - kx - d\dot{x}.$$

This is a well-studied second-order linear differential equation, often written in the form

$$m\ddot{x} + d\dot{x} + kx = f_e.$$

The special case, where the externally applied force $f_e = 0$, is known as the homogeneous form of the equation

$$m\ddot{x} + d\dot{x} + kx = 0.$$

If an initial displacement $x = x_0$ and initial velocity $\dot{x} = v_0$ are applied to the system, the homogeneous form of the equation describes how the system will behave over time, if undisturbed by outside forces. In order to understand how a strut behaves, let us examine what solutions to the equation look like if we set each of the parameters to 0, in turn, before looking at the solution to the full equation.

8.1.1.1 Massless Spring-Damper

If we set the mass $m = 0$, and then arrange the equation to solve for the highest derivative we have

$$\dot{x} = -\frac{k}{d}x.$$

Note that this equation is of the same form as the equation for exponential decay that we saw in Section 7.5, with time constant $T = \frac{d}{k}$. Thus, the solution is

$$x(t) = x_0 e^{-\frac{k}{d}t},$$

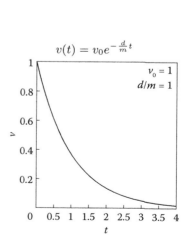

yielding an exponential decay from the initial position x_0. What we can learn from this exercise is that a strut, attached to a very small mass, will smoothly move the mass to the rest position of the strut, with a time constant of

$$T = \frac{d}{k}.$$

So, to slow down the motion either the damping constant d should be raised, or the spring constant k should be decreased. The key point to remember is that the time constant is a ratio, dependent on both the spring stiffness and the damping strength of the strut.

8.1.1.2 Springless Mass-Damper

If we set the spring stiffness $k = 0$, and then arrange the equation to solve for the highest derivative, we have

$$\ddot{x} = -\frac{d}{m}\dot{x},$$

which can be rewritten in terms of velocity as

$$\dot{v} = -\frac{d}{m}v.$$

This equation is also in the form of an exponential decay with time constant

$$T = \frac{m}{d},$$

but this time the decay is in velocity, not position. Thus, the solution is the exponential decay

$$v(t) = v_0 e^{-\frac{d}{m}t}.$$

This can be integrated once to yield the position

$$x(t) = x_0 + v_0 \frac{m}{d}(1 - e^{-\frac{d}{m}t}).$$

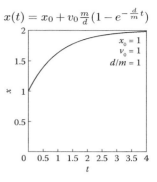

$$x(t) = x_0 + v_0 \frac{m}{d}(1 - e^{-\frac{d}{m}t})$$

Therefore, a strut with a very weak spring will smoothly slow down any initial motion of the mass until it comes to a stop. This will happen with a time constant of $T = \frac{m}{d}$. So, to more quickly bring the mass to a rest, either the mass m must be decreased or the damping constant d must be increased. Again, the time constant is a ratio, in this case dependent on both the mass and the damping strength of the strut.

8.1.1.3 Damperless Spring-Mass

If we set the damping constant $d = 0$, and then arrange the equation to solve for the highest derivative, we have

$$\ddot{x} = -\frac{k}{m}x.$$

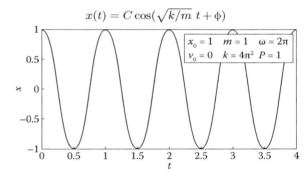

$$x(t) = C \cos(\sqrt{k/m}\, t + \phi)$$

Note that this equation is of the same form as the equation for sinusoidal oscillation that we also saw in Section 7.5, with solution

$$x(t) = C \cos(\sqrt{k/m}\, t + \phi).$$

The amplitude C and phase angle ϕ are determined by the initial position x_0 and velocity v_0 by the relationships

$$\phi = -\tan^{-1}\left(\sqrt{\frac{m}{k}}\frac{v_0}{x_0}\right), \quad \text{and}$$

$$C = \sqrt{x_0^2 + \frac{m}{k}v_0^2}.$$

Therefore, a strut with very little damping will oscillate in a sinusoidal fashion, with frequency

$$\omega = \sqrt{k/m}, \quad \text{or period } \; P = 2\pi\sqrt{m/k}.$$

To increase the period of the oscillation either the mass m can be increased or the spring constant k can be decreased. Again, we have a ratio, in this case dependent on both mass and spring stiffness.

8.1.1.4 Spring-Mass-Damper

From these three exercises, we can guess that the behavior of a strut must be some form of sinusoidal oscillation, but decaying over time in an exponential fashion. Further, the period of oscillation should be dependent on the ratio of mass to spring stiffness, and the exponential decay should be dependent on the ratios of damping to spring constant, and mass to damping.

In order to explore the solution to the full equation, the following substitutions have proven to be highly useful. First, divide the homogeneous equation by mass to yield

$$\ddot{x} + d/m\,\dot{x} + k/m = 0.$$

Note that the final term on the left-hand side is the square of the frequency obtained when there is no damping, so let us define the undamped natural frequency and the corresponding period to be

$$\omega_n = \sqrt{k/m}, \quad \text{and} \quad P_n = 2\pi\sqrt{m/k}.$$

A second substitution is to define a damping factor

$$\zeta = \frac{d}{2\sqrt{km}}.$$

Applying these substitutions to the differential equation gives us

$$\ddot{x} + 2\zeta\omega_n\dot{x} + \omega_n^2 = 0,$$

which has the solution

$$x(t) = Ce^{-\zeta\omega_n t}\cos(\omega_n\sqrt{1-\zeta^2}\,t + \phi), \quad \text{or}$$
$$x(t) = Ce^{-2\pi\zeta t/P_n}\cos(2\pi\sqrt{1-\zeta^2}\,t/P_n + \phi),$$

for ζ in the range $[0, 1]$. Most real materials have damping factors much less than 1, so this solution is generally applicable to most damped spring problems. For example, metals usually have damping factors less than 0.01, rubber around 0.05, and auto shock absorbers around 0.3.

The result is the product of an exponential decay with time constant

$$x(t) = e^{-\zeta\omega_n t}\cos(\omega_n\sqrt{1-\zeta^2}\,t + \phi)$$

$x_0 = 1$	$m = 1$	$\omega_n = 2\pi$
$v_0 = 0$	$k = 4\pi^2$	$P_n = 1$
$d = 0.8\pi$	$\zeta = 0.2$	

$$T = \frac{1}{\zeta\omega_n} = \frac{2m}{d},$$

and a sinusoidal oscillation with frequency

$$\omega = \omega_n\sqrt{1-\zeta^2},$$

or

$$\omega = \sqrt{k/m - (d/2m)^2}.$$

When the damping factor ζ is high, the time constant is small, meaning that the oscillation will die out quickly. If the damping factor is small, the oscillation will tend to persist. The frequency is also dependent on the damping factor. If the damping factor is small, the term $\sqrt{1-\zeta^2}$ will be nearly 1, so the frequency of oscillation will be very close to the undamped natural frequency $\omega_n = \sqrt{k/m}$. If the damping factor is larger, the frequency will be decreased significantly below the natural frequency.

It is important to note that if the damping factor ζ is greater than 1, this solution is no longer valid, because the term within the square root, $1-\zeta^2$, is negative. The solution in this case is in the form of a damped exponential. This reflects the fact that when the damping factor becomes large, motion is damped out before any oscillation takes place. When $\zeta = 0$ the system is called *undamped*, when $0 < \zeta < 1$ it is called *underdamped*, when $\zeta = 1$ it is called *critically damped*, and when $\zeta > 1$ it is called *overdamped*.

8.2   SPRINGY MESHES

We can construct a springy mesh by replacing the edges of a polygonal model by a spring-mass-damper system that produces forces tending to keep the edges at their original lengths, while allowing them to compress and elongate in response to outside forces. This is the basic idea of a springy-mesh model, but we will see that additional supports will be needed to maintain the stability of the model's shape. We begin by modeling the edges and then progress to addressing the structural stability problem.

8.2.1 Strut—A 3D Structural Element for a Springy Mesh

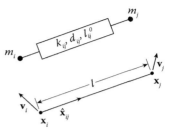

In order to make the spring-mass-damper system useful for constructing a springy mesh, we first need to move from the 1D model that we used to analyze the behavior of a door closer to a full 3D model. The above figure shows the abstraction that we will use, which we call a *strut*. It can be thought of abstractly as a tube containing a spring and a damper, as shown at the top of the figure. This is connected on each end to point masses m_i and m_j, and has three associated constants: k_{ij} specifying its spring stiffness, d_{ij} specifying its damping strength, and l_{ij}^0 specifying the rest length of the strut. At the bottom of the figure is a diagram showing the key variable computational elements of the strut. The two masses are at positions $\mathbf{x}_i$ and $\mathbf{x}_j$, and are moving with velocities $\mathbf{v}_i$ and $\mathbf{v}_j$. The vector from mass i to mass j is $\mathbf{x}_{ij}$, which has length $l = \|\mathbf{x}_{ij}\|$, and direction vector $\hat{\mathbf{x}}_{ij} = \mathbf{x}_{ij}/l$. All forces produced by the strut must be aligned with this direction. We can define these forces in terms of the positions and velocities of the two point masses.

The forces on the masses due to the spring in the strut come from elongation or compression of the spring from its rest length, which is measured by the difference $l_{ij} - l_{ij}^0$. Therefore, the spring force on mass i will be

$$\mathbf{f}_i^s = k_{ij}(l_{ij} - l_{ij}^0)\hat{\mathbf{x}}_{ij},$$

and by Newton's third law, the spring force on mass j will be equal and opposite:

$$\mathbf{f}_j^s = -\mathbf{f}_i^s.$$

The force on the masses due to the damper in the strut comes from a resistance to the rate of change in the length of the strut. This is measured by the component of the difference in the velocities of the two masses along the direction of the strut, $(\mathbf{v}_j - \mathbf{v}_i) \cdot \hat{\mathbf{x}}_{ij}$. Therefore, the force on mass i due to the damper will be

$$\mathbf{f}_i^d = d_{ij}[(\mathbf{v}_j - \mathbf{v}_i) \cdot \hat{\mathbf{x}}_{ij}]\hat{\mathbf{x}}_{ij},$$

and by Newton's third law, the damping force on mass j will be

$$\mathbf{f}_j^d = -\mathbf{f}_i^d.$$

8.2.2 Building a Springy Mesh Using Struts

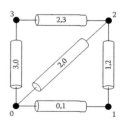

A polygonal mesh can be turned into a springy mesh by representing each edge between two vertices by a strut identified by the two vertex indices, and each vertex by a particle. The above example shows one way that this could be done for a mesh consisting of two triangles, whose vertices are numbered

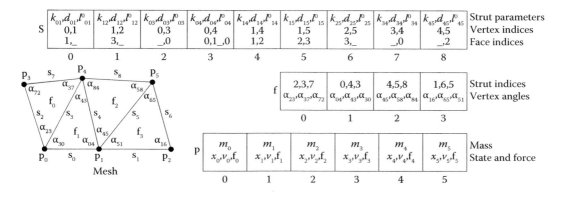

FIGURE 8.2 Data structure for a springy mesh, with example mesh.

from 0 to 3. Normally, the rest length of each strut should be set to the edge length of its corresponding edge in the mesh.

A simple data structure to support this representation is shown in Figure 8.2, together with an example mesh. The three arrays s, f, and p store information for the struts (i.e., the edges), faces, and vertex particles of the springy mesh. Each strut stores its spring, damper, and rest-length parameters, and the indices of the particles at its two ends. Each face stores the indices of the struts adjacent to it. Finally, each particle stores its mass, position, and velocity, as well as its accumulated force. We will see, later in the chapter, that for handling air resistance and torsional springs, and for distributing mass, it will be useful for each strut to also store the indices of the one or two faces adjacent to it, and for each face to store (or compute) the angle at each of its vertices.

If a consistent springiness of each strut is desired, a spring and damping constant should be chosen based on the desired strength of an edge of some nominal length L. Then, each strut's spring and damping constants should be scaled by the ratio L/l^0_{ij}. In this way, shorter edges will have stiffer

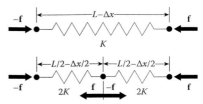

springs than longer edges. This is because we want a fixed length to have a fixed springiness, whether or not it is represented by one or several struts placed end to end. The diagram shows why this works. The force exerted by a spring of rest length L and spring constant K, when compressed the distance Δx, will be $K\Delta x$. If two identical springs of spring constant k and length $L/2$ are placed end to end, and this assembly is compressed the distance Δx, each of the small springs will be compressed the distance $\Delta x/2$. Since the force generated by the small spring will be $k\Delta x/2$, for the force to match the force of the long spring, it must be that $k = 2K$, i.e., the small springs are twice as stiff as the long spring. To convince yourself that this is correct, try the following experiment. Cut a rubber band to make a single strand, and pull on it to feel its strength. Then, cut this strand in half, and pull on one of the halves. Does it have the same strength as the original long strand?

8.2.3   Air Resistance and Wind

Since a springy mesh will usually be considered to have a surface made of polygons, adding air resistance and wind forces is no longer as simple as it was in the case of particles. Air resistance must now be considered to be acting across each polygonal face, rather than just on the particles making up the vertices of the polygons. Consider a flag made from a springy mesh. If wind forces act only on the vertex particles, the wind will push the particles in the direction of the wind, but will not cause the flapping behavior typical of flags. The flag will simply try to stretch in the direction of the wind. Instead, each polygon of the flag should be treated like a little wing. The lift and drag on a polygon will vary with its orientation to the wind, producing forces that have a component orthogonal to the wind direction, causing the flag to exhibit the nice flapping motion that is illustrated in Figure 8.3.

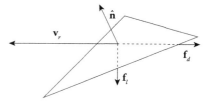

If we assume that all polygons are triangles, the figure to the right shows how lift force $\mathbf{f}_l$, and drag force $\mathbf{f}_d$ are related to the relative velocity $\mathbf{v}_r$ of the center of the triangle through the air. If $\mathbf{w}$ is the local wind velocity vector, and $\mathbf{v}$ is the triangle's velocity, $\mathbf{v}_r = \mathbf{v} - \mathbf{w}$, i.e., the velocity with which the polygon is pushing through the local air mass. For nearly equilateral triangles, the triangle's velocity at its center is well approximated by simply taking

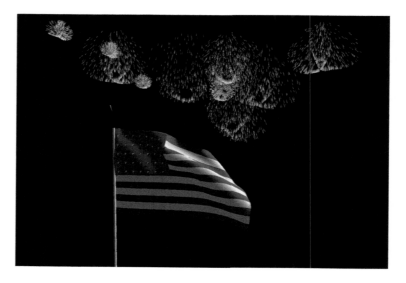

FIGURE 8.3   A frame from a Fourth-of-July flag and fireworks animation. (Courtesy of Nathan Newsome.)

the average of the velocities of its three vertices. Drag force is similar to the air resistance force on a single particle, in that it is always opposite to the direction of the velocity. Lift force is taken to be orthogonal to drag force. In the example figure, the triangle is moving to the left, and is oriented so it is tipped down in the direction of motion, so the lift force will push the triangle down. If, instead, the triangle were tipped up, the lift force would push it up.

The magnitude of both the lift and drag forces will be proportional to the square of the relative velocity of the polygon through the air, and to the effective area A_e of the triangle. The actual area A of the triangle, as demonstrated in Appendix F, is half the magnitude of the cross-product of any two of its edges. If the triangle's normal and relative velocity are exactly aligned, as in the top figure, the full area of the triangle must push through the air. If the triangle's normal and relative velocity are orthogonal, as in the bottom figure, the triangle is sliding through the air edge-on, so the effective area is 0. In general, as indicated in the middle figure, the triangle's effective area is the actual area of the triangle, scaled by the cosine of the angle between the triangle's surface normal and the relative velocity vector, i.e.,

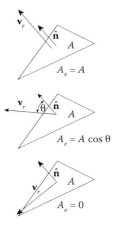

$$A_e = A(\hat{\mathbf{n}} \cdot \hat{\mathbf{v}}_r).$$

Thus, after some algebraic simplification, the drag and lift forces are given by

$$\mathbf{f}_d = -C_d A(\hat{\mathbf{n}} \cdot \mathbf{v}_r)\mathbf{v}_r, \quad \text{and}$$
$$\mathbf{f}_l = -C_l A(\hat{\mathbf{n}} \cdot \mathbf{v}_r)\left(\mathbf{v}_r \times \frac{\hat{\mathbf{n}} \times \mathbf{v}_r}{\|\hat{\mathbf{n}} \times \mathbf{v}_r\|}\right),$$

where C_d and C_l are drag and lift coefficients that are tunable by the user to obtain the desired behavior.

Once the force is calculated for a triangle, the force needs to be propagated to the vertices. One way to do this is to apply force to each vertex proportional to the triangle angle associated with that vertex. Since the angles of a triangle always total 180°, the fraction of the triangle's mass distributed to its vertex with angle θ, measured in degrees, would be $\frac{\theta}{180}$. For example, an equilateral triangle with three angles of 60° will have each vertex receive one third of the total force, while a 30° × 60° × 90° triangle will have one vertex receiving one sixth of the force, another receiving one third, and the last receiving one half.

8.2.4 Simulation of a Springy Mesh

The calculation of accelerations on each particle of a springy mesh would proceed as follows:

1. Loop over all of the particles, setting each particle's force to the accumulation of all external forces acting directly on each particle, such as air drag, friction, or gravity.

2. Loop over all of the struts, adding each strut's spring and damper forces to the forces acting on the two particles it is connected to.

3. Loop over all of the polygonal faces, distributing lift and drag forces acting on the faces to each of the faces's vertex particles.

4. Loop over all of the particles, dividing the particle's total applied force by its mass to obtain its acceleration.

8.2.5 Structural Rigidity

The goal of building springy objects is that the objects should roughly maintain their original shape but be able to deform moderately in response to forces. For example, the soft rolling ball in Figure 8.4 deforms under gravity and as it goes over the small beads on the floor, but still looks like a ball. Unfortunately, simply replacing polygon edges by struts will not always achieve the desired affect.

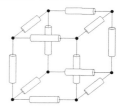

The figure to the right shows how a cube might be envisioned if all of its edges were replaced by springy struts, and each vertex by a point mass. Each edge is now free to elongate or shorten, with the spring tending to keep the edges at their original lengths. The problem with this configuration is that the point masses will act like ball joints connected to the edges.

FIGURE 8.4 A very soft ball rolling over some beads. (Courtesy of Chaorin Li.)

Since there is nothing in the system tending to keep the angles at the vertices at 90°, the cube can collapse, as depicted above. In fact, it can flatten completely, so that all of its faces lie in a single plane. This is clearly not the behavior that we would like from a springy object.

Figure 8.5 shows one approach that can be used to provide some structural stability to a springy object. The left column shows a diamond with its edges replaced by struts, and two ways that the diamond can be deformed. It can hinge within the plane of the diamond, shearing it in either direction until it collapses into a single line. It can also hinge out of the plane of the diamond by rotating about an axis formed by either of its two diagonals. In the extreme, it can collapse into a single triangle by rotating through a full 180°. The in-plane shearing problem can be fixed by attaching an additional strut across one of the diagonals. However, this does not fix the out-of-plane problem. Both problems are solved by inserting struts across both diagonals.

One way of guaranteeing structural stability is to connect every pair of vertices with a strut. Considering the cube, a cube could be given structural integrity by supplying 16 additional struts: one connected across each of the 12 face diagonals, and four across the internal diagonals of the cube. The resulting connections create too much clutter to show in a diagram, but are easy to imagine. Often, however, structural integrity can be achieved with significantly fewer struts. For example, in the cube, integrity can be achieved by adding just the four internal diagonals, or

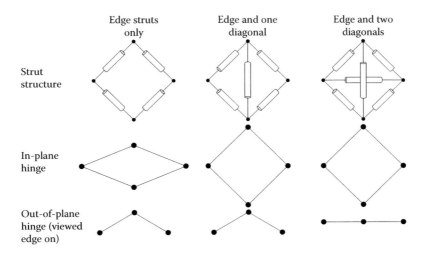

FIGURE 8.5 Adding reinforcing struts can solve the in-plane and out-of-plane rigidity problem with springy meshes.

by adding one diagonal strut on each of the six faces. The choice of which support struts to add and what parameters to use for each of them can play a major role in the overall behavior of the object.

Note that these support struts might not have an associated face in the strut array. For example, internal diagonal struts associated with a cube do not have any associated face, and if both diagonals are used across each of the six cube faces, they cannot both be associated with faces.

Another approach to providing structural stability is to take advantage of the fact that a springy tetrahedron, built with a strut for each edge, will always tend to maintain its shape. It cannot collapse, because all rotations at a vertex are inherently counteracted by the other edges. Therefore, if a geometric object can be represented by a set of tetrahedra it will form a springy 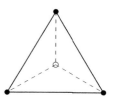 object that will be able to maintain its shape. For example, if the faces of a cube are cut diagonally to form 12 triangles, and the corners of these triangles are connected to a single vertex at the center of the cube, the cube will be formed from the resulting 12 tetrahedra, and will be able to maintain its shape.

8.3 TORSIONAL SPRINGS

The problem with fixing the structural problems of a springy mesh by adding cross-diagonal struts, or building it out of tetrahedra, is that neither approach scales easily to objects much more complex than a cube. For example, building a stable mesh to model a bunny or a teapot would be extremely complex, and involve a huge number of extra struts. Using tetrahedra to tile the volume is a better idea, but still highly complex. In this section, we present a different approach that is relatively easy to implement.

The structural stability of a springy object could be assured if, wherever two polygons on the object's surface share a common edge, the angle between these adjacent faces is maintained. A method for doing this, which is consistent with the use of springs to maintain edge lengths, is to introduce torsional springs across all adjacent faces. Since the analysis is simplified if the polygonal faces are all triangles, we will consider only this case. This is generally sufficient, because most geometric models are constructed from triangles, or from polygons, like quadrilaterals, that are easily subdivided into triangles.

The figure to the right shows conceptually how a torsional spring works. Two triangles are connected along an edge that is treated like a hinge around which the triangles can rotate. The torsional spring is attached on each end to a triangle face, so that when the triangles are rotated around the hinge, with respect to each other, a torque is exerted by the spring. This torque tends to rotate the triangles back to the position where the angle between the faces matches the *rest angle*

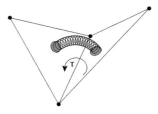

of the spring (i.e., the angle at which the spring is neither compressed nor stretched). If θ_0 is the rest angle, and θ is the current angle between the triangles, then the magnitude of the torque $\boldsymbol{\tau}$ will be proportional to the angular difference from the rest angle,

$$\|\boldsymbol{\tau}\| = k_\theta |\theta - \theta_0|,$$

where k_θ represents the strength of the spring. The direction of the torque will tend to increase the angular difference when the spring is compressed, and decrease the angular difference when it is stretched.

8.3.1 Torque

Torque is to rotational motion as force is to translational motion. Torque produces an angular acceleration, changing the velocity at which a body is rotating about some center. Like force, torque is a vector quantity, but unlike force, the direction of the torque vector is not in the direction of motion. If we think of a particle rotating 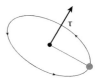 around an axis, the particle will sweep out a circle lying in a plane perpendicular to the axis. The torque vector is aligned with the axis around which the rotation is taking place, and thus orthogonal to the plane of the rotation. The magnitude of the torque is equal to the rate of change of angular momentum of the particle, so an object rotating at a fixed angular velocity is experiencing no net torque—just as an object translating at a fixed velocity is experiencing no net force.

Torque is an artifact of constrained motion. Consider a torque arising from a force being applied to a body, rigidly attached at a distance, to some sort of rotational joint. The diagram shows the relationship between the force $\mathbf{f}$ and the resultant torque $\boldsymbol{\tau}$, when the force is being ap- 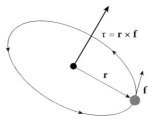 plied at position $\mathbf{r}$ from the joint. Only the component of the force perpendicular to the rigid attachment will result in rotation, since the force component parallel to the attachment is completely counteracted by the internal strength of the attachment. The resulting torque is perpendicular to both the force vector $\mathbf{f}$ and the vector $\mathbf{r}$ between the joint and the position on the object at which the force is being applied. If the force is applied close to the rotational joint, little torque is generated, but if the same force is applied far from the joint, the torque will be large. These three concepts are encapsulated in the relation

$$\boldsymbol{\tau} = \mathbf{r} \times \mathbf{f}, \tag{8.1}$$

relating torque to a force being applied at a distance from a rotational joint.

8.3.2 Computation of Torque from a Torsional Spring

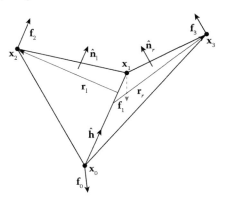

This figure attempts to represent the torsional spring problem in the form of a vector diagram needed to convert the problem, expressed in terms of a torque, into a problem involving only forces. We number each of the vertices of the two triangles as shown. We let the edge vector from vertex i to vertex j be denoted $\mathbf{x}_{ij} = \mathbf{x}_i - \mathbf{x}_j$, the edge length be $l_{ij} = \|\mathbf{x}_{ij}\|$, and the edge direction be $\hat{\mathbf{x}}_{ij} = \mathbf{x}_{ij}/l_{ij}$. We note that the hinge around which the triangles are rotating corresponds with the edge $\mathbf{x}_{01}$, so for convenience we define the hinge direction vector $\hat{\mathbf{h}} = \hat{\mathbf{x}}_{01}$. We denote attributes of the left triangle with a subscript l, and the right triangle with the subscript r. The up-facing surface normal for the left triangle is $\hat{\mathbf{n}}_l$, and for the right triangle is $\hat{\mathbf{n}}_r$. We also define $\mathbf{r}_l$ and $\mathbf{r}_r$ to be the vectors formed by lofting a perpendicular from the hinge edge $\mathbf{x}_{01}$ up to the outside vertices $\mathbf{x}_2$ and $\mathbf{x}_3$. They are given by

$$\mathbf{r}_l = \mathbf{x}_{02} - (\mathbf{x}_{02} \cdot \hat{\mathbf{h}})\hat{\mathbf{h}}, \quad \text{and}$$
$$\mathbf{r}_r = \mathbf{x}_{03} - (\mathbf{x}_{03} \cdot \hat{\mathbf{h}})\hat{\mathbf{h}}.$$

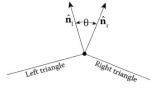

We will measure the rest angle θ_0 and the current angle θ between the two triangles as the angle between their surface normals, as shown in the above figure. Therefore, two coplanar triangles will be at $\theta = 0$, and two triangles on adjacent faces of a cube will be at $\theta = 90°$. Using this convention, the cosine of the angle between the triangles is $\cos\theta = \hat{\mathbf{n}}_l \cdot \hat{\mathbf{n}}_r$. However, the cosine only uniquely determines the angle across two quadrants, since $\cos\theta = \cos(-\theta)$. To establish the angle over a full 360° we also need to determine the sine. For this we turn to the cross-product. Note that $\hat{\mathbf{n}}_l \times \hat{\mathbf{n}}_r$ is guaranteed to be parallel to the hinge vector $\hat{\mathbf{h}}$, and oriented in the same direction as $\hat{\mathbf{h}}$ if θ is positive, as it is in the diagram. Therefore, $\sin\theta = (\hat{\mathbf{n}}_l \times \hat{\mathbf{n}}_r) \cdot \hat{\mathbf{h}}$. And we have,

$$\theta = \tan^{-1}\frac{(\hat{\mathbf{n}}_l \times \hat{\mathbf{n}}_r) \cdot \hat{\mathbf{h}}}{\hat{\mathbf{n}}_l \cdot \hat{\mathbf{n}}_r}.$$

Note that knowing the signs of the numerator and denominator in this relationship is necessary to determine the correct quadrant for the angle. Thus, in coding it is important to use a function like the C++ function `atan2()`, which takes the numerator and denominator as separate arguments and returns a full 360° angle, rather than `atan()`, which takes the ratio of the numerator and denominator as one argument and returns an angle resolved to only 180°.

If we compute the angle θ using the method described above, the torque exerted by the spring will be

$$\boldsymbol{\tau}_k = k_\theta(\theta - \theta_0)\hat{\mathbf{h}},$$

producing a rotation that decreases the angular difference when the torque vector is in the same direction as the hinge vector and increases the angular difference when it is in the opposite direction.

Analogous to linear struts, a torsional spring should also include a damping term, so that any oscillation produced by the spring is damped out. The components of the velocities of the outside vertices in the direction of their respective surface normals, divided by the distance of the vertex from the hinge, will give the angular velocity of that face around the hinge. The above figure shows how this works. In the figure

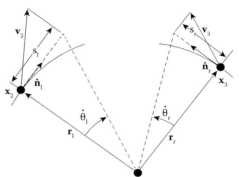

$\mathbf{v}_2$ is the velocity of the outside vertex on the left triangle. The speed of this vertex in the direction of the face normal is $s_l = \mathbf{v}_2 \cdot \hat{\mathbf{n}}_l$. The corresponding rotational speed in radians per second about the hinge axis is

$$\dot{\theta}_l = s_l/\|\mathbf{r}_l\|.$$

Similarly, the speed of vertex $\mathbf{v}_3$ on the right triangle in the direction of its face normal is $s_r = \mathbf{v}_3 \cdot \hat{\mathbf{n}}_r$, and the rotational speed of the right face is

$$\dot{\theta}_r = s_r/\|\mathbf{r}_r\|.$$

The sum of these two angular velocities is a measure of how rapidly the faces are approaching each other, and thus how fast the spring is stretching or compressing, and can be used to add a damping torque

$$\boldsymbol{\tau}_d = -d_\theta(\dot{\theta}_l + \dot{\theta}_r)\hat{\mathbf{h}},$$

tending to reduce the net angular velocity at the hinge. The constant d_θ determines the damping strength of the torsional spring.

Finally, the total torque produced by the torsional spring and damper will be

$$\boldsymbol{\tau} = \boldsymbol{\tau}_k + \boldsymbol{\tau}_d = [k_\theta(\theta - \theta_0) - d_\theta(\dot{\theta}_l + \dot{\theta}_r)]\hat{\mathbf{h}}.$$

8.3.3 Computation of the Vertex Forces from a Torsional Spring

Our goal is to compute the forces acting on the four vertices accounting for the torque exerted by the torsional spring. We associate a force $\mathbf{f}_i$ with each vertex i.

Since there are no outside forces acting on the triangle-spring system, it must be true that

$$\mathbf{f}_0 + \mathbf{f}_1 + \mathbf{f}_2 + \mathbf{f}_3 = 0.$$

If this were not true, the center of mass of the body would be able to accelerate due only to forces being generated within the body. Thus, if we can find three of the forces, the fourth is uniquely determined. We will use this fact in the analysis below, first finding $\mathbf{f}_1$, $\mathbf{f}_2$, and $\mathbf{f}_3$, so that

$$\mathbf{f}_0 = -(\mathbf{f}_1 + \mathbf{f}_2 + \mathbf{f}_3).$$

Since the forces $\mathbf{f}_2$ and $\mathbf{f}_3$ at the two outside vertices are produced by the torque, they must be parallel to the surface normals $\hat{\mathbf{n}}_l$ and $\hat{\mathbf{n}}_r$. Looking first at the force on the outside vertex of the left triangle, the torque-force relationship 8.1 gives,

$$\boldsymbol{\tau} = \mathbf{r}_l \times \mathbf{f}_2.$$

Taking the dot product of both sides with the hinge vector, and factoring out the magnitude of the vector $\mathbf{r}_l$ gives

$$\frac{\boldsymbol{\tau} \cdot \hat{\mathbf{h}}}{\|\mathbf{r}_l\|} = (\hat{\mathbf{r}}_l \times \mathbf{f}_2) \cdot \hat{\mathbf{h}}.$$

Now, since $\hat{\mathbf{r}}_l$, $\mathbf{f}_2$, and $\hat{\mathbf{h}}$ are all mutually orthogonal, and the direction of $\mathbf{f}_2$ is parallel to the surface normal of the left triangle, we have

$$\mathbf{f}_2 = \frac{\boldsymbol{\tau} \cdot \hat{\mathbf{h}}}{\|\mathbf{r}_l\|} \hat{\mathbf{n}}_l.$$

The force $\mathbf{f}_3$ on the outside vertex of the right triangle is found in similar fashion, beginning with the relationship

$$\boldsymbol{\tau} = \mathbf{r}_r \times \mathbf{f}_3,$$

and yielding

$$\mathbf{f}_3 = \frac{\boldsymbol{\tau} \cdot \hat{\mathbf{h}}}{\|\mathbf{r}_r\|} \hat{\mathbf{n}}_r.$$

This gives us two of the required three forces. To find a third, we will look at the balance of torques in the system.

Although we have not yet determined all of them, we have four forces acting on the hinged pair of triangles, which if considered with respect to any arbitrary point in the system must result in four torques, $\boldsymbol{\tau}_0, \boldsymbol{\tau}_1, \boldsymbol{\tau}_2$, and $\boldsymbol{\tau}_3$. Just as the four forces must balance so that there is no net acceleration on the system, the four resultant torques must balance, so that the system does not experience a change in angular momentum coming from torques generated strictly within the system. Therefore, we can write the torque balance equation

$$\boldsymbol{\tau}_0 + \boldsymbol{\tau}_1 + \boldsymbol{\tau}_2 + \boldsymbol{\tau}_3 = 0.$$

The diagram to the right shows one way to view the torque balance. If we look along the hinge vector, we can look at the forces exerting torques causing the hinge vector to rotate. Note, that any rotation of the hinge should be impossible since the only applied torque is parallel to the hinge. We will examine the torques, about the vertex at $\mathbf{x}_0$, resulting from the four

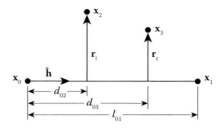

forces. We define $d_{02} = \mathbf{x}_{02} \cdot \hat{\mathbf{h}}$ and $d_{03} = \mathbf{x}_{03} \cdot \hat{\mathbf{h}}$ to be the distances along the hinge, from $\mathbf{x}_0$, at which the forces $\mathbf{f}_2$ and $\mathbf{f}_3$ are applied. The forces $\mathbf{f}_0$ and $\mathbf{f}_1$ are applied at the two ends of the hinge. Since the distance of force $\mathbf{f}_0$ from vertex $\mathbf{x}_0$ is 0, by Equation 8.1, $\boldsymbol{\tau}_0 = 0$. The other three torques are

$$\boldsymbol{\tau}_1 = l_{01} \hat{\mathbf{h}} \times \mathbf{f}_1,$$
$$\boldsymbol{\tau}_2 = d_{02} \hat{\mathbf{h}} \times \mathbf{f}_2, \quad \text{and}$$
$$\boldsymbol{\tau}_3 = d_{03} \hat{\mathbf{h}} \times \mathbf{f}_3.$$

Setting the sum of these three torques to 0, isolating $\mathbf{f}_1$ on one side of the equation, and factoring out the cross-product with the hinge vector yields

$$\hat{\mathbf{h}} \times \mathbf{f}_1 = \hat{\mathbf{h}} \times -\frac{d_{02}\mathbf{f}_2 + d_{03}\mathbf{f}_3}{l_{01}}.$$

Since $\mathbf{f}_1, \mathbf{f}_2$, and $\mathbf{f}_3$ are all perpendicular to the hinge $\hat{\mathbf{h}}$, the only way that this equation can be satisfied is if

$$\mathbf{f}_1 = -\frac{d_{02}\mathbf{f}_2 + d_{03}\mathbf{f}_3}{l_{01}}.$$

Since this was a rather involved derivation, let us summarize the calculations needed to compute the forces resulting from applying a torsional spring across the faces of two adjacent triangles:

$\mathbf{x}_{ij} = \mathbf{x}_j - \mathbf{x}_i$	$l_{ij} = \|\mathbf{x}_{ij}\|$	$\hat{\mathbf{h}} = \mathbf{x}_{01}/l_{01}$	
$d_{02} = \mathbf{x}_{02} \cdot \hat{\mathbf{h}}$	$d_{03} = \mathbf{x}_{03} \cdot \hat{\mathbf{h}}$	$\mathbf{r}_l = \mathbf{x}_{02} - d_{02}\hat{\mathbf{h}}$	$\mathbf{r}_r = \mathbf{x}_{03} - d_{03}\hat{\mathbf{h}}$
$\theta = \tan^{-1} \frac{(\hat{\mathbf{n}}_l \times \hat{\mathbf{n}}_r) \cdot \hat{\mathbf{h}}}{\hat{\mathbf{n}}_l \cdot \hat{\mathbf{n}}_r}$	$\dot{\theta}_l = \frac{\mathbf{v}_2 \cdot \hat{\mathbf{n}}_l}{\|\mathbf{r}_l\|}$	$\dot{\theta}_r = \frac{\mathbf{v}_3 \cdot \hat{\mathbf{n}}_r}{\|\mathbf{r}_r\|}$	$\boldsymbol{\tau} = [k_\theta(\theta - \theta_0) - d_\theta(\dot{\theta}_l + \dot{\theta}_r)]\hat{\mathbf{h}}$
$\mathbf{f}_3 = \frac{\boldsymbol{\tau} \cdot \hat{\mathbf{h}}}{\|\mathbf{r}_r\|} \hat{\mathbf{n}}_r$	$\mathbf{f}_2 = \frac{\boldsymbol{\tau} \cdot \hat{\mathbf{h}}}{\|\mathbf{r}_l\|} \hat{\mathbf{n}}_l$	$\mathbf{f}_1 = -\frac{d_{02}\mathbf{f}_2 + d_{03}\mathbf{f}_3}{l_{01}}$	$\mathbf{f}_0 = -(\mathbf{f}_1 + \mathbf{f}_2 + \mathbf{f}_3)$

8.3.4 Simulation of a Mesh with Torsional Springs

To build a springy-mesh system with torsional springs across all edges requires augmenting the mesh data structure shown in Figure 8.2, by providing a torsional spring constant for each strut that is adjacent to two faces, across which there is a torsional spring. The calculation of accelerations on each particle of a springy mesh, augmented with torsional springs, would also require the computation of hinge forces when looping over each strut.

8.4 CHOOSING GOOD PARAMETERS

When setting up a springy-mesh system, choosing a set of parameters that gives a desired behavior can be confusing, since the the parameter settings all interact to affect the important behavioral characteristics of the mesh. The following is a cookbook way to approach the parameter setting that will allow the animator to quickly get to settings that produce a desired effect.

The easiest parameter to set is mass. All of us have a strong intuitive feel for what the approximate weight of an object should be, so it makes sense to start with a good guess at what the real-world mass would be for a particular model. A bowling ball would have a mass of about 7 kg, a tennis ball about 0.06 kg, and a ping-pong ball about 0.003 kg. These are approximate numbers—the important thing is that the mass be in the right range.

The usual beginner's mistake is to set the mass to 1, with unspecified units, with the idea being that it simplifies all of the equations. The problem with this is that if we make a tennis ball's mass 1, then the mass of a bowling ball will have to be 116, and the mass of a ping-pong ball will have to be 0.05 if they are to occupy the same world and behave consistently. If all of them are given the mass of 1 then the world will behave strangely indeed! If each mass is chosen to have physically realistic values, according to your favorite measuring system, then the animated world will have a reasonable physical consistency, which will be reflected in the observed behavior.

Once a mass for an object is chosen, it must be distributed across the vertices of the model. If the object's mass is M, and its model has N vertices, then the mass of each vertex i, could be set to $m_i = M/N$. An even better approach would be to adjust each vertex' mass according to the fraction of the total area of the surface represented by the triangles adjacent to that vertex.

Consider a cube, represented by triangular faces, as shown in the figure to the right. If the side of the cube is of length L, then the total surface area of the cube will be $A = 6L^2$, and the area of each triangular face will be $L^2/2$. Thus, if M is the total mass of the cube, each triangle would account for mass $M/12$. As with distributing lift forces, the trick is to distribute this mass to the vertices of each triangle according to the angle of the triangle at that vertex. Consider vertex 0. It has four adjacent triangles, two with angle 45° and two with angle 90°.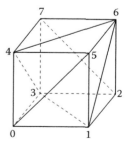
So the total mass distributed to vertex 0 would be $\frac{1}{4}(M/12) \times 2 + \frac{1}{2}(M/12) \times 2 = M/8$. Vertex 1 has 5 adjacent triangles, four with angle 45° and one with angle 90°, so its total mass would be $\frac{1}{4}(M/12) \times 4 + \frac{1}{2}(M/12) \times 1 = M/8$. By similar

reasoning, the areas adjacent to the other vertices can be calculated, accounting for the total area of the cube. For this simple case this gives us the expected equal weights of $M/8$ at each vertex. For a more complex case, with varying triangle sizes and angles, the mass distribution will not be equal at each vertex but will be well represented.

Once appropriate point masses have been determined, choosing the spring and damping constants for the struts comes down to deciding how quickly spring oscillations should be damped out, and what period the spring oscillations should have. Let us take for example the ball attached to the ceiling by a springy strut shown in the figure. Let us say that we want the ball to bounce up and down at a specified rate, and that we want the bounces to die down to less than 95% of full amplitude after a certain time. In animators' terms, we want to specify the number

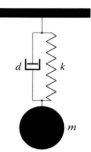

of frames per bounce, and the number of total frames for the complete bouncing sequence. As derived in Section 8.1.1, the time constant T and undamped period P_n of a strut are given by

$$T = \frac{2m}{d}, \quad \text{and}$$
$$P_n = 2\pi\sqrt{m/k}.$$

Since we have already selected the mass m, from the equation for the period we see that the spring and damping constants needed to achieve the desired damping time constant, and oscillation period would be

$$d = \frac{2m}{T}, \quad \text{and}$$
$$k = \frac{4\pi^2 m}{P_n^2}.$$

```
            1
                                              ┌──────────────────────┐
                                              │ x₀ = 1   m = 7   P = 5 │
Deflection from rest height, meters  0.5      │ v₀ = 0   k = 11.1 T = 5│
                                              │          d = 2.8  ζ = 0.2│
            0                                 └──────────────────────┘

          -0.5

           -1
             0    2    4    6    8    10   12   14
                        Time, seconds
```

Let us say that the ball is a bowling ball of mass $m = 7$ kg, we want the period of oscillation to be $P = 5$ seconds, and we want the oscillations to die out by three periods, so that the time constant should be $T = \frac{3P}{3} = 5$ seconds. Therefore, by the equations above, we would have to set the damping constant $d = 2.8$, and the spring constant $k = 11.1$. The figure above is a graph of the simulated height of the ball as a function of time, using $m = 7$ kg, $d = 2.8$ N-s/m, and $k = 11.1$ N/m, and starting with a 1 m initial deflection of the ball from its rest position. The graph shows that the oscillation does indeed have a period of 5 seconds, and that it is dying out with a time constant of 5 seconds.

This analysis is an oversimplification of the problem, because an interconnected system of springs and masses will have system-wide time constants and oscillation frequencies coming from the interactions among elements. These can be determined by eigenvalue analysis of the interconnected system, which is beyond the scope of this book but is well covered in Strang [2009]. Nevertheless, getting the individual struts to behave according to the design of the animator is a key first step in a process of finding the right parameter settings to achieve the desired frame rates and durations. Experimentation, making only small parameter adjustments, should then suffice to achieve the desired behavior.

The setting of torsional springs can proceed following the same approach, but modifying the period and time constant calculations to account for the rotational inertia of the hinge system. If r is the distance of the mass from the hinge axis (in a triangle this is the height of the triangle), wherever mass m appears in the translational equations, the moment of inertia mr^2 appears in the rotational equations. Thus, the torsional damping time constant and period are given by

$$T_\theta = \frac{2mr^2}{d_\theta}, \quad \text{and}$$
$$P_\theta = 2\pi r \sqrt{m/k_\theta}.$$

In our experience, we have observed that the time constants and periods for torsional springs need to be set much shorter than those for the struts. Otherwise, the object will be too weak to maintain its shape. In practical terms, it is a safe bet that the torsional spring and damping constants k_θ and d_θ should be set one or two orders of magnitude larger than the corresponding strut parameters.

8.5 COLLISIONS

Now that we are dealing with 3D objects with volume, and not just individual points, we need to reconsider how collisions should work. There are two main differences from collisions of point objects (recall Section 3.1). First, the collisions will no longer be just a point hitting a surface, but rather will involve more complicated geometric structures (vertices, edges, and faces); this will affect collision detection and determination. Second, the objects can now collide with each other, which is not the case for individual points moving around; this will affect collision response.

8.5.1 Types of Collisions

Our objects, both the ones undergoing simulation and those in the static environment, are represented as sets of vertices, edges, and faces. In order to find collisions, we need to be able to recognize them between each of the different types of geometric structures. Thus, we might need to check whether the faces, edges, and vertices of one object are colliding with the faces, edges, and vertices of another. So, there would be nine combinations of collision types to handle.

Fortunately, this problem can be simplified considerably by understanding the concept of *genericity*. Genericity refers to objects being in "general position," which you can think of, roughly, as an object being in a position where a tiny perturbation does not change the nature of its interaction with the stuff around it. Objects not in general position are said to be in *degen-*

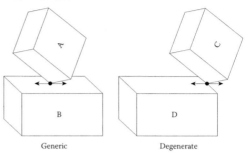

Generic   Degenerate

erate configurations. In the figure, objects A and B are in a general contact position with respect to each other, since either object can move in the contact plane in any direction, without changing the fact that a vertex of A is in contact with a face of B. Objects C and D are in a degenerate configuration, with a vertex of C in contact with an edge of D. Moving object C slightly to the left changes the contact from a vertex-edge contact to a vertex-face contact, moving it slightly to the right breaks the contact completely, while moving it to the right and down changes the contact to an edge-edge contact. Objects positioned in a truly random fashion will never be in degenerate configurations.

If you consider the ways that two objects can collide, it should quickly become apparent that there are only two generic types of collisions: between vertices and faces, and between pairs of edges. The other types of collisions are all degenerate, so that a very small perturbation will remove them as possibilities. We summarize the results in the following table, where V, E, and F refer to vertices, edges, and faces, and G and D refer to general position and degenerate.

		Object A		
		V	E	F
Object B	V	D	D	G
	E	D	G	D
	F	G	D	D

In a practical sense, this means that we can build our collision detection and collision determination code to consider only vertex-face and edge-edge collisions. We will describe below how we find these collisions.

Now, unfortunately, we do not typically set up our simulation environments in truly random positions. As a result we often will encounter degenerate, or nearly degenerate, configurations of objects. For this reason, some people will implement additional code to check for and handle degenerate collisions, but doing so is beyond the scope of this book. Note, though, that even degenerate collisions have generic collisions

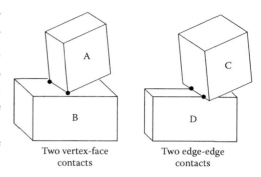

Two vertex-face contacts   Two edge-edge contacts

occurring as part of them. For example, an edge-face collision occurs when there are two vertex-face (objects A and B) or edge-edge collisions (objects C and D) happening simultaneously. Thus, handling generic collisions is critical, even for degenerate cases.

8.5.2 Determining Collisions

Notice that the collision detection process, between even two objects, can involve many vertex-face and edge-edge tests. However, since for any one object, the vertices, faces, and edges tend to be grouped nearby, if two objects are sufficiently far apart, there is no need to perform all the individual vertex-face and edge-edge tests between them. Based on this, there are a number of methods for speeding up the collision detection process, and it becomes more important to make use of these as we deal with more complex geometry. Rather than get sidetracked here, we will discuss these methods in more detail in Chapter 9, when we study rigid body dynamics.

8.5.2.1 Vertex-Face Tests

The vertex-face collision process is equivalent to the point-polygon collisions we have seen previously (see Section 3.5). We must consider the collision of each vertex of one object (the point), with each face of the other object (the polygon). Note that collision checks assume that the faces will be planar polygons. For a springy-mesh object, a nontriangular face can bend out-of-plane (e.g., imagine one vertex being pulled out of the face of a cube), but handling the resulting curved surfaces in a collision test is very difficult. When determining collisions, the models should be represented as a set of triangular faces.

A key difference from prior point-polygon checks is that, in this case, the polygonal faces themselves are moving. There is no difference in the actual mechanism for detecting and determining collisions, i.e., taking the face normal and determining whether the point is above or below, and then determining whether the point is inside or outside of the polygon. However, we must be sure to calculate the current vertices of the polygon at every fractional timestep. The estimates of the time and location at which a collision occurs will be off due to the relative motion.

8.5.2.2 Edge-Edge Tests

Edge-edge collisions require a different test. To perform edge-edge collision tests, we need to be able
to determine the closest point on each of the edges.
Consider the diagram, where we have nonparallel
edges $\mathbf{p}_1\mathbf{p}_2$ and $\mathbf{q}_1\mathbf{q}_2$. Let $\mathbf{p}_a$ be the closest point
on the first edge to the second one, and $\mathbf{q}_a$ be the
closest point on the second edge to the first one.
If the two lines are intersecting, then $\mathbf{p}_a = \mathbf{q}_a$. If
we consider the parametric form of each edge (see

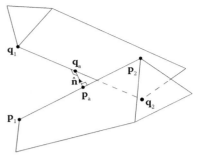

Appendix A.6), then the first edge can be denoted as $\mathbf{p}_1 + (\mathbf{p}_2 - \mathbf{p}_1)s = \mathbf{p}_1 + \mathbf{a}s$
and the second as $\mathbf{q}_1 + (\mathbf{q}_2 - \mathbf{q}_1)t = \mathbf{q}_1 + \mathbf{b}t$. Our goal is to find the value of s
corresponding to $\mathbf{p}_a$ and of t corresponding to $\mathbf{q}_a$.

Notice that the line segment $\mathbf{p}_a\mathbf{q}_a$ must be perpendicular to both of the edges,
since it represents the shortest distance between the two lines. Given that $\mathbf{a}$ and $\mathbf{b}$
are vectors along each edge,

$$\hat{\mathbf{n}} = \frac{\mathbf{a} \times \mathbf{b}}{\|\mathbf{a} \times \mathbf{b}\|}$$

gives the direction of $\mathbf{p}_a\mathbf{q}_a$.

We can calculate the value of s and t for
$\mathbf{p}_a$ and $\mathbf{q}_a$ by considering what the two edges
would look like if projected into the plane
with normal $\hat{\mathbf{n}}$. Notice that in this plane,
the points $\mathbf{p}_a$ and $\mathbf{q}_a$ would coincide, where
the line segments for the two edges cross
each other. Thus we need to calculate the
intersection point of the lines in this plane.

First, form the vector from $\mathbf{p}_1$ to $\mathbf{q}_1$:

$$\mathbf{r} = \mathbf{q}_1 - \mathbf{p}_1.$$

We will also form the axis $\hat{\mathbf{b}} \times \hat{\mathbf{n}}$. Then, the overall length of $\mathbf{p}_1\mathbf{p}_2$ projected on this
axis, corresponding to s values from 0 to 1, is $\mathbf{a} \cdot (\hat{\mathbf{b}} \times \hat{\mathbf{n}})$. Likewise, the projection
of $\mathbf{r}$ along this axis, corresponding to s values from 0 to where $\mathbf{p}_a$ is, is given by
$\mathbf{r} \cdot (\hat{\mathbf{b}} \times \hat{\mathbf{n}})$. Thus, the value of s corresponding to $\mathbf{p}_a$ is

$$s = \frac{\mathbf{r} \cdot (\hat{\mathbf{b}} \times \hat{\mathbf{n}})}{\mathbf{a} \cdot (\hat{\mathbf{b}} \times \hat{\mathbf{n}})}.$$

Likewise, the value of t corresponding to $\mathbf{q}_a$ is

$$t = \frac{-\mathbf{r} \cdot (\hat{\mathbf{a}} \times \hat{\mathbf{n}})}{\mathbf{b} \cdot (\hat{\mathbf{a}} \times \hat{\mathbf{n}})}.$$

By using the parametric forms, we can find $\mathbf{p}_a = \mathbf{p}_1 + s\mathbf{a}$ and $\mathbf{q}_a = \mathbf{q}_1 + t\mathbf{b}$.
Note that if either s or t falls outside of the $[0, 1]$ range, then that means the closest

point between the lines corresponding to the two edges is outside of the actual edge. In this case, there is not a collision between the edges, and in fact it is some other feature of the object (possibly one of the vertices of the edge) that is closest to the other object.

Using the technique described, we can determine whether a collision has occurred in a few different ways. One way is to compute the vector $\mathbf{m} = \mathbf{q}_a - \mathbf{p}_a$. If $\|\mathbf{m}\| = 0$ (within some tolerance), then we are at the point of collision. Although $\mathbf{m}$ will vary as the objects move, if there is a collision, the direction of the vector will reverse. Thus, if we know $\mathbf{m}^-$ in the step before, and $\mathbf{m}^+$ in the step afterward, then if $\mathbf{m}^- \cdot \mathbf{m}^+ < 0$, there was a collision.

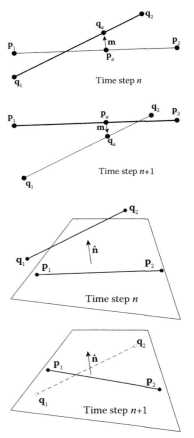

Another method for detecting an edge-edge collision is to consider a plane formed from the point $\mathbf{p}_1$ and the normal $\hat{\mathbf{n}}$. The line segment $\mathbf{q}_1\mathbf{q}_2$ must be parallel to this plane, since it is orthogonal to $\hat{\mathbf{n}}$. So, a collision occurs when a point on that line segment, e.g., $\mathbf{q}_1$, moves from one side of the plane to the other. This can be computed as a change in the sign of $(\mathbf{q}_1 - \mathbf{p}_1) \cdot \hat{\mathbf{n}}$. It is important to use the same $\hat{\mathbf{n}}$ for both checks, since the direction of $\hat{\mathbf{n}}$ can change when the two edges become parallel. If this happened between the two checks, the sign would appear to change, due to the reversed direction of $\hat{\mathbf{n}}$, and a collision would be reported incorrectly. Note that since all we care about is the sign, we can actually just use $\mathbf{n} = \mathbf{a} \times \mathbf{b}$ instead of the normalized $\hat{\mathbf{n}}$.

8.5.3 Collision Response for Springy Objects

Prior discussions of collision response dealt with a single point encountering a static object. Now, we have a point on a moving object, possibly encountering a point on another moving object. As a result, the collision response calculation must be changed. Before continuing, it may be helpful to review the process for collision response for particles as described in Section 3.2.

8.5.3.1 Collisions with Static Objects

If one of the objects is fixed, the task is relatively simple. If a vertex of the moving object encounters a static face, we can handle collision response just like we did for particles. If the moving object has an edge or face that collides, we need to calculate the information about the point of contact, in order to compute collision response.

Our collision determination process will have located the point of collision. We need to calculate the velocity for this point in order to compute the collision response. If the point is on an edge, we can interpolate the velocity of the collision point from the two vertices at the ends of the edge. A linear interpolation is sufficient, here. Likewise, if the collision point is on a face, we can use a weighting based on the barycentric coordinates of the collision point relative to the vertices of the face. Either way, we will compute the velocity of the nominal collision point and we can compute a collision response for this point in the same way we did for particles. Note that the collision response calculation requires a normal. For a face-vertex collision, the face normal can be used. For an edge-edge collision, the direction $\hat{\mathbf{n}}$ is taken from the cross-product of the two edges, as demonstrated in the previous section.

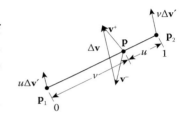

Once we know what the new velocity of the collision point should be, we need to adjust the velocities of the mesh vertices accordingly. One way of doing this is to just set the velocities of all the vertices on the edge or face to the new velocity. However, this will create unrealistic responses, where points far away from the collision change velocity more than is reasonable. We want vertices closer to the collision point to receive more velocity change than those farther away. To do this we will use the barycentric weighting scheme. To illustrate, assume that the collision point $\mathbf{p}$ is on an edge between points $\mathbf{p_1}$ and $\mathbf{p_2}$, so that $\mathbf{p} = u\mathbf{p_1} + v\mathbf{p_2}$, where $v = 1 - u$. If the velocities of $\mathbf{p}$ before and after collision are $\mathbf{v}^-$ and $\mathbf{v}^+$, respectively, then we need to adjust the velocity of $\mathbf{p}$ by $\Delta\mathbf{v} = \mathbf{v}^+ - \mathbf{v}^-$. We want to find a new velocity change $\Delta\mathbf{v}'$ that we can apply to $\mathbf{p_1}$ and $\mathbf{p_2}$, i.e., so that $\mathbf{v}_1^+ = \mathbf{v}_1^- + u\Delta\mathbf{v}'$ and $\mathbf{v}_2^+ = \mathbf{v}_2^- + v\Delta\mathbf{v}'$. All of this must result in a change of $\Delta\mathbf{v}$ in point $\mathbf{p}$, given by

$$\Delta\mathbf{v} = u\Delta\mathbf{v}_1 + v\Delta\mathbf{v}_2, \quad \text{or}$$
$$\Delta\mathbf{v} = u(u\Delta\mathbf{v}') + v(v\Delta\mathbf{v}'),$$

so that

$$\Delta\mathbf{v}' = \frac{\Delta\mathbf{v}}{(u^2 + v^2)}.$$

Likewise, if the collision point were on a triangular face, where $\mathbf{p} = u\mathbf{p_1} + v\mathbf{p_2} + w\mathbf{p_3}$ and $w = 1 - u - v$, we would use a value

$$\Delta\mathbf{v}' = \frac{\Delta\mathbf{v}}{(u^2 + v^2 + w^2)},$$

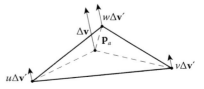

and adjust the velocities by $u\Delta\mathbf{v}'$, $v\Delta\mathbf{v}'$, and $w\Delta\mathbf{v}'$.

8.5.3.2 Collisions between Moving Objects

The method just described allows us to adjust the velocity at a collision point. For static objects, the collision response, i.e., the new velocity of the point after collision, is computed as in Section 3.2. For two moving objects, though, the new velocity must be computed differently, and the change in velocity must affect both points. That is, we have two collision points, **p** on object A and **q** on object B, and we need to find the new velocity for each of those points.

To account for collisions between objects, we will make use of Newton's third law, which states that the collision forces for the two objects should be equal but in opposite directions. Since the collision takes place in the same amount of time for both objects, this gives us a conservation of momentum. Momentum of an object, which is usually designated as **P**, is defined as the product of the mass and the velocity: $\mathbf{P} = m\mathbf{v}$. Notice that for a constant mass object, force ($m\mathbf{a}$) is the derivative of momentum, so if the two objects have an equal and opposite force applied during the very short pe-

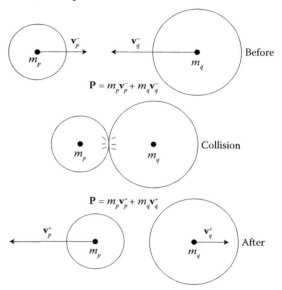

riod of time of the collision, the result is that each has an equal and opposite change in momentum. Conservation of momentum states that the total momentum of the system must remain unchanged. The figure illustrates this. Two objects with masses m_p and m_q, and with velocities $\mathbf{v}_p^-$, and $\mathbf{v}_q^-$ before their collision, will have $\mathbf{v}_p^+$, and $\mathbf{v}_q^+$ after collision such that the sum of their momenta stays constant.

For a springy object with mass distributed at vertex particles, we need to compute the effective mass for the collision point so that, as the collision begins, the collision point **p** on the first object will have an effective mass m_p and velocity $\mathbf{v}_p^-$, and the collision point **q** on the second object will have an effective mass m_q and velocity $\mathbf{v}_q^-$. Finding these masses m_p and m_q requires a weighted barycentric combination of the masses at the vertices. If the collision point has barycentric coordinates (u, v) where $v = 1 - u$ for an edge, or (u, v, w) where $w = 1 - u - v$ for a point on a triangular face, then we can compute the mass as

$$m = \frac{um_1 + vm_2}{u^2 + v^2}, \quad \text{or} \quad m = \frac{um_1 + vm_2 + wm_3}{u^2 + v^2 + w^2},$$

where the m_i are the masses at the vertices. Note that the denominator in these equations (which matches the denominator in the computation of $\Delta v'$, earlier) is needed to conserve momentum.

We need to find the velocities after collision, $\mathbf{v}_p^+$ and $\mathbf{v}_q^+$. We can use the same basic approach used previously for collision with a static object, but apply it to the two moving objects. The overall process will be as follows:

1. Compute the center of momentum $\mathbf{c}_m$.

2. Compute the velocities of $\mathbf{p}$ and $\mathbf{q}$ relative to $\mathbf{c}_m$.

3. Find the normal and tangential components of these velocities.

4. Compute the collision response due to elasticity and friction.

5. Add the $\mathbf{c}_m$ back to the resulting velocities to get back to the original frame of reference.

For the two objects, or in this case just the points of collision $\mathbf{p}$ and $\mathbf{q}$ from each, the overall momentum can be computed, and since we know momentum is conserved, we have

$$m_p \mathbf{v}_p^- + m_q \mathbf{v}_q^- = m_p \mathbf{v}_p^+ + m_q \mathbf{v}_q^+.$$

Each side of this equation gives a vector that describes the overall momentum of the system. Dividing this by the total mass gives the "center of momentum"

$$\mathbf{c}_m = \frac{m_p \mathbf{v}_p^- + m_q \mathbf{v}_q^-}{m_p + m_q}.$$

We can then define the motion of the two objects relative to this point, i.e.,

$$\acute{\mathbf{v}}_p^- = \mathbf{v}_p^- - \mathbf{c}_m, \quad \text{and} \quad \acute{\mathbf{v}}_q^- = \mathbf{v}_q^- - \mathbf{c}_m,$$

where the $´$ indicates that we are dealing with terms relative to the center of momentum.

With these velocities relative to the center of momentum, we can compute the response for each object around the normal, in the same way we did before. We will break the velocity into normal and tangential components, and apply the elasticity and friction responses to each component separately, using the simple friction model described in Section 3.2. The normal and tangential velocity components for object p before collision are

$$\acute{\mathbf{v}}_{p,n}^- = (\acute{\mathbf{v}}_p^- \cdot \hat{\mathbf{n}})\hat{\mathbf{n}}, \quad \text{and} \quad \acute{\mathbf{v}}_{p,t}^- = \acute{\mathbf{v}}_p^- - \acute{\mathbf{v}}_{p,n}^-,$$

and after collision they are

$$\acute{\mathbf{v}}_{p,n}^+ = -c_r \acute{\mathbf{v}}_{p,n}^-, \quad \text{and} \quad \acute{\mathbf{v}}_{p,t}^+ = (1 - c_f)\acute{\mathbf{v}}_{p,t}^-.$$

Therefore $\mathbf{p}$'s velocity after collision is

$$\acute{\mathbf{v}}_p^+ = \acute{\mathbf{v}}_{p,n}^+ + \acute{\mathbf{v}}_{p,t}^+.$$

The velocity $\acute{\mathbf{v}}_q^+$ of $\mathbf{q}$ after collision is computed in the same way. Note that these are still relative to the center of momentum, so we must finally readjust to the overall velocities

$$\mathbf{v}_p^+ = \acute{\mathbf{v}}_p^- + \mathbf{c}_m, \quad \text{and} \quad \mathbf{v}_q^+ = \acute{\mathbf{v}}_q^- + \mathbf{c}_m.$$

Notice that for static objects, where we assume the velocity is 0 and the mass is infinite (i.e., $\mathbf{v}_q^- = 0$ and $m_q = \infty$), then $\mathbf{c}_m = 0$ and the remaining equations are identical to what we have used earlier.

Given the new velocity for the collision points, these need to be propagated to the vertices, as described earlier. The reader may verify that the total change in momentum is not affected by this distribution.

It is apparent that the simplicity of a spring system, with mass at the vertices, connected by faces and edges having no mass of their own, leads to complications when it comes to handling collisions. In Chapters 9 and 10, covering rigid body simulation, we will describe ways of modeling objects and their collisions that account for the distribution of mass throughout a body.

8.6   LATTICE DEFORMERS

From the above discussion, it should be clear that building a structurally stable springy mesh, for a complex geometric model, will require many thousands of struts and torsional springs. Even worse, a refined model, containing many very small triangles, will result in very short struts, whose spring constants are very large, and whose vertex masses are very small. Since the vibration period of these struts ($P = 2\pi\sqrt{m/k}$) decreases with increasing spring constant k and also decreases with decreasing mass m, tiny triangles will have very short periods of oscillation P. Since the simulation timestep h must be a fraction of this period, we not only have to do computations for large numbers of elements, but we must use a very small timestep to avoid instability. For detailed models, these factors combine to make springy meshes very computationally expensive to simulate.

A *lattice deformer* provides a mechanism for applying the springy-mesh ideas to highly complex geometric models, without incurring the cost of providing springy struts for every triangle edge, or for dealing with small triangles. The idea is to embed 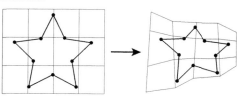 the model in a rectangular lattice, make the lattice into a springy object, simulate the lattice deforming, and move the model vertices so that they always maintain a fixed position relative to the lattice. The above figure shows this idea in 2D. Using this approach, the simulation is only done on the lattice, reducing the number of struts needed by orders of magnitude, and eliminating struts with very short rest lengths. The main idea behind lattice deformers was introduced to the graphics community by Sederberg and Parry [1986], who presented a modeling method that

FIGURE 8.6 A lattice deformer being used to animate the Eiffel Tower. (Courtesy of Jianwei Liu.)

they called *Free Form Deformations* (FFDs). Lattice deformers are one way to implement FFDs, that is especially suitable to the animation of polygonal models. An example 3D lattice placed over an Eiffel Tower model is shown in Figure 8.6.

This diagram to the right shows how a single vertex i in the geometric model, whose position is $\mathbf{x}_i$, would be handled within a cell of the lattice. On the left of the figure is the undeformed lattice cell, with its four vertices $\mathbf{p}_0 \cdots \mathbf{p}_3$, and the undeformed position of the vertex. Vertex i is assigned lattice cell coordinates

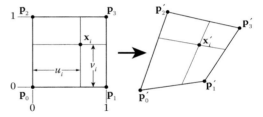

(u_i, v_i), indicating the fraction of vertex i's distance from the left, and from the bottom of the cell. If vertex i were on the left side of the lattice cell, u_i would be 0, and on the right side, u_i would be 1. Likewise, vertical position v_i would be 0 at the bottom of the cell and 1 at the top. On the right-hand side of the figure, the lattice cell is shown in a deformed position, with its vertices now at positions $\mathbf{p}'_0 \cdots \mathbf{p}'_3$. The problem is to compute the corresponding position $\mathbf{x}'_i$ of model vertex i.

The process of finding the transformed position of vertex i within a grid cell is known as bilinear interpolation. The above figure shows what we are doing geometrically to position the vertex. We can think of the lattice edge from $\mathbf{p}'_0$ to $\mathbf{p}'_1$ as the vector $\mathbf{p}'_{01} = \mathbf{p}'_1 - \mathbf{p}'_0$. We can scale this vector by u_i and use it to measure from $\mathbf{p}'_0$ to locate the point $\mathbf{p}_b$, on the bottom edge. We can use a similar process for edge 2-3 to locate the

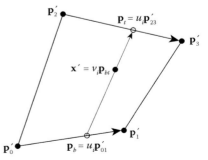

point $\mathbf{p}_t$ on the top edge. Using these points to form the vector $\mathbf{p}_{bt} = \mathbf{p}_t - \mathbf{p}_b$, we can scale this vector by v_i and use it to measure from $\mathbf{p}_b$ to locate the transformed vertex $\mathbf{x}'$.

This seems like a lot of work, but thankfully bilinear interpolation can be made much easier. The process we described above is equivalent to taking a sum of the lattice vertices, weighted by how close they are, in the u and v directions, from the model vertex we are trying to locate. The position of the modified vertex is given by

$$\mathbf{x}' = (1 - u_i)(1 - v_i)\mathbf{p}'_0 + u_i(1 - v_i)\mathbf{p}'_1 + (1 - u_i)v_i\mathbf{p}'_2 + u_iv_i\mathbf{p}'_3.$$

The reader might want to verify this equation by expanding and combining the calculations described in the previous paragraph.

In a physically based simulation, this process needs to be converted to 3D. This is also quite easy. Each lattice cell is a rectangular solid in 3D, and fractional distances within a cell are measured in (u, v, w) coordinates. Note that to maintain a right-handed coordinate system, the w value should be 0 at the back of the cell and 1 at the front. The interpolation used is trilinear interpolation, taking a weighted sum of the positions of the eight vertices of the lattice cell containing the model vertex, as given by

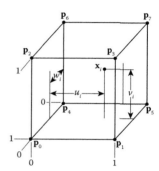

$$\begin{aligned}
\mathbf{x}' = {} & (1 - u_i)(1 - v_i)w_i\mathbf{p}'_0 + u_i(1 - v_i)w_i\mathbf{p}'_1 \\
& + (1 - u_i)v_iw_i\mathbf{p}'_2 + u_iv_iw_i\mathbf{p}'_3 \\
& + (1 - u_i)(1 - v_i)(1 - w_i)\mathbf{p}'_4 + u_i(1 - v_i)(1 - w_i)\mathbf{p}'_5 \\
& + (1 - u_i)v_i(1 - w_i)\mathbf{p}'_6 + u_iv_i(1 - w_i)\mathbf{p}'_7.
\end{aligned}$$

The 3D lattice would typically be sized and positioned by creating an axis-aligned bounding box around the model. The bounding box would then be broken into rectangular cells, by uniformly subdividing along each of the three axes. Each vertex of the model would then be mapped to the cell of the lattice it is contained in, and (u, v, w) coordinates assigned to the vertex. The easiest way to make the lattice deformable is by representing each cell edge by a strut, and supplying diagonal struts across each cell face and across its diagonals, to maintain structural stability. The simulation would involve only the deformable lattice, while at each timestep the (x, y, z) coordinates of each vertex are calculated relative to the lattice, using trilinear interpolation. The samurai animation sequence shown in Figure 8.7 was done using a lattice constructed in this way.

A tetrahedral mesh can serve as an alternative to a lattice deformer. With a bounding tetrahedral mesh, a set of tetrahedra are created to encompass the model. A potential advantage over the lattice deformers is that the tetrahedral mesh bounding volume can potentially be much closer to the original object than an

FIGURE 8.7 A lattice deformer being used to animate a complex samurai model. (Courtesy of Zach Shore.)

axis-aligned bounding lattice would be. For a tetrahedral mesh, each of the vertices of the object is located inside of one tetrahedron and expressed with barycentric coordinates relative to the four vertices (see Appendix F). As the tetrahedral mesh deforms, the object inside will deform along with it.

8.7 CLOTH MODELING

Woven cloth is especially interesting for animators, since a wide variety of animatable objects, from clothing to flags to bed sheets to tents, are made from woven cloth. Because of its underlying structure, woven cloth can be cut, sewn, pressed, and formed in ways that facilitate the design of complex garments and structures. And, when it folds and drapes it forms interesting complex shapes, and has a graceful flowing motion when moved through the air, as demonstrated by the examples in Figure 8.8. Particle methods for the simulation of woven cloth were first introduced in the paper *A Physically-Based Particle Model of Woven Cloth* by Breen, House, and Getto [Breen et al., 1992], and later refined to produce predictable behavior of

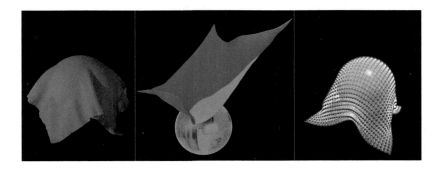

FIGURE 8.8 Examples of woven cloth draping over spheres. (From left to right: Courtesy of Timothy Curtis, Le Liu, Brian Peasley.)

particular cloth types [Breen et al., 1994]. Another landmark in the cloth simulation literature was the paper *Large Steps in Cloth Simulation* by Baraff and Witkin [1998], which provided the structure of a cloth simulation algorithm that allowed timesteps large enough to make it practical to consider adding simulated clothing to animated characters.

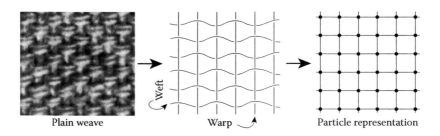

Plain weave   Warp   Particle representation

The figure above-left shows a magnified view of a section of plain-woven cloth, and the middle figure indicates how the weave is structured. Parallel warp yarns are tightly stretched on a loom. Weft yarns are woven across the warp yarns, and in a plain weave, go alternately under and over the warp yarns. As each new weft yarn is added, it is beaten down firmly against the weft yarns that are already in place. When the weaving is finished and the cloth is removed from the loom, the release of tension on the warp pulls all of the yarns tightly together, creating a structure that is held together by frictional forces and the interlocking of tiny fibers. The resulting structure is not so much a homogeneous material, like foil, plastic, or paper, but rather a mechanical structure at a micro scale. The right-hand figure shows how this structure is turned into a model for simulation. Each yarn crossing point is represented by a small point mass, and the warp and weft yarns are treated as connections between these points, creating a lattice of small quadrilaterals with mass points at the corners. Since the scale of a typical woven fabric is such that there are tens or several tens of warp yarns woven to create a single centimeter of fabric, the number of lattice cells in a square meter of fabric will be too large to be practical for simulation. Consequently, simulation models usually represent the fabric at a much coarser resolution, while maintaining the same pattern of connectivity that exists in the real cloth.

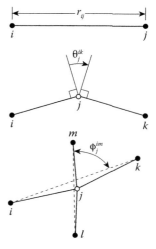

Cloth simulation is governed by forces meant to represent the types of bending and stretching that occur in the cloth as it moves. All particle-based cloth models attempt to account for at least three different types of forces within the material, and represent these forces as occurring at the crossing points of the warp and weft yarns. These forces are due to tensile stretching, out-of-plane bending, and in-plane shearing, within the woven structure. The above figure shows how these forces are parameterized. Tensile stretching is a function of the distance r_{ij} between any pair of adjacent points i and j in the lattice, and are equal and opposite at each vertex. If vertices i, j, and k are adjacent vertices on a warp or a weft yarn, out-of-plane bending at vertex j along this yarn can be parameterized by the angle θ_j^{ik} formed by perpendiculars to the edges i–j, and j–k. If vertices l, j, and m are adjacent vertices on a weft yarn, crossing the warp yarn with adjacent vertices i, j, and k, in-plane shearing is parameterized at vertex j by the angle ϕ_j^{im} formed between the straight lines connecting weft vertices i and k, and warp vertices l and m.

Unlike the struts described in Section 8.1, a realistic cloth simulation will not use a linear spring model, since the forces produced in cloth are highly nonlinear. In addition, the tensile strength of woven cloth tends to be very high compared with its strength preventing shearing. And, the strength preventing shearing tends to be very high compared with its strength preventing out-of-plane bending. In a cloth model attempting to be reasonably true to the real material, tensile strength should be one or two orders of magnitude larger than shear strength, and shear strength should be at least an order of magnitude larger than out-of-plane bending strength. A small experiment with a pocket handkerchief will prove this to you. Hold the handkerchief on two opposite sides and attempt to stretch it. Then, still holding two opposite sides, pull it tight and move the sides parallel to each other in opposite directions. Finally, lay the handkerchief across your hand and let it drape down. You will note that you have to pull very hard to stretch the handkerchief even a small amount. Shearing the handkerchief by pulling the edges in opposite directions is much easier but there is some noticeable resistance. On the other hand, out-of-plane bending is achieved simply due to the tiny gravitational forces acting on the light handkerchief. If high fidelity to woven cloth is desired, force functions parameterized by r_{ij}, θ_j^{ik}, and ϕ_j^{im} must be defined that attempt to match actual measured forces in real cloth. Attempting to do this accurately is beyond the scope of this book, but the interested reader might want to investigate attempts that have been made to do exactly this, using a mechanical testing system known as the Kawabata Evaluation System [Kawabata, 1980; Pabst et al., 2008], or using photogrammetry techniques to track the deformation of cloth under loads [Bhat et al., 2003].

Here we will confine ourselves to constructing a model approximating real woven cloth, using a spring configuration that will allow the generation of the three types of forces used in these models. The above figure shows how springs can be connected to achieve a cloth-like behavior. We begin with a set of particles uniformly spaced on a rectangular grid. We can consider the the warp direction to be vertical and the weft direction to be horizontal. Tensile forces are realized

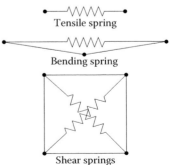
Tensile spring

Bending spring

Shear springs

by connecting springs between each particle and its immediate neighbors in the warp and weft directions. These springs should have their rest lengths set to the initial distance between the particles. Out of plane bending forces are realized by connecting springs from each particle to their one-away neighbor in the warp and weft directions, with their rest lengths set to twice the initial distance between neighboring particles. Shear forces are realized by connecting springs across the diagonals of each square formed by four neighboring particles.

To account for the high tensile strength of woven cloth, the tensile springs should have a high spring constant, and would typically be nonlinear. Instead of the spring's force being proportional to the difference between its actual length and its rest length, it can be made proportional to a power of this length difference. Making the force cubic is convenient, since it preserves the sign of the force. The bending springs should be at least two orders of magnitude weaker than the tensile springs, so that they have negligible effect when being stretched in the tensile direction but will still provide some force to prevent bending when the three particles that it extends over move out of line with each other, as indicated in the diagram above. The shear springs should be of intermediate strength, at least an order of magnitude weaker than the tensile springs.

Since the tensile springs in a woven cloth model must be made very stiff, and thus have very small time constants, an explicit integration scheme will need to use very small timesteps to keep the tensile springs stable. Since the bending and shearing time constants are orders of magnitude larger, this is especially inefficient. For this reason, it is usually recommended to use implicit integration for computing a cloth model, so that large timesteps can be taken without resulting in instability. Although this does solve the instability problem, it also introduces a large amount of numerical damping, which may be undesirable for animators, because it tends to reduce the responsiveness of the cloth, giving it a heavy look. Other approaches to dealing with instability, due to high tensile strength springs, have been to reduce the tensile spring constants but adjust vertex positions at each timestep to limit tensile stretching to a small percentage of the rest length [Provot, 1995; Ozgen and Kallmann, 2011], to replace the tensile springs by length constraints [House et al., 1996; Goldenthal et al., 2007], or to run the simulation using different timesteps for the tensile, shear, and bending components [Müller, 2008].

8.8 SUMMARY

The primary points to remember from this chapter were:

- The spring-mass-damper system provides a flexible means to define behavior between pairs of points.

- Spring-mass-damper systems act as a combination of an oscillating behavior and an exponential damping function.

- When creating a spring-mass-damper system, choosing good parameters is critical to getting the desired behavior. It is usually the *ratios* between the mass, spring constant, and damping coefficient that govern the behavior.

- Springs can be assembled between point masses to form 3D structures, with springs representing both external and internal edges.

- Sets of springs can be used to define the faces for a 3D object. Forces and collision response impulses can be applied to the edges or faces of the object, and these can be propagated to the point masses.

- Torsional springs can be used to maintain the angle between faces of an object, applying a torque to each face to maintain a given angle.

- Spring-mass-damper systems serve as the foundation for many different simulation-based computations. These include lattice deformers and simulations of cloth behavior.

III

Rigid Bodies and Constrained Dynamics

CHAPTER 9

Rigid Body Dynamics

WHILE THE SPRINGY-MESH MODELS we have seen previously offer some nice characteristics, they do not capture the true behavior of a 3D rigid object. In the real world, we do not have mass located at just a point, and we do not have edges and faces with no mass of their own. Instead, real objects are made up of volumes with some density, and an accurate simulation treats them this way.

Rigid body simulation allows us to simulate the tumbling behavior of solid 3D objects like the coins shown in Figure 9.1. The term *rigid bodies* refers to objects that do not deform as they go through motions and collisions. Because rigid bodies do not deform, we do not need to keep track of the state for each individual vertex, but rather just the state of the overall object. However, since we are no longer dealing with just points, the equations of motion become more complicated, as does the collision response.

9.1   RIGID BODY STATE

To represent a rigid object, we need to first keep track of the center of mass of the object. The center of mass will have a 3D position $\mathbf{x}$ and a velocity $\mathbf{v}$, just like we have had for points. Coupled with the mass of the overall object, we can think of modeling the linear or translational part of the rigid body's motion in the same way that we kept track of particles.

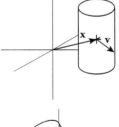

However, rigid bodies also have an *orientation*, i.e., the way that the object is rotated about its center of mass. Orientation is sometimes referred to as *pose*. Objects have three *degrees of freedom* in orientation. That is, specifying orientation in 3D requires knowing three values. There are multiple ways of representing and operating on orientation, including quaternions and Euler angles, which we will discuss later in this chapter.

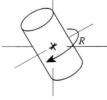

For now, though, we will give our description using a rotation matrix R since we are already familiar with this way of describing orientation. Recall (see Appendix D)

FIGURE 9.1 Coins tossed onto a tabletop. (Courtesy of Zhaoxin Ye.)

that a rotation matrix describes how we move from one coordinate frame to another. Now, we will take the point of view that we are using them to describe how the object being simulated is transformed from its original (or "base") orientation to its current orientation.

We will assume that each object is described originally with its base orientation, and with its center of mass at the origin.[*] This will be called the *body coordinate system* or *local coordinate system*, since it is a coordinate system describing the rigid body by itself, ignoring all the rest of the world.

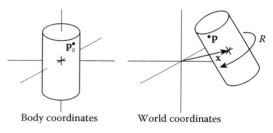

The rigid body, and the other objects we are simulating, will exist within the *world coordinate system*. To specify how the rigid body is placed in the world, we specify its position $\mathbf{x}$ and its orientation R, which defines a way of transforming between local and world coordinates. So, a point $\mathbf{p}_0$ in local coordinates will correspond to a point

$$\mathbf{p} = \mathbf{x} + R\mathbf{p}_0 \qquad (9.1)$$

in world coordinates.

We want to see how this point in world coordinates will change over time, so we can take its derivative with respect to time. The time derivative of Equation 9.1, denoted by the ˙ notation, is

$$\dot{\mathbf{p}} = \dot{\mathbf{x}} + R\dot{\mathbf{p}}_0 + \dot{R}\mathbf{p}_0.$$

---

[*]It is possible to work with an object whose center of mass in its local coordinate frame is not at the origin, but this complicates the mathematics significantly.

Notice that $\dot{\mathbf{p}}_0 = \mathbf{0}$ since the local coordinates of the object do not change for a rigid body, so this reduces to

$$\dot{\mathbf{p}} = \mathbf{v} + \dot{R}\mathbf{p}_0. \qquad (9.2)$$

This is a simple result, but leaves us needing to determine what the rate of change of orientation is, i.e., what is the time derivative of rotation matrix R.

To understand how the orientation is changing over time, we need to introduce the concept of *angular velocity*. Just as linear velocity describes the rate of change in position, angular velocity describes the rate of change in orientation. Typically, people think of this as "the way an object is spinning." Both linear velocity and angular velocity are typically represented as 3D

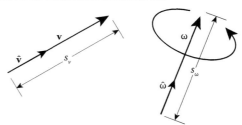

vectors. As shown in the figure, linear velocity $\mathbf{v}$ can be thought of as a speed $s_v = \|\mathbf{v}\|$, in the direction $\hat{\mathbf{v}} = \mathbf{v}/s_v$, or $\mathbf{v} = s_v\hat{\mathbf{v}}$. Angular velocity is usually represented by the Greek letter $\boldsymbol{\omega}$, and consists of an angular speed $s_\omega = \|\boldsymbol{\omega}\|$ and a direction $\hat{\boldsymbol{\omega}} = \boldsymbol{\omega}/s_\omega$, or $\boldsymbol{\omega} = s_\omega\hat{\boldsymbol{\omega}}$. The difference is that in the case of angular velocity, the direction $\hat{\boldsymbol{\omega}}$ is not the direction of motion, but instead gives the axis around which the object is spinning, and the speed s_ω is the rate of rotation, typically measured in radians per second. The convention that we will follow in this book is that the positive direction of rotation follows the right-hand rule (see Appendix D).

Given an orientation matrix R and an angular velocity $\boldsymbol{\omega}$, we need to understand how R changes with time. We know (Appendix D) that the columns of R are the direction vectors of the rotated coordinate frame, i.e.,

$$R = \begin{bmatrix} \hat{\mathbf{u}}_x & \hat{\mathbf{u}}_y & \hat{\mathbf{u}}_z \end{bmatrix}.$$

Therefore, the first time derivative of R is formed from the derivatives of these direction vectors:

$$\dot{R} = \begin{bmatrix} \dot{\hat{\mathbf{u}}}_x & \dot{\hat{\mathbf{u}}}_y & \dot{\hat{\mathbf{u}}}_z \end{bmatrix}.$$

Now, determining $\dot{R}$ is reduced to the problem of determining the derivative of a vector undergoing rigid rotation—i.e., a vector that is rotating but not changing length.

To understand this, let us first look at how a rotating point changes with time due to its angular velocity $\boldsymbol{\omega}$. The point is at position $\mathbf{p}$ relative to a center of rotation $\mathbf{x}$, and the vector from the center of rotation to $\mathbf{p}$ is $\mathbf{r}$. The problem is then to determine the rate of change of the $\mathbf{r}$. Since $\mathbf{p}$ is rotating with angular velocity $\boldsymbol{\omega}$, its instantaneous velocity must be perpendicular to the vectors $\mathbf{r}$ and $\boldsymbol{\omega}$, otherwise it would be changing its distance from $\mathbf{x}$ or its distance from the axis of rotation. Therefore, if we apply the right-hand rule for rotation about

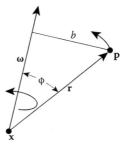

$\boldsymbol{\omega}$ the direction of this instantaneous velocity is given by $\boldsymbol{\omega} \times \mathbf{r}$. From inspection of the figure, it can be seen that the radius of rotation is given by $b = \|\mathbf{r}\| \sin \phi$, where ϕ is the angle between $\mathbf{r}$ and $\boldsymbol{\omega}$. The magnitude of the rate of change of $\mathbf{p}$ will be $\|\boldsymbol{\omega}\| b$, or $\|\boldsymbol{\omega}\| \|\mathbf{r}\| \sin \phi$. Thus, the direction of the rate of change of $\mathbf{p}$ is in the direction of the cross-product $\boldsymbol{\omega} \times \mathbf{r}$ and its magnitude is identical to the magnitude of the same cross-product, leading us to conclude that

$$\dot{\mathbf{r}} = \boldsymbol{\omega} \times \mathbf{r}.$$

Applying this result to the rotation matrix, we can now write the time derivative of the rotation matrix as

$$\dot{R} = \begin{bmatrix} \boldsymbol{\omega} \times \hat{\mathbf{u}}_x & \boldsymbol{\omega} \times \hat{\mathbf{u}}_y & \boldsymbol{\omega} \times \hat{\mathbf{u}}_z \end{bmatrix}.$$

This form is not very handy for computation, since we have to individually operate on each column of the matrix R in order to determine its derivative. Fortunately, the cross-product can be written in the form of a matrix by the equivalence relation

$$\mathbf{a} \times \mathbf{b} = a^* \mathbf{b},$$

where the matrix

$$a^* = \begin{bmatrix} 0 & -a_z & a_y \\ a_z & 0 & -a_x \\ -a_y & a_x & 0 \end{bmatrix}.$$

The reader is invited to carry out the cross-product and matrix-vector operations to verify that they are identical.

Using this representation of the cross-product, we arrive at a convenient form for the derivative of the rotation matrix,

$$\dot{R} = \omega^* R.$$

Finally, there is one more factor that we must account for, *inertia*. In order to understand inertia, we will first describe *momentum*. Here again, we have an analogous situation to linear motion. Just as Newton's first law implies that linear momentum is conserved, it also implies that angular momentum is conserved.

We have seen momentum $\mathbf{P}$ in the linear case as the product of mass and velocity,

$$\mathbf{P} = m\mathbf{v}.$$

In the angular case, we have a close analog, where angular momentum $\mathbf{L}$ is defined as the product of moment of inertia I and angular velocity.[*] So,

$$\mathbf{L} = I\boldsymbol{\omega}.$$

---

[*]It is an unfortunate accident of history that the convention of using I for the moment of inertia tensor is identical to the notation I to represent the identity matrix. In situations where there may be confusion, the notation $\mathbf{1}$ may be used for the identity matrix.

Now, while mass m is a scalar value, the moment of inertia I is instead a tensor (i.e., expressed as a 3×3 matrix) that describes how mass is distributed in an object. The matrix form of I allows it to describe how inertia varies in each direction.

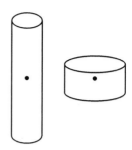

To give an intuitive sense of why the moment of inertia is not just a scalar, consider the two cylinders shown in the figure. They are sized so that they have identical mass; however, the long, thin cylinder will have a different moment of inertia than the short, squat cylinder. You can probably guess that it will take more effort to rotate the long cylinder about a horizontal axis than to rotate the squat cylinder. On the other hand, it will take less effort to rotate the long cylinder about its vertical axis than the squat cylinder. The moment of inertia matrix captures how these differences in mass distribution affect rotational inertia around the three coordinate axes.

You have probably encountered descriptions of inertia and conservation of angular momentum in an introductory physics class. The typical example used to illustrate angular motion is an ice skater spinning on the ice. When the skater's arms are held out far from the body, the moment of inertia is relatively large (for the direction of spin). As the skater's arms are brought into the body, the moment of inertia decreases. This means that the skater will spin faster, since the overall angular momentum is being conserved. You can verify this yourself by sitting on a stool or chair that is spinning while holding your arms out, and seeing how you spin faster by bringing your arms in. The effect is even more pronounced if you hold weights in each hand.

Notice, though, that this effect of inertia varies based on the direction of spin. If the skater, instead of staying upright, were to have fallen down and been spinning while lying flat on the ice, the moment of inertia would be quite different! If you lie on your back on the stool and try to spin, you will spin quite differently than if you are sitting upright, even if your body is in the same position. It should be intuitive, then, that the moment of inertia needs to have a different effect depending on the direction of spin. That is, $I\omega$ will be different in magnitude for one direction of ω than for another, so I cannot be a single scalar value.

Just to clarify terminology, often people will refer to the "moment of inertia" as the moment of inertia for rotation about some specific axis, and refer to the matrix as the moment of inertia tensor (or matrix). We will just use the term "moment of inertia" to refer to the tensor.

A typical representation for I is as a symmetric 3×3 matrix. We will see below how to compute I. An entry of this matrix indicates how much the spin in one direction affects the momentum in another. Since I is a matrix, the overall magnitude of $I\omega$ can vary considerably as ω changes direction.

We can summarize the linear (translational) and rotational components of rigid body motion in the following way:

Linear	Angular
Mass: m	Moment of Inertia: I
Position: $\mathbf{x}$	Orientation: R
Velocity: $\mathbf{v}$	Velocity: $\boldsymbol{\omega}$
Momentum: $\mathbf{P}$	Momentum: $\mathbf{L}$

9.2 PROPERTIES OF RIGID BODIES

In order to simulate rigid bodies, we must know their inherent properties, such as center of mass and moment of inertia. In earlier examples based on particles, we cared only about overall mass, which could be arbitrarily specified by an artist. For realistic rigid body motion, though, properties such as center of mass and moment of inertia must be computed so that they match the geometry of the objects being simulated.

9.2.1 Center of Mass

In order to ensure that an object is centered at its center of mass in the local coordinate frame, you must first compute its center of mass.

The general definition of the center of mass of an object is the point at which the mass is equally distributed in all directions. We can find this by integrating the density-weighted position, as follows:

$$\mathbf{c} = \frac{\int_V \rho(\mathbf{x})\mathbf{x}\,dV}{\int_V \rho(\mathbf{x})\,dV}.$$

Note that we usually cannot compute the integral directly, since we rarely have a continuous definition. Also, we often assume the density is uniform, so that it factors out of the two integrals removing it as a factor in the equation.

If the object were made up of a set of discrete points with mass (as in the springy-mesh models we used before), we could just take a weighted average of the points to find the center of mass. That is, if the points have position $\mathbf{x}_i$ and mass (or weight) m_i, then the center of mass is

$$\mathbf{c} = \frac{\sum m_i \mathbf{x}_i}{\sum m_i}.$$

In 3D computer graphics, most models are typically specified by a triangular mesh of the surface. There are two main ways that we can compute the center of mass from such an object.

Voxelization: One method, which is a direct extension of the point-mass method, is to divide the object into small volumes (voxels), and then treat each of those volumes as a point mass. A typical way of doing this is to define a space encompassing the object, and place a regular 3D grid of points through that space. Each point can be classified as either inside or outside of the object. In the 2D snowman example in the figure, the gray cells are considered as inside since the center point of the cell is inside the snowman. The object is then approximated as a set of points, each with the same mass. This further simplifies the center of mass computation, so that if there are n points in the object

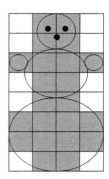

$$\mathbf{c} = \frac{1}{n}\sum \mathbf{x}_i.$$

There are a variety of ways of performing voxelization, and we will describe just one here. To classify points as inside or outside, a common approach that can be used is a ray-shooting test. By shooting a ray from a point, if the ray intersects the surface an odd number of times, that starting point must be inside the object, while an even number of intersections implies that the starting point is outside. For voxelizing an object, though, we can simplify our calculations considerably, since we know that all points lie on a regular grid. If we pick one plane, and shoot rays from outside the encompassing volume along each grid direction, we can classify

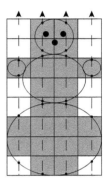

points much more easily. First, by shooting in one of the primary axis directions, the process of intersecting with any polygon is simplified. Second, because several grid points lie along that one ray, we can classify all the points along that one ray at the same time. All points along the ray until the first surface is hit are outside, then all those on the ray until the next surface is hit are inside, and so on. In the 2D snowman figure here, the four rays shown intersect the model several times, as marked with dots. By classifying the centers of the cells relative to these entry and exit points, we can classify all the voxels along one ray. These four rays are sufficient to classify all the voxels as inside or outside.

The voxelized approach is an approximation, but the smaller the voxels, the more accurate the approximation is.

Direct Calculation: There are other methods for calculating the center of mass more precisely. First you can pick a point (any point will do, but typically the origin of the original coordinate system is used), and create tetrahedra where that point is the apex, and the triangles on the surface are the bases. This construction is shown in the figure for a cylinder with hexagonal end caps. The bolded lines show how tetrahedra are defined for two of the front faces and one of the top faces. To finish the construction, all of the

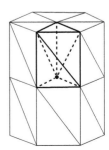

vertices of the remaining faces would also be connected to the central point. The tetrahedral volumes can be computed to determine the mass of each, and the center of mass of each tetrahedron computed from the four vertices. Each tetrahedron then defines a point mass and position, and we can use the weighted sum of these points to find the overall volume. Note, however, that the tetrahedra must have a *signed volume*, i.e., if the apex is on the "inside" of the object relative to that one surface triangle, it has a positive volume, and if it is on the "outside" relative to that one surface triangle, it has a negative volume.

To compute the volume of a tetrahedron, if the vertices of the triangle on the surface are $\mathbf{d}$, $\mathbf{e}$, and $\mathbf{f}$, and the apex point is at the origin, the volume is just

$$V = \frac{1}{6}\mathbf{d} \cdot (\mathbf{e} \times \mathbf{f}).$$

This is a signed volume. If we assume the vertices are in counterclockwise order when viewed from outside the model, it is positive if the origin is inside relative to that face, and negative if it is outside.

Likewise the center of the tetrahedron is the average of the four vertices, one of which is the origin: $\mathbf{x} = \frac{1}{4}(\mathbf{d} + \mathbf{e} + \mathbf{f})$. It is thus relatively easy to compute the center of mass of the object precisely, if we assume uniform density:

> WeightedPosition = 0; Volume = 0;
> **forall the** *Triangles on surface* **do**
> > *Assume triangle vertices are* $\mathbf{d}$, $\mathbf{e}$, *and* $\mathbf{f}$, *and that they are in counterclockwise order when viewed from outside the object.*
> > $V = \frac{1}{6}\mathbf{d} \cdot (\mathbf{e} \times \mathbf{f})$;
> > $\mathbf{x} = \frac{1}{4}(\mathbf{d} + \mathbf{e} + \mathbf{f})$;
> > WeightedPosition = WeightedPosition + $V\mathbf{x}$;
> > Volume = Volume + V;
> **end**
> $\mathbf{c}$ = WeightedPosition / Volume;

9.2.2 Moment of Inertia

When computing the moment of inertia matrix, we will first compute the matrix for the local coordinate frame (i.e., assuming the object's center of mass is at the origin).

The moment of inertia can be represented as a 3×3 matrix whose entries are defined as

$$I = \begin{bmatrix} \int_V (\mathbf{x}_y^2 + \mathbf{x}_z^2)\rho(\mathbf{x})dV & -\int_V (\mathbf{x}_x\mathbf{x}_y)\rho(\mathbf{x})dV & -\int_V (\mathbf{x}_x\mathbf{x}_z)\rho(\mathbf{x})dV \\ -\int_V (\mathbf{x}_x\mathbf{x}_y)\rho(\mathbf{x})dV & \int_V (\mathbf{x}_x^2 + \mathbf{x}_z^2)\rho(\mathbf{x})dV & -\int_V (\mathbf{x}_y\mathbf{x}_z)\rho(\mathbf{x})dV \\ -\int_V (\mathbf{x}_x\mathbf{x}_z)\rho(\mathbf{x})dV & -\int_V (\mathbf{x}_y\mathbf{x}_z)\rho(\mathbf{x})dV & \int_V (\mathbf{x}_x^2 + \mathbf{x}_y^2)\rho(\mathbf{x})dV \end{bmatrix},$$

where $\mathbf{x}_i$ is the i component of the position, $\mathbf{x}$. Again, note that ρ is often treated as a constant, 1. Notice that the matrix is symmetric, and thus there are really just six values to compute.

If we assume we have a set of point masses, this matrix becomes

$$I = \begin{bmatrix} \sum(y_i^2 + z_i^2)m_i & -\sum(x_i y_i)m_i & -\sum(x_i z_i)m_i \\ -\sum(x_i y_i)m_i & \sum(x_i^2 + z_i^2)m_i & -\sum(y_i z_i)m_i \\ -\sum(x_i z_i)m_i & -\sum(y_i z_i)m_i & \sum(x_i^2 + y_i^2)m_i \end{bmatrix},$$

where x_i, y_i, and z_i are the x, y, and z coordinates of the ith point and m_i is its mass.

Again, there is more than one way to compute this matrix in practice.

Voxelization: If we have a voxelized object, as described in the center of mass computation above, we can use these voxels to compute the moment of inertia, using the point-mass formulation given above. We will visit each voxel and sum its contribution to each of the elements of the moment of inertia matrix. As with the center of mass, this is not a precise method, but the finer the grid of voxels, the more accurate it will be. Also, if the masses are all equal, we can factor that out, and just multiply the whole matrix by m_i.

Direct Calculation: The direct calculation of the moment of inertia for a triangulated object is somewhat more complex. The essential process is similar to that for computing center of mass directly: forming tetrahedra and then summing up the contribution from each. However, the contribution for a moment of inertia for each tetrahedron is more complex than for the calculation of the center of mass. Each tetrahedron will have its own local moment of inertia, which must then be offset from the center of mass of the object, using the parallel axis theorem. Other direct approaches involve rewriting volume integrals and surface integrals, and computing more quickly using those.

Specific procedures for computing this moment of inertia matrix directly are more than we will delve into here, but some good references for how to compute this are the papers by Mirtich [1996a] and Eberly [2003].

For some shapes, the moment of inertia is computable as a formula. For instance, the moment of inertia tensor for a solid sphere is

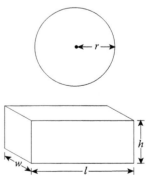

$$I = \begin{bmatrix} \frac{2}{5}mr^2 & 0 & 0 \\ 0 & \frac{2}{5}mr^2 & 0 \\ 0 & 0 & \frac{2}{5}mr^2 \end{bmatrix},$$

and that for a solid box of length l in x, w in z, and h in y is

$$I = \begin{bmatrix} \frac{m}{12}(w^2 + h^2) & 0 & 0 \\ 0 & \frac{m}{12}(l^2 + w^2) & 0 \\ 0 & 0 & \frac{m}{12}(l^2 + h^2) \end{bmatrix}.$$

There are similar formulas for many other basic shapes, such as cylinders. If you know you have such a simple shape, you can write the moment of inertia directly.

Moment of Inertia in World Coordinates: For a rigid object, the moment of inertia I_0 in the local coordinate frame will not change. However, the moment of inertia in world coordinates will change, depending on the current orientation of the object. Each row and column of the moment of inertia matrix corresponds to one of the coordinate directions, so depending on the current orientation of an object, the moment of inertia for that object will change.

Fortunately, if we know the moment of inertia in the local coordinate frame, we can quickly compute it for a different orientation. If our orientation matrix is R, and the moment of inertia in the local coordinate frame is I_0, then the moment of inertia for the object in the world coordinate frame is

$$I = RI_0R^T.$$

You can verify this by examining how each of the elements in the moment of inertia matrix changes for a different orientation. A derivation can also be found in Witkin and Baraff [2001].

As we will see shortly, we often want the inverse of the moment of inertia, I^{-1}. Fortunately, and remembering that for rotation matrices $R^{-1} = R^T$, if we know the inverse of the moment of inertia in local coordinates, the computation is still straightforward:

$$I^{-1} = (RI_0R^T)^{-1}, \quad \text{or} \quad I^{-1} = (R^T)^{-1}I_0^{-1}(R)^{-1}.$$

Therefore,

$$I^{-1} = RI_0^{-1}R^T.$$

9.3 RIGID BODY MOTION

Recall from Section 9.1 that for a rigid body, we have both a linear and an angular state. As we simulate rigid bodies, we must update both of these states. This will allow us to capture both the rotational motion and the translational motion of rigid bodies, like the dominos in Figure 9.2, as they move in space.

First, recall the way that forces are used to update linear position, such as for particles. We have a position $\mathbf{x}$, a mass m, and a velocity $\mathbf{v}$, giving us a linear momentum $\mathbf{P} = m\mathbf{v}$. Notice that for a force $\mathbf{F}$ we have $\mathbf{F} = m\mathbf{a} = m\dot{\mathbf{v}} = \dot{\mathbf{P}}$. That is, the force is the time rate of change of linear momentum.

We have an analogous process for changes in angular momentum, namely that the time rate of change of angular momentum is *torque*.

FIGURE 9.2 Dominoes rotating and translating as they fall and collide with each other. (Courtesy of Jordan Gestring.)

9.3.1 Torque

Torque is the rotational analogy to force. Just as force induces a change in linear momentum, torque induces a change in angular momentum, so

$$\boldsymbol{\tau} = \dot{\mathbf{L}}.$$

In other words, torque is the basic measure for change in angular momentum. To understand the motion of rigid bodies, it is necessary to understand the relationship between torque and force.

Given an object with center of mass $\mathbf{x}$, imagine we are applying a force $\mathbf{f}$ at a point $\mathbf{p}$. Any force applied to a rigid body at a position other than the center of mass will induce a torque. To determine this torque, we first form what is called the *moment arm*, $\mathbf{r} = \mathbf{p} - \mathbf{x}$, i.e., the vector from the center of mass to the point of application of the force. The resulting torque is given by

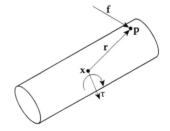

$$\boldsymbol{\tau} = \mathbf{r} \times \mathbf{f}. \qquad (9.3)$$

Notice a few things about torque. First, its magnitude is proportional to both the force and to the length of the moment arm. So, a longer moment arm will mean a greater torque, even with the same applied force. This is the familiar principle of the lever that goes back to Archimedes. Also, the more perpendicular the force is to the moment arm, the stronger the torque, since the cross-product scales the force with the sine of the angle between the moment arm and the force. Finally, notice that the torque is a vector quantity whose direction is perpendicular to both the moment arm and the force. The direction of the torque vector can be thought of as the axis around which the object will spin, due to the torque.

While one could imagine a simulation in which we just apply torque with no forces, the typical conditions in which we encounter torque are based on forces. For example, we might have a spring attached to one point of a rigid object: the spring is applying a force at that point, which induces an overall torque on the object. To calculate torque, we must know both the force, and the position at which the force is applied on an object.

It is important to realize that if a force is applied uniformly over an object, no net torque is induced. Such a force is called a *body force*—gravity and centrifugal force are primary examples of body forces. For example, in a gravitational field the same force is being applied to every molecule of the object, and though each of those forces would create a torque, they will "balance out" over the entire object, with every torque from one part of the object being cancelled by an opposing torque from another part.

Finally, note that the torque applies to the entire rigid body. It can be thought of as the torque "through" the center of mass. Different torques can be combined by vector addition. If we have two torques τ_1 and τ_2 applied to an object, the net torque is $\tau = \tau_1 + \tau_1$.

9.3.2 Updating Rigid Body State

We can consider the state of a rigid body to be

$$\mathbf{S} = \begin{bmatrix} \mathbf{x} \\ R \\ \mathbf{P} \\ \mathbf{L} \end{bmatrix},$$

which consists of the current position and momentum in both linear and angular terms. Therefore, the derivative of this state will be

$$\dot{\mathbf{S}} = \begin{bmatrix} \mathbf{v} \\ \omega^* R \\ \mathbf{F} \\ \tau \end{bmatrix}.$$

Recall that $\mathbf{v} = \frac{1}{m}\mathbf{P}$, and that $\omega = I^{-1}\mathbf{L}$, so velocity information can be directly derived from the state. Also, $\mathbf{F}$ is the total force (i.e., the sum of all forces) on the object, and τ is the total torque (i.e., the sum of all torques) on the object.

We can update the rigid body state by integrating the derivative of the state, just as we have done previously. The only difference is that now the state contains four elements, instead of two, and one of these is a matrix instead of a vector. In an implementation, the state will contain 18 scalar values instead of the 6 in a particle state. Fortunately, we can reduce this to 13 scalar values by representing rotation by a quaternion instead of a matrix.

9.3.3   Quaternion Representation

Although the expression of orientation by a rotation matrix R is the method we have followed up until now in this book, this method creates problems during integration. Imagine a simple Euler integration technique, considering only the update of orientation. Using matrix notation we would have

$$R^{[n+1]} = R^{[n]} + h\boldsymbol{\omega}^* R^{[n]},$$

which involves the addition of matrices. In most cases, the new orientation matrix, $R^{[n+1]}$, will no longer be an orthonormal set of vectors, and thus the matrix is no longer a true rotation matrix! The consequence for your simulation would be that, over time, your objects may undergo shear or nonuniform scaling, thus changing their shapes. While we could continually modify R to return it to the nearest true rotation matrix, this is a cumbersome process that introduces more potential error. A better option is to use an alternative representation for orientation: quaternions. The mathematical background for quaternions is described in Appendix E.

Just as R expressed a rotation from the original state, we can alternatively use a quaternion $\mathbf{q}$ to represent rotation from the original state. Quaternions have the advantage that they have only four elements that must be integrated, and they do not have a requirement for orthonormality. All that is required to maintain a true rotation is to keep them scaled to unit length. Thus, quaternions accumulate error more slowly than orientation matrices, and are easier to return to a valid orientation.

The derivative of the quaternion orientation is given by

$$\dot{\mathbf{q}} = \frac{1}{2}\boldsymbol{\omega}\mathbf{q}.$$

The proof of this is given below. Note that we must convert $\boldsymbol{\omega}$ into a quaternion $(0, \boldsymbol{\omega})$ to perform the quaternion multiplication.

Now, when integrating, we will end up adding quaternions (e.g., for Euler integration: $\mathbf{q}^{[n+1]} = \mathbf{q}^{[n]} + h\dot{\mathbf{q}}^{[n]}$). Doing this will cause the quaternions to become nonunit quaternions, meaning they are no longer valid representations of orientation. Fortunately, it is easy to correct this by renormalizing all quaternions after each integration—that is divide each quaternion by its magnitude to scale it to length 1.

Thus, the preferred representation of state and its derivative for rigid bodies incorporate quaternions and are given by

$$\mathbf{S} = \begin{bmatrix} \mathbf{x} \\ \mathbf{q} \\ \mathbf{P} \\ \mathbf{L} \end{bmatrix}, \quad \dot{\mathbf{S}} = \begin{bmatrix} \mathbf{v} \\ \frac{1}{2}\boldsymbol{\omega}\mathbf{q} \\ \mathbf{F} \\ \boldsymbol{\tau} \end{bmatrix}.$$

A note here is that although we no longer have the rotation matrix as part of the state, we still need it to compute the moment of inertia tensor in the rotated

Proof that $\dot{\mathbf{q}} = \frac{1}{2}\boldsymbol{\omega}\mathbf{q}$. At time t, the quaternion $\mathbf{q}(t)$ encodes the rotation up to that point in time. We wish to see how the rotation quaternion evolves when subjected to fixed angular velocity $\boldsymbol{\omega} = \hat{\mathbf{u}}\dot{\theta}$ for a small period of time, Δt. Converting the angular velocity to a quaternion and multiplying by the current quaternion we have

$$\mathbf{q}(t+\Delta t) = \left(\cos\frac{\dot{\theta}\Delta t}{2}, \ \hat{\mathbf{u}}\sin\frac{\dot{\theta}\Delta t}{2} \right)\mathbf{q}(t).$$

Differentiating this expression with respect to Δt yields

$$\frac{d\mathbf{q}}{d\Delta t} = \left(-\frac{\dot{\theta}}{2}\sin\frac{\dot{\theta}\Delta t}{2}, \ \hat{\mathbf{u}}\frac{\dot{\theta}}{2}\cos\frac{\dot{\theta}\Delta t}{2} \right)\mathbf{q}(t),$$

or, in the limit as Δt vanishes,

$$\frac{d\mathbf{q}}{dt} = (0, \ \frac{1}{2}\boldsymbol{\omega})\mathbf{q}.$$

In more convenient notation this is written

$$\dot{\mathbf{q}} = \frac{1}{2}\boldsymbol{\omega}\mathbf{q}.$$

coordinate frame of the body. Unfortunately, there is no simple way to update the moment of inertia directly using the quaternion. Fortunately, it is very simple to compute the rotation matrix from the quaternion, as described in Appendix E. Therefore, with this state representation, if we let forces applied at a point $\mathbf{r}$ relative to the center of mass be represented by $\mathbf{f}$ and body forces by $\mathbf{g}$, the elements of the derivative are computed from the state by the sequence of steps:

$$\mathbf{v} = \frac{1}{m}\mathbf{L},$$
$$R = R(\mathbf{q}), \quad \text{i.e., the rotation matrix derived from } \mathbf{q},$$
$$I^{-1} = RI_0^{-1}R^T,$$
$$\boldsymbol{\omega} = I^{-1}\mathbf{L},$$
$$\mathbf{F} = \sum_i \mathbf{g}_i + \sum_j \mathbf{f}_j,$$
$$\boldsymbol{\tau} = \sum_j (\mathbf{r}_j \times \mathbf{f}_j).$$

9.4   IMPLEMENTATION

The algorithm `ComputeRigidDerivative` on the next page encapsulates the process for implementing basic rigid body motion simulation using the quaternion representation of rotation. Notice that we are not including collisions yet. This will be the subject of Chapter 10.

For ease of description, we will show integration for a single rigid body, however it is straightforward to extend this to multiple rigid bodies, by just extending the state vector.

State ComputeRigidDerivative(State S, float m, Matrix3 × 3 I_0^{-1})
State is a vector of three vector elements and a quaternion. The vectors are position
x, linear momentum P, and angular momentum L, and the quaternion is orientation
q. The mass of the object is m, and the inverse of the moment of inertia in its original
(body) coordinate system is I_0^{-1}.
begin

> State $\dot{S}$;
>
> $\dot{S}.x = S.P/m$;
>
> Matrix3 × 3 $R = $ Quaternion2Matrix($S.q$);
> Matrix3 × 3 $I^{-1} = RI_0^{-1}R^T$;
> Vector3 $\omega = I^{-1}L$;
> Quaternion $\omega_q = $ Quaternion$(0, \omega)$;
> $\dot{S}.q = \frac{1}{2}\omega_q\, S.q$;
>
> $\dot{S}.P = 0 = \dot{S}.L = 0$;
> **for each** *Vector3 F_i* **do**
>> $\dot{S}.P \mathrel{+}= F_i$;
>>
>> *compute torque for each non-body force;*
>> **if** F_i *is applied at a point p_i* **then**
>>> Vector3 $r = p_i - S.x$;
>>> $\dot{S}.L \mathrel{+}= r \times F_i$;
>
> **end**
>
> **return** $\dot{S}$;

end

A simple Euler integration of this would proceed as below. It is straightforward to extend this to a different integration scheme.

RigidMotion()
Simulate a rigid body in motion.
begin

> State $S, S_{\text{new}}, \dot{S}$;
>
> Initialize(S, m, I);
>
> **while** $t < t_{max}$ **do**
>> $\dot{S} = $ ComputeRigidDerivative(S, m, I);
>> $S_{\text{new}} = S + \dot{S}h$;
>> Normalize($S_{\text{new}}.q$);
>>
>> **if** $t > t_{output}$ **then**
>>> Output(S_{new});
>>> $t_{output} \mathrel{+}= $ SimulationTimeBetweenOutputs;
>>
>> $S = S_{\text{new}}$;
>> $t \mathrel{+}= h$;
>
> **end**

end

9.5 SUMMARY

Here are some of the main concepts to understand about rigid body dynamics:

- To represent rigid body state, we need to consider not only the position but also the orientation of the object. Likewise, we will have not only linear velocity that describes change in position, but also angular velocity, describing change in orientation.

- Rigid body dynamics requires a representation of the moment of inertia for the object. The moment of inertia is, roughly, the angular motion equivalent to mass for linear motion.

- The moment of inertia is typically expressed as a matrix in the world coordinate system. This matrix can be computed by transforming a matrix expressed in local coordinates.

- Rigid objects can have forces applied, causing change in linear momentum, or torque applied, causing changes in angular momentum. Force applied at a single point on an object generates a corresponding torque.

- Representing and computing the orientation of an object can be done in multiple ways, including rotation matrices and quaternions. However, quaternions provide a more compact form that is more robust to errors introduced by numerical computation.

CHAPTER 10

Rigid Body Collisions and Contacts

A S FIGURE 10.1 DEMONSTRATES, some of the most interesting rigid body motion comes about when rigid bodies come into contact. Collisions create some of the most spectacular effects, but having objects come to rest in stacked and piled situations is also visually interesting.

Also, collisions are one of the most common ways that objects receive changes in angular momentum. While forces such as gravity that act on the entire body (and thus do not produce torque) are common, it is less common for a model to include continuous forces applied at a point, which would induce rotation.

In this chapter, we discuss how collisions between rigid bodies can be handled.

10.1 COLLISIONS OF RIGID BODIES

To illustrate the process for finding and resolving collisions, we first give a simple example of one moving object and one stationary object, and then expand to pairs of moving objects.

Recall that handling collisions involves three phases: collision detection, collision determination, and collision response. In Section 8.5 we already described the basic collision detection and determination process, and it would be worthwhile reviewing that section before proceeding. The three key points to take away are as follows:

- Collision testing for polygon objects can be reduced to vertex-face and edge-edge collisions—all other interesting cases can be reduced to some combination of these.

- Vertex-face collisions are done using point-polygon intersection methods.

- Edge-edge collisions are done by finding the closest point between the two edges, and checking to see if it has moved from one side to the other of the plane defined by a point on one of the edges and the cross-product between the edges.

FIGURE 10.1 A rigid ball crashes into a collection of rigid blocks. (Courtesy of Alex Beaty.)

FIGURE 10.2 The cue ball breaks the rack. (Courtesy of Christopher Thomas.)

Moving surfaces, rotational motion, and higher-order integration all make the collision detection process more difficult. In particular, it can be possible for a simulation of an object that is spinning quickly to "miss" a collision that occurs during a timestep, as a point on the object sweeps through some other object. Even if a collision is detected, it can be difficult to estimate the fraction of the timestep at which the collision occurred, since it is undergoing nonlinear motion, and often is integrated with a higher-order integrator.

We will have much more to say about ways to speed up collision detection in practical ways in Section 10.2. For now, assume that we can determine the point in time (within some tolerance) at which two objects collide.

Collision determination involves finding the collision point $\mathbf{p}$ where there is a vertex-face or edge-edge collision. Typically this collision determination stage occcurs during collision detection.

Our challenge, therefore, is in determining what the collision response should be in the rigid body state. This will allow us to capture the interesting motion, like the pool ball break shown in Figure 10.2, that is the result of the response to rigid body collisions.

10.1.1 Frictionless Collision with a Static Object

We first assume that we have a moving object that we designate with the subscript a, colliding with a static, unmoving object b. The moving object will have position $\mathbf{x}_a$, linear velocity $\mathbf{v}_a$, and angular velocity $\boldsymbol{\omega}_a$. We assume that the collision is at the point

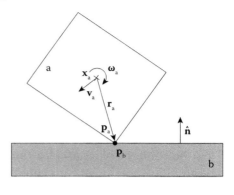

$$\mathbf{p} = \mathbf{p}_a = \mathbf{x}_a + \mathbf{r}_a.$$

Thus, $\mathbf{r}_a$ is defined as the vector from the center of mass $\mathbf{x}_a$ to the collision point $\mathbf{p}$. $\mathbf{p}_a$ denotes the point of collision on the moving object, while $\mathbf{p}_b$ denotes the point of collision on the static object.

While it is obvious that $\mathbf{p}_a = \mathbf{p}_b$, the velocities of the points are different, with $\dot{\mathbf{p}}_b = 0$ and

$$\dot{\mathbf{p}}_a = \mathbf{v}_a + \boldsymbol{\omega}_a \times \mathbf{r}_a.$$

Just as in our collisions with springy meshes, we will assume that we have a normal $\hat{\mathbf{n}}$ for the collision. For a vertex-face collision, $\hat{\mathbf{n}}$ is the face normal, while for an edge-edge collision, $\hat{\mathbf{n}}$ is formed from the cross product of the two edge vectors.

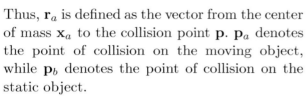

We will decompose the relative velocity along this collision normal, obtaining both a normal component to the velocity and a tangential component. The velocity in the normal direction prior to collision will be

$$v^- = \dot{\mathbf{p}}_a \cdot \hat{\mathbf{n}}.$$

The superscript $-$ indicates that this is the velocity at the time of collision but just before the collision response. A superscript $+$ will indicate a value immediately after collision response. Assuming the moving object is on the positive side of the normal $\hat{\mathbf{n}}$, we must have $v^- < 0$ for there to be a collision response, since otherwise the objects are moving apart.

We will consider here only collision response in the normal direction, ignoring the frictional component in the tangential direction.

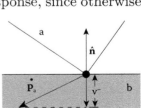

If we assume an elastic collision, similar to the one defined in Section 3.2.1, we should have a velocity in the normal direction after collision of

$$v^+ = -c_r v^-, \tag{10.1}$$

where c_r is the coefficient of restitution.

We will obtain this change by applying an *impulse*

$$\mathbf{J} = j\hat{\mathbf{n}}$$

to the body at the collision point. The only question is what j should be. An impulse can be thought of as a *delta function*, which is a function that obtains an infinitely large value for an infinitesimally small amount of time. Such a function mimics applying a very large force for a very short amount of time, the combination of which results in a finite change in momentum. Of course, this is just an approximation of what really happens during the collision, but at the time scale of a rigid body simulation this proves to be a very good approximation.

If we apply an impulse $\mathbf{J}$ at point $\mathbf{p}$, the impulse will change both the linear and angular momentum of the object, as given by

$$\Delta \mathbf{P} = \mathbf{J}, \quad \text{and} \tag{10.2}$$

$$\Delta \mathbf{L} = \mathbf{r}_a \times \mathbf{J} = j(\mathbf{r}_a \times \hat{\mathbf{n}}). \tag{10.3}$$

Thus, the change in linear velocity is

$$\Delta \mathbf{v}_a = \frac{1}{m}\Delta \mathbf{P}, \quad \text{or} \quad \Delta \mathbf{v}_a = \frac{1}{m}j\hat{\mathbf{n}},$$

and the change in angular velocity is

$$\Delta \boldsymbol{\omega}_a = I^{-1}\Delta \mathbf{L}, \quad \text{or} \quad \Delta \boldsymbol{\omega}_a = jI^{-1}(\mathbf{r}_a \times \hat{\mathbf{n}}).$$

Therefore, the final velocity after the collision is

$$\dot{\mathbf{p}}_a^+ = (\mathbf{v}_a + \Delta \mathbf{v}_a) + (\boldsymbol{\omega}_a + \Delta \boldsymbol{\omega}_a) \times \mathbf{r}_a$$
$$= \mathbf{v}_a + \boldsymbol{\omega}_a \times \mathbf{r}_a + \Delta \mathbf{v}_a + \Delta \boldsymbol{\omega}_a \times \mathbf{r}_a$$
$$= \dot{\mathbf{p}}_a + \Delta \mathbf{v}_a + \Delta \boldsymbol{\omega}_a \times \mathbf{r}_a,$$

or

$$\dot{\mathbf{p}}_a^+ = \dot{\mathbf{p}}_a + j\left(\frac{1}{m}\hat{\mathbf{n}} + I^{-1}(\mathbf{r}_a \times \hat{\mathbf{n}}) \times \mathbf{r}_a\right).$$

Remembering that our interest is only in the normal direction, we can take the dot product with the normal, yielding

$$\hat{\mathbf{n}} \cdot \dot{\mathbf{p}}_a^+ = \hat{\mathbf{n}} \cdot \left[\dot{\mathbf{p}}_a + j\left(\frac{1}{m}\hat{\mathbf{n}} + I^{-1}(\mathbf{r}_a \times \hat{\mathbf{n}}) \times \mathbf{r}_a\right)\right], \quad \text{or}$$

$$v^+ = v^- + j\left[\frac{1}{m} + \hat{\mathbf{n}} \cdot \left(I^{-1}(\mathbf{r}_a \times \hat{\mathbf{n}}) \times \mathbf{r}_a\right)\right].$$

Now if we substitute Equation 10.1 for v^+, we have

$$-c_r v^- - v^- = j\left[\frac{1}{m} + \hat{\mathbf{n}} \cdot \left(I^{-1}(\mathbf{r}_a \times \hat{\mathbf{n}}) \times \mathbf{r}_a\right)\right],$$

and therefore,

$$j = \frac{-(1+c_r)v^-}{\frac{1}{m} + \hat{\mathbf{n}} \cdot \left(I^{-1}(\mathbf{r}_a \times \hat{\mathbf{n}}) \times \mathbf{r}_a\right)}. \tag{10.4}$$

So, to determine a collision response, we first calculate j using Equation 10.4. Then, given j, we can form $\mathbf{J} = j\hat{\mathbf{n}}$, and use this to update both $\mathbf{P}$ and $\mathbf{L}$ according to Equations 10.2 and 10.3. Although the formula for j might appear complex, all components of the formula, c_r, v^-, m, $\hat{\mathbf{n}}$, I^{-1}, and $\mathbf{r}_a$, are easy to compute from known quantities.

10.1.2 Frictionless Collision of Two Moving Objects

The collision response for a pair of moving objects closely follows that for a single moving object colliding with a static object. Assume that we have determined a collision point $\mathbf{p}$ where objects a and b are colliding. In reference to the individual objects, this is defined

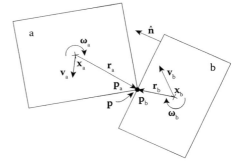

$$\mathbf{x}_a + \mathbf{r}_a = \mathbf{p}_a = \mathbf{p} = \mathbf{p}_b = \mathbf{x}_b + \mathbf{r}_b.$$

Although the positions of $\mathbf{p}_a$ and $\mathbf{p}_b$ are the same, the velocities of the points are different, with

$$\dot{\mathbf{p}}_a = \mathbf{v}_a + \boldsymbol{\omega}_a \times \mathbf{r}_a, \quad \text{and}$$
$$\dot{\mathbf{p}}_b = \mathbf{v}_b + \boldsymbol{\omega}_b \times \mathbf{r}_b.$$

As in the case of static collision, we can define a normal $\hat{\mathbf{n}}$ for the collision, formed from either the face normal of one object (in the case of a face-vertex collision) or the cross-product of the colliding edge vectors (for an edge-edge collision). We will take this normal to be facing from object b, toward object a.

We will again use the superscript $-$ to indicate velocity at the time of collision but just before the collision response and a superscript $+$ to indicate a value immediately after collision response.

We want to compute the relative velocity in the normal direction,

$$v_{rel}^- = \hat{\mathbf{n}} \cdot (\dot{\mathbf{p}}_a^- - \dot{\mathbf{p}}_b^-), \tag{10.5}$$

at the instant of collision between the objects.

If not done already in the collision determination phase, we should check the relative velocity between the objects in the normal direction, to ensure that the objects are moving toward each other. Since object a is on the positive side of the normal, the requirement is that

$$v_{rel}^- < 0.$$

We will apply an impulse $\mathbf{J}_a = j\hat{\mathbf{n}}$ to object a, and the equal and opposite impulse $\mathbf{J}_b = -j\hat{\mathbf{n}}$ to object b. As in the collision with a static object, our goal is to find the magnitude j of this impulse.

By following the same derivation used to obtain Equation 10.4, but now including both bodies, we find the required impulse magnitude

$$j = \frac{-(1+c_r)v_{rel}^-}{\frac{1}{m_a} + \frac{1}{m_b} + \hat{\mathbf{n}} \cdot \left(I_a^{-1}(\mathbf{r}_a \times \hat{\mathbf{n}}) \times \mathbf{r}_a + I_b^{-1}(\mathbf{r}_b \times \hat{\mathbf{n}}) \times \mathbf{r}_b\right)}. \tag{10.6}$$

The resulting updates in momenta and angular momenta are

$$\Delta\mathbf{P}_a = j\hat{\mathbf{n}} \qquad\qquad \Delta\mathbf{L}_a = j(\mathbf{r}_a \times \hat{\mathbf{n}})$$
$$\Delta\mathbf{P}_b = -j\hat{\mathbf{n}} \qquad\qquad \Delta\mathbf{L}_b = -j(\mathbf{r}_b \times \hat{\mathbf{n}})$$

10.2 COLLISION DETECTION

In a highly dynamic scene, there can be many different objects moving around, each with complex geometry. It is reasonable to have dozens, hundreds, or even thousands of objects simultaneously in motion and colliding with each other, as in Figure 10.3. It is also common that each of the objects may have complex geometry, making the problem even more difficult than handling the simple cubes in the figure. To determine whether there are any collisions occurring, performing an $O(N^2)$ pairwise comparison between pairs of N different geometric elements becomes impracticably slow as the number of objects becomes large. As a result, a variety of techniques have been developed to improve the performance of collision detection.

FIGURE 10.3 A large collection of falling, colliding blocks. (Courtesy of Jay Steele.)

These collision detection techniques tend to fall into two categories, labeled *broad phase* and
narrow phase. The broad phase
refers to trying to find out whether

Broad phase – separated   Broad phase – not separated   Broad phase – not separated
                     Narrow phase – not colliding   Narrow phase – colliding

or not two objects moving in space are clearly separated so that a collision cannot
occur. This is meant to be a conservative test, to eliminate pairs of objects that
cannot possibly be colliding. Following this, the narrow phase is designed to look
at the geometric elements in two individual objects, and to identify whether, and
where, there is a collision. The figure shows the three possible cases that can occur.
The pair of stars on the left will not be passed to the narrow phase detection algorithm because they are clearly separated, whereas the middle and right-hand stars
will be tested by the narrow phase. Only the stars on the right will be detected as
actually colliding.

10.2.1   Bounding Volumes

Both the broad phase and the narrow phase rely on the notion of a *bounding volume*.
A bounding volume is a region that encompasses all of the object or geometry that
is being tested for collision. The bounding volume should have geometry that is
much simpler than that of the object or geometry it surrounds.

The key idea of bounding volumes is: if there is not a collision with the bounding
volume, then there cannot be a collision with any of the geometry within the
bounding volume. Thus, if we find that a bounding volume is not colliding with
some other region, we have eliminated all the objects and geometry within that
region from collision.

There is a variety of bounding volume styles, with each style having its own
positives and negatives. We will review the most common ones here, giving a brief
description of each and highlighting some of the advantages and disadvantages
relative to other bounding volumes.

Spheres: A *bounding sphere* encloses the geometry of the
object within a sphere. It stores a position of the center (x, y, z)
and a radius r.

Bounding sphere

Computing: For an entire object, it is common to fix the position of the center to be the center of mass. If the center is not
given, then finding the center for a minimal bounding sphere
is surprisingly hard, and most practical algorithms are only
approximate. If you need to compute this, Ritter's algorithm
[Ritter, 1990] is relatively straightforward and provides a reasonable approximation.
Once the center is determined, the radius is determined by examining all vertices
and finding the distance to the farthest vertex.

To detect overlap between two spheres, the distance between their centers can be calculated, and this compared to the sum of the radii. To avoid the square root operation when computing distance, often the square of the distance will be compared to the square of the sum of the radii, as in the expression

$$(x_1 - x_2)^2 + (y_1 - y_2)^2 + (z_1 - z_2)^2 < (r_1 + r_2)^2.$$

If the left-hand side is less than the right-hand side, the spheres are overlapping, and the objects inside might be colliding.

Advantages: For a sphere centered at an object's center of mass, the bounding sphere is independent of the orientation of the object. As an object moves, only the position of the center needs to be updated; the radius does not change. Detecting collisions between spheres is reasonably fast, though not as fast as other bounding volumes.

Disadvantages: Spheres tend to be much larger in volume than the objects they enclose. This empty space tends to lead to more "false-positive" intersections than with the other bounding volume types. If the sphere is not centered on the object's center of mass, then the computation of the bounding sphere is somewhat more complicated, though this only needs to be done once.

AABBs: An *Axis-Aligned Bounding Box (AABB)* is a box aligned to the world x, y, and z axes. Storing an AABB consists of storing the minimum and maximum extents along each axis. These six numbers are stored either as minimum and maximum values $(x_{min}, x_{max}, y_{min}, y_{max}, z_{min}, z_{max})$, or else as a center (x, y, z) and half-extents in each direction $(x_{ext}, y_{ext}, z_{ext})$. Notice that $x_{min} = x - x_{ext}$, $x_{max} = x + x_{ext}$, etc.

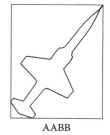
AABB

Computing: Computing an AABB for geometry is straightforward. All vertices are examined, and the minimum and maximum extents along all axes are stored.

Occasionally, AABBs will be computed from a bounding sphere. In this case, the center of the AABB is the center of the sphere, and $x_{ext} = y_{ext} = z_{ext} = r$. Notice that this formulation is even less compact than the bounding sphere, but has the advantage over an AABB fit directly to the object that the bounding box is invariant with respect to object rotation.

To find collisions between two AABBs, the extents along all three axes are checked for overlap. If the two extents overlap along all three axes, then the AABBs are colliding. If they do not overlap along any one axis, then they are not colliding.

This can be written as follows:

Boolean `AreAABBsColliding`$\big((x_{min,1}, x_{max,1}, y_{min,1}, y_{max,1}, z_{min,1}, z_{max,1}),$
$\qquad\qquad\qquad\qquad (x_{min,2}, x_{max,2}, y_{min,2}, y_{max,2}, z_{min,2}, z_{max,2}) \big)$
Inputs are the AABB extents for objects 1 and 2.
begin
    if $(x_{min,2} > x_{max,1})$ **or** $(x_{min,1} > x_{max,2})$ **or** $(y_{min,2} > y_{max,1})$ **or**
      $(y_{min,1} > y_{max,2})$ **or** $(z_{min,2} > z_{max,1})$ **or** $(z_{min,1} > z_{max,2})$ **then**
        return False ;
    end
    Overlapping in all dimensions, so return True.
    return True;
end

Advantages: Most computations with AABBs are very fast. Computing the AABB itself is straightforward, although it takes time proportional to the number of vertices. Checking for collisions is about as efficient as possible, with no computation required beyond a set of at most six comparisons.

Disadvantages: As objects change orientation, the AABB needs to be recomputed. For objects in free motion, this can mean recomputing the entire AABB at every timestep, and if the object contains many vertices, this could be a slow process. While generally more tight-fitting than a bounding sphere, there is typically still a lot of "empty" volume enclosed, meaning that intersections will often be over-reported.

k-dops: The k-*dop* bounding volume style, short for k-*discrete orientation polytopes*, can be thought of as an extension of AABBs. While AABBs define the bounding volume by a minimum and maximum along three axes, k-dops define the bounding volume by finding a minimum and maximum along additional axes, as well. The k in a k-dop refers to the number of directions in which an extent is measured. Since each axis has two extents (maximum and minimum), a k-dop is defined by $k/2$ different axes. An AABB is thus an instance of a 6-dop.

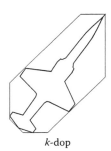

k-dop

Storing a k-dop involves storing a maximum and minimum for each of the $k/2$ axes. Like AABBs, the axes are chosen in a global frame of reference, and are the same for all objects. The first three axes are the three coordinate axes: x, y, and z. Most commonly, one or both of two additional sets of axes are also added. First are the six formed from pairs of the coordinate axes:

$$x+y, x-y, x+z, x-z, y+z, y-z.$$

If you imagine a cube, with the coordinate axes piercing the center of each face, these six axes are those that pierce the centers of the edges. Next are the four axes formed from triples of the coordinate axes:

$$x+y+z, x+y-z, x-y+z, x-y-z.$$

In the cube analogy, these can be thought of as the axes piercing the corners of the cube. Thus, the common bounding volumes used are the 6-dop (i.e., the AABB), 18-dop, 14-dop, or 26-dop. In theory, an arbitrary set of additional axes could be used, but there are diminishing gains as additional axes are added. In practical terms, either the 18-dop or 14-dop seems to give the best trade-off of performance/cost.

Computing: Computing the maxima and minima along each axis is only slightly more complex than for AABBs. We can examine each vertex of the object, and compute its projection along a given axis. For the pairwise axes, this is just the sum of the coordinates divided by $\sqrt{2}$, and for the axes formed from triples, this is the sum of the coordinates divided by $\sqrt{3}$. For example, a point $(2, 3, 7)$ projected on the $x + y - z$ axis would project to the value $-2\sqrt{3}$ along that axis. Since we care more about relative position than absolute position along an axis, often the $\sqrt{2}$ or $\sqrt{3}$ can be ignored throughout.

To compare two k-dops, we again use an extended version of the algorithm used for AABBs. Two k-dops are intersecting if and only if they overlap along all axes. Thus, by comparing the maximum and minimum extents of the two objects along each axis, we can determine whether or not they overlap. We will not write the algorithm explicitly, but it is a direct extension of **AreAABBsColliding**, as shown above.

Advantages: For typical objects, k-dops can provide a significantly tighter bounding volume than AABBs. The cost for this tighter fit is only slightly more than that for AABBs, involving only a few extra comparisons when checking for collisions, and a small factor of additional time when computing a new bounding box.

Disadvantages: Like AABBs, k-dops are dependent on the current orientation of the object, so as objects rotate, their k-dop must be updated. Forming a k-dop around a bounding sphere, so that the k-dop does not need to be updated as the object rotates, loses the benefit of having a tightly fitting bounding box.

OBBs: Oriented bounding boxes, or OBBs, consist of a bounding box where the three axes are not necessarily aligned with the global x, y, and z axes. Instead, three other axes are chosen, relative to the object's local (modeling) frame, and the bounding volume is set relative to those axes. Then, as the object moves around, the bounding box does not change in dimensions, but does rotate with the object.

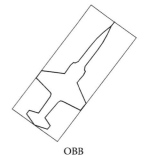

OBB

Each OBB thus stores a set of three orthonormal axes, along with the minimum and maximum along those axes, relative to the center of mass of the object.

Computing: To form an OBB, the three axes to use must be determined first. These are determined in the object's rest frame. Finding an optimally minimal box is an ill-defined problem, since it is not clear what is best to minimize (e.g., is it better to minimize overall volume of the OBB or the maximum dimension along an axis, or something else). However, three orthonormal axes can be obtained by performing a principal components analysis of the vertex positions of the object, to find the directions of greatest to least variance. These axes tend to produce a tight-fitting box.

Alternatively, if the object is in a "good" orientation in its local (modeling) frame, as is often the case when modeling, one can form an OBB using the x, y, and z axes from the local frame.

Given the three axes, the maximum and minimum along each of those axes must be determined. This can be found by projecting the position of the vertices relative to the center of mass onto all three axes, and looking for the maximum and minimum of each.

To check for collisions between two OBBs, we project them along an axis, called a *separating axis*, and determine whether they overlap along that axis. If the projections are not overlapping, then the objects are not overlapping. The converse, however, is not true; if two volumes overlap when projected onto an axis, it does not mean the volumes themselves overlap. The key is to find a small set of axes along which, if the objects overlap in all axes, the volumes do overlap. Testing these axes is enough to guarantee that the objects are not overlapping.

Note that when comparing AABBs or k-dops, we could rely on knowing a specific set of axes along which we would need to test for overlaps. We would like to have something similar for OBBs, but run into difficulty since each OBB is defined with its own set of axes. To resolve this problem and find collisions between two OBBs, we must rely on the *separating axis theorem*.

The separating axis theorem states that a complete set of separating axes can be found from the following:

- The normals of the faces of the first object

- The normals of the faces of the second object

- The cross-products of an edge of one object with an edge of the other object

For OBBs, this gives three axes for the faces from the first object, three more for the faces from the second object, and nine from the cross-products of the edges, for 15 total axes. In practice, however, one does not need to test all 15 axes for OBBs, since the test for overlap is a conservative one: we just need to eliminate cases that are not overlapping, not find cases where there is overlapping. Thus, it can be feasible to test only a limited set of axes that will still catch most cases, such as the six face normals. Notice that for AABBs, because the face normals align with the edges for both objects, there are only three axes to test (the x, y, and z axes).

Advantages: Unlike AABBs or k-dops, the OBB does not need to be completely recalculated as the object rotates. The direction of the axes needs to be updated, but this is a much simpler operation than completely recomputing the volume. OBBs are relatively tight-fitting. They are at least as tight-fitting as an AABB, and typically are more tight-fitting, sometimes even tighter than k-dops. Furthermore, if an object is subdivided into smaller and small parts, compared with AABB's, OBBs converge much more quickly to the underlying surface, as demonstrated in the diagram.

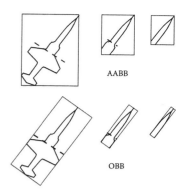

Disadvantages: The primary downside to using OBBs is that the collision detecion computation is more complicated than for spheres, AABBs, or k-dops. Typically more axes must be checked, and the volume (i.e., the eight vertices) must be projected onto each axis. This involves several computations, in contrast to a very small number of computations (for spheres) or just comparisons (for AABBs and k-dops). The initial cost of computing an OBB is relatively high, but this only needs to be done once, as a precomputation, rather than repeatedly during a simulation.

Convex Hulls: The convex hull of a set of points is defined as the smallest set of points for which convex combinations of those points encompass every point in the object. A convex combination of two points is basically the points on the line segment between the points; for three points it is the triangle formed by those points; for four points, it is the tetrahedron formed by those points. In 2D, the convex hull can be thought of as the shape formed by stretching a rubber band around the object and letting it go, and in 3D the analogy is similar to shrink-wrapping the

Convex hull

object. The convex hull is, by definition, the tightest-fitting convex polyhedron possible for a set of points.

Storing the convex hull of an object means storing a set of vertices, edges, and faces that make up the hull. Unlike the other bounding volumes we have discussed, storing the convex hull information requires much more than a few values, and can be quite complex in some cases.

Computing: Computing a convex hull is a long-standing problem in computational geometry, with many different implementations. We will not discuss the process here, but various algorithms can be found in almost any computational geometry text. The *Handbook of Discrete and Computational Geometry* is a standard reference [Goodman and O'Rourke, 2004].

Detecting collisions between two convex hulls can be done using the separating axis theorem. However, since each convex hull can have numerous faces and edges, there could be a very large number of axes required, making the process quite slow.

Advantages: The primary advantage of the convex hull as a bounding volume is its tightness of fit. It minimizes any wasted space. The convex hull can also be precomputed for an object, and the hull rotated as the object changes orientation. The entire hull does not need to be recomputed from scratch as an object rotates, unlike AABBs and k-dops.

Disadvantages: Detecting collisions between convex hulls is very slow, to the point that convex hulls are rarely used in practice for collision detection. However, there are cases where just one or two objects are being checked for collisions, and in these cases the relatively slow performance may still be acceptable, especially if one wishes to minimize the chances of a false-positive intersection. The Lin-Canny algorithm [Lin and Canny, 1991] is an example of a collision detection algorithm relying on the convex hull. In that case, the closest point between two bounding volumes is kept track of continuously, and in this case, since there are few objects, and a very tight fit is desired, the convex hull is an appropriate choice.

10.2.2   Broad Phase Collision Detection

The goal of broad phase collision detection is to eliminate pairs of objects that are clearly not colliding. Following the broad phase there should be a list of pairs of objects that are potentially colliding. Actual object collisions are not determined during the broad phase.

In the broad phase, we will typically use a sphere bounding volume, centered at the center of mass. Because the sphere is centered on the center of mass, this volume will enclose the object regardless of its orientation. As the object moves around, we will need to update the position of the sphere, but not its radius.

There are two major approaches to the broad phase of collision detection: spatial subdivision and sweep-and-prune.

Spatial Subdivision: In Section 6.3, we introduced several spatial data structures: the uniform grid, the octree, and the kd-tree. For broad phase collision detection, we use one of these spatial subdivisions, and place the object in *all* spatial regions that the object (or the object's bounding volume) overlaps.

During the broad phase of collision detection, we need to check only between pairs of objects that lie in the same spatial subdivision region. Note that if objects span many regions (e.g., along a thin object covering many voxels), there may be times that the same pair of objects is compared in many voxels. If this is likely to be a common problem, an additional list or hash table of checked pairs can be maintained and used to avoid unnecessary comparisons. However, for the broad phase, the comparison between any two objects's spheres is typically simple enough that this overhead does not pay off unless there will be a very large number of such cases.

Object pairs whose bounding volumes are found to overlap are passed to the narrow phase for subsequent determination of whether or not a collision between the objects themselves has actually occurred.

Sweep-and-prune: An alternative broad-phase approach is the Sweep-and-Prune algorithm [Baraff, 1992]. In this approach, each object is surrounded by an AABB.[*] Two objects pass the broad phase if their AABBs overlap. This means that the AABBs will overlap in extents along the x, y, and z axes.

The idea of sweep-and-prune is to identify overlapping pairs along each axis quickly and in a way that overlapping pairs can be updated easily over time. We find overlapping pairs along one axis, then the others; pairs are reported as overlapping only if they overlap along all three axes.

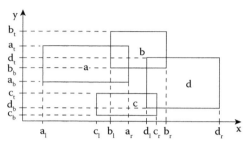

To find overlapping pairs along one axis, we first sort the starting and ending point of the AABBs along the axis. For n objects there will be $2n$ points to sort. The sweep operation will begin at the lowest point and sweep to the highest point, maintaining a list of "active" AABBs. As a starting point is passed, the appropriate AABB is added to the active list, and an overlap is reported with every other AABB already in the list. As an end point is passed, the AABB is removed from the active list. The result is that all the non-overlapping pairs (along that axis) are pruned away from the list. For example, in the figure above, a, b, c, and d represent bounding volumes for four objects. Sweeping along the x axis will consecutively find the overlaps a-c, a-b, c-b, c-d, and b-d. Along the y axis, the overlaps will be c-d, a-d, d-b, a-b, leaving only a-b, c-d, and b-d that appear in both lists. Starting from scratch, including the sort, this whole process will take time $O(n \lg n + k)$ where n is the number of objects and k is the number of overlapping pairs.

This algorithm can also exploit *temporal coherence*. As objects move, their position from one time step to the next does not change by a large amount. The new positions will be very near the old positions, or stated in terms of the sweep-and-prune algorithm, the positions of the starting and ending points of the AABBs will not move much. Most intervals overlapping at one timestep will still overlap in the next, and vica-versa. Each AABB interval needs to only update its position, which might possibly involve overlapping a new interval. On detection, this new overlap is added to the list of overlapping pairs. Similarly, if an AABB is detected as no longer overlapping one it was previously overlapping, it is removed from the list. In any case, this "re-sorting" of the endpoints will involve only a small move up or down in the list of sorted endpoints, which can be done in nearly constant time per object. An insertion sort or even a bubble sort can be used to update the nearly sorted list from the last timestep very quickly. Thus, the sweep-and-prune algorithm can be run in approximately $O(n + k)$ time, after the initial run of the algorithm.

---

[*]This could be an AABB around a bounding sphere, so that it does not need to be updated as orientation changes.

10.2.3 Narrow Phase Collision Detection

The narrow phase of collision detection is usually handled through bounding volume hierarchies. The idea is to form a tree of bounding volumes covering progressively fewer and fewer of the polygons making up the object's boundary.

At the base level, the top node of the tree, is a bounding volume covering the entire object. The children nodes represent a partitioning of the polygons in the parent node. Each child node has a bounding volume of its own, and it is further partitioned into smaller and smaller regions. Finally, the leaf nodes of the tree will represent a bounding volume for one or a few individual triangles. The bounding volume tree is often binary, but it is possible to have multiple children nodes. The figure illustrates three levels, showing how a single object might be hierarchically subdivided, with OBB bounding volumes computed at each subdivision in the hierarchy.

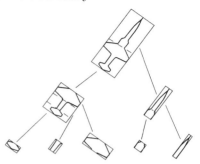

To check for a collision between two objects, a recursive procedure is followed. First, the bounding volumes for the top level nodes are compared for overlap. If they do not intersect, then the polygons within the bounding regions cannot intersect. If these do intersect, then the pairs of child nodes are checked. This continues recursively until a pair of intersecting leaf nodes is detected. At this point, the individual polygons represented by that leaf node are checked for intersection. Typically, this means that two triangles are checked for intersection.

The triangle intersection test is more complex than a bounding volume intersection test, and the whole point of the bounding volume hierarchy is to minimize the number of these tests. The basic process for determining whether and where two triangles intersect is to determine the intersection of one triangle with the plane containing the other triangle. This will form a line segment, the endpoints of which are determined by finding the intersection points of a triangle's edges with the plane. Note that the two edges that intersect the plane can be identified by finding the two edges whose vertices are on opposite sides of the plane. Then, the process is repeated for the other triangle, forming a second line segment. Finally, the two line segments, which must lie along the same line (the line of intersection between the two planes), are checked for overlap. If this line segment overlaps then the triangles are intersecting.

10.3 LINEAR COMPLEMENTARITY PROBLEMS

In this section we focus on the problem of handling collisions among multiple bodies, and on maintaining resting contact for rigid body configurations when a number of objects are resting on each other. We look at how the correct forces and impulses can be created to keep objects from passing through each other, and how to compute friction forces at contact points. First, however, we must develop a mathematical framework for looking at these sorts of problems.

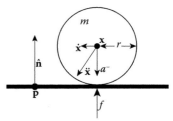

Consider the resting contact problem shown to the right. A ball of mass m and radius r is positioned with its center at $\mathbf{x}$, above a surface defined by the normal $\hat{\mathbf{n}}$, and a point on the surface $\mathbf{p}$. The ball's velocity is $\dot{\mathbf{x}}$, and it is accelerating with acceleration $\ddot{\mathbf{x}}$. A potential resting contact is established if, within some small tolerance,

$$(\mathbf{x} - \mathbf{p}) \cdot \hat{\mathbf{n}} = r, \quad \text{and}$$

$$\dot{\mathbf{x}} \cdot \hat{\mathbf{n}} = 0.$$

We define the component of the acceleration normal to the contact, before any force from the floor is applied, as

$$a^- = \ddot{\mathbf{x}} \cdot \hat{\mathbf{n}},$$

and the component of the acceleration after any force from the floor is applied as a^+. For example, for a ball resting on a horizontal floor and acting under gravitational acceleration g, $a^- = -g$ and $a^+ = 0$.

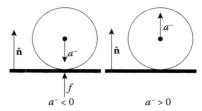

As indicated in this picture, there are two cases to be considered. Either the ball's acceleration is opposite to the direction of the surface normal, making a^- negative, or the acceleration is in the direction of the surface normal, making a^- positive. If a^- is negative, the floor will have to exert an opposing force $f = -ma^-$, so that $a^+ = 0$. But, if a^- is positive, the ball is accelerating away from the floor, so the floor can exert no force on the ball, therefore $f = 0$ and $a^+ = a^-$.

This is the simplest example of a configuration that can be posed as a *Linear Complementarity Problem*, or *LCP*. As an LCP, this problem is summarized by the linear relationship

$$\frac{1}{m}f + a^- = a^+, \tag{10.7}$$

subject to the conditions

$$a^+ \geq 0, \quad f \geq 0, \quad \text{and} \quad fa^+ = 0.$$

The condition that a^+ and f must be nonnegative, and the *complementarity condition* that either one or the other of a^+ or f must be 0, provide enough constraints for the single Equation 10.7 to have a solution for its two unknowns. The solution of this equation depends on the sign of a^-. If $a^- > 0$, the problem requires that $f = 0$ and therefore $a^+ = a^-$. But, if $a^- < 0$, the problem requires that $a^+ = 0$ and so $f = -ma^-$.

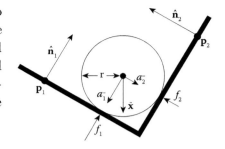

The problem illustrated by this figure has two potential resting contacts, one against a surface with normal $\hat{\mathbf{n}}_1$ passing through point $\mathbf{p}_1$, and one against an orthogonal surface with normal $\hat{\mathbf{n}}_2$ passing through point $\mathbf{p}_2$. There are two normal accelerations before any resisting forces are applied:

$$a_1^- = \ddot{\mathbf{x}} \cdot \hat{\mathbf{n}}_1, \quad \text{and} \quad a_2^- = \ddot{\mathbf{x}} \cdot \hat{\mathbf{n}}_2.$$

Because the surfaces are orthogonal to each other, any force f_1 exerted by surface 1 will be parallel to surface 2, and any force f_2 exerted by surface 2 will be parallel to surface 1. Thus, there is no interaction between these forces and their resulting accelerations. Such a system can be posed as two independent LCP's,

$$\frac{1}{m} f_1 + a_1^- = a_1^+, \quad \text{and}$$
$$\frac{1}{m} f_2 + a_2^- = a_2^+,$$

subject to the conditions

$$a_1^+, a_2^+ \geq 0, \quad f_1, f_2 \geq 0, \quad f_1 a_1^+ = 0, \quad \text{and} \quad f_2 a_2^+ = 0.$$

Each of these equations can be solved separately, with solutions depending upon the signs of a_1^- and a_2^-, just as we solved Equation 10.7 above.

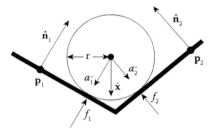

The problem illustrated by this figure presents additional complexities. It also has two potential resting contacts against surfaces 1 and 2, but because the surfaces are not orthogonal to each other, contact forces will interact. A force f_1, exerted by surface 1, will have a non-zero component in the direction of $\hat{\mathbf{n}}_2$, likewise force f_2 will have a component in the direction of $\hat{\mathbf{n}}_1$. Therefore, the two equations governing these forces are

$$\frac{1}{m} f_1 + \frac{1}{m} \hat{\mathbf{n}}_1 \cdot \hat{\mathbf{n}}_2 f_2 + a_1^- = a_1^+, \quad \text{and}$$

$$\frac{1}{m} \hat{\mathbf{n}}_1 \cdot \hat{\mathbf{n}}_2 f_1 + \frac{1}{m} f_2 + a_2^- = a_2^+.$$

These two equations can be written more compactly by the linear system

$$\frac{1}{m} \begin{bmatrix} 1 & \hat{\mathbf{n}}_1 \cdot \hat{\mathbf{n}}_2 \\ \hat{\mathbf{n}}_1 \cdot \hat{\mathbf{n}}_2 & 1 \end{bmatrix} \begin{bmatrix} f_1 \\ f_2 \end{bmatrix} + \begin{bmatrix} a_1^- \\ a_2^- \end{bmatrix} = \begin{bmatrix} a_1^+ \\ a_2^+ \end{bmatrix},$$

again subject to the conditions

$$a_1^+, a_2^+ \geq 0, \quad f_1, f_2 \geq 0, \quad f_1 a_1^+ = 0, \quad \text{and} \quad f_2 a_2^+ = 0.$$

The complementarity condition leaves us with four cases to consider, based on the signs of a_1^- and a_2^-. If both a_1^- and a_2^- are positive, $f_1, f_2 = 0$, and $a_1^+ = a_1^-$ and $a_2^+ = a_2^-$. If both a_1^- and a_2^- are negative, $a_1^+, a_2^+ = 0$, and by inverting the matrix we have the solution

$$\begin{bmatrix} f_1 \\ f_2 \end{bmatrix} = -\frac{m}{1 - (\hat{\mathbf{n}}_1 \cdot \hat{\mathbf{n}}_2)^2} \begin{bmatrix} 1 & -\hat{\mathbf{n}}_1 \cdot \hat{\mathbf{n}}_2 \\ -\hat{\mathbf{n}}_1 \cdot \hat{\mathbf{n}}_2 & 1 \end{bmatrix} \begin{bmatrix} a_1^- \\ a_2^- \end{bmatrix}.$$

In the two remaining cases, on the other hand, we have the two sub-cases indicated in this figure. In the case where $\hat{\mathbf{n}}_1 \cdot \hat{\mathbf{n}}_2 > 0$, a force f_1 exerted by the floor at contact point 1 will have a component tending to accelerate the ball away from contact 2. In the case where $\hat{\mathbf{n}}_1 \cdot \hat{\mathbf{n}}_2 < 0$, f_1

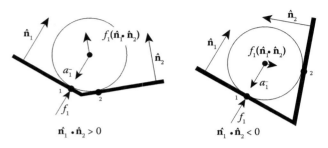

will tend to accelerate the ball toward contact 2. Consider what happens when $a_1^- < 0$ but $a_2^- > 0$. It might be expected that $a_1^+ = 0$ and $f_2 = 0$. In this case, the unknowns are f_1 and a_2^+. Solving the remaining linear equations yields

$$f_1 = -ma_1^-, \quad \text{and} \quad a_2^+ = a_2^- + (\hat{\mathbf{n}}_1 \cdot \hat{\mathbf{n}}_2)\frac{1}{m}f_1.$$

If $\hat{\mathbf{n}}_1 \cdot \hat{\mathbf{n}}_2 \geq 0$, then this is the final solution. However, if $\hat{\mathbf{n}}_1 \cdot \hat{\mathbf{n}}_2 < 0$, and f_1 is large enough, this solution may violate the requirement $a_2^+ \geq 0$. To get a solution will require solving the system allowing f_2 to be non-zero, and therefore $a_2^+ = 0$. There is a similar conundrum in the remaining case where $a_1^- > 0$ but $a_2^- < 0$. Therefore, solving an LCP can be seen to be a search process, to find a solution that meets the complementarity and positivity constraints. With only four main cases to consider, this can be done easily, but for larger problems we will need an efficient general approach.

The general form of an LCP problem with N variables is

$$K\mathbf{f} + \mathbf{a}^- = \mathbf{a}^+, \tag{10.8}$$

where K is a known $N \times N$ matrix, $\mathbf{a}^-$ is a known N element vector, and $\mathbf{f}$ and $\mathbf{a}^+$ are N element vectors to be determined, subject to the conditions for each element $0 \leq i < N$ that

$$a_i^+ \geq 0, \quad f_i \geq 0, \quad \text{and} \quad f_i a_i^+ = 0.$$

The development of the mathematics to solve this problem is outside of the scope of this book, but LCPs are a type of quadratic optimization problem, with a number of robust solvers available to link to your code. One of the better ones is available on the *Geometric Tools* website [Eberly, 2015]. Here we will focus on how to pose the problem correctly, and how to set up the matrix K for some typical configurations found in rigid body simulation.

10.3.1   Handling Multiple Contacting Rigid Bodies

It is not unusual for multiple contacts to exist in a rigid body simulation at the same time point. Each contact may be either a colliding contact or a resting contact, depending upon the relative velocities and accelerations between the bodies at the contact point. Assume that we have advanced the simulation clock to the point where there are no interpenetrations but several contacts coexist. Now, consider the contact point of two objects a and b that we covered in Section 10.1.2. Their relative velocity v^-_{rel}, which is the difference in their velocities in the direction of the collision surface normal as given by Equation 10.5, will be negative if the bodies are colliding, zero (within a tolerance) if the bodies are resting on each other, and positive if the bodies are receding from each other. If the bodies are receding, no action need be taken. If the bodies are colliding, they can be prevented from interpenetrating by applying the correct impulse. If the bodies are resting on each other, we need to look at their relative acceleration

$$a^-_{\text{rel}} = \hat{\mathbf{n}} \cdot (\ddot{\mathbf{p}}^-_a - \ddot{\mathbf{p}}^-_b).$$

If this is positive, the objects are accelerating away from each other already, and no action needs to be taken. Otherwise, they must be prevented from interpenetrating by applying the correct contact force. Both the collision and resting contact problems can be solved using an LCP formulation.

The figure shows a 2D configuration consisting of a fixed floor A, in contact with four rigid bodies B, C, D, and E. Eight numbered vertex-face contacts are shown in this configuration, with the direction of the surface normal at each contact indicated by arrows. An impulse or force exerted at any one of these 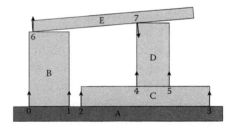 contacts will produce a corresponding impulse or force that will be felt at every one of the other contacts. Therefore, the problem will require a simultaneous solution. This can be set up as an LCP, if we can determine the elements of the matrix K and the vector $\mathbf{a}^-$ in Equation 10.8.

Let us consider the case where all of the contact points are in resting contact. The elements of $\mathbf{a}^-$ are easy to determine if we assume that the only force acting is gravitational, with acceleration constant g in the negative y direction. Elements a^-_0 through a^-_6 correspond to vertical facing normals, so they will have value $-g$. Element a^-_7, however, has a downward facing normal, so it will be positive, with value g scaled by the y component of the normal $\hat{\mathbf{n}}_7$.

The elements of the 8×8 matrix K are more difficult to determine, and require the application of rigid body mechanics. Its elements k_{ij} account for the effect of a force acting at contact j on contact i. There will be an equal and opposite effect of contact i on contact j, so the matrix will be symmetric and only the upper triangular terms need be determined. Contributing to the effect of contact j on contact i, will be the masses and moments of inertia of the bodies involved, the vector between each contact and the centers of mass of the affected bodies, and the normal vectors at each contact.

One approach to computing the elements of K is to apply test impulses normal to each of the contact points and note how velocity changes are propagated to the objects involved. In the figure, the test impulse $\delta\hat{\mathbf{n}}_0$ is applied at contact 0. Its direct rotational and translational effects on the other bodies, and thus on the other contact points, are noted. Body A is

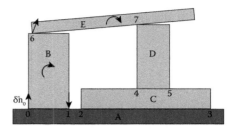

unaffected since it is a fixed floor. Body B will have a change in angular and translational velocities directly induced by the impulse and registered at contacts 0, 1, and 6. Body E, which is in direct contact with B at contact 6, will have a consequent change in its angular and translational velocities. The effect of any contact on any other contact will be 0 unless there is direct contact between the bodies involved, so that the effects on contacts 2, 3, 4, 5, and 7 are all 0. Chaining effects will be accounted for by applying test impulses at each of the contacts, in turn, and noting how they are directly propagated.

The algorithm `BuildKMatrix` on the next page shows how this is done. Below we provide the mathematical details required for implementation.

In the algorithm, the type **Contact** contains references to the two rigid bodies involved in the contact, as well as the spatial position of the contact point $\mathbf{p}$, the contact normal $\hat{\mathbf{n}}$, and the relative velocity v_{rel} of the two bodies in the direction of the contact normal. The convention is that the direction of the normal vector is away from body 2 and toward body 1. Either a vertex on body 1 is in contact with a plane on body 2, or the contact is edge-edge, in which case the edges on the two bodies will also be noted.

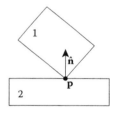

The `ApplyImpulse(p,` $\hat{\mathbf{n}}$`)` method for rigid body 1 applies a unit impulse at point $\mathbf{p}$ in the direction of the normal vector $\hat{\mathbf{n}}$, thus changing body 1's velocity and angular velocity. Therefore, if the impulse is of unit magnitude in the direction of $\hat{\mathbf{n}}$, the velocity updates will be

$$\Delta\mathbf{v}_1 = \frac{1}{m_1}\hat{\mathbf{n}}, \quad \text{and} \quad \Delta\boldsymbol{\omega}_1 = I_1^{-1}[(\mathbf{p} - \mathbf{x}_1) \times \hat{\mathbf{n}}].$$

The `GetPointVelocity(p)` method determines the velocity of point $\mathbf{p}$ on rigid body 1 as

$$\dot{\mathbf{p}} = \mathbf{v}_1 + \boldsymbol{\omega}_1 \times (\mathbf{p} - \mathbf{x}_1),$$

where $\mathbf{v}_1$ is the velocity of the center of mass of body 1 and $\boldsymbol{\omega}_1$ is its angular velocity.

```
Matrix BuildKMatrix(Contact C[], int N)
C is the current list of contacts, N is the number of contacts.
begin
    Matrix K[N][N];

    apply a test impulse at each contact in the contact list C.
    for i = 0 to N-1 do
        save the velocities and angular velocities of contact i's bodies
        C[i].SaveState();

        apply opposite unit impulses to the two bodies at contact i
        C[i].Body1.ApplyImpulse(C[i].p, C[i].n̂);
        C[i].Body2.ApplyImpulse(C[i].p, -C[i].n̂);

        note the effect on bodies directly in contact with Body1 or Body2.
        for j = i to N-1 do
            compute the current relative normal velocity at contact point j
            Vector3 v₁ = C[j].Body1.GetPointVelocity(C[j].p);
            Vector3 v₂ = C[j].Body2.GetPointVelocity(C[j].p);
            float v⁺ᵣₑₗ = (v₁ − v₂) · C[j].n̂ⱼ;

            Kᵢ,ⱼ and Kⱼ,ᵢ reflect relative velocity change at contacts i & j
            K[i][j] = K[j][i] = v⁺ᵣₑₗ − C[j].vᵣₑₗ;
        end

        restore the velocities and angular velocities of contact i's bodies
        C[i].RestoreState();
    end
    return the completed interaction matrix.
    return K;
end
```

10.3.2 Multiple Colliding and Resting Contacts as LCPs

The problem of mixed multiple contacts between rigid bodies is handled in two
steps. First a list of all contact points with zero or negative relative velocities is
built, and the matrix K is constructed using the algorithm **BuildKMatrix**. To
account for the energy loss at the collision, each relative velocity is scaled by the
coefficient of restitution at the contact. We then solve the LCP

$$K\mathbf{j} + \mathbf{v}^- = \mathbf{v}^+,$$

subject to the conditions, for each element of the N element contact list,

$$v_i^+ \geq 0, \quad j_i \geq 0, \quad \text{and} \quad j_i v_i^+ = 0.$$

The solution gives us the list of impulse magnitudes $\mathbf{j}$ required to prevent interpen-
etration, where the elements of $\mathbf{j}$ are denoted j_i, the required impulse magnitude at

contact i. These impulses are then applied toward the two bodies at each contact point, and their relative velocities are again computed. Each contact where this relative velocity is now positive can be removed from the contact list, as can any contact where the relative acceleration is positive. With this reduced contact list, the matrix K is again constructed and we solve the LCP

$$K\mathbf{f} + \mathbf{a}^- = \mathbf{a}^+,$$

subject to the conditions, for each element of the reduced contact list,

$$a_i^+ \geq 0, \quad f_i \geq 0, \quad \text{and} \quad f_i a_i^+ = 0.$$

The solution gives us the list of constraint force magnitudes $\mathbf{f}$.

10.3.3 Friction as an LCP

To obtain realistic rigid body behavior when contacts are involved, it is necessary to model frictional as well as support forces. The Coulomb model of friction limits the amount of frictional force at a contact to μf_n, where μ is the coefficient of friction at the contact, and f_n is the force normal to the surface at the contact. The direction of the force will be in opposition to the tangential velocity of the contact, or in the absence of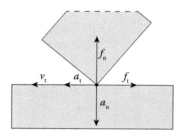
tangential velocity, in the direction of any applied force. In addition, frictional force is purely dissipative—it cannot cause the contact's motion to reverse direction—so the total force that can be realized in any timestep of a simulation must never be more than is needed to bring the tangential motion at the contact to a stop. Therefore, either the full force of friction is being felt, where $f_t = \mu f_n$, or a force less than this is being applied that brings the contact to a stop. In reality, the full acceleration due to friction is felt until the object stops. In a simulation, we can model this for a timestep by scaling the total acceleration to that which is exactly required to stop the object at the end of the timestep. In other words, $a_t^+ = -v_t/h$.

An LCP, proposed by Kokkevis [2004] for a frictional sliding contact is summarized by the three complementarity conditions:

1. $a_n^+ \geq 0$ complementary to $f_n \geq 0$

2. $a_t^+ + v_t^-/h + \lambda \geq 0$ complementary to $f_t \geq 0$

3. $\mu f_n - f_t \geq 0$ complementary to $\lambda \geq 0$

Condition 1 handles the relationship between normal force and acceleration that we have already covered in the frictionless condition. Condition 2 handles the relationship between tangential force and acceleration, including the requirement that the tangential acceleration cannot exceed that needed to stop a moving object.

Condition 3 assures that the Coulomb friction force limit is not exceeded. It also introduces a new non-negative variable λ, which is used to couple conditions 2 and 3.

Here is how this coupling works. If in condition 3, $f_t < \mu f_n$, then $\lambda = 0$, and $a_t^+ = -v_t^-/h$, which is exactly enough acceleration to bring the contact to rest in one timestep. However, if in condition 3 $f_t = \mu f_n$, then $\lambda \geq 0$ and $a_t^+ = -v_t^-/h - \lambda$. Therefore, either the full frictional force limit is not reached and the contact comes to a stop in one timestep, or the force limit is reached, and the contact is slowed but no more than would bring it to rest.

Since there are three conditions, involving the three unknowns f_n, f_t, and λ, each frictional contact must be modeled as a 3×3 system of equations

$$\begin{bmatrix} k_{nn} & k_{tn} & 0 \\ k_{nt} & k_{tt} & 1 \\ \mu & -1 & 0 \end{bmatrix} \begin{bmatrix} f_n \\ f_t \\ \lambda \end{bmatrix} + \begin{bmatrix} a_n^- \\ a_t^- + v_t^-/h \\ 0 \end{bmatrix} = \begin{bmatrix} a_n^+ \\ a_t^+ \\ \lambda^+ \end{bmatrix}.$$

The constant k_{nn} scales force in the normal direction into a normal acceleration, k_{tn} scales force in the tangential direction into normal acceleration, k_{nt}, which equals k_{tn}, scales normal force into tangential acceleration, and k_{tt} scales tangential force into tangential acceleration. The new dummy variable λ^+ allows the inequality in condition 3 to be expressed as an equality. The non-negative value λ^+ is allowed to vary as needed by the LCP solver. The purpose of the LCP solution is to determine f_n, f_t, and λ. As a by-product, the solver will compute a_n^+, a_t^+, and λ^+ but their values are unneeded. Also, since λ's only purpose is in coupling constraints 2 and 3, its value can be ignored.

For a simple single particle contact, with no rotational inertia and the center of mass at the contact point, the constants in the equation will be $k_{nn}, k_{tt} = \frac{1}{m}$ and $k_{tn}, k_{nt} = 0$. Notice, in this case, the equation represented by the top row can be written

$$f_n = m(a_n^+ - a_n^-),$$

which is simply Newton's second law applied to the net normal acceleration, and corresponds with the first complementarity condition. The second and third rows correspond with the other two complementarity conditions.

However, for contacts between rigid bodies, both the geometry of the objects and their rotational inertia must be considered in computing k_{nn} and k_{tt}, and the coupling constants $k_{tn} = k_{nt}$ will be non-zero. The figure shows that when a_n is downward the resulting constraint force f_n

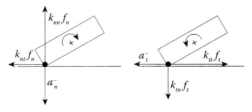

not only supports the body but also induces a rotation, which results in a tangential acceleration $k_{nt}f_n$. Likewise, a tangential friction force f_t opposing a_t^- induces a rotation, which results in a normal acceleration $k_{tn}f_t$. Since all of the geometric and inertial conditions are identical in both cases, $k_{nt} = k_{tn}$.

These elements can be computed by a modified version of the `BuildKMatrix` test-impulse algorithm for frictionless contacts, described above. The algorithm must be extended by adding additional impulses in the tangential direction. The direction of the tangential impulse should be chosen based on the current relative tangential velocity and acceleration at the contact point. If the relative tangential velocity is non-zero (within a tolerance), the impulse direction should be opposite the tangential velocity direction. If the tangential velocity is 0, the bodies are not moving relative to each other and the impulse direction should be opposite the tangential acceleration, thereby opposing movement. If both relative tangential velocity and acceleration are zero, an arbitrary impulse direction can be chosen— Kokkevis suggests using the last valid direction encountered in the simulation.

Therefore, when friction is being considered, the LCP matrix for multiple contacts will require a 3×3 submatrix for each contact, meaning that for N contacts, the matrix will be $3N \times 3N$. There are many ways that this can be organized, but a suggested organization is to group the like terms together in submatrices, giving the structure

$$
K = \begin{bmatrix}
\begin{bmatrix} k_{n_0 n_0} & \cdots & k_{n_{N-1} n_0} \\ \vdots & \ddots & \vdots \\ k_{n_0 n_{N-1}} & \cdots & k_{n_{N-1} n_{N-1}} \end{bmatrix} & \begin{bmatrix} k_{t_0 n_0} & \cdots & k_{t_{N-1} n_0} \\ \vdots & \ddots & \vdots \\ k_{t_0 n_{N-1}} & \cdots & k_{t_{N-1} n_{N-1}} \end{bmatrix} & \mathbf{0} \\
\begin{bmatrix} k_{n_0 t_0} & \cdots & k_{n_{N-1} t_0} \\ \vdots & \ddots & \vdots \\ k_{n_0 t_{N-1}} & \cdots & k_{n_{N-1} t_{N-1}} \end{bmatrix} & \begin{bmatrix} k_{t_0 t_0} & \cdots & k_{t_{N-1} t_0} \\ \vdots & \ddots & \vdots \\ k_{t_0 t_{N-1}} & \cdots & k_{t_{N-1} t_{N-1}} \end{bmatrix} & \mathbf{1} \\
\begin{bmatrix} \mu_0 & & \\ & \ddots & \\ & & \mu_{N-1} \end{bmatrix} & -\mathbf{1} & \mathbf{0}
\end{bmatrix},
$$

where $\mathbf{0}$ is the $N \times N$ zero matrix, and $\mathbf{1}$ is the $N \times N$ identity matrix. This allows the f_n, f_t, λ and other terms to be grouped into N element vectors, e.g., $\mathbf{f_n}$, $\mathbf{f_t}$, and $\boldsymbol{\lambda}$, giving the final linear system the form

$$
K \begin{bmatrix} \mathbf{f_n} \\ \mathbf{f_t} \\ \boldsymbol{\lambda} \end{bmatrix} + \begin{bmatrix} \mathbf{a_n^-} \\ \mathbf{a_t^-} + \frac{1}{h}\mathbf{v_t^-} \\ \mathbf{0} \end{bmatrix} = \begin{bmatrix} \mathbf{a_n^+} \\ \mathbf{a_t^+} \\ \boldsymbol{\lambda}^+ \end{bmatrix}.
$$

In this form, the known parameters can be handed to an LCP solver, which will return the resulting forces and λ values.

10.4 SUMMARY

Here are some key points to understand about rigid body collisions and contacts:

- Collisions of rigid bodies involve collision detection, determination, and response. We can model a collision response as an impulse.

- Impulses introduce both linear motion (instantaneous force) applied to the center of mass, and angular motion (instantaneous torque) applied at the point of collision. The result of the impulse will change the velocity of the point of collision on the object.

- The collision detection process is often the slowest part of the collision process, and different techniques can be used to speed it up. These are usually divided into a broad phase, where possible collisions between objects are identified, and a narrow phase, where specific collisions between polygons of the objects are identified.

- Broad phase collision detection is usually accelerated by either a spatial subdivision approach (only objects in the same spatial region can collide) or the sweep-and-prune algorithm (identifying objects with overlapping bounding boxes).

- Narrow phase collision detection is usually accelerated through the use of bounding volume hierarchies, progressively giving a tighter and tighter fit of volumes around an object.

- Several different bounding volumes can be used, with differing trade-offs in tightness of fit and speed of various computations.

- Linear complementarity can be used to express the relationships between multiple bodies in contact at the same time, including objects at rest. Multiple bodies colliding and in contact can be solved for simultaneously by a linear complementarity system.

- Linear complementarity can be used to model friction and sliding contacts in addition to collision responses and resting contacts.

CHAPTER 11

Constraints

M OST OF THIS BOOK has been dedicated to describing the dynamics of systems that are fundamentally unconstrained. By that, we mean that a particle, or rigid body is free to move in any direction, subject only to internal and external forces acting on it. However, there have been some exceptions. Particles cannot penetrate the walls of objects or fall through a floor—so they are constrained to move only in the region free of solid boundaries. The same is true for rigid bodies— they can tumble and fall freely, but cannot penetrate another solid. These are examples of problems that are usually solved as if there were no constraints, and then the constraints are handled as special cases, such as in the collision detection and response modules of a particle or rigid body simulation.

In physically based animation, however, there are many important problems that inherently involve constraints. At the physical level, all constraints come from forces being exerted on objects that prevent any motion that violates the constraint. For example, a train rolling on tracks is constrained to follow the tracks by forces exerted by the steel rails on the wheels of the train. The rails exert a force upward to support the weight of the train, and they exert sideward forces to keep the wheels aligned with the tracks when the tracks go around a curve. In this chapter, we will examine methods of maintaining constraints that explicitly compute the forces needed to maintain the constraints, but we will also look at the constraints as reducing the number of *degrees of freedom* of an object's motion.

An unconstrained particle problem has three *translational degrees of freedom*—a particle can move in the x, y, and z directions. An unconstrained rigid body has six degrees of freedom, since besides the three translational degrees of freedom, it has three *rotational degrees of freedom*, about the x, y, and z axes.

The figure to the right shows two constrained dynamics problems that can be understood in terms of the number of translational degrees of freedom. The box, sliding along

the floor, is an example of a problem that we have already seen—that of resting-contact. The box is being supported by the floor. It is free to bounce up, or continue on the floor, but cannot move down into the floor. This is an example of a constrained dynamics problem that does not reduce the number of degrees of freedom. The box can move in all directions, it is just that it cannot move down below the floor height in the y direction. The problem of roller coaster cars on a track is fundamentally different. The track is a complex curve that can wind in any direction. But, since the cars are constrained to move only on the track, at any instant the cars have only one degree of freedom—they can only roll in the direction of the track. They cannot rise above, or fall below the track, nor can they turn against the track's direction. When the cars are at a particular position on the track, the track provides a local coordinate frame, within which the cars can move only backward or forward along one direction.

The three-jointed arm in this figure is an example of a constrained dynamics problem, where the constraints are rotational rather than translational. The segments of the arm can be translated and rotated in space, but only in configurations permitted by the set of possible joint angles. The number of degrees of freedom of each individual joint is one, a rotation about the axis of the joint. The entire arm configuration has three degrees of freedom, one for each joint.

11.1 PENALTY METHODS

The simplest way to maintain a constraint is via the *penalty method*. In this approach, motion is computed based on external and internal forces, without considering any constraints, and then forces are applied to counteract any deviation from the desired constrained motion. A way to think about this approach is to think of there being a *control system* that has a sensor measuring any deviation from the constraint, and a servo motor that exerts a correcting force based on this measured deviation.

Since the penalty approach depends on the deviation from the constraint in order to generate a correcting force, no penalty method is able to maintain a *hard constraint*. A hard constraint is one that can never be violated, even to a small degree. If a hard constraint is needed, other methods must be used. But, in many cases a *soft constraint*, where small deviations from the constraint can be temporarily tolerated, will work. In this case the penalty method's simplicity and ease of implementation make it very handy to have in the tool set of an animator.

11.1.1 P Control: Proportional

The simplest control system that can be used for the penalty method is known as a *proportional* or *P controller*, which exerts a force that is directly proportional to the measured constraint deviation. The construction of the controller is as follows. Consider the case of a gray bead constrained to follow along a wire, as shown in the figure. The thin line indicates the constraint path or wire, while the actual path of the bead is shown as a bold line. The position of the center of the bead is $\mathbf{x}(t)$, the nearest point on the constraint path to the bead is $\mathbf{c}(\mathbf{x})$, and the vector measuring the error, or deviation from the constraint, is $\mathbf{e}(\mathbf{x}) = \mathbf{x}(t) - \mathbf{c}(\mathbf{x})$. A P controller, whose strength constant is k_p, would exert the correcting force

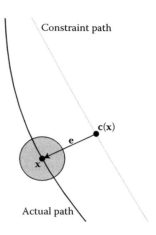

$$\mathbf{f}_p = -k_p \mathbf{e}.$$

Note that this construction is identical to having a spring of rest length 0 connecting the constraint path to the bead, where one end of the spring is free to slide along the path.

In an implementation, for each object using a P controller to enforce a constraint via the penalty method, the corresponding constraint force $\mathbf{f}_p$ would have to be added into the sum of forces acting on the object. This assumes that an error function $\mathbf{e}(\mathbf{x})$ is known for each such object.

The figure to the right shows what the gray bead's motion might look like if it were constrained to travel along a parabolic track using a P controller. The thin line denotes the track, and the darker line shows the path that the bead might follow under the influence of gravity, air resistance, and the controller. While the

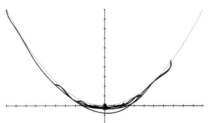

bead generally tries to follow the constraint path, there are large deviations and oscillations in the distance between the bead and the path. In addition, when the bead comes to rest, there is a constant offset from the path, where the force due to gravity exactly counteracts the force exerted by the controller.

11.1.2 PD Control: Proportional + Derivative

The large swings in error exhibited by the proportional or P controller are due to the fact that it does not exert a force to hold a constraint until the constraint has already been violated. A P controller can be greatly improved by the addition of a *derivative* term, giving it the ability to anticipate future changes in the error.

The derivative term adds a force proportional to the rate of change of the error in the direction of the error vector, so that the controller's total force is given by

$$\mathbf{f}_{pd} = -\left[k_p\mathbf{e} + k_d(\dot{\mathbf{e}} \cdot \hat{\mathbf{e}})\hat{\mathbf{e}}\right],$$

where k_d is an adjustable gain (scale factor) on the error derivative. Note, that this formulation is identical to adding a damper to a spring of rest length 0, connecting the bead to the constraint path. Such a controller is called a *proportional plus derivative* or *PD controller*.

In an implementation, for each object using a PD controller to enforce a constraint via the penalty method, the corresponding constraint force $\mathbf{f}_{pd}$ would have to be added into the sum of forces acting on the object. This assumes that an error function $\mathbf{e}(\mathbf{x})$ and its first time derivative $\dot{\mathbf{e}}$ are known for each such object. If the function $\mathbf{e}$ is known analytically, it can be differentiated via the chain rule to obtain

$$\dot{\mathbf{e}} = \frac{\partial\mathbf{e}}{\partial\mathbf{x}}\frac{d\mathbf{x}}{dt}, \quad \text{or} \quad \dot{\mathbf{e}} = \frac{\partial\mathbf{e}}{\partial\mathbf{x}}\mathbf{v}.$$

Often there is no convenient analytic form for the error function. As long as we can compute $\mathbf{e}$, we can use the error at the current timestep n, and the error at the previous timestep $n - 1$ to approximate the rate of change of error at the current timestep:

$$\dot{\mathbf{e}}^{[n]} \approx (\mathbf{e}^{[n]} - \mathbf{e}^{[n-1]})/h.$$

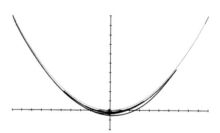

The figure shows the path of the gray bead following a parabolic path, using a PD controller to maintain the constraint. The large swings and oscillations exhibited by the P controller have been eliminated. However, the constant offset from the path when the bead comes to rest is identical to that obtained with the P controller, because the derivative term can exert no force unless the error is changing.

11.1.3 PID Control: Proportional + Integral + Derivative

The rest state error problem with the P and PD controllers can be solved by adding an *integral* term, which exerts a force proportional to the integral of the error. Such a controller is called a *proportional plus integral plus derivative* or *PID controller*. The total force exerted by a PID controller is given by

$$\mathbf{f}_{pid} = -\left[k_p\mathbf{e} + k_d(\dot{\mathbf{e}} \cdot \hat{\mathbf{e}})\hat{\mathbf{e}} + k_i\int_0^t \mathbf{e}\,dt\right],$$

where k_i is an adjustable gain on the error integral.

In an implementation, for each object using a PID controller to enforce a constraint via the penalty method, the corresponding constraint force $\mathbf{f}_{pid}$ would have to be added into the sum of forces acting on the object. The first two terms of the PID controller are computed just as for a PD controller. To compute the integral term, all that we need is to be able to compute **e** at each timestep. The integral of the error is simply the sum of the values for **e**, scaled by the timestep. We can maintain a vector variable **E** to hold this sum. In the simplest implementation, using Euler integration, as we advance to timestep n from timestep $n-1$,

$$\mathbf{E}^{[n]} = \mathbf{E}^{[n-1]} + \mathbf{e}^{[n]} h.$$

A very clean way to do the integration is to include **E** in the state vector, and in the system dynamics function set $\dot{\mathbf{E}} = \mathbf{e}(\mathbf{x})$. Then, the integral of the error will be automatically calculated by whatever integration scheme is being used.

Another implementation issue with PID controllers is that if the system is wildly out of constraint, the integrator will rapidly accumulate a very high value, which can take a long time to dissipate as the system comes into constraint. A standard way of overcoming this problem with the integral term is to establish a maximum limit on the integrator's magnitude. If the magnitude of the integrator's output exceeds this value, the integrator output is held clamped so that it cannot exceed this limit.

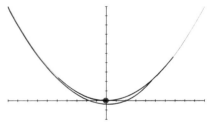

The figure shows a path obtained with a PID controller. Initially, the motion is nearly identical to that obtained with the PD controller, but as the bead slows it comes very close to the constraint path, and in the final rest configuration it exactly meets the constraint. This is because the integral term will exert a force that increases as long as the constraint is not met, so it is able to provide a force that eventually will exactly compensate for the force due to gravity.

Penalty constraint controllers can be used to good effect in a number of important animation applications. One of the most time-consuming tasks in a simulation for animation is collision detection and response, since computing these accurately can involve complex geometric calculations to determine a collision, and stopping and restarting the simulation to handle the response accurately. One of the ways in which the penalty method has been used successfully is to anticipate and prevent collisions from actually occurring.

A popular approach is to make a rough distance test between objects that may collide. If the objects appear to be headed for collision, a one-way PD controller that exerts force only in the direction preventing collision can be attached between the objects—this would function like a damped spring that acts to prevent the objects from approaching each other but exerts no force tending to pull the objects together. The picture illustrates, from top to bottom, how this might work over several timesteps in a simulation. A damped spring, with a non-zero rest length, is attached to the ball as it nears the vertical wall. The spring makes contact with the wall and is compressed by the ball's motion, producing a force pushing the ball back away from the wall. This causes the ball to bounce away from the wall without ever having to do accurate collision detection and response tests. As the ball moves away from the wall, the damped spring is removed. This approach has been used in cloth simulation to prevent cloth from self-penetrating [Baraff and Witkin, 1998]. One approach to quickly determine the distance between objects in a rigid body simulation is to maintain a signed distance field to indicate distance from fixed obstacles [Guendelman et al., 2003].

11.2 CONSTRAINED DYNAMICS

While penalty methods provide an easy way to maintain constraints, they have the problem that they cannot exactly model a hard constraint. This is because they require there to be some detectable constraint violation error before they are able to generate forces to counteract that error. In a classic set of SIGGRAPH Course Notes, Andrew Witkin [Witkin and Baraff, 2001] developed the mathematics of what he calls *constrained dynamics*. This is a way of guaranteeing maintenance of hard constraints by generating forces that counteract applied forces, to prevent any constraint violation from ever occurring. Here we summarize that method, beginning with a simple one degree of freedom example, containing only one constraint, and then showing how the method can be generalized to handle problems with multiple constraints.

11.2.1 One Constraint

We will look first at the problem of simulating the constrained dynamics of a pendulum undergoing motion in 2D—i.e., the pendulum's motion remains in a single plane. The figure to the right shows how this might be configured. The position $\mathbf{x}_0$ is at the fulcrum of the pendulum, so all motion should be a rotation about this position. The pendulum has a spherical bob of mass m, mounted at the end of a solid shaft of length r, that is assumed to be of negligible mass. We will let the variable $\mathbf{x}$ be the position of the center of the bob, and the force $\mathbf{f}_a$ is the sum of all external forces applied to the pendulum's

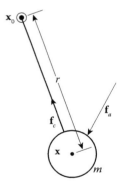

bob. What we seek to do is to always generate a constraint force $\mathbf{f}_c$ that exactly counteracts any component of $\mathbf{f}_a$ that will tend to cause the shaft's length to change. Intuitively, for this problem we can see that the constraint force should act along the direction of the shaft.

A key element of the constrained dynamics approach is to define, for each constraint in the system, a constraint function that goes to 0 when, and only when, the constraint is met. We start the system so that all constraints are satisfied, and then guarantee that there is no change in the constraint functions by making sure that their first and second time derivatives are always 0. Therefore, if a system is in constraint, it will always remain in constraint. For this to work, the constraint function has to be chosen such that it has a non-zero first spatial derivative when the constraint is being met.

For example, for the pendulum problem, we could pick the most obvious constraint function

$$c(\mathbf{x}) = \|\mathbf{x} - \mathbf{x}_0\| - r.$$

Clearly, this goes to 0 when the distance between $\mathbf{x}$ and $\mathbf{x}_0$ is exactly r. In addition, its derivative with respect to $\mathbf{x}$ is non-zero at this distance. (It is the direction vector from $\mathbf{x}_0$ to $\mathbf{x}$.) The only problem with this constraint function is that taking the norm of a vector requires a square root, and thus its derivative is harder to compute than is necessary. Instead, we could pick the constraint function

$$c(\mathbf{x}) = \frac{1}{2}[(\mathbf{x} - \mathbf{x}_0)^2 - r^2]. \tag{11.1}$$

Notice that this function still goes to 0 when the distance between $\mathbf{x}$ and $\mathbf{x}_0$ is exactly r. However, its derivative

$$\frac{\partial c}{\partial \mathbf{x}} = c' = \mathbf{x} - \mathbf{x}_0 \tag{11.2}$$

is very simple, and is clearly non-zero when $\|\mathbf{x} - \mathbf{x}_0\| = r$.

If we start a simulation with $c = 0$, it will stay at 0 as long as $\frac{\partial c}{\partial t} = \dot{c} = 0$, and $\dot{c}$ will remain at 0 as long as $\frac{\partial^2 c}{\partial t^2} = \ddot{c} = 0$. By the chain rule,

$$\dot{c} = \frac{\partial c}{\partial \mathbf{x}} \frac{d\mathbf{x}}{dt} = c'\dot{\mathbf{x}}.$$

Thus, by Equation 11.2 we have

$$\dot{c} = (\mathbf{x} - \mathbf{x}_0) \cdot \dot{\mathbf{x}}, \tag{11.3}$$

and differentiating this, with respect to time, gives

$$\ddot{c} = \dot{\mathbf{x}}^2 + (\mathbf{x} - \mathbf{x}_0) \cdot \ddot{\mathbf{x}}. \tag{11.4}$$

The total force acting on the bob is the sum of the applied and constraint forces, so by Newton's second law

$$\ddot{\mathbf{x}} = \frac{1}{m}(\mathbf{f}_a + \mathbf{f}_c). \tag{11.5}$$

Now, since we need to constrain $\dot{c}$ to be zero, by Equation 11.3

$$(\mathbf{x} - \mathbf{x}_0) \cdot \dot{\mathbf{x}} = 0. \tag{11.6}$$

Note, that this requires that the bob's velocity $\dot{\mathbf{x}}$ must always be perpendicular to the vector $(\mathbf{x} - \mathbf{x}_0)$ along the pendulum's shaft, which can be understood as the condition that all motion be circular about the pendulum's fulcrum. Also, since we need to constrain $\ddot{c}$ to be zero, we can set Equation 11.4 to zero, replace $\ddot{\mathbf{x}}$ by Equation 11.5 and rearrange to give us the constraint force expression

$$\frac{1}{m}(\mathbf{x} - \mathbf{x}_0) \cdot \mathbf{f}_c = -\dot{\mathbf{x}}^2 - \frac{1}{m}(\mathbf{x} - \mathbf{x}_0) \cdot \mathbf{f}_a. \tag{11.7}$$

We can now invoke the principle of *virtual work*. Briefly stated, this principle requires that constraint forces can do no work on a system. The work done by a force is defined to be the integral, over a motion path, of the component of the force in the direction of motion. But, since virtual work requires that no work ever be done by the constraint force, the integrand must always be zero, meaning that a constraint force can never act in the direction of the velocity. In the pendulum problem, this means that the constraint force of the shaft on the bob can neither speed up nor slow down the bob. Therefore, we require that

$$\mathbf{f}_c \cdot \dot{\mathbf{x}} = 0. \tag{11.8}$$

Equation 11.6 requires that the shaft vector always be perpendicular to the velocity of the bob, and Equation 11.8 requires that the constraint force also always be perpendicular to the velocity. Therefore, since all motion is in a single plane, the constraint force must be parallel to the shaft, so that we can write

$$\mathbf{f}_c = \lambda(\mathbf{x} - \mathbf{x}_0), \tag{11.9}$$

where λ is a scale factor to be determined.

This gives mathematical form to our original intuition that the constraint force acts only along the shaft. The constraint force is parallel to the shaft vector $(\mathbf{x} - \mathbf{x}_0)$, and we need only to find its magnitude and sign by solving for the scale factor λ. This also turns the problem of finding the constraint force into a scalar problem, rather than a vector problem. Once the correct value for λ is known, Equation 11.9 uniquely determines $\mathbf{f}_c$.

If we apply this to Equation 11.7, we can solve for λ:

$$\frac{\lambda}{m}(\mathbf{x} - \mathbf{x}_0)^2 = -\dot{\mathbf{x}}^2 - \frac{1}{m}(\mathbf{x} - \mathbf{x}_0) \cdot \mathbf{f}_a, \quad \text{or}$$

$$\lambda = -\frac{m\dot{\mathbf{x}}^2 + (\mathbf{x} - \mathbf{x}_0) \cdot \mathbf{f}_a}{(\mathbf{x} - \mathbf{x}_0)^2}. \tag{11.10}$$

One small practical implementation problem remains. Since we are maintaining the pendulum shaft length by computing a constraint force at each timestep, there is bound to be some small numerical drift of the constraint, simply due to the accumulation of computation round-off error over many timesteps. This drift will manifest itself in the constraint function and its first derivative moving slightly away from 0. Witkin suggests that this problem can be handled by augmenting the value for λ by a penalty term, using a PD controller that takes c and $\dot{c}$ as its error signals. Augmenting Equation 11.10 by this controller gives us

$$\lambda = -\frac{m\dot{\mathbf{x}}^2 + (\mathbf{x} - \mathbf{x}_0) \cdot \mathbf{f}_a}{(\mathbf{x} - \mathbf{x}_0)^2} - k_p c - k_d \dot{c}, \qquad (11.11)$$

where k_p and k_d are adjustable proportional and derivative constants. In practice, the amount of numerical drift will be quite small, so the solution will not be especially sensitive to the values of these constants.

So, the system dynamics function for the pendulum first requires the computation of all external forces acting on the pendulum, in order to determine $\mathbf{f}_a$, then Equation 11.11 is used to compute the scale factor λ to be applied in Equation 11.9 to compute the constraint force $\mathbf{f}_c$. Given $\mathbf{f}_a$ and $\mathbf{f}_c$, Equation 11.5 is used to compute the total acceleration on the bob.

11.2.2   Multiple Constraints

Now that we have seen how constrained dynamics works for a small problem, with only one constraint, we can generalize the approach to handle more complex systems with multiple constraints. We will use the figure to the right to give us a concrete example, but the equations we develop will be applicable to more general problems. Here we have three masses, attached together by two rigid rods, with the joints at the middle mass free to rotate in all directions. Thus, the rods act as distance constraints between the masses that they are connected to.

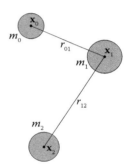

The three masses are at positions $\mathbf{x}_0$, $\mathbf{x}_1$, and $\mathbf{x}_2$, and the two distance constraints are r_{01} and r_{12}. Now, we need to design two constraint functions. Following the pendulum example, these could be

$$c_0(\mathbf{x}_0, \mathbf{x}_1) = \frac{1}{2}[(\mathbf{x}_1 - \mathbf{x}_0)^2 - r_{01}^2] \text{ and,}$$

$$c_1(\mathbf{x}_1, \mathbf{x}_2) = \frac{1}{2}[(\mathbf{x}_2 - \mathbf{x}_1)^2 - r_{12}^2].$$

In any problem like this, the constraints will be functions of the positions of the objects being constrained. We can then generalize by organizing the positions into a vector $\mathbf{X}$, and the constraints into a vector $\mathbf{C}(\mathbf{X})$. In this example,

$$\mathbf{X} = \begin{bmatrix} \mathbf{x}_0 \\ \mathbf{x}_1 \\ \mathbf{x}_2 \end{bmatrix},$$

and

$$\mathbf{C} = \begin{bmatrix} c_0(\mathbf{X}) \\ c_1(\mathbf{X}) \end{bmatrix}.$$

In order to maintain a constraint that is already being met, we need to hold the first and second time derivatives of the constraint vector to be $\mathbf{0}$. The first derivative is

$$\dot{\mathbf{C}} = \frac{\partial \mathbf{C}}{\partial \mathbf{X}} \frac{d\mathbf{X}}{dt},$$

or

$$\dot{\mathbf{C}} = \mathbf{J}\dot{\mathbf{X}},$$

where $\mathbf{J}$ is the Jacobian matrix of $\mathbf{C}$, as defined in Section 7.7.2. In our three mass—two constraint example,

$$\mathbf{J} = \begin{bmatrix} \frac{\partial c_0}{\partial \mathbf{x}_0} & \frac{\partial c_0}{\partial \mathbf{x}_1} & \frac{\partial c_0}{\partial \mathbf{x}_2} \\ \frac{\partial c_1}{\partial \mathbf{x}_0} & \frac{\partial c_1}{\partial \mathbf{x}_1} & \frac{\partial c_1}{\partial \mathbf{x}_2} \end{bmatrix},$$

and

$$\dot{\mathbf{X}} = \begin{bmatrix} \dot{\mathbf{x}}_0 \\ \dot{\mathbf{x}}_1 \\ \dot{\mathbf{x}}_2 \end{bmatrix}.$$

Therefore, if there are m constraints and n masses, the matrix $\mathbf{J}$ is $m \times n$, and the vector $\dot{\mathbf{X}}$ is $n \times 1$. $\mathbf{C}$ and its derivatives, $\dot{\mathbf{C}}$ and $\ddot{\mathbf{C}}$, are $m \times 1$ vectors.

However, each of the terms in the Jacobian matrix is itself a row vector of three elements. For example,

$$\frac{\partial c_0}{\partial \mathbf{x}_0} = \begin{bmatrix} \frac{\partial c_0}{\partial x_0} & \frac{\partial c_0}{\partial y_0} & \frac{\partial c_0}{\partial z_0} \end{bmatrix},$$

and each of the elements of the vector $\dot{\mathbf{X}}$ is a three-element column vector. For example,

$$\dot{\mathbf{x}}_0 = \begin{bmatrix} \dot{x}_0 \\ \dot{y}_0 \\ \dot{z}_0 \end{bmatrix}.$$

Therefore, if we think of $\mathbf{J}$ as a matrix of scalars and $\dot{\mathbf{X}}$ as a vector of scalars, $\mathbf{J}$ is $m \times 3n$ and $\dot{\mathbf{X}}$ is $3n \times 1$. The vectors $\mathbf{C}$ and its time derivatives are $m \times 1$ vectors of scalars.

Differentiating $\dot{\mathbf{C}}$ to obtain the second time derivative of $\mathbf{C}$, gives us

$$\ddot{\mathbf{C}} = \dot{\mathbf{J}}\dot{\mathbf{X}} + \mathbf{J}\ddot{\mathbf{X}}.$$

If we now define a vector of n applied forces $\mathbf{F}_a$ and a vector of constraint forces $\mathbf{F}_c$, we can write Newton's second law for the constrained dynamics problem as

$$M\ddot{\mathbf{X}} = \mathbf{F}_a + \mathbf{F}_c,$$

where M is a $3n \times 3n$ diagonal matrix, known as the *matricized mass*. This matrix is 0 except for its diagonal elements, which are each of the masses, repeated three times.

This equation can be solved for the acceleration on the system

$$\ddot{\mathbf{X}} = M^{-1}(\mathbf{F}_a + \mathbf{F}_c).$$

Now, setting $\ddot{\mathbf{C}} = \mathbf{0}$, substituting the above equation for $\ddot{\mathbf{X}}$, and isolating $\mathbf{F}_c$ on the left-hand side gives us

$$\mathbf{J}M^{-1}\mathbf{F}_c = -\dot{\mathbf{J}}\dot{\mathbf{X}} - \mathbf{J}M^{-1}\mathbf{F}_a. \qquad (11.12)$$

This equation cannot be solved for the constraint forces, because the matrix $\mathbf{J}M^{-1}$ is $m \times n$, which will typically be non-square, and thus has no inverse. We can resolve this using the principal of virtual work together with the condition that $\dot{\mathbf{C}} = \mathbf{0}$.
    Since $\dot{\mathbf{C}} = \mathbf{0}$,

$$\mathbf{J}\dot{\mathbf{X}} = 0.$$

By the principle of virtual work, none of the constraint forces can have a component aligned with the velocity of the mass that it is applied to, so

$$\mathbf{F}_c \cdot \dot{\mathbf{X}} = 0.$$

The first of these conditions requires that each row of $\mathbf{J}$ be orthogonal to $\dot{\mathbf{X}}$. For the second condition to be true, it must be possible to represent the constraint forces as linear combinations of vectors orthogonal to $\dot{\mathbf{X}}$. Combining these two conditions, mathematically $\mathbf{F}_c$ must lie in the row space of $\mathbf{J}$. Therefore,

$$\mathbf{F}_c = \mathbf{J}^T\boldsymbol{\lambda}, \qquad (11.13)$$

where $\boldsymbol{\lambda}$ is a $m \times 1$ vector of scalars, with one element for each of the constraints.
    Equation 11.13 is the key equation in the constrained dynamics method. It states that the constraint force vector $\mathbf{F}_c$ is a weighted sum of the rows of $\mathbf{J}$. The weight for each row is the element of the vector $\boldsymbol{\lambda}$ corresponding to that row. Therefore, instead of needing to solve for the vector elements of the constraint force vector $\mathbf{F}_c$, we need only solve for the scalar elements of $\boldsymbol{\lambda}$. Once we know $\boldsymbol{\lambda}$, Equation 11.13 gives us $\mathbf{F}_c$.
    Substituting Equation 11.13 for $\mathbf{F}_c$ in Equation 11.12 gives us

$$\mathbf{J}M^{-1}\mathbf{J}^T\boldsymbol{\lambda} = -\dot{\mathbf{J}}\dot{\mathbf{X}} - \mathbf{J}M^{-1}\mathbf{F}_a. \qquad (11.14)$$

The matrix $\mathbf{J}M^{-1}\mathbf{J}^T$ is $m \times m$, so a solution to this equation is possible.
    As with our single constraint example, implementations should add a PD controller to eliminate any numerical drift in $\mathbf{C}$, so we would actually use

$$\mathbf{J}M^{-1}\mathbf{J}^T\boldsymbol{\lambda} = -\dot{\mathbf{J}}\dot{\mathbf{X}} - \mathbf{J}M^{-1}\mathbf{F}_a - k_p\mathbf{C} - k_d\dot{\mathbf{C}}. \qquad (11.15)$$

If we are to handle large systems of constraints, solving this equation can become a bottleneck in the system force calculations. Fortunately, the matrix $\mathbf{J}M^{-1}\mathbf{J}^T$

tends to be quite sparse, so the solution to Equation 11.15 can be attained with a solver designed to take advantage of that sparsity, with great savings in both time and space. The biconjugate gradient method described in *Numerical Recipes* [Press et al., 2007] is a commonly used approach. It has the advantage that it will arrive at a least-squared-error solution, even if the problem is overconstrained (i.e., maintaining all of the constraints simultaneously is impossible).

We can now complete the example that we began above by providing the necessary derivatives and matrices. The partial derivatives that are the elements of the Jacobian matrix J are

$$\frac{\partial c_0}{\partial \mathbf{x}_0} = -(\mathbf{x}_1 - \mathbf{x}_0)^T, \qquad \frac{\partial c_0}{\partial \mathbf{x}_1} = (\mathbf{x}_1 - \mathbf{x}_0)^T, \qquad \frac{\partial c_0}{\partial \mathbf{x}_2} = \mathbf{0}^T,$$

$$\frac{\partial c_1}{\partial \mathbf{x}_0} = \mathbf{0}^T, \qquad \frac{\partial c_1}{\partial \mathbf{x}_1} = -(\mathbf{x}_2 - \mathbf{x}_1)^T, \qquad \frac{\partial c_1}{\partial \mathbf{x}_2} = (\mathbf{x}_2 - \mathbf{x}_1)^T.$$

Therefore, the Jacobian matrix is

$$\mathbf{J} = \begin{bmatrix} -(\mathbf{x}_1 - \mathbf{x}_0)^T & (\mathbf{x}_1 - \mathbf{x}_0)^T & \mathbf{0}^T \\ \mathbf{0}^T & -(\mathbf{x}_2 - \mathbf{x}_1)^T & (\mathbf{x}_2 - \mathbf{x}_1)^T \end{bmatrix},$$

and its first time derivative is

$$\dot{\mathbf{J}} = \begin{bmatrix} -(\dot{\mathbf{x}}_1 - \dot{\mathbf{x}}_0)^T & (\dot{\mathbf{x}}_1 - \dot{\mathbf{x}}_0)^T & \mathbf{0}^T \\ \mathbf{0}^T & -(\dot{\mathbf{x}}_2 - \dot{\mathbf{x}}_1)^T & (\dot{\mathbf{x}}_2 - \dot{\mathbf{x}}_1)^T \end{bmatrix}.$$

If we let I be the 3×3 identify matrix, and 0 be the 3×3 zero matrix, then the matricized mass is

$$M = \begin{bmatrix} m_0 I & 0 & 0 \\ 0 & m_1 I & 0 \\ 0 & 0 & m_2 I \end{bmatrix},$$

and its inverse is

$$M^{-1} = \begin{bmatrix} \frac{1}{m_0} I & 0 & 0 \\ 0 & \frac{1}{m_1} I & 0 \\ 0 & 0 & \frac{1}{m_2} I \end{bmatrix}.$$

11.3 REDUCED COORDINATES

The constrained dynamics method is one approach to achieving constraints. The problem is typically posed in the usual 3D Cartesian frame, and forces are computed that exactly counteract any tendency to violate constraints. Thus, the constrained dynamics approach simply adds another source of forces to the system. Once these constraint forces are added, the simulation proceeds in the usual fashion, integrating accelerations to update velocities, and integrating velocities to update positions.

In this section, we look at an entirely different way of handling constraints—that is to pose the problem in a coordinate frame in which only motion in the allowed directions is possible. Let us use the 2D pendulum problem shown in the figure to illustrate what we mean. The pendulum's bob with mass m is constrained to always be at a fixed distance r from the axis of the pendulum. On the left, we

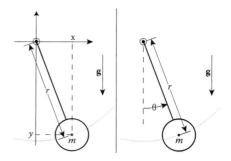

see the problem posed in a 2D Cartesian coordinate frame. At any point in time, the center of the pendulum's bob is at position $[x(t), y(t)]$, always subject to the constraint that

$$x^2(t) + y^2(t) = r^2.$$

To maintain this constraint, using the method of constrained dynamics described in Section 11.2, we would compute a constraint force exactly canceling any component of the gravitational force in the direction of the pendulum's shaft. On the right, the problem is posed in a polar coordinate frame. Here, the only variable is the angle that the pendulum's shaft makes from the vertical, and the center of the pendulum's bob is at $[r, \theta(t)]$. Therefore, the shaft-length constraint is always satisfied, and no additional forces need to be calculated to maintain this constraint.

Note that the polar coordinate formulation will be different from the Cartesian formulation in that the dynamics will be rotational, rather than translational. The gravitational force will result in a torque, producing angular acceleration. To advance the simulation, this angular acceleration would be integrated to yield angular velocity, which in turn would be integrated to determine angle.

The pendulum example leads us to the fundamental idea of the reduced coordinates approach to simulation—we pose the problem in a coordinate frame that has only the degrees of freedom allowable in the problem. The primary mathematical tool in this approach is the *Lagrangian dynamics formulation*. Instead of posing the problem in terms of forces and torques, this approach looks at how kinetic and potential energy interact to govern the system's dynamics.

11.3.1 Kinetic and Potential Energy

A system's energy is defined as its capacity to do work. Kinetic energy is the energy of a system contained in its motion. In Newtonian mechanics, a rigid body of mass m and moment of inertia I that is translating with velocity $\mathbf{v}$ and rotating with angular velocity $\boldsymbol{\omega}$ has kinetic energy

$$T = \frac{1}{2}(m\mathbf{v}^2 + \boldsymbol{\omega}^T I \boldsymbol{\omega}).$$

Note that the derivative of kinetic energy with respect to velocities $\mathbf{v}$ and $\boldsymbol{\omega}$ is the system's total momentum, $m\mathbf{v} + I\boldsymbol{\omega}$. Potential energy is the energy stored in a system due to its position or spatial configuration. Potential energy can be turned into kinetic energy, under the right conditions. A typical example is

$$V = mgh,$$

which is the potential energy of a body with mass m, in a gravitational field with strength g, and that is at a distance h from the ground plane. Note that the derivative of V with respect to height is mg, which is the negative of the force due to gravity. Another example is the potential energy stored in a compressed spring. If the spring has stiffness constant k, rest length l^0, and current length l, its potential energy is

$$V = \frac{1}{2}k(l - l^0)^2.$$

Note that in this case the derivative of V with respect to l is $k(l - l^0)$, which is the negative of the force exerted by a compressed spring. In general, the negative of the gradient[*] of potential energy is the force that this potential exerts.

11.3.2 Lagrangian Dynamics Formulation

To support the Lagrangian dynamics formulation, we first define

T to be the kinetic energy of the system

V to be the potential energy of the system

$L = T - V$ to be the *Lagrangian* of the system

Inspection shows that the Lagrangian L describes the balance of kinetic and potential energy in the system.

In the Lagrangian formulation, motion is taken to be with respect to a *generalized coordinate frame* $\mathbf{q}$, with one element of the vector $\mathbf{q}$ for each degree of freedom of the system. For example, $\mathbf{q}$ might be a set of allowable displacements and angles, or any convenient parameters parameterizing position along a curve, surface, or volume. Only motions satisfying the constraints on the system can be described in this coordinate frame, and so all solutions are guaranteed to satisfy the system constraints.

---

[*]The gradient of a scalar field is defined to be the first spatial derivative of the field, taken in each coordinate direction, and arranged as a vector. Look ahead to Section 13.2 for a more complete description of scalar fields and the gradient operator.

The central equation of the Lagrangian dynamics formulation is

$$\frac{d(\frac{\partial L}{\partial \dot{\mathbf{q}}})}{dt} - \frac{\partial L}{\partial \mathbf{q}} = \mathbf{Q}. \tag{11.16}$$

This equation relates changes in the Lagrangian L to a set of *applied* or *dissipative* forces and torques $\mathbf{Q}$. An applied force or torque is any one acting outside of the system being modeled and that is not accounted for in the computation of potential or kinetic energy. For example, an electric motor could be modeled as providing an applied torque to a fan rotor. A dissipative force is any force acting to remove energy from the system. Friction and air resistance are two canonical examples of dissipative forces—friction turns kinetic energy into heat and noise, while air resistance transfers some of the kinetic energy of a moving body into motion of the surrounding air mass.

Note that since only the kinetic energy is affected by the velocities represented in $\dot{\mathbf{q}}$, $\frac{\partial L}{\partial \dot{\mathbf{q}}}$ is the momentum of the system, and $d(\frac{\partial L}{\partial \dot{\mathbf{q}}})/dt$ is the rate of change of momentum. In other words, this term corresponds to the term $m\mathbf{a}$ in Newton's second law. Since the potential energy is only affected by the configuration $\mathbf{q}$, the term $\frac{\partial L}{\partial \mathbf{q}}$ governs how potential energy changes as the system moves spatially, and gives the force $\mathbf{F}$ acting internally on the system as it stores or releases potential energy. Thus, this equation reduces to $m\mathbf{a} - \mathbf{F} = \mathbf{Q}$ or

$$m\mathbf{a} = \mathbf{F} + \mathbf{Q},$$

which is in the form already familiar to us. Also note that while the internal workings of the system are described in terms of energy in a generalized coordinate system, $\mathbf{Q}$ must be specified in terms of forces in this same coordinate system.

11.3.3 Falling Ball Example

To see how the Lagrangian dynamics formulation works, let us look at the simple example we started with in Chapter 2, a ball falling under the influence of gravity. Assume that we have a ball of mass m, acting under a gravitational field $\mathbf{g} = -g\hat{\mathbf{u}}_y$, where $\hat{\mathbf{u}}_y$ is the unit vector in the vertical direction, and the coordinate frame is the standard 3D Cartesian coordinate system. The ball's position is $\mathbf{x} = \begin{bmatrix} x & y & z \end{bmatrix}^T$, and its velocity is $\mathbf{v} = \begin{bmatrix} v_x & v_y & v_z \end{bmatrix}^T$, so that, $\mathbf{q} = \mathbf{x}$, and $\dot{\mathbf{q}} = \mathbf{v}$. We will assume that the ball is not rotating, so it has no rotational inertia. Therefore, its kinetic energy is

$$T = \frac{1}{2}m\mathbf{v}^2.$$

The ball's potential energy is

$$V = \int_0^y mg\,dy, \quad \text{or} \quad V = mg\,\hat{\mathbf{u}}_y \cdot \mathbf{x}.$$

Therefore, the Lagrangian is

$$L = \frac{1}{2}m\mathbf{v}^2 - mg\,\hat{\mathbf{u}}_y \cdot \mathbf{x},$$

and we have the partial derivatives

$$\frac{\partial L}{\partial \mathbf{q}} = \frac{\partial L}{\partial \mathbf{x}} = -mg\,\hat{\mathbf{u}}_y, \quad \text{and} \quad \frac{\partial L}{\partial \dot{\mathbf{q}}} = \frac{\partial L}{\partial \mathbf{v}} = m\mathbf{v},$$

so that

$$\frac{d(\frac{\partial L}{\partial \dot{\mathbf{q}}})}{dt} = m\dot{\mathbf{v}} = m\mathbf{a},$$

where $\mathbf{a}$ is the acceleration vector. Since we have already accounted for gravitational force in the formulation of the potential energy, and there are no other forces acting, $\mathbf{Q} = \mathbf{0}$. Therefore Equation 11.16 becomes

$$\frac{d(\frac{\partial L}{\partial \dot{\mathbf{q}}})}{dt} - \frac{\partial L}{\partial \mathbf{q}} = \mathbf{0}, \quad \text{or}$$

$$m\mathbf{a} + mg\,\hat{\mathbf{u}}_y = \mathbf{0} \quad \text{and thus,}$$

$$\mathbf{a} = -g\,\hat{\mathbf{u}}_y.$$

This result is entirely unsurprising, as we knew the answer from the beginning, but the example serves to demonstrate how the various energies and derivatives are formulated, and how the partial derivatives are taken. It is also a first indication that the general Lagrangian dynamics formulation is correct.

If we considered air drag, then $\mathbf{Q}$ would be non-zero. If the drag were acting to oppose the ball's velocity, and proportional to its velocity with drag constant d, then the resulting dissipative force would be

$$\mathbf{Q} = -d\mathbf{v},$$

and Equation 11.16 would be

$$\frac{d(\frac{\partial L}{\partial \dot{\mathbf{q}}})}{dt} - \frac{\partial L}{\partial \mathbf{q}} = -d\mathbf{v}, \quad \text{or}$$

$$\mathbf{a} = -g\,\hat{\mathbf{u}}_y - \frac{d}{m}\mathbf{v}.$$

Again, this matches the solution we obtained by simply applying Newton's second law in Cartesian coordinates, in Section 2.7.2.

11.3.4 Pendulum Example

Given this success with a simple problem, let us look again at
the pendulum problem, expressed in polar coordinates. The only
coordinate is θ so **q** is the scalar $q = \theta$, and its rate of change is
$\dot{q} = \dot{\theta} = \omega$. Since the pendulum is only rotating, its kinetic energy contains only the rotational term. For this one-dimensional
problem, $I = mr^2$, and ω is a scalar, so

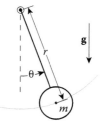

$$T = \frac{1}{2}mr^2\omega^2.$$

The potential energy increases linearly with the height y of the bob, which we can
pick to be 0 when the pendulum is at the same height as its axis, i.e., $\theta = 90°$, so
$y = -r\cos\theta$. Therefore, the potential energy is given by

$$V = -mgr\cos\theta,$$

and the Lagrangian is

$$L = \frac{1}{2}mr^2\omega^2 + mgr\cos\theta.$$

Now,

$$\frac{\partial L}{\partial \mathbf{q}} = \frac{\partial L}{\partial \theta} = -mgr\sin\theta, \quad \text{and} \quad \frac{\partial L}{\partial \dot{\mathbf{q}}} = \frac{\partial L}{\partial \omega} = mr^2\omega,$$

so that

$$\frac{d(\frac{\partial L}{\partial \dot{\mathbf{q}}})}{dt} = \frac{d(\frac{\partial L}{\partial \omega})}{dt} = mr^2\dot{\omega}.$$

Again, we have accounted for gravity and there are no other forces, so $Q = 0$, and
Equation 11.16 yields

$$\frac{d(\frac{\partial L}{\partial \omega})}{dt} - \frac{\partial L}{\partial \theta} = 0, \quad \text{or}$$
$$mr^2\dot{\omega} + mgr\sin\theta = 0 \quad \text{and thus,}$$
$$\dot{\omega} = \ddot{\theta} = -\frac{g}{r}\sin\theta,$$

which is the familiar solution to the pendulum problem. For small angles, $\theta \approx \sin\theta$
and the solution can be approximated as $\ddot{\theta} = -\frac{g}{r}\theta$. This can be seen to be an
oscillator with frequency $\omega = \sqrt{\frac{g}{r}}$ or period $P = 2\pi\sqrt{\frac{r}{g}}$, which for a pendulum
1 meter in length, on Earth, is approximately 2 seconds.

Adding air resistance to this formulation is easy. We assume that air resistance
will always result in a damping torque $\tau_d = -c_d r\dot{\theta}$ opposing the angular velocity,

where c_d is an air drag constant. This dissipative torque must be included in $\mathbf{Q}$ in Equation 11.16. We now have $Q = \tau_d = -c_d r\dot{\theta}$, so that

$$mr^2\ddot{\theta} + mgr \sin\theta = -c_d r\dot{\theta} \quad \text{or,}$$

$$\ddot{\theta} = -\frac{1}{r}\left(g\sin\theta + \frac{c_d}{m}\dot{\theta}\right).$$

This is the same solution that we had when air resistance was not included, but augmented by a term tending to reduce the angular acceleration by an amount proportional to the angular velocity.

11.3.5 Bead on a Wire Example

There is no reason that the generalized coordinates $\mathbf{q}$ must consist only of translations and rotations. The bead on a wire problem is a one-dimensional problem whose only coordinate is a parameter s, used to locate position along a curved path $\mathbf{c}$. Such a spatial curve would have 3D spatial coordinates given by

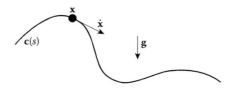

$$\mathbf{c}(s) = \begin{bmatrix} c_x(s) \\ c_y(s) \\ c_z(s) \end{bmatrix}.$$

If we think of this curve as a wire, and a bead with mass m and position $\mathbf{x}$ sliding along this wire, then clearly at any position s along the wire

$$\mathbf{x} = \mathbf{c}(s).$$

Differentiating the bead's position with respect to time, using the chain rule, gives the bead's velocity

$$\dot{\mathbf{x}} = \frac{\partial \mathbf{c}}{\partial s}\frac{ds}{dt} = \mathbf{c}'\dot{s}.$$

The bead's kinetic energy is given by

$$T = \frac{1}{2}m\dot{\mathbf{x}}^2 = \frac{1}{2}m\mathbf{c}'^2\dot{s}^2,$$

and if we assume the same gravitational system as in the previous problems, the bead's potential energy will be

$$V = mg\,\hat{\mathbf{u}}_y \cdot \mathbf{c}.$$

Therefore,

$$L = T - V = m\left(\frac{1}{2}\mathbf{c}'^2\dot{s}^2 - g\,\hat{\mathbf{u}}_y \cdot \mathbf{c}\right).$$

Now,

$$\frac{\partial L}{\partial q} = \frac{\partial L}{\partial s} = m\left(\mathbf{c}' \cdot \mathbf{c}'' \dot{s}^2 - g\, \hat{\mathbf{u}}_y \cdot \mathbf{c}'\right),$$

and

$$\frac{\partial L}{\partial \dot{q}} = \frac{\partial L}{\partial \dot{s}} = m\mathbf{c}'^2 \dot{s},$$

whose first time derivative is

$$\frac{d\left(\frac{\partial L}{\partial \dot{s}}\right)}{dt} = m\frac{d}{dt}\left(\mathbf{c}'^2 \dot{s}\right) = m\left(\mathbf{c}'^2 \ddot{s} + 2\mathbf{c}' \cdot \frac{\partial \mathbf{c}'}{\partial s}\frac{ds}{dt}\dot{s}\right) = m\left(\mathbf{c}'^2 \ddot{s} + 2\mathbf{c}' \cdot \mathbf{c}'' \dot{s}^2\right).$$

Since there are no applied or dissipative forces outside of gravity, $Q = 0$, and Equation 11.16 yields

$$\frac{d\left(\frac{\partial L}{\partial \dot{s}}\right)}{dt} - \frac{\partial L}{\partial s} = 0, \quad \text{or}$$

$$m\left(\mathbf{c}'^2 \ddot{s} + 2\mathbf{c}' \cdot \mathbf{c}'' \dot{s}^2 - \mathbf{c}' \cdot \mathbf{c}'' \dot{s}^2 + g\, \hat{\mathbf{u}}_y \cdot \mathbf{c}'\right) = 0 \quad \text{and thus,}$$

$$\ddot{s} = -\frac{\mathbf{c}' \cdot \mathbf{c}'' \dot{s}^2 + g\, \hat{\mathbf{u}}_y \cdot \mathbf{c}'}{\mathbf{c}'^2}.$$

A nice extension of the bead on a wire problem would be the problem of a character moving over a complex terrain. If the terrain is represented by NURBS patches, there will be two parameters u and v governing position on the surface, and the NURBS equations can be differentiated with respect to these parameters. In this case, $\mathbf{q} = \begin{bmatrix} u & v \end{bmatrix}^T$, and the derivatives of kinetic energy with respect to $\mathbf{q}$ and potential energy with respect to $\dot{\mathbf{q}}$ will also be vectors. The solution will determine accelerations in both the u and v directions, with the clear benefit that all positions will remain strictly on the surface.

Although Lagrangian dynamics, using generalized or reduced coordinates, is a powerful way of establishing and maintaining constraints, it is not often used in animation, simply because it is quite difficult to build into a modeling and animation package. Since each problem will have its own generalized coordinate system, and each will have a unique formulation for capturing the kinetic and potential energy of the system, there is no straightforward way to build this into a modeler.

11.4 SUMMARY

Here are some of the main points to take away from this chapter:

- The degrees of freedom of a dynamic simulation of an object are those distinct directions in which the the object can move. The degrees of freedom can be translational or rotational.

- A constrained dynamics problem is one in which motion may be restricted along one of the degrees of freedom, or motion along one or more degrees of freedom may be prevented.

- Penalty methods approximate constrained dynamics by exerting forces in response to deviations from the desired constrained motion. These cannot provide hard constraints on the motion since they only act in response to an error that has already occurred.

- The technique of Dynamic Constraints maintains hard constraints by introducing constraint forces canceling any applied forces that would tend to move the object out of constraint.

- The technique of Reduced Coordinates guarantees that constraints are always met by posing the problem in a generalized coordinate frame in which disallowed degrees of freedom are removed from the problem. Any solution in this coordinate frame will be guaranteed to be in constraint.

CHAPTER 12

Articulated Bodies

A WIDE VARIETY OF ANIMATED OBJECTS, most especially humans and animals with a skeleton, can be modeled as an articulated body, which is a tree of linked chains. The diagram shows abstractly how this could be done to model a puppet pulling a wagon. Most segments of the model are chains composed of rigid links, connected together by rotating 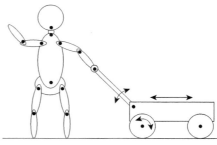 joints. The one exception to this is the wagon's body, which does not rotate, but can move back and forth parallel to the floor.

Simulating the dynamics of an articulated body can be approached in several ways, but the approach that has proven to be most useful in computer animation is the algorithm due to Featherstone [1983], who developed it for use in robotics. This algorithm was elaborated for practical use in graphics by Mirtich [1996a], and a particularly efficient implementation is described in Kokkevis [2004]. Here, we will follow closely the approach elaborated by Mirtich, because it is probably the easiest to follow. The reader wishing a fuller explanation of the method is directed to Chapter 4 of Mirtich's thesis [Mirtich, 1996b].

12.1   STRUCTURE OF AN ARTICULATED BODY

In a multilink chain, we consider each chain to have a *root* that can be used to place the object in space. The figure to the right shows a four-linked structure, mounted on a pedestal base, which serves as the chain's root. The $\oplus$ symbol indicates the center of mass of each link. A link's *inboard* joint connects to its neighboring link closer to the root. There can be zero, one, or more *outboard* joints connecting to neighboring links farther from the root. The structure would be placed in a 3D scene by positioning and orienting its root link. The rest of the structure 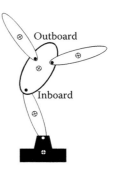 is defined relative to the position and orientation of the center of mass of the root. Although, in this example, the root serves as a base at the bottom of the chain, other articulated structures may have a root more centrally located. For example, in a model like the puppet, the link that would typically serve as the root would be the one representing the hips.

The two kinds of joints that can be used to connect the links in an articulated body are known as *revolute* and *prismatic*. This diagram shows how each type of joint is modeled. With respect to the joint connecting a link to its inboard neighbor, a link with a revolute joint can only rotate, and a link with a prismatic joint can only translate. In the puppet-with-wagon example, all of the links are revolute, except the wagon's body, which is prismatic.

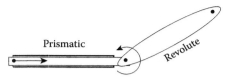

To simplify modeling, we can consider each joint to have only one degree of freedom. The requirement that each joint can have only one degree of freedom is not a limitation on the structure of the model, because multiple joints can be placed at the same location. Thus, a joint like the knuckle on a finger, which has one degree of rotational freedom, can be modeled by a single revolute joint, but a joint like the hip, which has two degrees of rotational freedom, would be modeled by two joints with a 0 length link between them.

We will define joint i to be the joint between link i and its inboard neighbor. Since this joint has only one degree of freedom, we need only the direction of the joint axis, and a single scalar parameter to describe the orientation of the joint relative to its inboard neighbor. We will use the symbol q_i to represent that parameter for joint i. If the joint connecting link i to its inboard neighbor is revolute, q_i is an angle of rotation about the axis defining the joint's rotational degree of freedom. If the joint is prismatic, q_i is a displacement in the direction of the joint's translational degree of freedom. Likewise, the first time derivative $\dot{q}_i$ of this joint parameter gives the angular speed of a revolute joint or the translational speed of a prismatic joint, and its second time derivative $\ddot{q}_i$ gives the angular acceleration of a revolute joint or the translational acceleration of a prismatic joint.

The entire collection of displacements for a multilink structure is known as its *configuration*. The positional state of an entire configuration of n links is represented by the vector

$$\mathbf{q} = \begin{bmatrix} q_1 & q_2 & \cdots & q_n \end{bmatrix}^T.$$

Note that there is no entry for q_0 since, by definition, it is always true that $q_0 = 0$. Because this vector represents a configuration of the structure, it is said to lie in *configuration space*.

Each model will be assembled from its individual links in a starting configuration that is called its *pose configuration*. The diagram to the right might be the pose configuration of a puppet. By definition, in pose configuration all joint angles or displacements are 0, thus $q_i = 0$ for all joints. In other words, the pose configuration is the origin of the configuration space,

$$\mathbf{q}_0 = \begin{bmatrix} 0 & 0 & \cdots & 0 \end{bmatrix}^T.$$

12.2 DYNAMIC STATE OF AN ARTICULATED BODY

The dynamic state of the multilink structure is compactly described by the configuration vector $\mathbf{q}$ and its first time derivative

$$\dot{\mathbf{q}} = \begin{bmatrix} \dot{q}_1 & \dot{q}_2 & \cdots & \dot{q}_n \end{bmatrix}^T.$$

Likewise, the rate of change of this dynamic state is described by $\dot{\mathbf{q}}$ and its second time derivative

$$\ddot{\mathbf{q}} = \begin{bmatrix} \ddot{q}_1 & \ddot{q}_2 & \cdots & \ddot{q}_n \end{bmatrix}^T.$$

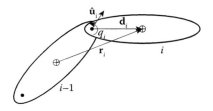

We start by considering chains where each link is connected to at most one outboard link, and order the links such that the inboard neighbor of link i is always link $i-1$. Later in this section we will generalize to handle trees of chains, where links may have more than one outboard link. The right figure is a vector diagram, set up for link i and its inboard neighbor. The direction vector $\hat{\mathbf{u}}_i$ indicates the direction of the degree of freedom of joint i, between links $i-1$ and i, and q_i is the joint's scalar displacement parameter. The vector $\mathbf{d}_i$ encodes the distance and direction from the position of joint i to the center of mass of link i, and vector $\mathbf{r}_i$ encodes the difference between the center of mass of link i and the center of mass of link $i-1$.

As a convention, all of the vectors for link i will be represented in the model space of link i. The center of mass of the link will be the origin $\mathbf{0}$ of the link's model space, and its joint direction vector $\hat{\mathbf{u}}_i$ is fixed in this space. For a link with a revolute joint, $\mathbf{d}_i$ is also fixed. For a prismatic joint, $\mathbf{d}_i$ is always parallel to $\hat{\mathbf{u}}_i$, but varies in length. Because the joint between links $i-1$ and i has only a single degree of freedom, the transformation from the model space of link $i-1$ to that of link i is straightforward, involving only a rotation and a translation. We will call this transformation $_iT_{i-1}$. Its inverse $_{i-1}T_i$ transforms from the model space of link i to that of link $i-1$. The representation of this transformation will be detailed below, after we develop the required mathematical framework.

We can start by defining the angular velocity $\boldsymbol{\omega}_i^0$ and the velocity $\mathbf{v}_i^0$ of the center of mass of link i, relative to its inboard link. These are the velocities it would have if the motions of its neighboring links are ignored, and only the rate of change $\dot{q}_i$

of the joint's configuration parameter q_i is considered. For a prismatic joint

$$\boldsymbol{\omega}_i^0 = \mathbf{0}, \text{ and}$$
$$\mathbf{v}_i^0 = \dot{q}_i \hat{\mathbf{u}}_i, \tag{12.1}$$

and for a revolute joint

$$\boldsymbol{\omega}_i^0 = \dot{q}_i \hat{\mathbf{u}}_i, \text{ and}$$
$$\mathbf{v}_i^0 = \dot{q}_i \hat{\mathbf{u}}_i \times \mathbf{d}_i. \tag{12.2}$$

To understand this last equation, recall from Section 9.1 that the derivative of a vector $\mathbf{a}$ undergoing pure rotation with angular velocity $\boldsymbol{\omega}$ is given by $\dot{\mathbf{a}} = \boldsymbol{\omega} \times \mathbf{a}$, and note that $\dot{q}_i \hat{\mathbf{u}}_i$ is the angular velocity of joint i.

The state of each link can now be defined inductively, starting at the root and working out. To simplify the notation, we will assume that all vectors have already been transformed into the model space of link i. The root link will have a specified position $\mathbf{x}_0$, and its velocities will be

$$\boldsymbol{\omega}_0 = \mathbf{0}, \text{ and } \mathbf{v}_0 = \mathbf{0}.$$

At each subsequent link,

$$\mathbf{x}_i = \mathbf{x}_{i-1} + \mathbf{r}_i,$$
$$\boldsymbol{\omega}_i = \boldsymbol{\omega}_{i-1} + \boldsymbol{\omega}_i^0, \text{ and}$$
$$\mathbf{v}_i = \mathbf{v}_{i-1} + \boldsymbol{\omega}_{i-1} \times \mathbf{r}_i + \mathbf{v}_i^0. \tag{12.3}$$

We see that the state of the entire chain is uniquely determined from its configuration $\mathbf{q}$ and its rate of change $\dot{\mathbf{q}}$, using Equations 12.1, 12.2, and 12.3.

The acceleration of the configuration can be determined by differentiating the rotational and translational velocities to obtain the rotational acceleration $\boldsymbol{\alpha}_i$ and translational acceleration $\mathbf{a}_i$. Since the vector $\mathbf{r}_i$ in Equation 12.3 is both rotating and changing in length, its time derivative is $\dot{\mathbf{r}}_i = \boldsymbol{\omega}_{i-1} \times \mathbf{r}_i + \mathbf{v}_i^0$. Therefore, the link accelerations defined inductively are

$$\boldsymbol{\alpha}_i = \boldsymbol{\alpha}_{i-1} + \dot{\boldsymbol{\omega}}_i^0, \text{ and,}$$
$$\mathbf{a}_i = \mathbf{a}_{i-1} + \boldsymbol{\alpha}_{i-1} \times \mathbf{r}_i + \boldsymbol{\omega}_{i-1} \times (\boldsymbol{\omega}_{i-1} \times \mathbf{r}_i) + \boldsymbol{\omega}_{i-1} \times \mathbf{v}_i^0 + \dot{\mathbf{v}}_i^0. \tag{12.4}$$

In order to complete the computation of the accelerations for each joint i, we still need to determine the accelerations $\dot{\boldsymbol{\omega}}_i^0$ and $\dot{\mathbf{v}}_i^0$. Differentiating Equation 12.1 for a prismatic joint we obtain

$$\dot{\boldsymbol{\omega}}_i^0 = \mathbf{0}, \text{ and}$$
$$\dot{\mathbf{v}}_i^0 = \ddot{q}_i \hat{\mathbf{u}}_i + \boldsymbol{\omega}_{i-1} \times \dot{q}_i \hat{\mathbf{u}}_i, \tag{12.5}$$

and differentiating Equation 12.2 for a revolute joint we obtain

$$\dot{\boldsymbol{\omega}}_i^0 = \ddot{q}_i \hat{\mathbf{u}}_i + \boldsymbol{\omega}_{i-1} \times \dot{q}_i \hat{\mathbf{u}}_i, \text{ and}$$
$$\dot{\mathbf{v}}_i^0 = \ddot{q}_i \hat{\mathbf{u}}_i \times \mathbf{d}_i + \boldsymbol{\omega}_{i-1} \times \dot{q}_i \hat{\mathbf{u}}_i \times \mathbf{d}_i + \dot{q}_i \hat{\mathbf{u}}_i \times (\dot{q}_i \hat{\mathbf{u}}_i \times \mathbf{d}_i). \quad (12.6)$$

Note that since Equations 12.5 and 12.6 require the joint's parametric acceleration $\ddot{q}_i$, we cannot calculate the accelerations inductively in the same way that we did for velocities.

The algorithm proposed by Featherstone, elaborated by Mirtich, and refined by Kokkevis uses a three-step process to complete the computation of the configuration acceleration. First, a loop over the links proceeding outward from the root uses the current state to compute the translational and angular velocities of all links. Then, an opposite inward loop uses these velocities together with applied torques and forces to compute quantities necessary for the computation of the accelerations of each link, which are then computed in a second outward loop. Before describing this algorithm, we first need to develop a system of mathematical notation that will allow us to hide some of the complexity of the computations. For this we will use *spatial algebra*.

12.3   SPATIAL ALGEBRA

Spatial algebra is a mathematical system providing a unified treatment of both translational and rotational dynamics across multiple coordinate frames. We have seen that the description of the state and the rate of change of state of an articulated body is mathematically complex, and the underlying equations take different forms depending upon whether a link is revolute or prismatic. Spatial algebra will give us a representation that unifies the treatment of the two types of links, and greatly simplifies the notation required to describe articulated body dynamics.

12.3.1   Spatial Velocity and Acceleration

The *spatial vector*

$$\check{\mathbf{v}} = \begin{bmatrix} \boldsymbol{\omega} \\ \mathbf{v} \end{bmatrix},$$

represents the velocity of an object. It is composed of two 3D vectors: angular velocity $\boldsymbol{\omega}$ and translational velocity $\mathbf{v}$. Just as $\check{\mathbf{v}}$ represents spatial velocity,

$$\check{\mathbf{a}} = \begin{bmatrix} \boldsymbol{\alpha} \\ \mathbf{a} \end{bmatrix}$$

represents spatial acceleration, where $\boldsymbol{\alpha} = \dot{\boldsymbol{\omega}}$, and $\mathbf{a} = \dot{\mathbf{v}}$. Consistent with these two definitions, in the following text the ˘ annotation will be used on any variable expressed in spatial algebra.

12.3.2 Spatial Transforms

Transformations between coordinate frames can be expressed in the form of *spatial matrices*. Consider the rigid body in the right figure. It contains two coordinate frames, F and G that are simply translates of each other. Let $\mathbf{r}$ be the vector from the origin of frame F to frame G, expressed in frame G. And, let $\boldsymbol{\omega}$ be the angular velocity of the body, which will be identical in both frames. Now, if $\mathbf{v}_F$ is a velocity expressed in frame F, and $\mathbf{v}_G$ is the same velocity expressed in frame G, it is clear that

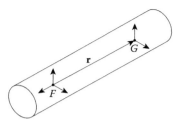

$$\mathbf{v}_G = \mathbf{v}_F + \boldsymbol{\omega} \times \mathbf{r}.$$

Let us define $\mathbf{1}$ to be the 3×3 identity matrix, $\mathbf{0}$ to be a 3×3 matrix of 0's, and $\mathbf{r}^*$ to be the 3×3 matrix equivalent of $\mathbf{r} \times$ (as defined in Section 9.1). Then the full spatial transformation of velocity between frames F and G can be written

$$\check{\mathbf{v}}_G = \begin{bmatrix} \boldsymbol{\omega} \\ \mathbf{v}_G \end{bmatrix} = \begin{bmatrix} \boldsymbol{\omega} \\ \mathbf{v}_F + \boldsymbol{\omega} \times \mathbf{r} \end{bmatrix} = \begin{bmatrix} \mathbf{1} & \mathbf{0} \\ -\mathbf{r}^* & \mathbf{1} \end{bmatrix} \begin{bmatrix} \boldsymbol{\omega} \\ \mathbf{v}_F \end{bmatrix}.$$

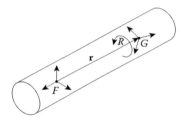

If, as in the figure to the left, the two coordinate frames are not only translated but rotated with respect to each other, the spatial transform would also need to include a rotation to align the frames, before the translation. Because of this rotation, the body's angular velocity vector would be oriented differently in the two frames, so we will use $\boldsymbol{\omega}_F$ and $\boldsymbol{\omega}_G$ to represent these two vectors. If the rotation from the orientation of frame F to frame G is expressed as the 3×3 rotation matrix R, then the full transform would be

$$\check{\mathbf{v}}_G = \begin{bmatrix} \boldsymbol{\omega}_G \\ \mathbf{v}_G \end{bmatrix} = \begin{bmatrix} R\boldsymbol{\omega}_F \\ R\mathbf{v}_F + R\boldsymbol{\omega}_F \times \mathbf{r} \end{bmatrix} = \begin{bmatrix} \mathbf{1} & \mathbf{0} \\ -\mathbf{r}^* & \mathbf{1} \end{bmatrix} \begin{bmatrix} R & \mathbf{0} \\ \mathbf{0} & R \end{bmatrix} \begin{bmatrix} \boldsymbol{\omega}_F \\ \mathbf{v}_F \end{bmatrix}.$$

Therefore, the fully general spatial matrix encoding the transform converting spatial quantities from an arbitrary frame F to an arbitrary frame G is

$$_G\check{\mathbf{T}}_F = \begin{bmatrix} R & \mathbf{0} \\ -\mathbf{r}^*R & R \end{bmatrix}.$$

12.3.3 Spatial Force

A spatial force is given by

$$\check{\mathbf{f}} = \begin{bmatrix} f \\ \boldsymbol{\tau} \end{bmatrix}.$$

The transformation of force from a frame F to a frame G simply requires a rotation, so $\mathbf{f}_G = R\mathbf{f}$, where matrix R is the rotation from frame F to frame G. The transform of torque requires a rotation and a cross-product, so $\boldsymbol{\tau}_G = R\boldsymbol{\tau} - \mathbf{r} \times R\mathbf{f}$, where $\mathbf{r}$ is the vector from the origin of the original frame to the origin of frame G. Therefore,

$$\check{\mathbf{f}}_G = \begin{bmatrix} \mathbf{f}_G \\ \boldsymbol{\tau}_G \end{bmatrix} = \begin{bmatrix} R\mathbf{f}_F \\ -\mathbf{r} \times R\mathbf{f}_F + R\boldsymbol{\tau}_F \end{bmatrix} = \begin{bmatrix} R & \mathbf{0} \\ -\mathbf{r}^* R & R \end{bmatrix} \begin{bmatrix} \mathbf{f}_F \\ \boldsymbol{\tau}_F \end{bmatrix}.$$

We see that the same spatial matrix that is used to transform spatial velocity and accelerations between coordinate frames can also be used to transform spatial forces.

12.3.4 Spatial Transpose

The *spatial transpose* of a spatial vector

$$\check{\mathbf{x}} = \begin{bmatrix} \mathbf{a} \\ \mathbf{b} \end{bmatrix}$$

is defined

$$\check{\mathbf{x}}^T = \begin{bmatrix} \mathbf{b}^T & \mathbf{a}^T \end{bmatrix}.$$

12.3.5 Spatial Inner Product

The spatial transpose is used to define the *spatial dot product* or *spatial inner product* as

$$\check{\mathbf{x}} \cdot \check{\mathbf{y}} = \check{\mathbf{x}}^T \check{\mathbf{y}}.$$

For example, the inner product of force and velocity is

$$\check{\mathbf{f}} \cdot \check{\mathbf{v}} = \begin{bmatrix} \boldsymbol{\tau}^T & \mathbf{f}^T \end{bmatrix} \begin{bmatrix} \boldsymbol{\omega} \\ \mathbf{v} \end{bmatrix} = \boldsymbol{\tau} \cdot \boldsymbol{\omega} + \mathbf{f} \cdot \mathbf{v}.$$

12.3.6 Spatial Cross-Product

The spatial cross-product operation is given by

$$\check{\mathbf{x}} \check{\times} = \begin{bmatrix} \mathbf{a}^* & \mathbf{0} \\ \mathbf{b}^* & \mathbf{a}^* \end{bmatrix}.$$

12.4 ACCELERATION PROPAGATION IN SPATIAL NOTATION

Examining Equation 12.4, we see that the propagation of acceleration from frame $i-1$ to frame i can be written in the spatial form

$$\check{\mathbf{a}}_i = \check{\mathbf{a}}_{i-1} + \begin{bmatrix} \dot{\boldsymbol{\omega}}_i^0 \\ \mathbf{a}_{i-1} \times \mathbf{r}_i + \boldsymbol{\omega}_{i-1} \times (\boldsymbol{\omega}_{i-1} \times \mathbf{r}_i) + \boldsymbol{\omega}_{i-1} \times \mathbf{v}_i^0 + \dot{\mathbf{v}}_i^0 \end{bmatrix}.$$

Therefore, for a prismatic joint, by Equation 12.5,

$$\check{\mathbf{a}}_i = \check{\mathbf{a}}_{i-1} + \begin{bmatrix} \mathbf{0} \\ \mathbf{a}_{i-1} \times \mathbf{r}_i + \boldsymbol{\omega}_{i-1} \times (\boldsymbol{\omega}_{i-1} \times \mathbf{r}_i) + 2\boldsymbol{\omega}_{i-1} \times \dot{q}_i \hat{\mathbf{u}}_i + \ddot{q}_i \hat{\mathbf{u}}_i \end{bmatrix},$$

and for a revolute joint, by Equation 12.6,

$$\breve{\mathbf{a}}_i = \breve{\mathbf{a}}_{i-1} + \begin{bmatrix} \ddot{q}_i \hat{\mathbf{u}}_i + \boldsymbol{\omega}_{i-1} \times \dot{q}_i \hat{\mathbf{u}}_i \\ \mathbf{a}_{i-1} \times \mathbf{r}_i + \boldsymbol{\omega}_{i-1} \times (\boldsymbol{\omega}_{i-1} \times \mathbf{r}_i) + 2\boldsymbol{\omega}_{i-1} \times (\dot{q}_i \hat{\mathbf{u}}_i \times \mathbf{d}_i) + \\ \dot{q}_i \hat{\mathbf{u}}_i \times (\dot{q}_i \hat{\mathbf{u}}_i \times \mathbf{d}_i) + \ddot{q}_i \hat{\mathbf{u}}_i \times \mathbf{d}_i \end{bmatrix}.$$

With these definitions, we can arrange the expression for the propagation of acceleration for a prismatic joint by grouping terms involving accelerations at joint $i-1$, terms involving accelerations at joint i, and terms involving only velocities, giving

$$\begin{bmatrix} \boldsymbol{\alpha}_i \\ \mathbf{a}_i \end{bmatrix} = \begin{bmatrix} \boldsymbol{\alpha}_{i-1} \\ -\mathbf{r}_i \times \mathbf{a}_{i-1} + \mathbf{a}_{i-1} \end{bmatrix} + \ddot{q}_i \begin{bmatrix} \mathbf{0} \\ \hat{\mathbf{u}}_i \end{bmatrix} + \begin{bmatrix} \mathbf{0} \\ \boldsymbol{\omega}_{i-1} \times (\boldsymbol{\omega}_{i-1} \times \mathbf{r}_i) + 2\boldsymbol{\omega}_{i-1} \times \dot{q}_i \hat{\mathbf{u}}_i \end{bmatrix}.$$

Similarly, for a revolute joint we can write

$$\begin{bmatrix} \boldsymbol{\alpha}_i \\ \mathbf{a}_i \end{bmatrix} = \begin{bmatrix} \boldsymbol{\alpha}_{i-1} \\ -\mathbf{r}_i \times \mathbf{a}_{i-1} + \mathbf{a}_{i-1} \end{bmatrix} + \ddot{q}_i \begin{bmatrix} \hat{\mathbf{u}}_i \\ \hat{\mathbf{u}}_i \times \mathbf{d}_i \end{bmatrix}$$
$$+ \begin{bmatrix} \boldsymbol{\omega}_{i-1} \times \dot{q}_i \hat{\mathbf{u}}_i \\ \boldsymbol{\omega}_{i-1} \times (\boldsymbol{\omega}_{i-1} \times \mathbf{r}_i) + 2\boldsymbol{\omega}_{i-1} \times (\dot{q}_i \hat{\mathbf{u}}_i \times \mathbf{d}_i) + \dot{q}_i \hat{\mathbf{u}}_i \times (\dot{q}_i \hat{\mathbf{u}}_i \times \mathbf{d}_i) \end{bmatrix}$$

Now, let us define the *spatial joint axis* for a prismatic joint i as

$$\breve{\mathbf{s}}_i = \begin{bmatrix} \mathbf{0} \\ \hat{\mathbf{u}}_i \end{bmatrix},$$

and for a revolute joint as

$$\breve{\mathbf{s}}_i = \begin{bmatrix} \hat{\mathbf{u}}_i \\ \hat{\mathbf{u}}_i \times \mathbf{d}_i \end{bmatrix}.$$

We can also define what will will call the *spatial Coriolis force*[*] for a prismatic joint i as

$$\breve{\mathbf{c}}_i = \begin{bmatrix} \mathbf{0} \\ \boldsymbol{\omega}_{i-1} \times (\boldsymbol{\omega}_{i-1} \times \mathbf{r}_i) + 2\boldsymbol{\omega}_{i-1} \times \dot{q}_i \hat{\mathbf{u}}_i \end{bmatrix},$$

and for a revolute joint as

$$\breve{\mathbf{c}}_i = \begin{bmatrix} \boldsymbol{\omega}_{i-1} \times \dot{q}_i \hat{\mathbf{u}}_i \\ \boldsymbol{\omega}_{i-1} \times (\boldsymbol{\omega}_{i-1} \times \mathbf{r}_i) + 2\boldsymbol{\omega}_{i-1} \times (\dot{q}_i \hat{\mathbf{u}}_i \times \mathbf{d}_i) + \dot{q}_i \hat{\mathbf{u}}_i \times (\dot{q}_i \hat{\mathbf{u}}_i \times \mathbf{d}_i) \end{bmatrix}.$$

With these definitions, the reader can verify that using spatial notation, for either prismatic or revolute joints, the spatial Coriolis force can be written in the form

$$\breve{\mathbf{c}}_i = \breve{\mathbf{v}}_i \overset{\times}{\times} \breve{\mathbf{s}}_i \dot{q}_i. \tag{12.7}$$

---

[*]Note that this term includes both Coriolis and centripetal forces. The centripetal force is the constraint force required to keep the joint length constant. The Coriolis force is a virtual force that is required to correct motion in a rotating coordinate frame, due to the fact that points in the frame are moving faster away from the origin than near the origin.

Likewise, the propagation of acceleration can be written compactly as

$$\breve{\mathbf{a}}_i = {}_i\breve{\mathbf{T}}_{i-1}\,\breve{\mathbf{a}}_{i-1} + \breve{\mathbf{s}}_i\ddot{q}_i + \breve{\mathbf{c}}_i. \tag{12.8}$$

Since these equations hide the distinction between revolute and prismatic joints in the definition of the spatial joint axis $\breve{\mathbf{s}}_i$, they are ideal for use in algorithm development.

12.5 SPATIAL ISOLATED QUANTITIES

The *spatial isolated* quantities of a link incorporate its mechanical properties if the link is considered on its own, ignoring its inboard and outboard connections.

We define the *spatial isolated inertia* of link i with mass m_i and moment of inertia tensor I_i as

$$\breve{\mathbf{I}}_i = \begin{bmatrix} \mathbf{0} & M_i \\ I_i & \mathbf{0} \end{bmatrix},$$

where $\mathbf{1}$ is the 3×3 identity matrix, $\mathbf{0}$ is the 3×3 matrix of 0's, and $M_i = m_i\mathbf{1}$ is called the matricized mass of the link.

We define the *spatial isolated zero acceleration force*, as the force that would have to be applied at the position of the inboard joint to keep the link from accelerating. If $\mathbf{f}_i$ is the sum of all forces acting externally on the link, and $\boldsymbol{\tau}_i$ is the sum of all torques being applied, including any torques induced at the link's center of mass due to applied forces, then the force needed to counteract the applied forces is $-\mathbf{f}_i$, and the torque needed is $-\boldsymbol{\tau}_i$. If the link is rotating with angular velocity $\boldsymbol{\omega}_i$, then its instantaneous rate of change of translational momentum due to this angular velocity will be $\boldsymbol{\omega}_i \times m_i\mathbf{v}_i$, and its instantaneous rate of change of angular momentum will be $\boldsymbol{\omega}_i \times I_i\boldsymbol{\omega}_i$. Therefore, the spatial isolated zero acceleration force needed to oppose these forces would be

$$\breve{\mathbf{z}}_i = \begin{bmatrix} \boldsymbol{\omega}_i \times m_i\mathbf{v}_i - \mathbf{f}_i \\ \boldsymbol{\omega}_i \times I_i\boldsymbol{\omega}_i - \boldsymbol{\tau}_i \end{bmatrix}.$$

If we define the spatial applied force to be

$$\breve{\mathbf{f}}_i = \begin{bmatrix} \mathbf{f}_i \\ \boldsymbol{\tau}_i \end{bmatrix},$$

then the spatial isolated zero acceleration force can be written as

$$\breve{\mathbf{z}}_i = \breve{\mathbf{v}}_i \breve{\times} \breve{\mathbf{I}}_i\breve{\mathbf{v}}_i - \breve{\mathbf{f}}_i.$$

12.6 FIRST OUTWARD LOOP

The algorithm to perform the first outward loop is given in Figure 12.1. It follows closely the algorithm outlined by Kokkevis [2004]. As we indicated above, in this loop we determine the velocity and angular velocity of each link, and thus each link's

```
ComputeLinkVelocities(Link L[ ], int n)
L is an array of n Links. Each Link contains q, q̇, x, d, r, û, š, and v̌
To simplify the notation, xᵢ is used as a stand-in for L[i].x
begin
    v̌₀ = 0̌;
    for i = 1 to n do
        determine ᵢŤ₍ᵢ₋₁₎;  the transform from the frame of link i − 1 to link i
        v̌ᵢ = ᵢŤ₍ᵢ₋₁₎ v̌₍ᵢ₋₁₎ + šᵢ q̇ᵢ;  spatial velocity of link i

        ž̌ᵢ = v̌ᵢ ×̃ Ǐᵢ v̌ᵢ − f̌ᵢ;  isolated zero acceleration force for link i
        č̌ᵢ = v̌ᵢ ×̃ šᵢ q̇ᵢ;  Coriolis force for link i

    end
end
```

FIGURE 12.1 First outward loop to compute link velocities and internal forces.

spatial velocity. In addition to spatial velocity, we can also compute the spatial isolated Coriolis and zero acceleration forces for each link, since they depend only on known applied forces and torques, and known characteristics of the link. These characteristics include its moment of inertia I_i and mass m_i, the rate of change of its orientation parameter q_i, its spatial joint axis $\check{\mathbf{s}}_i$, and its spatial velocity $\check{\mathbf{v}}_i$. We will need these quantities in the second inward loop to compute the *spatial articulated inertia* $\check{\mathbf{I}}_i^A$, and the *spatial articulated zero acceleration force* $\check{\mathbf{z}}_i^A$, of each link i.

12.7 COMPUTING SPATIAL ARTICULATED QUANTITIES

The spatial articulated quantities of a link account for the fact that a joint acting on an outboard child link sees not only the forces and torques applied to the child link but also those applied to all of the links outboard from the child link. Likewise, the mass and moment of inertia seen by the joint will include the masses and moments of inertia of all outboard links.

In order to describe the construction of spatial articulated quantities Mirtich defines an *articulated body* of an original serial linkage to be the subchain consisting of a link and all of its outboard children, as if it were severed from all of the inboard links. If the subchain starts at link i, link i is known as the *handle* of the articulated body. The right figure shows an articulated body whose handle is link 2 and includes links 2, 3, and 4. Links 3 and 4, if taken by themselves, would constitute trivial articulated bodies with no outboard links.

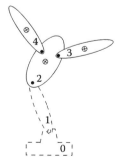

We have already defined the spatial acceleration of each link to be $\check{\mathbf{a}}_i$. We can now also define the spatial force exerted by the link's inboard joint as $\check{\mathbf{f}}_i^I$, and that exerted by its outboard joint as $\check{\mathbf{f}}_i^O$. These forces will be expressed in the link's own coordinate frame and referred to the origin of that frame. With these definitions, we can develop an inward loop to determine the forces required at each joint such that the joint will not accelerate.

In order to keep the derivation of this algorithm simple, let us first consider a simple linked chain, as indicated in the right figure. Link n is at the end of the chain, and thus is the only trivial link. For link n, there are no outboard links, so

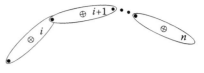

$$\check{\mathbf{f}}_n^O = 0.$$

The force on the link needed to provide articulated acceleration $\check{\mathbf{a}}_n$ is

$$\check{\mathbf{f}}_n^I = \check{\mathbf{I}}_n \check{\mathbf{a}}_n + \check{\mathbf{z}}_n,$$

by Newton's second law. Note that $\check{\mathbf{z}}_n$ is the spatial isolated zero acceleration force computed in the first outward loop, and $\check{\mathbf{I}}_n$ is the spatial isolated inertia of the link, which is constant and can be precomputed. Now, since there are no outboard links, the spatial articulated and spatial isolated quantities for the trivial links are identical and we have

$$\check{\mathbf{I}}_n^A = \check{\mathbf{I}}_n, \quad \text{and,}$$
$$\check{\mathbf{z}}_n^A = \check{\mathbf{z}}_n.$$

So, for the outermost link n in a chain

$$\check{\mathbf{f}}_n^I = \check{\mathbf{I}}_n^A \check{\mathbf{a}}_n + \check{\mathbf{z}}_n^A.$$

Our goal in the derivation below is to obtain the general expression at each link i for inboard force

$$\check{\mathbf{f}}_i^I = \check{\mathbf{I}}_i^A \check{\mathbf{a}}_i + \check{\mathbf{z}}_i^A. \tag{12.9}$$

In order to do this, we need to be able to compute the spatial articulated zero acceleration force $\check{\mathbf{z}}_i^A$, and the spatial articulated inertia $\check{\mathbf{I}}_i^A$.

Now, for each inboard link i we can proceed to calculate forces inductively, assuming that we already know the inboard force $\check{\mathbf{f}}_{i+1}^I$ on the next outboard link. Since each inboard link has both outboard and inboard joints,

$$\check{\mathbf{f}}_i^I + \check{\mathbf{f}}_i^O = \check{\mathbf{I}}_i \check{\mathbf{a}}_i + \check{\mathbf{z}}_i.$$

But, force $\check{\mathbf{f}}_i^O$ must be equal and opposite to $\check{\mathbf{f}}_{i+1}^I$, so in the coordinate frame of link i

$$\check{\mathbf{f}}_i^O = -\,_i\check{\mathbf{T}}_{i+1}\,\check{\mathbf{f}}_{i+1}^I.$$

Therefore,

$$\check{\mathbf{f}}_i^I = \check{\mathbf{I}}_i \check{\mathbf{a}}_i + \check{\mathbf{z}}_i + \,_i\check{\mathbf{T}}_{i+1}\,\check{\mathbf{f}}_{i+1}^I.$$

But,

$$\check{\mathbf{f}}_{i+1}^{I} = \check{\mathbf{I}}_{i+1}^{A} \check{\mathbf{a}}_{i+1} + \check{\mathbf{z}}_{i+1}^{A}.$$

Therefore, substituting Equation 12.8 for spatial acceleration $\check{\mathbf{a}}_{i+1}$, we have

$$\check{\mathbf{f}}_{i}^{I} = \check{\mathbf{I}}_{i} \check{\mathbf{a}}_{i} + \check{\mathbf{z}}_{i} + {}_{i}\check{\mathbf{T}}_{i+1} \left[\check{\mathbf{I}}_{i+1}^{A} ({}_{i+1}\check{\mathbf{T}}_{i} \check{\mathbf{a}}_{i} + \check{\mathbf{s}}_{i+1} \ddot{q}_{i+1} + \check{\mathbf{c}}_{i+1}) + \check{\mathbf{z}}_{i+1}^{A} \right],$$

which can be rearranged to obtain

$$\check{\mathbf{f}}_{i}^{I} = \left[\check{\mathbf{I}}_{i} + {}_{i}\check{\mathbf{T}}_{i+1} \check{\mathbf{I}}_{i+1}^{A} {}_{i+1}\check{\mathbf{T}}_{i} \right] \check{\mathbf{a}}_{i} + \left[\check{\mathbf{z}}_{i} + ({}_{i}\check{\mathbf{T}}_{i+1} \check{\mathbf{s}}_{i+1} \ddot{q}_{i+1} + \check{\mathbf{c}}_{i+1} + \check{\mathbf{z}}_{i+1}^{A}) \right]. \qquad (12.10)$$

The only unknown term in this equation is $\ddot{q}_{i+1}$, which can be derived from the expression

$$Q_i = \check{\mathbf{s}}_i^T \check{\mathbf{f}}_i^I, \qquad (12.11)$$

giving the resultant force and torque magnitude at joint i. Note that this is the dot product of the spatial joint axis with the spatial force, giving the component of spatial force in the direction of this axis.

Since

$$\check{\mathbf{f}}_{i+1}^{I} = \check{\mathbf{I}}_{i+1}^{A} ({}_{i+1}\check{\mathbf{T}}_{i} \check{\mathbf{a}}_{i} + \check{\mathbf{s}}_{i+1} \ddot{q}_{i+1} + \check{\mathbf{c}}_{i+1}) + \check{\mathbf{z}}_{i+1}^{A},$$

we can premultiply by $\check{\mathbf{s}}_{i+1}^{T}$ to obtain

$$Q_{i+1} = \check{\mathbf{s}}_{i+1}^{T} \check{\mathbf{I}}_{i+1}^{A} ({}_{i+1}\check{\mathbf{T}}_{i} \check{\mathbf{a}}_{i} + \check{\mathbf{s}}_{i+1} \ddot{q}_{i+1} + \check{\mathbf{c}}_{i+1}) + \check{\mathbf{s}}_{i+1}^{T} \check{\mathbf{z}}_{i+1}^{A},$$

which can be solved for $\ddot{q}_{i+1}$ to obtain

$$\ddot{q}_{i+1} = \frac{Q_{i+1} - \check{\mathbf{s}}_{i+1}^{T} \check{\mathbf{I}}_{i+1}^{A} {}_{i+1}\check{\mathbf{T}}_{i} \check{\mathbf{a}}_{i} - \check{\mathbf{s}}_{i+1}^{T} (\check{\mathbf{z}}_{i+1}^{A} + \check{\mathbf{I}}_{i+1}^{A} \check{\mathbf{c}}_{i+1})}{\check{\mathbf{s}}_{i+1}^{T} \check{\mathbf{I}}_{i+1}^{A} \check{\mathbf{s}}_{i+1}}. \qquad (12.12)$$

This can be substituted into Equation 12.10, and rearranged to obtain

$$\check{\mathbf{f}}_{i}^{I} = \left[\check{\mathbf{I}}_{i} + {}_{i}\check{\mathbf{T}}_{i+1} \left(\check{\mathbf{I}}_{i+1}^{A} - \frac{\check{\mathbf{I}}_{i+1}^{A} \check{\mathbf{s}}_{i+1} \check{\mathbf{s}}_{i+1}^{T} \check{\mathbf{I}}_{i+1}^{A}}{\check{\mathbf{s}}_{i+1}^{T} \check{\mathbf{I}}_{i+1}^{A} \check{\mathbf{s}}_{i+1}} \right) {}_{i+1}\check{\mathbf{T}}_{i} \right] \check{\mathbf{a}}_{i}$$

$$+ \check{\mathbf{z}}_{i} + {}_{i}\check{\mathbf{T}}_{i+1} \left[\check{\mathbf{z}}_{i+1}^{A} + \check{\mathbf{I}}_{i+1}^{A} \check{\mathbf{c}}_{i+1} + \frac{\check{\mathbf{I}}_{i+1}^{A} \check{\mathbf{s}}_{i+1} \left[Q_{i+1} - \check{\mathbf{s}}_{i+1}^{T} (\check{\mathbf{z}}_{i+1}^{A} + \check{\mathbf{I}}_{i+1}^{A} \check{\mathbf{c}}_{i+1}) \right]}{\check{\mathbf{s}}_{i+1}^{T} \check{\mathbf{I}}_{i+1}^{A} \check{\mathbf{s}}_{i+1}} \right].$$

Comparing this equation to Equation 12.9, we have our desired expressions for spatial articulated inertia and spatial articulated zero acceleration force. These are

$$\check{\mathbf{I}}_{i}^{A} = \check{\mathbf{I}}_{i} + {}_{i}\check{\mathbf{T}}_{i+1} \left(\check{\mathbf{I}}_{i+1}^{A} - \frac{\check{\mathbf{I}}_{i+1}^{A} \check{\mathbf{s}}_{i+1} \check{\mathbf{s}}_{i+1}^{T} \check{\mathbf{I}}_{i+1}^{A}}{\check{\mathbf{s}}_{i+1}^{T} \check{\mathbf{I}}_{i+1}^{A} \check{\mathbf{s}}_{i+1}} \right) {}_{i+1}\check{\mathbf{T}}_{i}, \qquad (12.13)$$

and

$$\check{\mathbf{z}}_{i}^{A} = \check{\mathbf{z}}_{i} + {}_{i}\check{\mathbf{T}}_{i+1} \left[\check{\mathbf{z}}_{i+1}^{A} + \check{\mathbf{I}}_{i+1}^{A} \check{\mathbf{c}}_{i+1} + \frac{\check{\mathbf{I}}_{i+1}^{A} \check{\mathbf{s}}_{i+1} \left[Q_{i+1} - \check{\mathbf{s}}_{i+1}^{T} (\check{\mathbf{z}}_{i+1}^{A} + \check{\mathbf{I}}_{i+1}^{A} \check{\mathbf{c}}_{i+1}) \right]}{\check{\mathbf{s}}_{i+1}^{T} \check{\mathbf{I}}_{i+1}^{A} \check{\mathbf{s}}_{i+1}} \right].$$

$$(12.14)$$

```
ComputeArticulatedInertia(Link L[ ], int n)
```
L *is an array of* n Links. *Each* Link *contains* q, $\dot{q}$, **x**, **d**, **r**, $\hat{\mathbf{u}}$, $\check{\mathbf{I}}$, $\check{\mathbf{s}}$, *and* $\check{\mathbf{v}}$
$_{i+1}\check{\mathbf{T}}_i$, $\check{\mathbf{v}}_{i+1}$, $\check{\mathbf{z}}_{i+1}$, *and* $\check{\mathbf{c}}_{i+1}$ *have been precomputed in the first outward loop.*
To simplify the notation, x_i *is used as a stand-in for* **L**$[i].x$
begin
$\quad$ $\check{\mathbf{I}}_n^A = \check{\mathbf{I}}_n$;
$\quad$ $\check{\mathbf{z}}_n^A = \check{\mathbf{z}}_n$;
$\quad$ **for** $i = $ *n-1* **downto** *1* **do**
$\qquad$ determine $_i\check{\mathbf{T}}_{i+1}$; $\quad$ *the transform from the frame of link* $i+1$ *to link* i

$\qquad$ $\check{\mathbf{I}}_i^A = $ spatial articulated inertia from Eq. 12.13;

$\qquad$ $Q_i = (L[i].\check{\mathbf{s}})^T \check{\mathbf{f}}_i^I$;
$\qquad$ $\check{\mathbf{z}}_i^A = $ spatial articulated zero acceleration force from Eq. 12.14;
$\quad$ **end**
end

FIGURE 12.2 Inward loop to compute spatial articulated inertia and zero acceleration force.

Given this analysis, we can now define the inward loop that computes spatial articulated quantities starting with the outermost link and working toward the root. The algorithm describing this loop is given in Figure 12.2.

12.8 COMPUTING LINK ACCELERATIONS

After computing the spatial articulated quantities, the final outward loop is used to compute the joint and link accelerations. The algorithm describing this loop is given in Figure 12.3.

```
ComputeLinkAccelerations(Link L[ ], int n)
```
L *is an array of* n Links. *Each* Link *contains* q, $\dot{q}$, **x**, **d**, **r**, $\hat{\mathbf{u}}$, $\check{\mathbf{I}}$, $\check{\mathbf{s}}$, *and* $\check{\mathbf{v}}$
$_{i+1}\check{\mathbf{T}}_i$, $\check{\mathbf{v}}_{i+1}$, $\check{\mathbf{z}}_{i+1}$, *and* $\check{\mathbf{c}}_{i+1}$ *have been precomputed in the first outward loop.*
$_i\check{\mathbf{T}}_{i+1}$, Q_i, $\check{\mathbf{I}}_{i+1}^A$, $\check{\mathbf{z}}_{i+1}^A$ *have been precomputed in the inward loop.*
To simplify the notation, x_i *is used as a stand-in for* **L**$[i].x$
begin
$\quad$ $\ddot{q}_0 = 0$;
$\quad$ $\check{\mathbf{a}}_0 = \check{\mathbf{0}}$;
$\quad$ **for** $i = $ *1* **to** n **do**
$\qquad$ $\ddot{q}_i = $ joint parametric acceleration from Eq. 12.12;
$\qquad$ $\check{\mathbf{a}}_i = $ link spatial acceleration from Eq. 12.8;
$\quad$ **end**
end

FIGURE 12.3 Second outward loop to compute link accelerations.

int NumberLinks(Link **L**[ ], int p, int i)
L *is an array of* Links. p *is the index of the current node's parent,*
i *is the index of the current node.*
The return value is one greater than the last index assigned.
begin
    $\mathbf{L}[i].parent = p$;
    $p = i$;
    int $index = i + 1$;
    for *each child j of the current node* **do**
        $\mathbf{L}[i].child[j] = index$;
        $index = $ NumberLinks($\mathbf{L}$, p, $index$);
    end
    return *index*;
end

FIGURE 12.4 Recursive scheme to number the links.

12.9 GENERALIZATION TO TREE-LIKE ARTICULATIONS

The algorithm can be generalized to handle tree-like articulated structures, where each link has only one inboard joint but may have more than one outboard joint. To provide a coherent set of link indices, they can be assigned using a recursive numbering scheme, which guarantees that each outboard link will have an index greater than its parent link. Such a numbering algorithm is shown in Figure 12.4. Link information is stored in an array of length n total links. To facilitate loop indexing using this scheme, each link holds a list of the indices of its outbound child branches, as well as the index of its parent link. In the initial call to this routine a parent index of -1 and a current index of 0 should be supplied as parameters.

Now, in the inward and outward loops, the branching structure needs to be taken into account. In the outward loops, each link can be considered in turn, assigning its parent index as the inbound link. In the inward loop, each link must iterate over its children to sum their contributions to the link's articulated inertia and articulated zero acceleration force.

12.10 SUMMARY

Here is a brief review of some of the main concepts to take away from this chapter:

- Articulated bodies are tree structures constructed from links, which are rigid bodies, and connected together at joints, which may be either rotational or prismatic.

- A rotational joint provides for one rotational degree of freedom about a single joint axis.

- A prismatic joint provides for one translational degree of freedom along a single direction.

- Multiple degree-of-freedom joints can be specified by placing multiple joints on top of each other.

- The state of an articulated body is captured by a set of scalars giving joint angle and angular velocity for rotational joints, or joint translation and translational velocity for prismatic joints.

- Computation of articulated motion is done in a three-step algorithm, with the first step computing link velocities, the second computing spatial articulated inertia and spatial articulated zero acceleration force, and the third computing the link accelerations.

- A spatial algebra, capturing both rotational and translational motion in a compact, unified form, provides the mathematical framework for expressing the algorithm.

IV

Fluid Simulation

CHAPTER 13

Foundations of Fluid Dynamics

BEFORE EMBARKING ON A DISCUSSION OF FLUID SIMULATION it is important to establish the notion that what we mean by a fluid is not necessarily a liquid, but includes all liquid and gaseous materials. In most animation situations, the fluids we will be considering are either water or air. The key point is that when dealing with fluids we are no longer dealing with discrete particles, but with continuous media.

Until now, the objects that we have been seeking to animate have been either particles, systems of particles, or rigid bodies. In each case, we have been dealing with individual elements whose behavior is tracked over time. The problem of animating fluids presents us with a very different situation. Consider the smoke simulation in Figure 13.1. On the left, the smoke is falling down and interacting with a set of stairs. On the right the smoke is rising in turbulent air, and being deflected by a ball. Instead of dealing with individual elements, we have a continuously deforming mass of material that has no distinct parts or pieces. Simulating continuous media will require us to develop a new set of mathematical tools, in particular the notion of a field and operators that act on fields. In addition, it suggests that we may need to look deeper at computational strategies for simulation.

In this chapter we attempt to lay the foundations for the study of fluid simulation. The reader who wishes to go more deeply into the subject should first turn to the excellent book by Bridson [2008], *Fluid Simulation for Computer Graphics*.

13.1 LAGRANGIAN VERSUS EULERIAN SIMULATION

There are two primary approaches to simulation, known as the *Lagrangian* and *Eulerian* approaches. In Lagrangian methods, the mass of the material is divided into discrete elements, each of whose motion is individually tracked. Thus, each discrete element has a position in space, and carries with it the momentum of the mass represented by the element. Everything in the previous chapters of this book

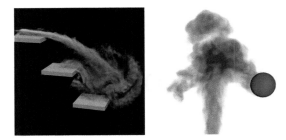

FIGURE 13.1 Simulations of smoke interacting with solid obstacles. (Courtesy of Ruoguan Huang.)

has been grounded in the Lagrangian approach, from particle systems to rigid body simulations. Eulerian methods use a very different approach. Instead of the material being represented by discrete elements, space itself is subdivided into discrete cells, with the simulated material being tracked by these cells as it moves through them. For example, in a fluid simulation space might be divided into a fixed spatial grid, with each grid cell recording the velocity and other properties of the fluid passing through it.

On the surface, it would seem that any simulation handling elements that are discrete would most naturally be done using a Lagrangian approach, and any simulation handling elements that are time-varying continuous media would most naturally be done using an Eulerian approach. For the most part this is true, but we run into problems created by the nature of these methods. Since Eulerian methods discretize space, it is often difficult to represent fine detail—for example, it is hard to capture the complex detail of splashing in a fluid simulation. Since Lagrangian methods discretize the material being simulated, bulk properties, other than total mass, are difficult to maintain—for example, it is difficult to maintain a constant volume or a constant density in a fluid simulation.

In the rest of this chapter we first lay out the mathematical foundations for treating continuous fields, describe the Navier-Stokes equations for fluid momentum update, and then go on to demonstrate the most popular Lagrangian and Eulerian methods for simulating fluids for computer animation.

13.2 MATHEMATICAL BACKGROUND FOR FLUID SIMULATION

13.2.1 Scalar and Vector Fields

The mathematical notion of a field is of a quantity defined everywhere in space, and whose value is spatially determined. Consequently, a field can be thought of as a function, mapping spatial position $\mathbf{x}$ to a unique quantity. Fields can be either fixed (sometimes called steady), in which case the notation would be $f(\mathbf{x})$, or time varying $f(\mathbf{x}, t)$. Abstractly, a field could return any type of quantity, but in physical simulation we will be concerned mainly with *scalar fields*, where the value returned by the function is a scalar, and *vector fields*, which return a vector quantity. A familiar example of a scalar field is pressure in a liquid medium. If your space is a swimming pool, then everywhere in the pool there is a pressure that grows with depth in the pool. Your ears tell you this if you dive deep into the pool. A familiar example of a vector field is velocity in a liquid medium. If your space is the surface of a river, then everywhere you paddle your kayak in the river you can feel the direction and speed of flow as you paddle with or against it. Clearly, the river has a velocity at every position on its surface. These quantities are different from quantities possessed by a particle—for example, a particle might have a weight and a velocity, but the pool and the river are continuous media, so it cannot be said that any particular "particle" of the medium has a pressure or a velocity. The medium as a whole has a pressure or a velocity that can be measured at any chosen position but that cannot be assigned to any particular unit of the substance of the medium.

13.2.2 Gradient

Given a scalar field $\phi(\mathbf{x})$, we can always use this to obtain a vector field $\nabla\phi(\mathbf{x})$, giving us a vector value at every position for which the function is defined. The operator ∇ is known as the *gradient operator* and in 3D Cartesian space is defined

$$
\nabla = \begin{bmatrix} \frac{\partial}{\partial x} \\ \frac{\partial}{\partial y} \\ \frac{\partial}{\partial z} \end{bmatrix}.
$$

From this definition it is apparent that the gradient operating on a scalar field forms a 3D vector from the spatial partial derivatives of this field, taken in the x, y, and z directions. For example, the gradient of a scalar field ϕ is

$$
\nabla\phi = \begin{bmatrix} \frac{\partial \phi}{\partial x} \\ \frac{\partial \phi}{\partial y} \\ \frac{\partial \phi}{\partial z} \end{bmatrix}.
$$

Since $\frac{\partial \phi}{\partial x}, \frac{\partial \phi}{\partial y}$, and $\frac{\partial \phi}{\partial z}$ indicate the local spatial rate of change in the scalar value if we move in the x, y, or z direction, the gradient at a point determines how the scalar field is changing spatially.

A way of understanding the gradient is to think of the scalar field as denoting height above a surface. Thought of in this way, the gradient of the scalar field is a vector that always points in the direction of steepest ascent from the point at which the gradient is taken. Conversely, the negative of the gradient points in the direction of steepest descent.

Another way of thinking of the gradient, at a point in space, is as a velocity that determines the speed and direction at which a massless particle would begin to move if placed in the scalar field at that point. A simple example will help to explain this.

Let us suppose that our scalar field is defined by the function $f(\mathbf{x}) = ax + by + cz$, so that its gradient is $\mathbf{u}(\mathbf{x}) = \begin{bmatrix} a & b & c \end{bmatrix}^T$. The scalar field varies linearly with position in space, so the gradient is constant everywhere. If we think of the gradient as a velocity field, then there is a constant velocity in the direction of the gradient, and a massless particle placed anywhere in this field will move with velocity $\mathbf{u} = \begin{bmatrix} a & b & c \end{bmatrix}^T$.

13.2.3 Divergence

Given a vector field $\mathbf{u}(\mathbf{x})$, we can obtain the scalar field $\nabla \cdot \mathbf{u}$, providing a scalar value at every position for which the function is defined. The operator $\nabla \cdot$ is known as the *divergence operator*. In 3D Cartesian space, the divergence operator, operating on the vector field $\mathbf{u} = \begin{bmatrix} u_x & u_y & u_z \end{bmatrix}^T$, yields

$$\nabla \cdot \mathbf{u} = \begin{bmatrix} \frac{\partial}{\partial x} \\ \frac{\partial}{\partial y} \\ \frac{\partial}{\partial z} \end{bmatrix} \cdot \begin{bmatrix} u_x \\ u_y \\ u_z \end{bmatrix} = \frac{\partial u_x}{\partial x} + \frac{\partial u_y}{\partial y} + \frac{\partial u_z}{\partial z}.$$

Thus, the divergence operator is analogous to a dot product, where partial spatial differentiation by term replaces multiplication. If we think of any infinitesimal volume about the point $\mathbf{x}$, the divergence at this point is a measure of how the vector field $\mathbf{u}$ is expanding locally.

To make a physical analogy, picture the tiny cube of space shown in the figure, with dimensions $\Delta x, \Delta y, \Delta z$. Imagine that the vector field $\mathbf{u} = \begin{bmatrix} u_x & u_y & u_z \end{bmatrix}^T$ is a fluid velocity field that the cube is immersed in. Then, $u_x \Delta y \Delta z$ is the rate of fluid flowing into the cell from the left, and $u_y \Delta x \Delta z$ and $u_z \Delta x, \Delta y$ are the rates of flow into the cell from below and from behind. The instantaneous rate of change of 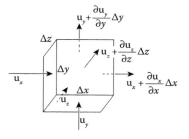 flow in the x direction is $\frac{\partial u_x}{\partial x}$. We can assume this value will be the same across the cell, which is more and more true as Δx shrinks to an infinitesimal. The rate of fluid flowing out of the cell on the right will be $(u_x + \frac{\partial u_x}{\partial x} \Delta x) \Delta y \Delta z$, with similar terms for flow out of the top and front of the cell. To obtain the net outflow from the cell, we subtract the inflow from the outflow to obtain

$$\left(\frac{\partial u_x}{\partial x} + \frac{\partial u_y}{\partial y} + \frac{\partial u_z}{\partial z} \right) \Delta x \Delta y \Delta z,$$

so that the outflow per unit volume $V = \Delta x \Delta y \Delta z$ is exactly the divergence. Thus, the divergence gives the net excess rate of outflow, compared to inflow, across the entire surface of the cube. If the divergence is positive, then more fluid is flowing out of the cube than is flowing in, and if it is negative, then more fluid is flowing in than is flowing out. Only if the total inflow matches the total outflow is the divergence 0.

A field is called *divergence free* if $\nabla \cdot \mathbf{u} = 0$ everywhere in the field. In the case of a fluid flow field, if the fluid is *incompressible* its velocity field must be divergence free. If the divergence were non-zero anywhere, the fluid would have to be compressing or expanding so that the rate of fluid entering a point could differ from the rate leaving that point.

13.2.4 Curl

The *curl operator* $\nabla \times$ operates on a vector field following the same pattern as is used in taking a cross product. Thus, the curl operator, operating on the vector field $\mathbf{u} = \begin{bmatrix} u_x & u_y & u_z \end{bmatrix}^T$, yields

$$
\nabla \times \mathbf{u} = \begin{bmatrix} \frac{\partial}{\partial x} \\ \frac{\partial}{\partial y} \\ \frac{\partial}{\partial z} \end{bmatrix} \times \begin{bmatrix} u_x \\ u_y \\ u_z \end{bmatrix} = \begin{bmatrix} \frac{\partial u_z}{\partial y} - \frac{\partial u_y}{\partial z} \\ \frac{\partial u_x}{\partial z} - \frac{\partial u_z}{\partial x} \\ \frac{\partial u_y}{\partial x} - \frac{\partial u_x}{\partial y} \end{bmatrix}.
$$

Note that in some regions the convention is to write the curl operation as *rot* $\mathbf{u}$, but we will use the cross product notation throughout.

The curl measures the rotation of the vector field about the point at which the curl is taken. A physical analogy that will help you to understand curl is to imagine the vector field as being a fluid velocity field. Taking the curl of this field at a point is equivalent to placing a very light ball in the field at this point and observing how the ball is rotated by the fluid. The axis of rotation is in the direction of the curl, following the right-hand rule for rotation, and the angular speed of the ball's rotation is proportional to the magnitude of the curl, with constant of proportionality $1/2$.

A more formal way of understanding curl is as the limit of a path integral. Let $\hat{\mathbf{n}}$ be the normal vector of a planar surface in 3D space, let C be a closed path on this surface surrounding the position $\mathbf{x}$, and let A be the area enclosed by C. Then

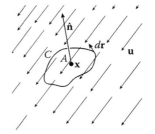

$$
[\nabla \times \mathbf{u}(\mathbf{x})] \cdot \hat{\mathbf{n}} = \lim_{A \to 0} \left(\frac{1}{A} \oint_C \mathbf{u} \cdot d\mathbf{r} \right),
$$

where $d\mathbf{r}$ is everywhere tangent to C.

An analogy that will help in understanding this integral is to think of $\mathbf{u}$ as the flow in a river, $\mathbf{n}$ as pointing straight up so that it is normal to the surface of the river, and C as the path of a kayak paddling in a closed path around the fixed point $\mathbf{x}$. Depending upon how the kayak's direction aligns with the flow direction it will speed up, or slow down. The integral is simply the sum of all of these speed changes. If the integral is zero, it must be that the kayak was sped up and slowed down equally as it traversed the full path. If the integral is non-zero, there must be a flow differential along the path of the kayak around $\mathbf{x}$, resulting in a net acceleration or deceleration. Dividing the result of this integral by the enclosed area A provides the scale factor to normalize the result based on the path size. Taking this to the limit, as the path length and its enclosed area go to zero, gives the local curl at point $\mathbf{x}$.

A field is called *curl free* if $\nabla \times \mathbf{u} = \mathbf{0}$ everywhere in the field. A fluid velocity field that is curl free is called *irrotational*. An important theorem states that a field is curl free if and only if the field can be expressed as the gradient of a scalar field:

$$\nabla \times \mathbf{u} = \mathbf{0} \text{ everywhere} \iff \mathbf{u} = \nabla \phi,$$

where ϕ is some scalar field. In other words, if you have a vector field that is curl free, then there exists some scalar field whose gradient is exactly this vector field. And, conversely, if you have a vector field that is the gradient of some scalar field, then it is guaranteed to be curl free.

13.2.5 Laplacian

The *Laplacian operator* $\nabla^2 = \nabla \cdot \nabla$ operates on either a vector or a scalar field, returning a field of the same type. We can write this operator:

$$\nabla^2 = \nabla \cdot \nabla = \begin{bmatrix} \frac{\partial}{\partial x} \\ \frac{\partial}{\partial y} \\ \frac{\partial}{\partial z} \end{bmatrix} \cdot \begin{bmatrix} \frac{\partial}{\partial x} \\ \frac{\partial}{\partial y} \\ \frac{\partial}{\partial z} \end{bmatrix} = \frac{\partial^2}{\partial x^2} + \frac{\partial^2}{\partial y^2} + \frac{\partial^2}{\partial z^2}$$

Note that in some fields the convention is to write the Laplacian operator as Δ, but we will use the dot product notation throughout, as it can be thought of as the divergence of the gradient of the field. When operating on a scalar field ϕ, the Laplacian operator yields

$$\nabla^2 \phi = \nabla \cdot \nabla \phi = \left(\frac{\partial^2}{\partial x^2} + \frac{\partial^2}{\partial y^2} + \frac{\partial^2}{\partial z^2} \right) \phi = \frac{\partial^2 \phi}{\partial x^2} + \frac{\partial^2 \phi}{\partial y^2} + \frac{\partial^2 \phi}{\partial z^2}.$$

If the scalar field is not static, and its time rate of change is proportional to the Laplacian of the field, with constant of proportionality α, we have

$$\frac{\partial \phi}{\partial t} = \alpha \nabla^2 \phi,$$

which is the well-known *heat equation*, and governs diffusion of the field. Diffusion is essentially a smoothing operation that results, at the differential level, in every point in the field attaining a value that is the average of all of the values in the point's surrounding neighborhood. Using a heat analogy, hot and cold spots diffuse out through the field, resulting in a more uniform distribution of temperature. The constant α controls the rate at which the diffusion takes place.

A vector field $\mathbf{u}$ can be thought of as three scalar fields u_x, u_y, and u_z. Therefore, the Laplacian operator applied to a vector field yields

$$\nabla^2 \mathbf{u} = \nabla \cdot \nabla \mathbf{u} = \left(\frac{\partial^2}{\partial x^2} + \frac{\partial^2}{\partial y^2} + \frac{\partial^2}{\partial z^2} \right) \begin{bmatrix} u_x \\ u_y \\ u_z \end{bmatrix} = \begin{bmatrix} \frac{\partial^2 u_x}{\partial x^2} + \frac{\partial^2 u_x}{\partial y^2} + \frac{\partial^2 u_x}{\partial z^2} \\ \frac{\partial^2 u_y}{\partial x^2} + \frac{\partial^2 u_y}{\partial y^2} + \frac{\partial^2 u_y}{\partial z^2} \\ \frac{\partial^2 u_z}{\partial x^2} + \frac{\partial^2 u_z}{\partial y^2} + \frac{\partial^2 u_z}{\partial z^2} \end{bmatrix}.$$

If the field $\mathbf{u}$ is a velocity field, and its rate of change is proportional to the Laplacian of the field, the result is very similar to velocity matching that we saw when studying flocking simulation in Section 6.5. The velocity field will undergo diffusion that will smooth the field such that, at the differential level, neighboring points will tend to have identical velocities.

13.3   THE NAVIER-STOKES EQUATIONS

By now, we are very used to using Newton's second law $\mathbf{f} = m\mathbf{a}$ to govern physical simulation by solving for the acceleration in terms of the sum of all applied forces:

$$\mathbf{a} = \frac{1}{m} \sum_i \mathbf{f}_i.$$

Another way to write this equation is in terms of the rate of change of momentum:

$$\frac{d(m\mathbf{v})}{dt} = \sum_i \mathbf{f}_i.$$

For fluid simulation we will use an equation of exactly this form, except that we will have to account for the fact that we are no longer solving for the rate of change of the velocity of discrete elements, but instead solving for a vector field that accounts for the rate of change of the velocity field, i.e., we are solving for an acceleration field. In addition, instead of elements that have distinct masses, we now have a material whose mass is distributed as a scalar field. Since there are no discrete elements to carry mass, we replace mass with a scalar density field whose units are mass per unit volume, and forces are replaced by force density, whose units are force per unit volume. Finally, because a fluid is a continuous medium, force applied anywhere in the medium is transmitted through the medium by the fluid pushing on itself. We account for this force transmission by another scalar field, known as the pressure field. Its units are force per unit area.

At each timestep, in a typical fluid simulation for computer animation, the system state is completely accounted for by the density field, which tells us the distribution of fluid material in space; the velocity field, which tells us the speed and direction of flow; and the pressure field, which tells us how force is being transmitted through the fluid. If we assume that the fluid is incompressible, then wherever we have fluid the density field must be constant, which imposes a key constraint on allowable velocity field solutions. We can compute the acceleration field for the fluid knowing only this state, and any external forces acting on the fluid.

We use the following notation in writing fluid simulation equations to indicate these space- and time-varying fields. We represent the fluid velocity field as $\mathbf{u}(\mathbf{x}, t)$, the acceleration field $\frac{\partial \mathbf{u}(\mathbf{x},t)}{\partial t}$ as $\dot{\mathbf{u}}(\mathbf{x}, t)$, the density field as $\rho(\mathbf{x}, t)$, and the pressure field as $p(\mathbf{x}, t)$. We will also need a field $\mathbf{g}(\mathbf{x}, t)$, to account for external accelerations acting on the body of the fluid, such as gravity. As a notational convenience, these will be written simply as $\mathbf{u}$, $\dot{\mathbf{u}}$, ρ, p, and $\mathbf{g}$, but the reader is cautioned to remember that these are always space- and time-varying fields, and not simple scalar or vector values.

An assumption that is almost always made in fluid simulation for animation is that the fluid is incompressible. For all practical purposes this is an excellent assumption for water simulation, and is also a good assumption for air flow up to speeds approaching 100 meters per second (roughly 200 miles per hour). Recall that this implies that the fluid velocity field should be divergence free.

Given the incompressibility assumption, and our chosen notational form, the Navier-Stokes momentum equation governing fluid flow is

$$\rho \frac{d\mathbf{u}}{dt} = -\nabla p + \eta \nabla^2 \mathbf{u} + \rho \mathbf{g}, \tag{13.1}$$

subject to the constraint that

$$\nabla \cdot \mathbf{u} = 0. \tag{13.2}$$

Note that $\frac{d\mathbf{u}}{dt}$ is the *total derivative* with respect to time, not the partial derivative $\dot{\mathbf{u}}$. Equation 13.1 relates the time rate of change of the velocity field to the sum of three sources of acceleration, resulting from both internal and external forces. The constraint on the fluid velocity field given by Equation 13.2 enforces incompressibility by assuring that the fluid flow remains divergence free.

The terms in Equation 13.1 all have SI units of N/m^3, and can be summarized as follows:

$-\nabla p$ This term accounts for the force due to the local *pressure gradient*. If a point in the field has a lower pressure than the surrounding fluid, fluid will tend to flow from the higher pressure region to the lower pressure region, following the negative of the gradient, to equilibrate the pressure. Pressure p has SI units N/m^2.

$\eta \nabla^2 \mathbf{u}$ This term is known as the *viscosity* or *diffusion* term, and accounts for shear forces in the fluid created by velocity differences in neighboring regions of the fluid. The constant η is known as the *dynamic viscosity* of the fluid, and can be thought of loosely as the "thickness" of the fluid, i.e., how much it tends to resist flowing. For example, the dynamic viscosity, at room temperature, of water is roughly 0.002, of SAE 30 motor oil is 0.2, and of honey is 2. All of these are in SI units of $N\text{-}s/m^2$ [Research Equipment

(London) Limited, 2015]. The effect of the viscosity term is to create forces that tend to diffuse velocities across the fluid, and can create turbulence in the flow if there are high-velocity gradients.

$\rho\mathbf{g}$ This term is the *external force* term, expressed directly as density times acceleration. In SI units the acceleration $\mathbf{g}$ would be in m/s^2, or equivalently N/kg, and density ρ has units kg/m^3. This term is normally used to capture the effects of *body forces* like gravity or centrifugal force that act uniformly across the fluid. Locally acting forces pushing on the fluid, for example from a boat propeller, are usually best handled by applying boundary conditions to the pressure and velocity fields.

Equation 13.1 is not usually presented in the given form. It is common to divide through by density, and to use the *kinematic viscosity* $\nu = \eta/\rho$, rather than the dynamic viscosity. Since the density of water is $1{,}000 \ kg/m^3$, the kinematic viscosity of water is 1/1,000th of its dynamic viscosity. This leaves the equation in the form

$$\frac{d\mathbf{u}}{dt} = -\frac{1}{\rho}\nabla p + \nu\nabla^2\mathbf{u} + \mathbf{g}. \tag{13.3}$$

Since the left-hand side of this equation represents the total time derivative of a field that is both time and space varying, it expands to

$$\frac{d\mathbf{u}}{dt} = \frac{\partial\mathbf{u}}{\partial t} + \frac{\partial\mathbf{u}}{\partial x}\frac{dx}{dt} + \frac{\partial\mathbf{u}}{\partial y}\frac{dy}{dt} + \frac{\partial\mathbf{u}}{\partial z}\frac{dz}{dt}.$$

The term $\frac{\partial\mathbf{u}}{\partial t}$ is the fluid acceleration that we will write $\dot{\mathbf{u}}$. The terms $\frac{dx}{dt}$, $\frac{dy}{dt}$, and $\frac{dz}{dt}$ are simply the velocity components u_x, u_y, and u_z. Thus, the total velocity time derivative can be rewritten

$$\frac{d\mathbf{u}}{dt} = \dot{\mathbf{u}} + u_x\frac{\partial\mathbf{u}}{\partial x} + u_y\frac{\partial\mathbf{u}}{\partial y} + u_z\frac{\partial\mathbf{u}}{\partial z},$$

which can be easily shown to be equivalent to

$$\frac{d\mathbf{u}}{dt} = \dot{\mathbf{u}} + (\mathbf{u}\cdot\nabla)\mathbf{u}.$$

The term $(\mathbf{u}\cdot\nabla)\mathbf{u}$ is known as the *convection* term, and accounts for how the material of the fluid is transported by the velocity field. Since the fluid material is being transported by convection, all attributes of that material are transported with it. For example, if part of the fluid is dyed red, the motion of the fluid will transport this dye with the fluid. The transport of the properties of the fluid by convection is called *advection*. This transport applies to any quantities carried by the fluid, including the fluid velocity itself. For example, an eddy in a river will move with the flow of the river, and not remain fixed in one place. Because the terms convection and advection are so closely related, they are often confused in discussions of fluid flow.

Applying this result to Equation 13.3 gives us the form of the Navier-Stokes equations for incompressible flow normally seen in the graphics literature:

$$\dot{\mathbf{u}} = -(\mathbf{u} \cdot \nabla)\mathbf{u} - \frac{1}{\rho}\nabla p + \nu\nabla^2\mathbf{u} + \mathbf{g}, \qquad (13.4)$$

subject to the constraint that

$$\nabla \cdot \mathbf{u} = 0. \qquad (13.5)$$

The following table lists densities (ρ), dynamic (η), and kinematic (ν) viscosities of liquids and gasses that might typically be used in a computer animation. All dynamic viscosities and fluid densities for liquids are from *Marks' Standard Handbook for Mechanical Engineers* [Avallone and Baumeister, 1996]. These entries are recorded for a standard temperature of 20°C. Gas densities are from the *Alicat Scientific* website [Alicat Scientific, 2015]. These entries are recorded for a standard temperature of 25°C, and at one atmosphere of pressure (76 mm of mercury, or 101.33 kN/m^2, or 14.7 psi). An excellent source for density and viscosity information on a large variety of materials is the *Viscopedia* website [Anton Parr, 2015].

	ρ kg/m^3	η kg/m-s	ν m^2/s
	Liquids		
Alcohol	789	834	1.05
Gasoline	675	286	0.424
Glycerine	1,260	1,410,000	1,120
Mercury	13,500	1,550	0.115
Heavy oil	903	453	0.502
Light oil	903	86.7	0.0960
Sea water	1,020	1,080	1.06
Water	998	1,000	1.00
	Gases		
Air	1.18	18.7	15.8
Carbon dioxide	1.81	14.8	8.18
Helium	0.164	19.4	118
Hydrogen	0.0824	8.75	106
Nitrogen	1.15	17.5	15.2
Oxygen	1.31	20.3	15.5

13.4   POTENTIAL FLOW FIELDS

The Navier-Stokes equations provide a full description of fluid flow for domains typically used in computer graphics, but the solution methods for these equations are many and varied. In this section we examine how a set of simplifying assumptions can be made that reduce the Navier-Stokes equations to a form that has straight-forward solutions, but that, nevertheless, can be quite useful for describing complex wind fields in animation applications.

In Section 5.1, when we discussed the effect of wind on a particle, we assumed that there is a constant wind, blowing at a constant speed, in a constant direction. In this section, we expand this notion to wind fields, where the direction and speed of the wind are a function of position in space. In this way, the flow of particles can be shaped by the wind field. The idea for the approach presented here was first described by Wejchert and Haumann [1991].

Potential flow is a mathematical abstraction, working from the Navier-Stokes equations, which makes the following assumptions:

1. The flow is *steady* (meaning that while the velocity field can vary spatially, it is not changing in time).

2. The flow is *inviscid* (meaning that we ignore any effects due to fluid viscosity, i.e., $v = 0$).

3. The flow is incompressible.

4. The flow is irrotational.

These assumptions have the following ramifications:

1. Since the flow is steady, the velocity is a non-time-varying field $\mathbf{u}(\mathbf{x})$.

2. Since the flow is inviscid, it will not become turbulent, so the flow can be modeled by a smooth function.

3. Since the flow is incompressible, its divergence must be zero everywhere, i.e., $\nabla \cdot \mathbf{u} = 0$.

4. Since the flow is irrotational $\nabla \times \mathbf{u} = \mathbf{0}$, so the flow can be expressed as the gradient of a scalar field ϕ: $\mathbf{u} = \nabla \phi$.

Combining conditions 3 and 4, we have

$$\nabla \cdot \nabla \phi = 0, \text{ or}$$
$$\nabla^2 \phi = 0,$$

which is known as Laplace's equation. Any scalar field ϕ satisfying this equation, subject to any externally imposed boundary conditions, can be used for describing potential flow. Such solutions have been well studied and cataloged.

Three well-known solutions to Laplace's equation are particularly well suited to defining a flow field, and can be easily integrated into a 3D modeling and animation environment. The first of these is uniform flow, defined by

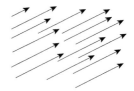

$$\phi = ax + by + cz,$$

$$\mathbf{u} = \nabla\phi = \begin{bmatrix} a \\ b \\ c \end{bmatrix}.$$

The scalar field varies linearly with position in space, so the velocity field is constant. In a modeling environment, this can serve as an overall or global wind direction. The second and third solutions to Laplace's equation lead directly to the definition of sources, sinks, and vortices, which can be used to add local detail to the flow.

Rather than being defined in Cartesian coordinates, the solutions for sources, sinks, and vortices are most easily defined in (r, θ, γ) spherical, or (r, θ, y) cylindrical coordinates. The r coordinate is distance from the origin and is always positive, thus $r \geq 0$. The θ coordinate is angular rotation about the Cartesian y axis, thus $-\pi \geq \theta \geq \pi$, and the γ coordinate is angular rotation above or below the z-x plane, thus $-\pi/2 \geq \gamma \geq \pi/2$. Quantities in spherical coordinates are converted to Cartesian coordinates via

$$x = r \cos\theta \cos\gamma,$$
$$y = r \sin\gamma,$$
$$z = -r \sin\theta \cos\gamma.$$

Quantities in cylindrical coordinates are converted to Cartesian coordinates via

$$x = r \cos\theta,$$
$$y = y,$$
$$z = -r \sin\theta.$$

Either of these coordinate systems can be aligned arbitrarily in Cartesian space by applying a rotation to the resulting (x, y, z) coordinates, and can be positioned arbitrarily in Cartesian space by a translation following the rotation. The gradient operator is defined differently in cylindrical and spherical coordinates. The gradient in spherical coordinates is given by

$$\nabla\phi = \begin{bmatrix} \frac{\partial\phi}{\partial r} \\ \frac{1}{r}\frac{\partial\phi}{\partial\theta} \\ \frac{1}{r\sin\theta}\frac{\partial\phi}{\partial\gamma} \end{bmatrix},$$

and the gradient in cylindrical coordinates is given by

$$\nabla \phi = \begin{bmatrix} \frac{\partial \phi}{\partial r} \\ \frac{1}{r}\frac{\partial \phi}{\partial \theta} \\ \frac{\partial \phi}{\partial y} \end{bmatrix}.$$

Sources and sinks can be specified in either spherical or cylindrical coordinates. In either case, their definition takes the form

$$\phi = \frac{a}{2\pi} \ln r,$$

$$\mathbf{u} = \nabla \phi = \begin{bmatrix} \frac{a}{2\pi r} \\ 0 \\ 0 \end{bmatrix}.$$

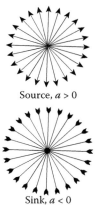

Source, $a > 0$

Sink, $a < 0$

The constant a in this equation is a strength parameter, which is positive for a source and negative for a sink. Since only the r coordinate is non-zero, flow arises from the origin of the coordinate frame, flowing in or out uniformly in all directions. In cylindrical coordinates, flow will be out from or in to the coordinate frame's y axis, rather than the origin. Note that the velocity of the flow decreases with the inverse of r, so the effect of a source or sink on the flow will be most significant near to the origin of its coordinate frame (or y axis).

A vortex is defined in cylindrical coordinates as

$$\phi = \frac{b}{2\pi}\theta,$$

$$\mathbf{u} = \nabla \phi = \begin{bmatrix} 0 \\ \frac{b}{2\pi r} \\ 0 \end{bmatrix}.$$

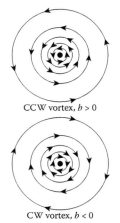

CCW vortex, $b > 0$

CW vortex, $b < 0$

The constant b is a strength parameter, whose sign determines the direction of the rotation of the flow: positive or negative around the y axis. Like a source or sink, the velocity of the vortex flow decreases with the inverse of r, so the effect of a vortex will also be most significant near to the y axis of its coordinate frame.

Note that the speed of a source, sink, or vortex is infinite at its origin. In a practical implementation of potential flow, a check on distance from the origin must be made to limit the flow to a large but finite speed.

Since the ∇^2 operator is a linear operator, if we have several scalar fields ϕ_1, ϕ_2, ϕ_3 each satisfying Laplace's equation, then a weighted sum of these fields $a\phi_1 + b\phi_2 + c\phi_3$ will also satisfy the equation, i.e., $\nabla^2(a\phi_1 + b\phi_2 + c\phi_3) = a\nabla^2\phi_1 + b\nabla^2\phi_2 + c\nabla^2\phi_3 = 0$. This means that solutions to Laplace's equation can be superimposed and scaled to build a more complicated scalar field, whose gradient is a more complicated potential flow field. Thus, source, sink, and vortex can be

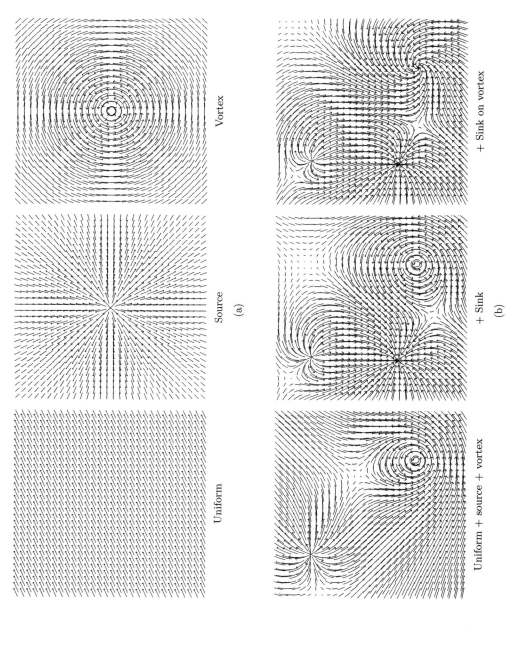

FIGURE 13.2 Potential flow solutions. (a) Primitives, (b) superimposed primitives.

The thoughtful reader will probably be asking, "How can a source or sink be divergence free, and how can a vortex be curl free?" The answer is that they are, except exactly at their centers. Any place in the scalar field where the gradient vanishes is known as a singularity in the field, and the gradient vanishes exactly at these centers. Removing singularity points from the flow field, a quick check on the source, sink, and vortex primitives will confirm that with $u = \nabla \phi$, $\nabla \cdot u$ and $\nabla \times u$ are zero everywhere. Returning to the *circularity* definition of irrotational: "if we travel in a closed curve in the flow field, we will be traveling with the velocity as much as we will be traveling against the velocity, so the net velocity effect on us will be 0," we must modify this to require that the closed path not enclose a singularity.

An intuitive way to understand what is happening here is to realize that a source, sink, or vortex is really a single point representation for a boundary condition in the field. A source is like a hose, injecting fluid into the flow field, a sink is like a drain removing fluid, and a vortex is like a paddle wheel rotating in the fluid. Source and sink are boundary conditions providing a fixed velocity expanding out from or into the hose or drain. Vortex is a boundary condition providing a fixed angular velocity along the blades of the paddle wheel. Thought of in this way, they are not part of the field at all, but are really finite size phenomena operating on the field. We reduce them to a single point as a convenient mathematical abstraction, but in doing analysis on the field they should not be included.

used as flow primitives that can be positioned within a geometric modeling system to create many interesting flow field configurations.

Figure 13.2 demonstrates how this can be done. The figure shows 2D fields, but the same principle applies in 3D. The top row of this figure shows vector diagrams indicating flow direction and magnitude for the uniform, source, and vortex flow primitives. The bottom row shows what the flow field looks like after successively adding additional primitives to an underlying uniform flow. The leftmost diagram shows a source and a vortex added to a uniform flow field. The central figure adds a sink to the field, and the right figure shows what happens when a sink primitive is placed exactly on top of a vortex; instead of a circular flow, the flow spirals in to create an effect like water draining from a tub. If we had added a source instead of a sink on top of the vortex, we would have created a pinwheel effect. All of these flows exhibit regions of high flow velocities near to the primitives and also *stagnation* regions, where the flow velocity goes to 0 surrounded by a saddle-shaped flow.

13.5 SUMMARY

Here are some of the main points to take away from this chapter:

- The term *fluid* includes both gasses and liquids.

- Fluid simulation methods fall into two categories: Lagrangian and Eulerian.

- Lagrangian simulations divide the material into small mass units and track them in time.

- Eulerian simulations divide space into cells and track the flow of mass through the space cells.

- A fluid simulation is attempting to compute entire scalar and vector fields, in particular the pressure and velocity fields.

- The differential operators used to do computation over these fields are gradient, divergence, curl, and the Laplacian.

- The Navier-Stokes equations for incompressible flow are most commonly used for simulating the dynamics of a fluid for animation purposes.

- One of these equations accounts for the forces acting to change fluid momentum, with forces expressed as pressures, i.e., force per unit area, and mass expressed as density, i.e., mass per unit volume.

- The other equation for incompressible flow is a constraint, requiring that the divergence of the velocity field be 0 everywhere.

- For the special case of steady, inviscid flow a fluid velocity field can be developed as a solution to Laplace's equation. Such a solution provides flow primitives like sources, sinks, and vortices that can be manipulated in a modeler to choreograph the flow.

CHAPTER 14

Smoothed Particle Hydrodynamics

I N THIS SECTION, WE LOOK AT THE MOST SUCCESSFUL LAGRANGIAN METHOD for doing incompressible fluid simulation, known as *Smoothed Particle Hydrodynamics*, or *SPH* for short. As the name implies, the fluid is represented by a large collection of individual fluid particles. These interact with each other following the laws of hydrodynamics—as captured by the Navier-Stokes equations. Figure 14.1 shows what a typical SPH water simulation might look like if the water particles were rendered as colored spheres. Note that the simulation is especially good at capturing detail in the splashing fluid motion. SPH found its original applications in the astrophysics community, with its underlying mathematical and physical elaboration developed in a paper by Monaghan [1992]. The SPH method was first introduced to the graphics community by Stam and Fiume [1995] for simulating fire, and soon after was used by Desbrun and Gascuel [1996] for simulating highly deformable objects. The paper that firmly established SPH as a method for fluid simulation was by Müller et al. [2003], entitled *Particle-Based Fluid Simulation for Interactive Applications*. As the title suggests, the original intent of SPH was to provide interactive fluid-like animation for applications like VR and video games.

14.1 SPATIAL SAMPLING AND RECONSTRUCTION

The basic idea of SPH is that the fluid mass is sampled onto a large system of interacting particles, so that each particle can be thought of as representing a small "chunk" or volume of the fluid. If the volume represented by particle i is V_i, centered at position $\mathbf{x}_i$, its mass will be

$$m_i = \rho(\mathbf{x}_i)V_i.$$

In standard SPH, a particle's mass remains constant throughout the simulation. The particle itself is free to move through space, so it does not remain in its initial position. It is typical, but not required, to make the assumption that the fluid

FIGURE 14.1 Frames from an SPH fluid simulation, showing a volume of water being dropped into a box. (Courtesy of Zhizhong Pan.)

density is initially constant across the entire medium, and to assign uniform volume and mass to each particle.

When field quantities, like pressure, are needed to compute the acceleration on a particular particle, they are estimated by considering all of the particles in the neighborhood of that particle. Thus, the entire method is dependent upon an initial sampling of the fluid field to generate a set of particles with their spatial positions and velocities, and then at every timestep to reconstruct all of the field quantities needed to compute accelerations.

In order to reconstruct a field from a set of particles, SPH depends on radially symmetric *kernel functions*, sometimes known as *blending functions*, that are used to spread the effect of a particle over its surrounding space. If $\mathbf{x}_i$ is the position of particle i, and $\mathbf{r} = \mathbf{x} - \mathbf{x}_i$ is a vector from this position to point $\mathbf{x}$ in space, kernel functions associated with particle i will have the form

$$w_i(\mathbf{r}) = w(\|\mathbf{r}\|),$$

i.e., they vary only with distance $r = \|\mathbf{r}\|$ from their center. In order to localize the effect of a single particle on its neighboring particles, the kernel functions are usually chosen to be of *finite support*, meaning that if $r_{\max}$ is the maximum support distance,

$$w(r) = 0, \text{ for all } r \geq r_{\max}.$$

The kernels are also normalized so that

$$\oint w(\mathbf{r})d\mathbf{r} = 1,$$

where the integral is taken over the entire support volume.

When the set of particles is created, each particle must be assigned a value for each property it will be keeping track of. Normally, this will include only the particle's velocity, as pressure and density will be computed on-the-fly at each timestep. But, it could include any other value that you would like to be advected by the fluid, such as fluid temperature.

In the discussion below, a field name Φ, written without a subscript, refers to the continuous field, but when written Φ_i it refers to the field value sampled at the position of particle i.

If it is necessary to know the field value of some field Φ at a position $\mathbf{x}$, the kernel weighted effects of all of the particles in the support neighborhood $N(\mathbf{x})$ of position $\mathbf{x}$ are summed, giving the reconstructed estimate

$$\Phi(\mathbf{x}) = \sum_{j \in N(\mathbf{x})} m_j \frac{\Phi_j}{\rho_j} w(\mathbf{x} - \mathbf{x}_j). \qquad (14.1)$$

Note that $m_j/\rho_j = V_j$, so that the summation is weighted by both the kernel value and the particle's volume—if particles are of nonuniform size, bigger particles will have more effect. In the equations below, we will assume that the summations are over the points within the neighborhood of the position indicated on the left-hand side of the equation.

While a particle's mass will remain constant, its density will not, since particles are free to separate or cluster together. Thus, when density ρ_i at the position of particle i needs to be known it is computed from Equation 14.1, with $\Phi_j \equiv \rho_j$. Thus, it follows that the density at any given position in space will be

$$\rho(\mathbf{x}) = \sum_j m_j w(\mathbf{x} - \mathbf{x}_j), \qquad (14.2)$$

so that for particle i,

$$\rho_i = \sum_j m_j w(\mathbf{x}_i - \mathbf{x}_j). \qquad (14.3)$$

14.2 PARTICLE ACCELERATION CALCULATION

Since the particles carry their own mass, their momenta are simply functions of time, and not space, so the Navier-Stokes equation in the form of Equation 13.3, can be used to calculate accelerations acting on the particles, eliminating the need for the convection term of Equation 13.4. This equation, as it would be applied to each particle, is

$$\frac{d\mathbf{u}_i}{dt} = -\frac{1}{\rho_i}\nabla p_i + \nu\nabla^2\mathbf{u}_i + \mathbf{g}_i. \tag{14.4}$$

Thus, at each timestep, we need to compute the pressure gradient, the Laplacian of the velocity field, and any externally applied acceleration at the position of each particle.

14.2.1 Pressure Gradient

Fluid pressure is related to density according to the relationship

$$p = \frac{k\rho_0}{\gamma}\left[\left(\frac{\rho}{\rho_0}\right)^{\gamma} - 1\right], \tag{14.5}$$

where ρ_0 is a reference density, and k is a stiffness parameter. For example, if we were computing air flow, we might pick ρ_0 to be a typical atmospheric pressure. Most SPH implementations take γ to be 1, so that for each particle i, after calculating the particle's density ρ_i, we determine its pressure to be

$$p_i = k(\rho_i - \rho_0).$$

Given the pressure and density for each particle, we can compute the gradient of the pressure/density ratio as

$$\nabla\left(\frac{p}{\rho}\right) = \frac{\rho\nabla p - p\nabla\rho}{\rho^2} = \frac{\nabla p}{\rho} - \frac{p\nabla\rho}{\rho^2},$$

allowing us to rewrite the pressure gradient term in Equation 14.4 as

$$\frac{\nabla p}{\rho} = \nabla\left(\frac{p}{\rho}\right) + \frac{p\nabla\rho}{\rho^2}.$$

We need to rewrite the terms on the right-hand side as summations over particles. Recalling Equation 14.3, we have

$$\nabla\rho_i = \nabla\left(\sum_j m_j w(\mathbf{x}_i - \mathbf{x}_j)\right) = \sum_j m_j \nabla w(\mathbf{x}_i - \mathbf{x}_j),$$

since m_j is constant. Likewise, from Equation 14.1,

$$\nabla \left(\frac{p_i}{\rho_i} \right) = \sum_j m_j \frac{\frac{p_j}{\rho_j}}{\rho_j} \nabla w(\mathbf{x}_i - \mathbf{x}_j) = \sum_j m_j \frac{p_j}{\rho_j^2} \nabla w(\mathbf{x}_i - \mathbf{x}_j).$$

Thus, the pressure gradient term, evaluated at the position of particle i, is

$$\frac{\nabla p_i}{\rho_i} = \nabla \left(\frac{p}{\rho} \right) + \frac{p \nabla \rho}{\rho^2}$$

$$= \sum_j m_j \frac{p_j}{\rho_j^2} \nabla w(\mathbf{x}_i - \mathbf{x}_j) + \frac{p_i}{\rho_i^2} \sum_j m_j \nabla w(\mathbf{x}_i - \mathbf{x}_j)$$

$$= \sum_j m_j \left(\frac{p_i}{\rho_i^2} + \frac{p_j}{\rho_j^2} \right) \nabla w(\mathbf{x}_i - \mathbf{x}_j). \tag{14.6}$$

In some computer graphics literature a different formulation of the pressure gradient is used, specifically

$$\frac{\nabla p_i}{\rho_i} = \sum_j m_j \frac{p_j}{\rho_i \rho_j} \nabla w(\mathbf{x}_i - \mathbf{x}_j).$$

However, this formulation assumes constant density, which may be a poor assumption, and leads to an asymmetric relationship in which Newton's third law is violated—i.e., particles i and j may not exert equal and opposite forces on each other. To fix this asymmetry, p_j may be replaced with $\frac{p_i + p_j}{2}$:

$$\frac{\nabla p_i}{\rho_i} = \sum_j m_j \frac{p_i + p_j}{2 \rho_i \rho_j} \nabla w(\mathbf{x}_i - \mathbf{x}_j).$$

This yields a symmetric relationship. However, Equation 14.6 is probably to be preferred. It is derived directly and is always symmetric.

14.2.2 Diffusion

Computing the Laplacian in the diffusion term in Equation 14.4, without considering any density gradient, also results in an asymmetry problem, and violates Newton's third law. Since the density field can vary, it is more accurate to begin with the momentum $\rho(\mathbf{x})\mathbf{u}(\mathbf{x})$, whose Laplacian is

$$\nabla^2(\rho \mathbf{u}) = \rho \nabla^2 \mathbf{u} + \mathbf{u} \nabla^2 \rho,$$

and therefore,

$$\nabla^2 \mathbf{u} = \frac{1}{\rho} \left(\nabla^2(\rho \mathbf{u}) - \mathbf{u} \nabla^2 \rho \right).$$

Notice that we can calculate

$$\nabla^2 \rho_i = \nabla^2 \left(\sum_j m_j \frac{\rho_j}{\rho_j} w(\mathbf{x}_i - \mathbf{x}_j) \right) = \sum_j m_j \nabla^2 w(\mathbf{x}_i - \mathbf{x}_j)$$

and likewise

$$\nabla^2(\rho_i \mathbf{u}_i) = \nabla^2 \left(\sum_j m_j \frac{\rho_j \mathbf{u}_j}{\rho_j} w(\mathbf{x}_i - \mathbf{x}_j) \right) = \sum_j m_j \mathbf{u}_j \nabla^2 w(\mathbf{x}_i - \mathbf{x}_j)$$

Applying these results together gives us a formulation for the Laplacian, which when evaluated at the position of particle i is

$$\nabla^2 \mathbf{u}_i = \frac{1}{\rho_i} \left(\nabla^2(\rho_i \mathbf{u}_i) - \mathbf{u}_i \nabla^2 \rho_i \right)$$

$$= \frac{1}{\rho_i} \left(\sum_j m_j \mathbf{u}_j \nabla^2 w(\mathbf{x}_i - \mathbf{x}_j) - \mathbf{u}_i \sum_j m_j \nabla^2 w(\mathbf{x}_i - \mathbf{x}_j) \right)$$

$$= \sum_j m_j \frac{\mathbf{u}_j - \mathbf{u}_i}{\rho_i} \nabla^2 w(\mathbf{x}_i - \mathbf{x}_j). \tag{14.7}$$

14.2.3 External Acceleration and Collisions

The external acceleration $\mathbf{g}_i$ in Equation 14.4 is normally used to represent gravity, so it is constant across all particles. But, in the SPH formulation, it provides a convenient place for the animator to produce unusual effects by applying accelerations in specific regions or on specific particles. Thus, this term should be the sum of all external accelerations applied to a specific particle. If it is desired to apply a force to a particle i, rather than to directly apply an acceleration, the force should be divided by the local density of the particle ρ_i.

Since SPH is an interacting particle method, all of the techniques that we have discussed earlier for handling particle collisions with external objects can be used without modification. This can include both particle bounce and friction. Therefore, it is easy to simulate constrained liquid flow, like pouring a liquid into a glass.

14.3 KERNEL FUNCTION

There is an infinite number of kernel functions that could be used for SPH, and the choice of a function is based largely on the properties the animator desires. Important considerations are that it should be symmetric, have finite support, and have an integrated volume equal to 1. Generally, it should decrease monotonically from the center, so that the influence of particles falls off the farther away they are. Another useful property is for the kernel and its derivatives to smoothly go to zero at the boundary of the region of support.

A spline-based 3D kernel function with nice properties was presented in the early SPH paper by Monaghan [1992]. If $r = \|\mathbf{r}\|$ is the distance from the kernel center, this kernel is given by

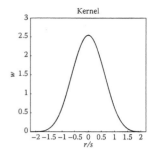

$$w(\mathbf{r}) = \frac{1}{\pi s^3} \begin{cases} 1 - \frac{3}{2}(\frac{r}{s})^2 + \frac{3}{4}(\frac{r}{s})^3 & \text{if } 0 \leq \frac{r}{s} \leq 1, \\ \frac{1}{4}(2 - \frac{r}{s})^3 & \text{if } 1 \leq \frac{r}{s} \leq 2, \\ 0 & \text{otherwise.} \end{cases}$$

This kernel has finite support radius $2s$, i.e., the kernel goes to exactly 0 beyond distance $2s$ from its center. Further, its first and second derivatives go to 0 at $2s$, providing smooth interpolation up to and beyond the support distance. As required, its volume integral is 1.

Given an appropriate kernel function w in closed form, ∇w, and $\nabla^2 w$ can also be computed in closed form, so that no numerical differentiation needs to be done. Since the kernel is radially symmetric, i.e., it is a function only of distance from its center, we need only compute its first and second derivatives with

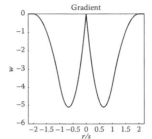
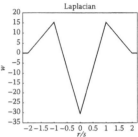

respect to r to determine its gradient and Laplacian. For example, for the kernel described above

$$\frac{dw}{dr} = \frac{1}{\pi s^4} \begin{cases} 3\frac{r}{s}(-1 + \frac{3}{4}\frac{r}{s}) & \text{if } 0 \leq \frac{r}{s} \leq 1, \\ -\frac{3}{4}(2 - \frac{r}{s})^2 & \text{if } 1 \leq \frac{r}{s} \leq 2, \\ 0 & \text{otherwise,} \end{cases}$$

and

$$\frac{d^2 w}{dr^2} = \frac{1}{\pi s^5} \begin{cases} 3(-1 + \frac{3}{2}\frac{r}{s}) & \text{if } 0 \leq \frac{r}{s} \leq 1, \\ \frac{3}{2}(2 - \frac{r}{s}) & \text{if } 1 \leq \frac{r}{s} \leq 2, \\ 0 & \text{otherwise.} \end{cases}$$

Thought of in this way, w, ∇w, and $\nabla^2 w$ are simply three different kernel functions. The fact that the gradient doesn't go smoothly to 0 at the center helps ensure that nearby particles receive an appropriate "push" in the pressure calculation.

14.4 THE FLUID SURFACE AND SURFACE TENSION

In our discussion of fluid simulation, so far, we have not addressed the issue of the fluid surface. Some fluid simulations, like most gas-flow simulations, may not require denoting a surface, as it may be sufficient to imagine the fluid as having an infinite 3D extent. But, when simulating liquids it is often desired to represent the fluid surface so that oceans, swimming pools, and glasses of water can all be simulated.

The surface of the SPH fluid is found by creating what is known as a scalar *color field* c, whose value is 1 at each particle position and goes to 0 beyond the region of support of all fluid particles. The smoothly varying field is computed

$$c(\mathbf{x}) = \sum_i m_i \frac{1}{\rho_i} w(\mathbf{x} - \mathbf{x}_i),$$

using the template of Equation 14.1, and setting the value of $c_i = 1$.

The gradient of the color field provides a vector valued surface field,

$$\mathbf{s}(\mathbf{x}) = \nabla c = \sum_i m_i \frac{1}{\rho_i} \nabla w(\mathbf{x} - \mathbf{x}_i),$$

whose magnitude is large near the fluid surface and nearly zero elsewhere. Therefore, $\|\mathbf{s}\|$ is a strong indicator of the interface between the region containing fluid particles, and the region containing no particles. The surface field points in the direction away from the nonfluid region toward the fluid region. Therefore, a thresholding operation on $\|\mathbf{s}\|$ will locate the fluid surface, and normalizing the negative of the gradient provides a surface normal field

$$\hat{\mathbf{n}} = -\mathbf{s}/\|\mathbf{s}\|,$$

that can be used for rendering. A raytracing renderer can render the surface directly by finding the ray intersection with the thresholded surface [Hart, 1993]. A polygon-based renderer can use *Marching Cubes* to create a set of surface triangles [Lorensen and Cline, 1987].

There have been various improvements suggested for extracting a surface for rendering from a particle-based simulation, including by Zhu and Bridson [2005]. The best current method is probably that of Yu and Turk [2013].

A final consideration regarding the surface of a fluid is surface tension. The molecules in a fluid exert intermolecular forces on each other due to uneven charge distribution. Interior to the fluid, these forces, balance each other, but at the surface they are unbalanced. For example, at the interface between water and air, the air molecules exert a weak influence on the surface water molecules, compared to the strong forces exerted by the interior water molecules. The result is that there is a net force tending to try to pull the molecules at the water's surface down into the body of the water. This gives the water surface some of the characteristics of an elastic membrane, allowing, for example, water insects to be able to glide along the water surface without sinking. It is also the force tending to pull water droplets into a spherical shape—the water surface will tend to maintain minimal curvature, and any deviation of the shape of a closed body from a sphere will require regions of the surface to have higher curvature. The divergence of the surface normal field

$$\kappa = \nabla \cdot \hat{\mathbf{n}}$$

provides a measure of surface curvature. The surface tension force is proportional to the local curvature, and in the direction toward the fluid, as given by

$$\mathbf{f}_s = \begin{cases} -\alpha \kappa \hat{\mathbf{n}} & \text{if } \|\mathbf{s}\| > \tau_s, \\ \mathbf{0} & \text{otherwise.} \end{cases}$$

The constant of proportionality α, and the level threshold τ_s are tunable by the animator to obtain the desired surface tension effect.

14.5 SIMULATION ALGORITHM

The basic SPH algorithm, as described by Müller et al. [2003], is an interacting particle algorithm whose structure is identical to that described in Section 6.1.3. A neighborhood of influence for each particle is determined. Then, over the neighborhood of each particle, pressure gradient, diffusion, and external accelerations are calculated and summed. For particles near the surface, surface tension is computed and treated as an external acceleration.

Managing the computational load of the SPH calculations is mainly a matter of efficiently determining the particles that are in the neighborhood of a particular particle. Since all of the SPH particles are moving, typically quite rapidly, using a data structure like an octree or a kd-tree is not very efficient, because these data structures will need to be rebuilt every timestep. For this reason, the acceleration method of choice is typically a spatial grid. This can be fixed or can be resized every timestep to conform to the bounding box of the fluid particles. In either case, the computational cost of rebuilding this data structure is linear in the number of particles.

A big problem with SPH, as elaborated above, is that this formulation violates the incompressibility constraint normally invoked in Navier-Stokes fluid simulations for animation. For this reason, fluids simulated by SPH tend to exhibit a "springiness" not seen in most real fluids. For example, the surface of an SPH fluid poured into a glass will appear to bounce up and down in an unrealistic way. This can be somewhat ameliorated by increasing the constants k and γ in the pressure-density relationship given by Equation 14.5, making the fluid "stiffer," but this approach suffers from requiring a shorter simulation timestep to maintain stability.

The compressibility problem in SPH was solved elegantly by Solenthaler and Pajarola [2009], in the paper *Predictive-Corrective Incompressible SPH*. Because of this improvement, SPH has moved beyond being merely a convenient real-time method, and has become the method of choice when highly detailed splashing effects are desired. The fundamental idea in the predictive-corrective approach is that accelerations due to diffusion and external forces are held fixed, while the pressure field is iteratively corrected to produce pressure gradient accelerations resulting in the desired constant density throughout the field. The pressure correction for each particle is based on the deviation of density at that particle from the desired density. The details of this method are beyond the scope of this book, but are fully explained in their paper.

14.6 SUMMARY

Here are some of the main points to take away from this chapter:

- SPH is the most popular Lagrangian approach to fluid simulation. It treats the fluid as a large collection of mass "particles," and derives their motion from both external forces and internal interparticle forces governed by the Navier-Stokes equations.

- SPH is particularly useful for interactive applications, or when high-detail effects, such as splashing, are required.

- Field quantities, such as pressure and velocity, are derived from these quantities measured at the individual particles, and then spread through the fluid volume by kernel functions. The net field value at a spatial position is then the kernel weighted sum of the values at particles in the neighborhood of that position.

- Constructing a fluid surface for rendering in an SPH simulation can be done implicitly by constructing a color field, whose gradient magnitude allows detection of the surface, and whose direction provides a surface normal.

- SPH is fully mass preserving, since the total number of mass particles does not change.

- SPH does not have an explicit mechanism to enforce volume preservation, so the fluid can look "springy" unless measures are taken to reduce this effect.

CHAPTER 15

Finite Difference Algorithms

15.1 FINITE DIFFERENCES

ULERIAN APPROACHES TO FLUID SIMULATION require sampling the space that the fluid is acting in, rather than sampling the fluid itself. Because Eulerian approaches begin by subdividing space, they typically require bounding the region over which a fluid simulation is done. This is in contrast to Lagrangian methods, where particles are free to move anywhere in space. In this section we present how this can be done using a uniform spatial grid, as described in Section 6.3.1. Assuming a gridded representation of space, we first lay the foundations for doing numerical computing over this grid, using *finite difference* representations of the differential operators appearing in the Navier-Stokes equations. We then describe two approaches for sampling fields onto the grid, and build on this to describe the two most popular simulation schemes built on this structure, the *semi-Lagrangian* and *FLIP* methods.

15.1.1 Numerical Differentiation

Given that we will sample the fluid simulation fields over a regular spatial grid, we need a way to define the differential operators of the Navier-Stokes equations under this sampling. This will require an approach to estimating first and second partial spatial derivatives.

Forward differencing: One technique for spatial numerical differentiation is *forward differencing*. This approach is depicted in the figure to the right. Consider the one-dimensional derivative of a spatial quantity $\phi(x)$, using the classical definition of the derivative,

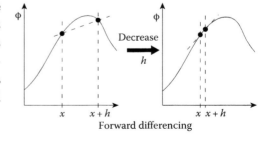

Forward differencing

$$\frac{d\phi}{dx} = \lim_{h \to 0} \frac{\phi(x+h) - \phi(x)}{h}.$$

This is the foundation of forward differencing. Moving from the left of the figure to the right shows that as we move closer to the limit, letting h become smaller but still finite, we get a better estimate of the slope of the curve at x. Now, suppose we have a one-dimensional field ϕ sampled on a regular interval Δx, with samples at $(\cdots, x_{i-1}, x_i, x_{i+1}, \cdots)$. Using forward differencing, the first derivative of ϕ at x_i would be estimated as

$$\frac{d\phi}{dx}\bigg|_{x_i} \approx \frac{\phi_{i+1} - \phi_i}{\Delta x}.$$

Backward differencing: Backward differencing is similar, but uses the derivative definition

$$\frac{d\phi}{dx} = \lim_{h \to 0} \frac{\phi(x) - \phi(x - h)}{h}.$$

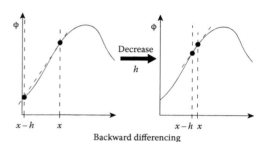

Backward differencing

Using backward differencing on a regular set of samples, the first derivative of ϕ at x_i would be estimated as

$$\frac{d\phi}{dx}\bigg|_{x_i} \approx \frac{\phi_i - \phi_{i-1}}{\Delta x}.$$

Central differencing: On the other hand, we could start with an alternate definition of the derivative, which is the foundation of central differencing,

$$\frac{d\phi}{dx} = \lim_{h \to 0} \frac{\phi(x + h/2) - \phi(x - h/2)}{h}.$$

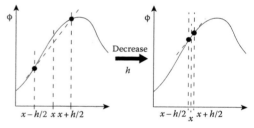

Central differencing

Central differencing explicitly places the derivative halfway between the two samples that it is derived from. With central differencing, the first derivative of ϕ at $x_i + \Delta x/2$ would be estimated as

$$\frac{d\phi}{dx}\bigg|_{x_i + \Delta x/2} \approx \frac{\phi_{i+1} - \phi_i}{\Delta x},$$

and at $x_i - \Delta x/2$ the central differencing estimate would be

$$\frac{d\phi}{dx}\bigg|_{x_i - \Delta x/2} \approx \frac{\phi_i - \phi_{i-1}}{\Delta x},$$

Although the three approaches are identical in the limit as Δx becomes vanishingly small, for a finite Δx central differencing explicitly places the estimate where it is most accurate. Therefore, in numerical calculations, it is best to use central differencing, whenever possible, to maintain the highest accuracy.

In some cases, we need to calculate the derivative of φ directly at a position x_i. In this case, we can use an alternative central differencing form

$$\left.\frac{d\phi}{dx}\right|_{x_i} \approx \frac{\phi_{i+1} - \phi_{i-1}}{2\Delta x}.$$

That is, we take the difference from a distance h on each side, instead of $h/2$. This has the potential advantage of making all the calculations of φ and its derivatives occur at the same points, without any bias in one direction or the other, as forward and backward differencing have. However, because the difference is taken over a larger region, it tends to cause more smoothing in the derivative calculation than is ideal.

Upwind differencing: There are situations where it is computationally inconvenient to place the derivative estimate halfway between two samples, and undesirable to have the excessive smoothing caused by a $2\Delta x$ region of central differencing. In this case, if we have a choice between either forward or backward differencing, the suggested approach is to make that choice using an *upwind differencing* scheme. In upwind differencing, if we are taking a derivative in the context of a vector field, such as a fluid flow field, we should choose the sample "upwind" (i.e., in the direction from which the flow is coming) of the current position when taking the difference. If the component of the flow field in the direction of the derivative is u_x, then the upwind scheme is concisely stated as

$$\left.\frac{d\phi}{dx}\right|_{x_i} \approx \begin{cases} \frac{\phi_i - \phi_{i-1}}{\Delta x} & \text{if } u_x \geq 0 \\ \frac{\phi_{i+1} - \phi_i}{\Delta x} & \text{if } u_x < 0. \end{cases}$$

Second difference: To estimate the second derivative at x_i, we would subtract forward and backward to compute central differences located at $x_i + \Delta x/2$, and $x_i - \Delta x/2$, and then difference again, using these estimates. Thus, the rule for estimating the second derivative is

$$\left.\frac{d^2\phi}{dx^2}\right|_{x_i} = \left.\frac{d(\frac{d\phi}{\partial x})}{dx}\right|_{x_i} \approx \frac{\left(\frac{\phi_{i+1} - \phi_i}{\Delta x}\right) - \left(\frac{\phi_i - \phi_{i-1}}{\Delta x}\right)}{\Delta x} = \frac{\phi_{i+1} - 2\phi_i + \phi_{i-1}}{\Delta x^2}.$$

The location of the second derivative, computed in this way, is at the original location x_i.

15.1.2 Differential Operators

In all of the figures and discussion below, the scalar pressure field is indicated by p, and the 3D vector velocity field by $\mathbf{u} = \begin{bmatrix} u & v & w \end{bmatrix}^T$. To simplify notation, we name the three velocity components $u \equiv u_x$, $v \equiv u_y$, and $w \equiv u_z$, and follow this convention throughout.

Gradient: If we have samples on a uniform 3D grid, the three spatial partial derivatives of a field ϕ would be estimated using central differencing as

$$\nabla \phi = \begin{bmatrix} \frac{\partial \phi}{\partial x} \\ \frac{\partial \phi}{\partial y} \\ \frac{\partial \phi}{\partial z} \end{bmatrix} \approx \begin{bmatrix} \frac{\phi_{i,j,k} - \phi_{i-1,j,k}}{\Delta x} \\ \frac{\phi_{i,j,k} - \phi_{i,j-1,k}}{\Delta y} \\ \frac{\phi_{i,j,k} - \phi_{i,j,k-1}}{\Delta z} \end{bmatrix}.$$

As central differences, the three components of the gradient would be located at the three different locations: $x_{i,j,k} - \Delta x/2$, $y_{i,j,k} - \Delta y/2$, and $z_{i,j,k} - \Delta z/2$. If the values $\phi_{i,j,k}$ are samples taken at the centers of the cells, the three components of the gradient will be located at the centers of the left, bottom, and back cell faces. Alternatively, this calculation could be done using upwind differencing, placing the gradient at $\mathbf{x}_{i,j,k}$. The upwind direction must be determined separately for each of the three coordinate directions.

Divergence: Since the divergence of the velocity field is used to measure the rate of change of total fluid in a cell, we will always want to know the divergence at the center of a cell. The divergence of a vector quantity $\mathbf{u}$ would be estimated as

$$\nabla \cdot \mathbf{u} = \frac{\partial \mathbf{u}}{\partial x} + \frac{\partial \mathbf{u}}{\partial y} + \frac{\partial \mathbf{u}}{\partial z}$$

$$\approx \frac{u_{i+1,j,k} - u_{i,j,k}}{\Delta x} + \frac{v_{i,j+1,k} - v_{i,j,k}}{\Delta y} + \frac{w_{i,j,k+1} - w_{i,j,k}}{\Delta z}.$$

For central differencing to be used, if the divergence is to be placed at the center of the cell, the vector components will have to lie on centers of the left, bottom, and back faces. If the vector components lie in the center of the cell, upwind differencing should be used, and will place the divergence at the center of the cell.

Laplacian: The Laplacian of a scalar field ϕ is given by

$$\nabla^2 \phi = \frac{\partial^2 \phi}{\partial x^2} + \frac{\partial^2 \phi}{\partial y^2} + \frac{\partial^2 \phi}{\partial z^2}$$

$$\approx \frac{\phi_{i+1,j,k} - 2\phi_{i,j,k} + \phi_{i-1,j,k}}{\Delta x^2} + \frac{\phi_{i,j+1,k} - 2\phi_{i,j,k} + \phi_{i,j-1,k}}{\Delta y^2}$$

$$+ \frac{\phi_{i,j,k+1} - 2\phi_{i,j,k} + \phi_{i,j,k-1}}{\Delta z^2}.$$

If samples are taken on a cubic lattice, so that $\Delta x = \Delta y = \Delta z$, then for cell (i,j,k) this simplifies to

$$\nabla^2 \phi_{i,j,k} \approx \frac{\phi_{i+1,j,k} + \phi_{i,j+1,k} + \phi_{i,j,k+1} - 6\phi_{i,j,k} + \phi_{i-1,j,k} + \phi_{i,j-1,k} + \phi_{i,j,k-1}}{\Delta x^2}.$$

The position of the Laplacian will be at the location $\mathbf{x}_{i,j,k}$. Similarly, for a 2D problem on a square grid, the Laplacian is given by

$$\nabla^2 \phi_{i,j} \approx \frac{\phi_{i+1,j} + \phi_{i,j+1} - 4\phi_{i,j} + \phi_{i-1,j} + \phi_{i,j-1}}{\Delta x^2}.$$

The Laplacian of a vector field $\mathbf{u}$ is given by

$$\nabla^2 \mathbf{u} = \begin{bmatrix} \frac{\partial^2 u}{\partial x^2} + \frac{\partial^2 u}{\partial y^2} + \frac{\partial^2 u}{\partial z^2} \\ \frac{\partial^2 v}{\partial x^2} + \frac{\partial^2 v}{\partial y^2} + \frac{\partial^2 v}{\partial z^2} \\ \frac{\partial^2 w}{\partial x^2} + \frac{\partial^2 w}{\partial y^2} + \frac{\partial^2 w}{\partial z^2} \end{bmatrix},$$

where each of the vector's components can be considered to be a separate scalar field. Thus, the estimation of the Laplacian of $\mathbf{u}$ in cell (i, j, k) on a cubic lattice will be

$$\nabla^2 \mathbf{u}_{i,j,k}$$

$$\approx \frac{1}{\Delta x^2} \begin{bmatrix} u_{i+1,j,k} + u_{i,j+1,k} + u_{i,j,k+1} - 6u_{i,j,k} + u_{i-1,j,k} + u_{i,j-1,k} + u_{i,j,k-1} \\ v_{i+1,j,k} + v_{i,j+1,k} + v_{i,j,k+1} - 6v_{i,j,k} + v_{i-1,j,k} + v_{i,j-1,k} + v_{i,j,k-1} \\ w_{i+1,j,k} + w_{i,j+1,k} + w_{i,j,k+1} - 6w_{i,j,k} + w_{i-1,j,k} + w_{i,j-1,k} + w_{i,j,k-1} \end{bmatrix}.$$

15.1.3   Sampling and Interpolation

The first step in representing fluid flow is to decide on how the continuous fluid fields are to be sampled, and reconstructed via interpolation, given a uniform grid representation. How sampling is done directly affects the differencing scheme that must be used, as we must always be aware of where the quantities we are computing are located in space. Recall that the scalar pressure field is indicated by p, and the 3D vector velocity field by $\mathbf{u} = \begin{bmatrix} u & v & w \end{bmatrix}^T$. The density field is not typically sampled, as in all of the methods we discuss, we assume that the fluid is incompressible, assuring that density will be held constant across the simulation.

Central sampling: One approach to sampling the pressure and velocity fields on a regular grid is to place all of the samples in the center of each grid cell, as shown in 2D, in the figure to the right. The extension to 3D is straightforward. Grid cells are shown in solid lines. Each 3D cell is of width Δx, height Δy, and depth Δz. The convention we will use is that column indices are labeled i, row indices j, and depth indices k, corresponding to the x, y, and z coordinate directions. The pressure and velocity sampled at the center of cell

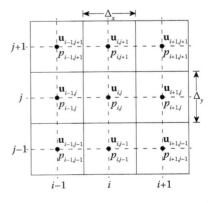

(i, j) have 2D sample values $\mathbf{u}_{i,j}$, and $p_{i,j}$. In 3D, they would be labeled $\mathbf{u}_{i,j,k}$, and $p_{i,j,k}$. Any other fields required by a particular simulation would also be sampled

at the cell centers. The spatial location for the set of samples at the center of cell (i,j,k) is

$$\mathbf{x}_{i,j,k} = \begin{bmatrix} x_0 + (i+0.5)\Delta x \\ y_0 + (j+0.5)\Delta y \\ z_0 + (k+0.5)\Delta z \end{bmatrix}, \tag{15.1}$$

assuming that the position (x_0, y_0, z_0) is the position of the back-left-bottom corner of the grid. Given an arbitrary spatial position $\mathbf{x}$, the indices of the cell that this point lies in are given by

$$(i,j,k) = \left(\left\lfloor \frac{x - x_0}{\Delta x} \right\rfloor, \left\lfloor \frac{y - y_0}{\Delta y} \right\rfloor, \left\lfloor \frac{z - z_0}{\Delta z} \right\rfloor \right).$$

From centrally placed samples, trilinear interpolation, as described in Section 8.6, can be used to estimate continuous field values at any location within the spatial bounds of the simulation. For trilinear interpolation, a dual grid is used, located with its corners at the centers of the regular grid cells, as shown with dashed lines in the diagram. The indices of the cell whose center is at the lower left corner of the dual cell that $\mathbf{x}$ lies in are

$$(i,j,k) = \left(\left\lfloor \frac{x - x_0}{\Delta x} - \frac{1}{2} \right\rfloor, \left\lfloor \frac{y - y_0}{\Delta y} - \frac{1}{2} \right\rfloor, \left\lfloor \frac{z - z_0}{\Delta z} - \frac{1}{2} \right\rfloor \right).$$

From these dual indices, the eight cells forming the corners of the dual cell, to be used for trilinear interpolation of values at $\mathbf{x}$, are (i,j,k), $(i+1,j,k)$, $(i,j+1,k)$, $(i+1,j+1,k)$, $(i,j,k+1)$, $(i+1,j,k+1)$, $(i,j+1,k+1)$, and $(i+1,j+1,k+1)$.

Since, in this sampling scheme, the velocity and pressure samples are located in the center of each grid cell, the spatial derivatives to compute the gradient of pressure and the divergence must be done using upwind differencing, so that they also lie in the center of the cell, or using central differencing across a larger region.

Staggered grid sampling: An alternative grid cell organization, known as a *staggered grid*, is shown in 2D in this figure. Pressure is still sampled at the center of the cell, but the components of the velocity are sampled at the centers of grid faces. In 2D, the u component of velocity is sampled at the center of the left cell edge, and the v component at the center of the bottom edge. In 3D, the u component is sampled at the center of the cell's left face, v at the center of the bottom face, and w at the center of the back face. For each of these, the positive direction is into the cell.

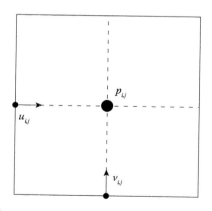

The staggered grid organization has the distinct advantage that central differencing can be used for all calculations, leaving computed differences where they are needed for the simulation. The pressure gradient, computed using central differences, will have its three components located on the centers of the cell faces where the velocity components are stored. The divergence of velocity, computed using central differences, will lie at the center of the cell. The only disadvantage to this organization is that the velocity components are located in different places, requiring a somewhat more complex interpolation scheme to compute the velocity at a particular position.

This figure shows how staggered grid cells tile over space, and will help to show how interpolation should be done with this organization. Interpolation of pressure will be exactly as for central sampling, but the interpolation scheme for velocity is different. Examining the figure, consider the positions within cell (i, j) indicated by the crosses labeled $\mathbf{x}_a$, $\mathbf{x}_b$, $\mathbf{x}_c$, and $\mathbf{x}_d$. Each lies in a different quadrant of cell (i, j). In the figure, look to find the four u velocity components that form the corners of a cell that $\mathbf{x}_a$ lies in. These are $u_{i,j}$, $u_{i+1,j}$, $u_{i,j+1}$, and

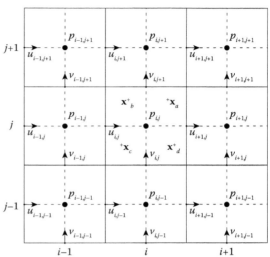

$u_{i+1,j+1}$. Now, note that $\mathbf{x}_b$ lies in the same cell. Similarly, it is easy to see that $\mathbf{x}_c$ and $\mathbf{x}_d$ lie in the cell whose corners are $u_{i,j-1}$, $u_{i+1,j-1}$, $u_{i,j}$, and $u_{i+1,j}$. On the other hand, the v component for $\mathbf{x}_a$ and $\mathbf{x}_d$ lie in the same cell whose corners are $v_{i,j}$, $v_{i+1,j}$, $v_{i,j+1}$, and $v_{i+1,j+1}$, while those for $\mathbf{x}_b$ and $\mathbf{x}_c$ lie in the cell $v_{i-1,j}$, $v_{i,j}$, $v_{i-1,j+1}$, and $v_{i,j+1}$. The figure below shows this in visual form.

Extrapolating this result to 3D, and generalizing algebraically, we have the following indexing scheme for finding the indices of the cell whose velocity component is at the lower-left-back corner of the cell formed from the eight velocity components that should be used for trilinear interpolation. When interpolating the u

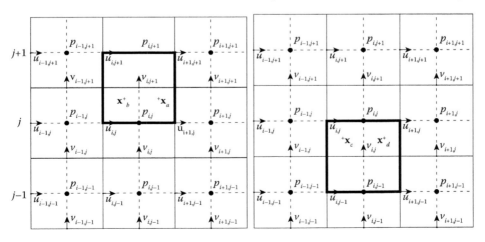

component,

$$(i, j, k) = \left(\left\lfloor \frac{x - x_0}{\Delta x} \right\rfloor, \left\lfloor \frac{y - y_0}{\Delta y} - \frac{1}{2} \right\rfloor, \left\lfloor \frac{z - z_0}{\Delta z} - \frac{1}{2} \right\rfloor \right).$$

When interpolating the v component,

$$(i, j, k) = \left(\left\lfloor \frac{x - x_0}{\Delta x} - \frac{1}{2} \right\rfloor, \left\lfloor \frac{y - y_0}{\Delta y} \right\rfloor, \left\lfloor \frac{z - z_0}{\Delta z} - \frac{1}{2} \right\rfloor \right).$$

And, when interpolating the w component,

$$(i, j, k) = \left(\left\lfloor \frac{x - x_0}{\Delta x} - \frac{1}{2} \right\rfloor, \left\lfloor \frac{y - y_0}{\Delta y} - \frac{1}{2} \right\rfloor, \left\lfloor \frac{z - z_0}{\Delta z} \right\rfloor \right).$$

15.1.4 CFL Condition

Just as there are accuracy and stability criteria based on time constants and oscillation periods for choosing a timestep for Lagrangian numerical simulation (see Section 7.5), Eulerian numerical simulation imposes its own limitations on timestep size. In their 1928 paper, reprinted in English in 1967, Courant, Friedrichs, and Lewy [Courant et al., 1967] lay out a criterion that has come to be known as the *CFL Condition*. Briefly, they outline a balance between spatial grid size, timestep size, and velocity. Roughly stated, the CFL Condition that is normally employed in fluid simulation for graphics is that the timestep needs to be small enough that a massless particle, moved by the fluid, cannot traverse more than one cell during one timestep. If the grid cells are cubic, this can be summarized in the relationship

$$h < \frac{\Delta x}{\|\mathbf{u}_{\max}\|},$$

meaning that the timestep h must be kept smaller than the ratio of grid size Δx and the maximum velocity $\mathbf{u}_{\max}$ in the fluid. If a larger timestep is desired, a corresponding coarsening of the grid size must be made, or a way of limiting the velocity of the fluid must be introduced. Thus, increasing spatial detail in the flow representation requires a proportional decrease in the size of the timestep.

15.2 THE SEMI-LAGRANGIAN METHOD

The *semi-Lagrangian* method for fluid simulation is fundamentally an Eulerian method, but with a Lagrangian approach to computing advection in the fluid. Eulerian fluid simulation was first introduced to the graphics community by Foster and Metaxas [1996], in their paper *Realistic Animation of Fluids*. The semi-Lagrangian algorithm followed the main ideas of this paper but resolved several of its numerical problems. The technique was introduced to the graphics community in the seminal paper by Stam [1999], entitled *Stable Fluids*. Later, in another key paper, entitled *Visual Simulation of Smoke*, Stam, along with Fedkiw and Jensen [Fedkiw et al., 2001] extended the method to enhance vortex activity, using an approach known as *vorticity confinement*. This adds interesting visual complexity to the flow, that tends to be damped out by the original method. Figure 15.1 shows two examples of a smoke simulation done using a modified version of the algorithm proposed by Stam. The simulation on the left uses a low-resolution spatial grid. The simulation on the right uses a higher-resolution grid and captures much more fine detail.

The Navier-Stokes equations for incompressible flow are repeated here for convenience. They are the momentum Equation 13.4,

$$\dot{\mathbf{u}} = -(\mathbf{u} \cdot \nabla)\mathbf{u} - \frac{1}{\rho}\nabla p + \nu\nabla^2\mathbf{u} + \mathbf{g},$$

(a) (b)

FIGURE 15.1 Semi-Lagrangian smoke simulations done at two different spatial resolutions. (a) Low resolution, (b) high resolution. (Courtesy of Ruoguan Huang.)

and the incompressibility constraint Equation 13.5,

$$\nabla \cdot \mathbf{u} = 0.$$

We might consider organizing an Eulerian fluid simulation as follows. Assume that the values of the velocity field $\mathbf{u}$ and pressure field p, sampled onto a uniform computational grid, are known at timestep n. We could imagine advancing a grid node to the next timestep $n + 1$ by computing and summing all of the terms on the right-hand side of Equation 13.4 at the node, giving the node's rate of change of velocity. After doing this for all nodes, we could then integrate the acceleration at each node to produce updated velocities.

This naive approach has two fundamental problems. First, it does not update the pressure field, which will be needed to compute accelerations at the next timestep. Second, there is nothing inherent in this calculation enforcing the divergence free criterion of Equation 13.5. These problems are highly interrelated, since pressure and fluid compressibility are tightly coupled. If we attempt to force more fluid into a cell that is already full, we will increase its pressure, and if we have a cell that has a higher pressure than its surrounding cells the pressure difference will tend to push fluid out to the surrounding cells.

The naive approach to solving the Navier-Stokes equations also has numerical problems. The convection term $(\mathbf{u} \cdot \nabla)\mathbf{u}$ has a tendency to cause instability in a numerical solver, because it involves the square of velocity. Any region of the flow with high velocity will tend to behave like a stiff spring in a springy mesh simulation, requiring a very small timestep to maintain stability. For highly viscous fluids, the diffusion term $\nu\nabla^2\mathbf{u}$ will also act like a stiff spring, again leading to instability.

The following algorithm outlines how the semi-Lagrangian method advances the current velocity field. Inputs to the algorithm are the current velocity vector field $\mathbf{u}$, the pressure field p, and the external acceleration vector field $\mathbf{g}$. These fields are sampled on a regular spatial grid, using either a central or staggered grid organization. Additional inputs are the constant fluid density ρ, and the timestep h. The algorithm's outputs are the updated velocity and pressure fields for the next timestep. The semi-Lagrangian method breaks the acceleration and integration processes into separate steps for each of the acceleration sources in Equation 13.4, using distinctly different approaches for handling each of them.

We present the algorithm first, followed by a brief description of the steps. Pseudo code for the algorithm is shown in Figure 15.2. The subsequent sections explain the steps in more detail.

First, the input velocity is accelerated by the external acceleration field, using forward integration, resulting in intermediate velocity field $\mathbf{w}_1$. The convection term is not computed and integrated, due to its inherent instability. Instead it is handled by explicitly computing the velocity advection that would take place due to this term. This is done using a Lagrangian approach, hence the name "semi-Lagrangian." Each sampled velocity in $\mathbf{w}_1$ is treated as if it were a particle. A backtracking algorithm traces back into the flow one timestep, to see what

```
(VectorField, ScalarField) semiLagrangian(VectorField u, VectorField g,
                                          float ρ, float h)
begin
    VectorField w₁, w₂, w₃, w₄;
    ScalarField φ, p;

    // Apply external accelerations and integrate using forward integration.
    w₁ = integrate(u, g, h);

    // Advect the velocity field using backtracing.
    w₂ = backtrace(w₁, h);

    // Apply acceleration due to viscosity, using implicit integration.
    w₃ = integrate(w₂, ν∇²w₃, h);

    // Project velocity to a divergence free field, and update pressure field.
    (w₄, p) = project(w₃, ρ, h);

    // Return updated velocity field, and corresponding pressure field.
    return (w₄, p);
end
```

FIGURE 15.2   Overview of the Semi-Lagrangian algorithm.

velocity this particle would have had one timestep ago, and then copies this velocity to the sampled velocity's position, in the field $\mathbf{w}_2$. The diffusion term can be quite stiff for high-viscosity fluids, so this acceleration is handled via implicit integration, using the Laplacian of the new field $\mathbf{w}_3$ to determine $\mathbf{w}_3$. Since all of the operations are linear, this is achieved by solving a linear system. Finally, the velocity field $\mathbf{w}_3$ is projected onto the nearest divergence free velocity field $\mathbf{w}_4$, and simultaneously the pressure field p is calculated. This can be done by solving a Poisson equation, or alternatively by a relaxation process.

15.2.1 $\mathbf{w}_1$−Adding External Accelerations

External accelerations on a real fluid would include gravity, and those due to any other forces directly applied to the fluid. Once computed, their application is self-explanatory, as simple Euler integration can be used:

$$\mathbf{w}_1 = \mathbf{u} + h\mathbf{g}.$$

15.2.2 $\mathbf{w}_2$−Lagrangian Advection via Backtracing

Instead of directly computing the acceleration due to the convection term in Equation 13.4, the effect of the convection term is approximated using a Lagrangian approach. Since the convection term accounts for fluid transport, it results in the advection of all properties of the fluid, including the fluid's velocity. To estimate this effect, each velocity sample in the computational grid is treated as if it were a particle. By following the velocity field backward one timestep, it is possible to estimate where in space this particle came from. Then, the velocity at its former position is copied to the sample's position:

$$\mathbf{w}_2 = \texttt{backtrace}(\mathbf{w}_1, h).$$

One version of the `backtrace` algorithm is shown below. It traces back through the velocity field in N substeps, to complete one full timestep h. It takes as input a velocity field sampled on a spatial grid, and the timestep. It returns as output the new velocity field resulting from advecting the velocities in the original field. The function $\mathbf{V}$ in the algorithm takes a gridded velocity field and a position in space, and returns the interpolated velocity at that position. The algorithm, as written, uses only first-order Euler integration to do the backtracing. It could be easily modified to use a higher-order integrator, like RK4, for improved advection accuracy. Also, as written, the algorithm assumes that a central sampling grid layout is being used, so that there is only one velocity sample per cell, located at the center of the cell. If a staggered grid distributed sampling layout is being used, the algorithm would have to be modified to loop through all three velocity samples in each cell, and to take the starting points for the traceback to be the centers of the left, bottom, and back cell faces. Since each of these locations holds only one component of the velocity, only this component should be copied when computing the advection.

```
VectorField backtrace(VectorField u, float h)
begin
    VectorField w;

    float s = h/N;
    for each cell u_{i,j,k} in u do
        x = location of velocity sample in cell u_{i,j,k};
        for i = 0 to N-1 do
            x = x − sV(u, x);
        end
        velocity sample in w_{i,j,k} = V(u, x);
    end

    return (w);
end
```

15.2.3 $\mathbf{w}_3$−Implicit Integration for Velocity Diffusion

Like the external acceleration calculation, the acceleration due to the diffusion term could be calculated and directly integrated using Euler integration:

$$\mathbf{w}_3 = \mathbf{w}_2 + h\nu\nabla^2\mathbf{w}_2.$$

This will be satisfactory for fluids with low viscosity, but for high-viscosity fluids it can easily lead to numerical instability due to excessive stiffness. To avoid instability, the integration can be set up in implicit form:

$$\mathbf{w}_3 = \mathbf{w}_2 + h\nu\nabla^2\mathbf{w}_3.$$

Since all of the operations in this equation are linear, this can be put into the form

$$(I - h\nu\nabla^2)\mathbf{w}_3 = \mathbf{w}_2. \tag{15.2}$$

The term in parentheses is a linear operator that can be represented as a matrix in the finite difference representation. Finally, $\mathbf{w}_3$ can be determined by solving the linear system. Because the matrix is sparse with a nice structure, it can be stored and solved efficiently. Note that since $\mathbf{w}_2$ and $\mathbf{w}_3$ are vector valued fields, this single equation really represents three scalar equations, and needs to be solved for the u, v, and w components of the velocity field.

15.2.4 $\mathbf{w}_4$—Achieving a Divergence Free Velocity Field

There is no reason to expect that the intermediate velocity field $\mathbf{w}_3$ will be divergence free. The solution to this problem is to compute a pressure field that will act on the velocity field to make it divergence free. In a real fluid, pressure will instantaneously change to prevent any change in local divergence. We can emulate this process numerically by computing a pressure field that will provide exactly the pressure gradient needed to adjust the velocity field so that it is divergence free.

Relaxation: One way of making the velocity field divergence free, and simultaneously finding the corresponding pressure field is by a relaxation approach. Here, we iteratively refine the pressure and velocity fields to achieve a divergence free velocity field. Begin with the candidate velocity field, $\mathbf{w}_3$ in this case. Then, compute the divergence of the candidate field in each cell, adjust the pressure in each cell to reduce the magnitude of its divergence, and finally adjust the candidate velocity field based on the pressure updates. Any cell that has a positive divergence, meaning that more fluid is flowing out than flowing in, will have its pressure dropped, and any cell that has a negative divergence will have its pressure raised. This process can then be iterated until the candidate velocity field has an acceptably small divergence in every cell. Since pressure updates can be done independently in every cell, this approach distributes very well over parallel processors, and therefore is easily implemented in a graphics processor.

The constants needed to perform this algorithm are derived from the Navier-Stokes equations, looking only at the pressure and velocity terms. The fluid acceleration due to the pressure gradient is

$$\dot{\mathbf{u}} = -\frac{1}{\rho}\nabla p.$$

This can be discretized into finite differences, yielding the change in the three velocity components, in one timestep h, due to a change in pressure:

$$\begin{bmatrix} \Delta u \\ \Delta v \\ \Delta w \end{bmatrix} = -\frac{h}{\rho} \begin{bmatrix} \frac{\Delta p}{\Delta x} \\ \frac{\Delta p}{\Delta y} \\ \frac{\Delta p}{\Delta z} \end{bmatrix}. \tag{15.3}$$

The divergence of the velocity field is

$$\nabla \cdot \mathbf{u} = \frac{du}{dx} + \frac{dv}{dy} + \frac{dw}{dz},$$

which can be discretized as

$$\delta = \frac{\Delta u}{\Delta x} + \frac{\Delta v}{\Delta y} + \frac{\Delta w}{\Delta z}.$$

To determine the pressure change needed to reduce the divergence to 0, we must determine how much a pressure change in one timestep will affect the divergence. This can be found by substituting the velocity-pressure relationship from Equation 15.3 into this equation, yielding

$$\delta = -\frac{h \Delta p}{\rho} \left(\frac{1}{\Delta x^2} + \frac{1}{\Delta y^2} + \frac{1}{\Delta z^2} \right).$$

In this form, we can solve for the required pressure change,

$$\Delta p = -\beta \delta, \quad \text{where} \quad \beta = \frac{\rho}{h \left(\frac{1}{\Delta x^2} + \frac{1}{\Delta y^2} + \frac{1}{\Delta z^2} \right)}.$$

To maintain numerical stability of the relaxation algorithm, a fraction $0 < f < 1$ of the required pressure change is applied at each iteration of the algorithm, so that the pressure update for each cell (i, j, k) is

$$\Delta p_{i,j,k} = -f \beta \delta_{i,j,k}.$$

Finally, if we assume a staggered grid layout, the corresponding velocity update from Equation 15.3, distributed equally across each cell, is

$$\Delta u_{i,j,k} = -\frac{h}{2\rho} \Delta p_{i,j,k} / \Delta x, \quad \Delta u_{i+1,j,k} = \frac{h}{2\rho} \Delta p_{i+1,j,k} / \Delta x,$$

$$\Delta v_{i,j,k} = -\frac{h}{2\rho} \Delta p_{i,j,k} / \Delta y, \quad \Delta v_{i,j+1,k} = \frac{h}{2\rho} \Delta p_{i+1,j,k} / \Delta y,$$

$$\Delta w_{i,j,k} = -\frac{h}{2\rho} \Delta p_{i,j,k} / \Delta z, \quad \Delta w_{i,j,k+1} = \frac{h}{2\rho} \Delta p_{i+1,j,k} / \Delta z.$$

Pressure projection: Another way of determining the pressure field, and a corresponding divergence free velocity field, uses a fundamental theorem from vector calculus, known as the *Helmholtz-Hodge Decomposition* [Bhatia et al., 2012]. Briefly, the theorem states that any sufficiently smooth vector field $\mathbf{w}$ can always be decomposed into the sum of two vector fields $\mathbf{u}$ and $\mathbf{v}$, such that $\mathbf{u}$ is divergence free, and $\mathbf{v}$ is curl free. In algebraic form,

$$\mathbf{w} = \mathbf{u} + \mathbf{v}, \tag{15.4}$$

where

$$\nabla \cdot \mathbf{u} = 0 \ \text{ and } \ \nabla \times \mathbf{v} = \mathbf{0}.$$

Recall that for any curl free vector field $\mathbf{v}$, there exists a scalar field ϕ such that

$$\mathbf{v} = \nabla \phi.$$

Applying this fact to Equation 15.4 allows us to rewrite the Helmholtz-Hodge Decomposition as

$$\mathbf{w} = \mathbf{u} + \nabla \phi. \tag{15.5}$$

Since $\nabla \cdot \mathbf{u} = 0$, taking the divergence of both sides of this equation gives us

$$\nabla^2 \phi = \nabla \cdot \mathbf{w}, \tag{15.6}$$

which is in the form of a famous equation, known as the *Poisson Equation*, and for which there are well-established techniques for solving for the unknown scalar field ϕ.

We can use this result to project any smooth vector field $\mathbf{w}$ onto a nearby divergence free field $\mathbf{u}$. First, we solve Equation 15.6 for ϕ. Then, it follows from Equation 15.5 that subtracting the gradient of ϕ from $\mathbf{w}$ yields its divergence free component,

$$\mathbf{u} = \mathbf{w} - \nabla \phi. \tag{15.7}$$

Because, from Equation 13.4, the rate of change of fluid velocity with respect the gradient of pressure is

$$\dot{\mathbf{u}} = -\frac{1}{\rho} \nabla p,$$

the discrete change of velocity in one timestep h, due to the pressure gradient, is

$$\frac{\Delta \mathbf{u}}{\Delta t} = -\frac{1}{\rho} \nabla p, \ \text{ or } \ \Delta \mathbf{u} = -\nabla \left(\frac{h}{\rho} \right) p,$$

after substituting $h = \Delta t$. From this, we see that the relationship of pressure to the scalar field ϕ, within a scalar constant, is

$$\phi = \left(\frac{h}{\rho} \right) p.$$

Therefore, the update steps from velocity field $\mathbf{w}_3$ to divergence free field $\mathbf{w}_4$ and pressure field p (again within a scalar constant) are

$$\nabla^2 \phi = \nabla \cdot \mathbf{w}_3, \quad \text{solved for } \phi,$$
$$\mathbf{w}_4 = \mathbf{w}_3 - \nabla \phi,$$
$$p = \frac{\rho}{h} \phi.$$

15.2.5 Organization of a Smoke Simulation Calculation

In order to understand how the equations above can be put into a useful computational form, let us first look at the simplest possible example. Consider the 2D problem represented by the 3×3 grid of cells pictured to the right, and imagine that we are doing a smoke simulation. The way this would work is that the space of the computation would be filled with massless particles, representing smoke particles. The fluid containing the smoke will be free to move in an unrestricted

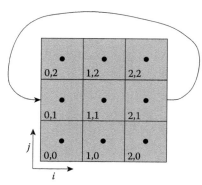

way around the grid. The smoke particles would be advected with the fluid at each timestep, with each particle being assigned the velocity at the particle's position, which would be integrated over the timestep to find the particle's new position. To make the problem unbounded, we will apply what are known as *periodic boundary conditions*, where we consider fluid leaving the right side of the grid to be entering back on the left, and fluid leaving the top of the grid entering back on the bottom. The same applies to pressure—e.g., pressure in the right-most grid cell will be felt on the left of the left-most grid cell on the same row. If you like topology, it is as if the fluid were on the surface of a torus. If you want a concrete example, think of the classic *Pac-Man* games—the ghosts do just what we are imagining the fluid to do.

In order to arrange the ϕ and divergence values in vectors, as required by Equation 15.6, and the velocity components, as required by Equation 15.2, it is helpful to use an alternative to the (i, j) coordinate pairs that identify each cell. This figure shows how this might be done. The (i, j) pairs in the lower left-hand corner of each cell indicate the column and row indices of the 2D array used to hold the data for each cell. The single number in the upper right-

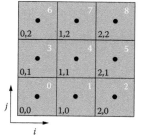

hand corner of each cell indicates the corresponding index into the vectors. In the simulation code, a mapping would have to be maintained between the vector indices, and the indices of the corresponding value in the spatial grid. Given this indexing scheme, Equation 15.6 would be rewritten

$$
\nabla^2
\begin{bmatrix}
\phi_0 \\
\phi_1 \\
\vdots \\
\phi_7 \\
\phi_8
\end{bmatrix}
=
\begin{bmatrix}
\nabla \cdot \mathbf{w}_{3|0} \\
\nabla \cdot \mathbf{w}_{3|1} \\
\vdots \\
\nabla \cdot \mathbf{w}_{3|7} \\
\nabla \cdot \mathbf{w}_{3|8}
\end{bmatrix}.
\tag{15.8}
$$

For this and all subsequent examples in this chapter, we assume that a staggered grid organization is being used, so that central differencing can be applied. This greatly simplifies computation, since if a central grid organization is used, tests will have to be done for every computation to determine the upwind differencing direction. Also, we assume in these examples that our cells are square (in 2D) or cubical (in 3D), so that $\Delta x = \Delta y = \Delta z$. This also simplifies our computations, since we can just use Δx in all computations.

Computing divergence values: The divergence values in each of the eight cells will be the sum of the per-unit-distance differences of the flow out on the right and in on the left, and out on the top and in on the bottom. For example, the divergence in the central cell 4 would be

$$
\nabla \cdot \mathbf{w}_{3|4} = \frac{u_5 - u_4}{\Delta x} + \frac{v_7 - v_4}{\Delta x}.
$$

Since we are using periodic boundary conditions, horizontal flow out of cell 5 on the right will match the horizontal flow into cell 3 on the left, so

$$
\nabla \cdot \mathbf{w}_{3|5} = \frac{u_3 - u_5}{\Delta x} + \frac{v_8 - v_5}{\Delta x}.
$$

Cell 8 has wrap-around flow in two directions, so

$$
\nabla \cdot \mathbf{w}_{3|8} = \frac{u_6 - u_8}{\Delta x} + \frac{v_2 - v_8}{\Delta x}.
$$

The remaining cells follow similar patterns.

Computing ϕ values to determine pressure: The linear operator ∇^2 in Equation 15.6 can be represented as a matrix, with each matrix row corresponding to the Laplacian operator applied at the center of a particular cell. Therefore, if there are N fluid cells, the matrix will be $N \times N$. In the central cell 4, central differencing would yield a Laplacian value

$$\nabla^2 \phi_4 = \frac{1}{\Delta x^2}(\phi_1 + \phi_3 - 4\phi_4 + \phi_5 + \phi_7).$$

Due to wrap-around, cell 5, adjacent to the right boundary, would yield

$$\nabla^2 \phi_5 = \frac{1}{\Delta x^2}(\phi_2 + \phi_4 - 4\phi_5 + \phi_3 + \phi_8),$$

and cell 8 would yield

$$\nabla^2 \phi_8 = \frac{1}{\Delta x^2}(\phi_5 + \phi_7 - 4\phi_8 + \phi_6 + \phi_2).$$

A similar analysis can be done for the remaining cells.

Matrix representation of Poisson equation: After numerically representing the divergence and Laplacian operations for each cell, the ∇^2 matrix in Equation 15.9 can be expanded to the form

$$
\begin{bmatrix}
-4 & 1 & 1 & 1 & 0 & 0 & 1 & 0 & 0 \\
1 & -4 & 1 & 0 & 1 & 0 & 0 & 1 & 0 \\
1 & 1 & -4 & 0 & 0 & 1 & 0 & 0 & 1 \\
1 & 0 & 0 & -4 & 1 & 1 & 1 & 0 & 0 \\
0 & 1 & 0 & 1 & -4 & 1 & 0 & 1 & 0 \\
0 & 0 & 1 & 1 & 1 & -4 & 0 & 0 & 1 \\
1 & 0 & 0 & 1 & 0 & 0 & -4 & 1 & 1 \\
0 & 1 & 0 & 0 & 1 & 0 & 1 & -4 & 1 \\
0 & 0 & 1 & 0 & 0 & 1 & 1 & 1 & -4
\end{bmatrix}
\begin{bmatrix}
\phi_0 \\ \phi_1 \\ \phi_2 \\ \phi_3 \\ \phi_4 \\ \phi_5 \\ \phi_6 \\ \phi_7 \\ \phi_8
\end{bmatrix}
= \Delta x
\begin{bmatrix}
u_1 - u_0 + v_3 - v_0 \\
u_2 - u_1 + v_4 - v_1 \\
u_0 - u_2 + v_5 - v_2 \\
u_4 - u_3 + v_6 - v_3 \\
u_5 - u_4 + v_7 - v_4 \\
u_3 - u_5 + v_8 - v_5 \\
u_7 - u_6 + v_0 - v_6 \\
u_8 - u_7 + v_1 - v_7 \\
u_6 - u_8 + u_2 - u_8
\end{bmatrix}.
$$

Unfortunately, this equation has no unique solution, because only the pressure gradient, and not absolute pressure, affects fluid acceleration in the Navier-Stokes equations. This problem is easily solved by fixing the ϕ value in one of the cells, and letting all of the other cells be defined relative to this. If we determine some ambient pressure p_a, and assign this to cell 8, then $\phi_8 = \frac{h}{\rho}p_a$. We can replace the bottom row of the matrix by this equation, resulting in the final computational form:

$$
\begin{bmatrix}
-4 & 1 & 1 & 1 & 0 & 0 & 1 & 0 & 0 \\
1 & -4 & 1 & 0 & 1 & 0 & 0 & 1 & 0 \\
1 & 1 & -4 & 0 & 0 & 1 & 0 & 0 & 1 \\
1 & 0 & 0 & -4 & 1 & 1 & 1 & 0 & 0 \\
0 & 1 & 0 & 1 & -4 & 1 & 0 & 1 & 0 \\
0 & 0 & 1 & 1 & 1 & -4 & 0 & 0 & 1 \\
1 & 0 & 0 & 1 & 0 & 0 & -4 & 1 & 1 \\
0 & 1 & 0 & 0 & 1 & 0 & 1 & -4 & 1 \\
0 & 0 & 0 & 0 & 0 & 0 & 0 & 0 & 1
\end{bmatrix}
\begin{bmatrix}
\phi_0 \\ \phi_1 \\ \phi_2 \\ \phi_3 \\ \phi_4 \\ \phi_5 \\ \phi_6 \\ \phi_7 \\ \phi_8
\end{bmatrix}
= \Delta x
\begin{bmatrix}
u_1 - u_0 + v_3 - v_0 \\
u_2 - u_1 + v_4 - v_1 \\
u_0 - u_2 + v_5 - v_2 \\
u_4 - u_3 + v_6 - v_3 \\
u_5 - u_4 + v_7 - v_4 \\
u_3 - u_5 + v_8 - v_5 \\
u_7 - u_6 + v_0 - v_6 \\
u_8 - u_7 + v_1 - v_7 \\
\frac{h}{\Delta x \rho}p_a
\end{bmatrix}.
$$

Matrix representation for implicit integration of diffusion term: Equation 15.2, which is the implicit integration of $\mathbf{w}_2$ to determine $\mathbf{w}_3$, also must be put into matrix form. This equation must actually be solved once for each of the 2D velocity components u and v, or three times for a 3D problem to also determine the w component. Looking only at the u component of the $\mathbf{w}_2$ and $\mathbf{w}_3$ velocity fields, we form the vectors $\mathbf{u}_2$ and $\mathbf{u}_3$, and rewrite Equation 15.2 as

$$(I - h\nu\nabla^2)\mathbf{u}_3 = \mathbf{u}_2.$$

We can use an analysis similar to the one used for computing the Laplacian of ϕ to write the following equation for cell 4:

$$u_{3|4} - \frac{h\nu}{\Delta x^2}(u_{3|1} + u_{3|3} - 4u_{3|4} + u_{3|5} + u_{3|7}) = u_{2|4}.$$

This can be rearranged to simplify the matrix elements by multiplying through by $\frac{\Delta x^2}{h\nu}$ to obtain

$$-u_{3|1} - u_{3|3} + \left(4 + \frac{\Delta x^2}{h\nu}\right)u_{3|4} - u_{3|5} - u_{3|7} = \frac{\Delta x^2}{h\nu}u_{2|4}.$$

Following a system similar to that used to construct the matrix for the Poisson equation, and letting $K = 4 + \frac{\Delta x^2}{h\nu}$, we have the implicit integration for the diffusion step:

$$
\begin{bmatrix}
K & -1 & -1 & -1 & 0 & 0 & -1 & 0 & 0 \\
-1 & K & -1 & 0 & -1 & 0 & 0 & -1 & 0 \\
-1 & -1 & K & 0 & 0 & -1 & 0 & 0 & -1 \\
-1 & 0 & 0 & K & -1 & -1 & -1 & 0 & 0 \\
0 & -1 & 0 & -1 & K & -1 & 0 & -1 & 0 \\
0 & 0 & -1 & -1 & -1 & K & 0 & 0 & -1 \\
-1 & 0 & 0 & -1 & 0 & 0 & K & -1 & -1 \\
0 & -1 & 0 & 0 & -1 & 0 & -1 & K & -1 \\
0 & 0 & -1 & 0 & 0 & -1 & -1 & -1 & K
\end{bmatrix}
\begin{bmatrix}
u_{3|0} \\ u_{3|1} \\ u_{3|2} \\ u_{3|3} \\ u_{3|4} \\ u_{3|5} \\ u_{3|6} \\ u_{3|7} \\ u_{3|8}
\end{bmatrix}
= \frac{\Delta x^2}{h\nu}
\begin{bmatrix}
u_{2|0} \\ u_{2|1} \\ u_{2|2} \\ u_{2|3} \\ u_{2|4} \\ u_{2|5} \\ u_{2|6} \\ u_{2|7} \\ u_{2|8}
\end{bmatrix}.
$$

A similar equation can be written to integrate the v component of velocity.

For this toy 2D problem, these equations are small enough to solve by matrix inversion, but for the much larger sized 3D problems encountered in fluid simulation for animation it is usual to take advantage of the sparsity of the matrices and solve the problem using an iterative solution technique like the *biconjugate gradient* method. These methods are available in most numerical linear algebra systems like *Eigen* [Inria, 2015], and are explained fully in Numerical Recipes [Press et al., 2007].

In order to produce an interesting looking smoke simulation it will be necessary to introduce some external forces to perturb the flow. This is usually done through the external force term in the Navier-Stokes equations, which can be used to provide forces due to user interaction, or from a procedural force generator.

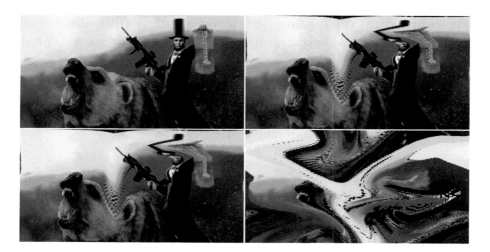

FIGURE 15.3 Fluid advection of texture coordinates. (Courtesy of Rui Icy Wang and Christopher Malloy.)

An interesting way to use a 2D semi-Lagrangian smoke simulation is to have its flow field advect (u, v) texture coordinates. Figure 15.3 is an example of what this might produce. Underlying the image is a 2D grid. Each vertex of the grid is initially assigned a u coordinate that corresponds with its fraction of the distance across the width of the image, and similarly a v coordinate as its fraction of the height of the image. At each step in the fluid simulation these coordinates are advected, using backtracing, just like the velocity field is advected. The updated texture coordinates are then used to render the image on the underlying grid. The figure uses a grid that is coarser than the original image, so results are somewhat blocky. This could be fixed by using a finer grid and a more sophisticated texture sampling approach.

15.2.6 Organization of a Water Simulation Calculation

Moving from a smoke simulation to a water simulation requires us to introduce the concepts of the fluid surface and boundaries. We will examine how this can be done by looking at the simple 2D swimming pool cross-section example shown in the figure. To make this as simple as possible, we use only a 5×5 computational grid. The methods described can be extrapolated to 3D, to larger grids, and to more complex configurations. The dark cells are considered to be *boundary* cells or wall cells. These would be like the walls of a swimming pool, through which no fluid can flow

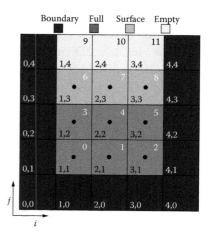

normal to the boundary. Walls also exert friction, resisting the flow of fluid, so we will also have to establish conditions on the boundary cells affecting the rate of flow parallel to the boundary. We will assume that the pressure in each boundary cell will be identical to the pressure in the fluid cell adjacent to it, so boundary cell pressures do not need to be calculated. The three white cells at the top are considered to be *empty* cells, containing no fluid to be simulated. For example, in a water simulation, these cells would contain only air. The three light gray cells just below the empty cells contain fluid, but are considered to be *surface* cells, since they have at least one face adjacent to an empty cell. Empty cells are given a vector index, because it is possible that, when we advance a timestep, fluid can begin flowing into them from an adjacent surface cell. We assume that, since surface cells are adjacent to the external space, their pressures will all be the same as the ambient pressure in the external environment. In a water simulation, this pressure would correspond with the ambient air pressure p_a. Therefore, the pressures of surface cells do not need to be calculated. The remaining six dark gray cells are the *full* cells containing only the fluid we are simulating, and for which we will need to compute a pressure. The assumptions about pressure in the empty, surface, and boundary cells will serve to provide boundary conditions for the pressure computation.

The cell numbering scheme, shown in the diagram, is similar to the one used in the smoke simulation example. Given this indexing scheme, Equation 15.6 would be rewritten

$$\nabla^2 \begin{bmatrix} \phi_0 \\ \phi_1 \\ \vdots \\ \phi_5 \\ \phi_6 \end{bmatrix} = \begin{bmatrix} \nabla \cdot \mathbf{w}_{3|0} \\ \nabla \cdot \mathbf{w}_{3|1} \\ \vdots \\ \nabla \cdot \mathbf{w}_{3|5} \\ \frac{h}{\rho} p_a \end{bmatrix}. \qquad (15.9)$$

Note that all surface cells share the same pressure value, and thus the same ϕ value, so we only include ϕ_6 in the vector of ϕ values. Because of this, the matrix will not be strictly a Laplacian matrix, but will be a 6×6 Laplacian matrix augmented by an extra row and column for the equation $\phi_6 = \frac{h}{\rho} p_a$.

Computing divergence values: The divergence values in each of the six full cells will be computed as in the smoke simulation, but accounting for the fact that there can be no flow into or out of a boundary cell. For example, the divergence in the central cell 4 would be

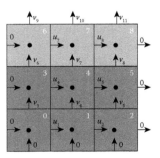

$$\nabla \cdot \mathbf{w}_{3|4} = \frac{u_5 - u_4}{\Delta x} + \frac{v_7 - v_4}{\Delta x},$$

but for cell 3, which is next to the left wall,

$$\nabla \cdot \mathbf{w}_{3|3} = \frac{u_4 - 0}{\Delta x} + \frac{v_6 - v_3}{\Delta x} = \frac{u_4 + v_6 - v_3}{\Delta x}.$$

Computing φ values to determine pressure:
Computing the Laplacian in each cell also parallels
the approach used in the smoke simulation. In the
central cell 4, central differencing would yield a
Laplacian value

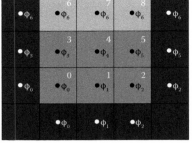

$$\nabla^2 \phi_4 = \frac{1}{\Delta x^2}(\phi_1 + \phi_3 - 4\phi_4 + \phi_5 + \phi_6).$$

Since boundary cells have identical pressure to an
adjacent full cell, cell 3, adjacent to the left boundary, would yield

$$\nabla^2 \phi_3 = \frac{1}{\Delta x^2}(\phi_0 - 3\phi_3 + \phi_4 + \phi_6).$$

Similarly, cell 0, in the bottom left corner would yield

$$\nabla^2 \phi_3 = \frac{1}{\Delta x^2}(-2\phi_0 + \phi_1 + \phi_3).$$

A similar analysis can be done for the remaining cells.

Matrix representation of Poisson equation: After numerically representing the divergence and Laplacian operations for each cell, Equation 15.9 can be expanded to its final computational form:

$$
\begin{bmatrix}
-2 & 1 & 0 & 1 & 0 & 0 & 0 \\
1 & -3 & 1 & 0 & 1 & 0 & 0 \\
0 & 1 & -2 & 0 & 0 & 1 & 0 \\
1 & 0 & 0 & -3 & 1 & 0 & 1 \\
0 & 1 & 0 & 1 & -4 & 1 & 1 \\
0 & 0 & 1 & 0 & 1 & -3 & 1 \\
0 & 0 & 0 & 0 & 0 & 0 & 1
\end{bmatrix}
\begin{bmatrix}
\phi_0 \\ \phi_1 \\ \phi_2 \\ \phi_3 \\ \phi_4 \\ \phi_5 \\ \phi_6
\end{bmatrix}
= \Delta x
\begin{bmatrix}
u_1 + v_3 \\
u_2 - u_1 + v_4 \\
-u_2 + v_5 \\
u_4 + v_6 - v_3 \\
u_5 - u_4 + v_7 - v_4 \\
-u_5 + v_8 - v_5 \\
\frac{h}{\Delta x \rho}p_a
\end{bmatrix}.
$$

Matrix representation for implicit integration of diffusion term: The
implicit integration of $\mathbf{w}_2$ to determine $\mathbf{w}_3$ using Equation 15.2 also follows a
procedure similar to the smoke simulation. We solve for each velocity component
independently. Because there cannot be any flow into a boundary, we know that
$u_{3|0} = u_{3|3} = u_{3|6} = 0$, and $v_{3|0} = v_{3|1} = v_{3|2} = 0$.

Because of friction, the rate of flow parallel to the boundary will be
affected by the presence of the boundary. A typical way of accounting
for this is to set *phantom* flow values parallel to the boundary within
each boundary cell, to be used in interpolating the flow at the boundary.
Consider the cell with index 1. Its horizontal velocity is u_1, and we can
imagine a velocity u_1' in the boundary cell below it. When horizontal

velocity is interpolated exactly at the boundary, it will be $u_{1b} = \frac{u_1 + u_1'}{2}$. If $u_1' = u_1$,
the horizontal velocity at the boundary will exactly match the velocity in cell 1.

This is called the *full slip* condition—corresponding to no friction between the wall and the fluid. On the other hand, if $u'_1 = -u_1$, the boundary's horizontal velocity will be 0. This is called the *no slip* condition—corresponding to very high friction. We can assign a parameter $0 \leq \mu \leq 1$, analogous to the coefficient of friction introduced in Section 3.2.2. If $\mu = 0$ corresponds to the full-slip condition, and $\mu = 1$ corresponds to the no-slip condition, the phantom horizontal or vertical velocity in the boundary cell adjacent to cell i will be given by

$$u'_{ib} = (1 - 2\mu)u_i, \quad \text{or} \quad v'_{ib} = (1 - 2\mu)v_i.$$

Unlike the pressure calculation, we will also need to compute the fluid velocity in each surface cell on any left or bottom boundary shared with a full cell or another surface cell. Therefore, we will need to include equations to compute u_7, and u_8, and also v_6, v_7, and v_8. So, the horizontal velocity vector will be of the form

$$\mathbf{u} = \begin{bmatrix} u_1 & u_2 & u_4 & u_5 & u_7 & u_8 \end{bmatrix}^T,$$

and the vertical velocity vector will be of the form

$$\mathbf{v} = \begin{bmatrix} v_3 & v_4 & v_5 & v_6 & v_7 & v_8 \end{bmatrix}^T,$$

Following the logic used in the smoke simulation, but considering boundaries, the horizontal velocity entering cell 4 from the left is represented in the numerical integration by the equation

$$-u_{3|1} + \left(4 + \frac{\Delta x^2}{h\nu}\right) u_{3|4} - u_{3|5} - u_{3|7} = \frac{\Delta x^2}{h\nu} u_{2|4}.$$

Cell 7 has a similar structure but has 0 horizontal velocities in the adjacent boundary and empty cells. The horizontal velocity entering cell 5 from the left is represented by

$$-u_{3|2} - u_{3|4} + \left(4 + \frac{\Delta x^2}{h\nu}\right) u_{3|5} - u_{3|8} = \frac{\Delta x^2}{h\nu} u_{2|5},$$

and cell 8 has a similar structure, modulo boundary and empty cells. Cells 1 and 2 must account for the slip condition at the boundary, so their horizontal velocities are given by

$$-(1-2\mu)u_{3|1} + (4+\frac{\Delta x^2}{h\upsilon})u_{3|1} - u_{3|2} - u3|4 = \frac{\Delta x^2}{h\upsilon}u_{2|1},$$

and

$$-(1-2\mu)u_{3|2} - u_{3|1} + (4+\frac{\Delta x^2}{h\upsilon})u_{3|2} - u_{3|5} = \frac{\Delta x^2}{h\upsilon}u_{2|2},$$

Letting $K = 4 + \frac{\Delta x^2}{h\upsilon}$, we have the implicit integration for the horizontal velocities in the diffusion step:

$$\begin{bmatrix} K-(1-2\mu) & -1 & -1 & 0 & 0 & 0 \\ -1 & K-(1-2\mu) & 0 & -1 & 0 & 0 \\ -1 & 0 & K & -1 & -1 & 0 \\ 0 & -1 & -1 & K & 0 & -1 \\ 0 & 0 & -1 & 0 & K & -1 \\ 0 & 0 & 0 & -1 & -1 & K \end{bmatrix} \begin{bmatrix} u_{3|1} \\ u_{3|2} \\ u_{3|4} \\ u_{3|5} \\ u_{3|7} \\ u_{3|8} \end{bmatrix} = \frac{\Delta x^2}{h\upsilon} \begin{bmatrix} u_{2|1} \\ u_{2|2} \\ u_{2|4} \\ u_{2|5} \\ u_{2|7} \\ u_{2|8} \end{bmatrix}.$$

A similar equation can be written to integrate the v component of velocity.

Again, these equations are best solved by exploiting the sparsity in the matrices, using an iterative solver.

Keeping track of the water surface: Since, in any interesting liquid simulation, the liquid surface will be moving, the surface, full, and empty cells in the computational grid must be relabeled at every timestep. For example, if a wave moves across the surface, empty cells may become surface cells, surface cells may become full or empty, and full cells may become surface cells. If the simulation is adhering to the CFL condition described in Section 15.1.4, it should not be possible for an empty cell to become full, or a full cell to become empty, in one timestep. The full complexity of this problem can be seen by examining the frames from the water sloshing simulation shown in Figure 15.4.

The simplest way to keep track of the surface is by the Marker and Cell, or MAC, technique [Foster and Metaxas, 1996]. When the simulation is initialized, a number of invisible massless particles should be assigned to each cell that initially contains fluid. Then, at each timestep, these particles can be advected by the fluid velocity field, and reassigned to the cell that they have moved to. At the start of a new timestep, any cell containing no particles is marked as an empty cell. The remaining cells all contain fluid. These are marked as either full or surface cells depending on whether or not they are adjacent to an empty cell. The marker particles can also be used to generate a fluid surface for rendering, in the same way that a surface can be rendered in SPH, as described in Section 14.4.

Although the Marker and Cell method has the advantage of simplicity, it is not a very accurate way of tracking the water surface, and constructing a surface

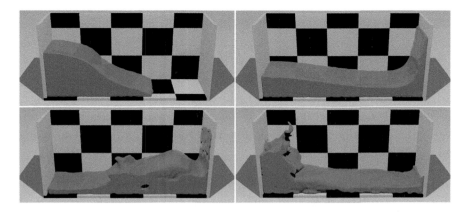

FIGURE 15.4 Water sloshing around in a box. (Courtesy of Ruoguan Huang.)

from a set of particles results in a bumpy, overly noisy look. An improved, hybrid approach is described in the paper *Practical Animation of Liquids* by Foster and Fedkiw [2001]. Besides advecting a set of particles, they maintain a *signed distance field* $s(\mathbf{x})$ that is advected with the fluid. This is a scalar field that returns the shortest distance to the fluid surface at spatial position $\mathbf{x}$. This distance is signed, typically with positive values being outside the fluid and negative values inside the fluid. In an algorithm, the signed distance field is stored in a spatial grid of higher resolution than the grid being used for fluid simulation. At each timestep, at the same time that the marker particles are advected by the fluid, the signed distance field s is updated via the update equation:

$$\frac{\partial s}{\partial t} = -\mathbf{u} \cdot \nabla s.$$

This approach of updating the surface by advecting the distance field is an example of a *level set method*.

A renderer can use a ray-marching approach to efficiently find the surface, where $s = 0$, since at each step in the ray march, the field itself gives the minimum distance to the surface, and thus the distance that the ray can march ahead without danger of missing the surface. When the surface is found, the normal to the surface is simply

$$\hat{\mathbf{n}} = \nabla s / \|\nabla s\|.$$

While this surface could be rendered alone, it has the opposite problem from surfaces obtained using particles. It will suffer from being too smooth in regions of splashing or complex surface motion. To obtain a surface that is smooth where needed but preserves detail where it should, Foster and Fedkiw recommend computing the local curvature of the surface

$$\kappa = \nabla \cdot (\nabla s / \|\nabla s\|),$$

for each view ray during rendering. If the curvature is low, the surface from the signed distance field is used, otherwise the surface is estimated using the particles.

The method described here is a basic one, and there have been various improvements in surface extraction for Eulerian simulations, including that of Bargteil et al. [2006].

Computing surface velocities: The velocities in the surface cells will be computed for any face that is shared with another cell containing liquid (either a full cell or another surface cell). However, velocities for faces of a surface cell that are shared with an empty cell will have no velocity computed. In our swimming pool example, these would be the vertical velocities v_9, v_{10}, and v_{11}. This problem is resolved by setting these velocities to values appropriate to enforce incompressibility in the surface cell, i.e., to make them divergence free. There is more than one way to do this, and we present here the method used by Foster and Metaxas [1996].

In the diagram, gray cells are fluid cells (full or surface), with the central cell (i, j) always being the surface cell for which we need to find missing velocities. Computed velocities are indicated by solid arrows, and missing velocities by dashed arrows. White cells are empty cells. In 2D, only the four distinct cases, shown in the diagram, need to be considered. All other cases are rotations or mirror reflections of these. Case I is when only one face of a surface cell is adjacent to an empty cell. In this case, the cell will be divergence free if

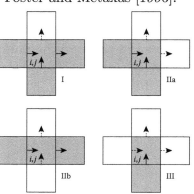

$$v_{i,j+1} = u_{i,j} - u_{i+1,j} + v_{i,j}.$$

In case IIa, we can make the cell divergence free by letting

$$u_{i+1,j} = u_{i,j} \quad \text{and} \quad v_{i,j+1} = v_{i,j},$$

setting the flow out equal to the flow in, in each of the two directions. In case IIb, we can let

$$v_{i,j} = -\frac{u_{i,j} - u_{i+1,j}}{2} \quad \text{and} \quad v_{i+1,j} = \frac{u_{i,j} - u_{i+1,j}}{2},$$

distributing the vertical flow out of both horizontal faces to one half of the residual horizontal flow into the cell. Finally, case III can be handled by setting

$$u_{i,j} = u_{i+i,j} = 0 \quad \text{and} \quad v_{i,j+1} = v_{i,j}.$$

The reader can easily extend this methodology to handle the eight unique 3D cases.

Initializing the simulation: It can be difficult to initialize a fluid simulation with the fluid already moving, so the typical procedure is to provide a quiescent initial state, and then perturb the fluid as the simulation proceeds. In the swimming pool example, a quiescent state is achieved if all of the initial velocities are 0, and the pressures are set to account for gravity. The mass of fluid in a cubic full cell is $\rho \Delta x^3$. If the gravitational acceleration constant is g, a full cell will exert the pressure $p = g\rho\Delta x^3/\Delta x^2 = g\rho\Delta x$ on the cell below it. The surface cells all have the ambient pressure p_a. Therefore, the first cell below the surface will have pressure $p_a + g\rho\Delta x$, and the nth cell below the surface will have pressure $p_a + ng\rho\Delta x$. Note that, when using the Poisson equation approach to compute the pressure at the next timestep, it is not necessary to initialize the pressures, but they should be initialized if the iterative relaxation approach is being used.

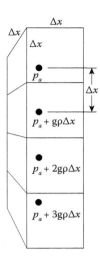

15.3 FLIP

The Fluid-Implicit-Particle or FLIP method for fluid simulation is a Lagrangian method, where a set of particles carries the momentum of the fluid, as well as any other fluid properties required by the simulation. In this way, the necessity for a backtracing advection scheme, such as that used in the semi-Lagrangian method, is eliminated. At each timestep, a regular computational grid is created and the particle velocities are averaged onto the nodes of this grid. This serves as a computational convenience, so that external, diffusion, and pressure force effects can be accounted for within a regular computational structure, creating a velocity field that is used to update particle momenta, and for advecting the particles. This is in contrast to SPH, which does all computations with respect to the nonuniformly distributed set of particles. FLIP was first proposed in the fluid dynamics research community by Brackbill and Ruppel [1986], and was introduced to the graphics community as a fluid animation method in the paper *Animating Sand as a Fluid* by Zhu and Bridson [2005].

One timestep of the FLIP method proceeds according to the algorithm shown in Figure 15.5. It takes as its primary input the current particle system **S**, providing the position and velocity of each of the fluid particles. The particle system can also carry any other values that are to be advected by the fluid. Additional inputs include a possible set of external accelerations **g**, the fluid density ρ, and the timestep h. The output of the algorithm is the updated particle system, with a new position and velocity for each particle.

Following the algorithm, FLIP builds a new staggered computational grid at each timestep, sized and positioned to contain the axis-aligned bounding volume around the particle system. Therefore, unlike Eulerian methods, FLIP simulations are spatially unbounded. Two grids are needed, **G**$_0$ and **G**$_1$, to hold the original and

ParticleSystem FLIP(ParticleSystem **P**, Scene S, VectorField **g**, float ρ, float h)
begin

> ParticleSystem $\mathbf{P}_{\text{new}}$;
>
> // *Construct bounding region with dimensions* **W** *and origin* $\mathbf{x}_0$ *around*
> // *particles and use to construct initial and final computational volumes*
> // $\mathbf{G}_0$ *and* $\mathbf{G}_1$.
> (Vector3d **W**, Vector3d $\mathbf{x}_0$) = BoundingVolume(**P**);
> StaggeredGrid $\mathbf{G}_0(\mathbf{W}, \mathbf{x}_0)$, $\mathbf{G}_1(\mathbf{W}, \mathbf{x}_0)$;
>
> // *Average particle velocities onto the initial computational grid, and*
> // *classify cells as boundary, empty, surface, or full.*
> $\mathbf{G}_0$ = AverageVelocitiesOntoGrid(**P**, **W**, $\mathbf{x}_0$);
> $\mathbf{G}_0$ = ClassifyCells($\mathbf{G}_0$, **P**, S);
>
> // *Advance the velocity field one timestep using the external force,*
> // *diffusion, and pressure projection steps of the semi-Lagrangian*
> // *method, but omitting advection.*
> $\mathbf{G}_1$ = VelocityUpdate($\mathbf{G}_0$, **g**, ρ, h);
>
> // *The difference between the initial and final grid velocities is used*
> // *to update the velocities (i.e., the momenta) carried by the particles.*
> //
> $\mathbf{P}_{\text{new}}$ = **P**;
> $\mathbf{P}_{\text{new}}.v$ += VelocityDifference($\mathbf{G}_1$, $\mathbf{G}_0$);
>
> // *Advect particles through the new velocity field by numerical integration.*
> $\mathbf{P}_{\text{new}}.x$ = integrate($\mathbf{P}_{\text{new}}$, $\mathbf{G}_1$, h);
>
> // *Return updated fluid particle system.*
> **return** $\mathbf{P}_{\text{new}}$;

end

FIGURE 15.5 Overview of the FLIP algorithm.

updated velocity fields. The u, v, and w components of the particle velocities are averaged onto the staggered grid nodes at the centers of the cell faces to initialize the computational grid. The grid cells are then classified into boundary, empty, surface, and full cells based on overlap of the grid cells with scene geometry, and the presence or absence of particles within a cell. Then, all of the same computations that are used in the semi-Lagrangian method, except for the advection step, are used to produce new velocity and pressure fields from the current velocity field. The new particle system $\mathbf{S}_{\text{new}}$ is initialized to the current particle positions and velocities, and then its velocities are incremented by the interpolated differences between the new and old velocity fields stored on the grids. The particles, together with their updated velocities, are then advected by numerical integration using the velocity field in the new grid $\mathbf{G}_1$. This integration can be done using a higher-order

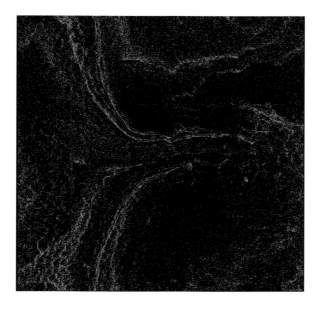

FIGURE 15.6 FLIP flow simulation visualized by drawing the moving particles. (Courtesy of Doug Rizeakos.)

integrator, like RK4, and the full timestep can be done in several substeps to take advantage of the detail in the flow field. Since this is the only integration done on the grid, the CFL condition can be set to match the size of the substeps, so that a relatively coarse grid can be used without fear of instability or numerical artifacts.

Figure 15.6 shows a collection of particles being moved by a FLIP simulation. This simulation was set up with periodic boundary conditions—that is, that flow out of the right-hand side enters on the left-hand side, and vice versa. The top and bottom boundaries work similarly.

Since FLIP is a Lagrangian method, the fluid surface should be constructed directly from the particles. Zhu and Bridson suggest an improved way of forming the fluid surface, and a more recent paper by Yu and Turk [2013] has an even better method.

15.4 SUMMARY

Here are some of the main points to take away from this chapter:

- A standard way of doing Eulerian fluid simulation is using finite difference methods. In this approach, a regular spatial grid is superimposed on the problem domain. This grid is used both to store field quantities, and to compute their derivatives.

- Each grid cell corresponds with a single sample of whatever fields are being tracked. Typically, in a fluid simulation these include at least the fluid velocity and the fluid pressure.

- Spatial derivatives are calculated by taking differences in sample values across cells and dividing by a cell width. These differences are taken in all three spatial directions to approximate partial spatial derivatives in these directions.

- Upwinding schemes choose the direction for taking a finite difference, along a row or column, corresponding to the direction of the flow component along that row or column.

- All of the differential operators, including gradient, divergence, and the Laplacian have discrete approximations depending on the differencing scheme being used.

- Either a central or staggered sampling method can be used in constructing the spatial grid.

- In the central sampling method, all samples are taken at the center of the cell, and differences must be computed using an upwinding scheme.

- In the staggered method, the pressure and any other scalar fields are sampled in the center of the cell, but velocity and any other vector fields are sampled per component, with each component sampled at the appropriate cell face center.

- In staggered sampling, central differences can used in almost all cases, locating the resulting derivatives exactly where they are needed for computation of accelerations.

- A CFL condition is one that relates the spatial resolution of a simulation grid to the maximum velocity expected in the simulation, and the simulation timestep size. For stability and accuracy, cell sizes should be kept such that an imagined fluid particle will not move across more than one cell in one simulation time step.

- The Semi-Lagrangian Method is a technique for efficiently computing the incompressible Navier-Stokes equations within a finite difference simulation. It obtains speed and stability by computing advection of the fluid velocity field using a Lagrangian approach, by solving for the velocity diffusion using an implicit integration scheme, and by enforcing the incompressibility constraint by solving a Poisson equation for the pressure correction term.

- The FLIP Method is fundamentally a Lagrangian approach. The fluid is represented by particles, as in SPH, but the method also uses a spatial grid, constructed at each timestep. The velocity field is sampled from the particles onto the grid, an updated velocity field is calculated, and the difference between the old and new velocity fields is projected back onto each particle to update its velocity. The particles are then moved by integrating their velocity over the timestep.

Vectors

To a mathematician, a vector is the fundamental element of what is known as a vector space, supporting the operations of scaling, by elements known as scalars, and also supporting addition between vectors. When using vectors to describe physical quantities, like velocity, acceleration, and force, we can move away from this abstract definition, and stick with a more concrete notion. We can view them as arrows in space, of a particular length and denoting a particular direction, and we can think of the corresponding scalars as simply the real numbers. Practically speaking, a vector is simply a way of simultaneously storing and handling two pieces of information: a direction in space and a magnitude or length.

An arrow is a convenient way to draw a vector; since both length and direction are clearly indicated. A real number is a convenient way to represent a scalar, which when multiplied by a vector changes its length. To the left are three visual representations of identical vectors. They are identical, since they are 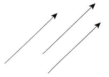 all of the same length and the same direction, i.e., they are parallel to each other. Their location within the space is irrelevant.

In the study of physically based animation, we will initially be interested in vectors in two-dimensional (2D) and in three-dimensional (3D) space, whose elements are real numbers. But, we will see later that vectors can be defined in a space of any number of dimensions, with elements that may themselves be multidimensional.

Notationally, a vector is usually denoted by a lower-case letter, which has a line over it, like $\bar{v}$, or is printed in bold type, like $\mathbf{v}$. For hand written notes, the line is most convenient, but in printed form the bold form is more usual. Throughout this book the form $\mathbf{v}$ is used.

A vector in 2D Euclidean space is defined by a pair of scalars arranged in a column, like

$$\mathbf{v} = \begin{bmatrix} v_x \\ v_y \end{bmatrix}.$$

Examining the diagram to the right, we see that v_x denotes the horizontal extent or *component* of the vector, and v_y its vertical component. Note, that in a computer program this structure can be easily represented as a two-element array of floating point numbers, or a struct containing two floats. When working in 2D, the direction of the vector can be given by the slope $m = v_y/v_x$. Its magnitude, also called its *norm*, is written $\|\mathbf{v}\|$. By the Pythagorean Theorem, $\|\mathbf{v}\| = \sqrt{v_x^2 + v_y^2}$.

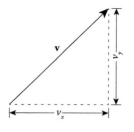

A vector in 3D space is defined by three scalars arranged in a column,

$$\mathbf{v} = \begin{bmatrix} v_x \\ v_y \\ v_z \end{bmatrix},$$

where v_x is the horizontal component, v_y the vertical component, and v_z the depth component. The norm of a 3D vector $\mathbf{v}$ is

$$\|\mathbf{v}\| = \sqrt{v_x^2 + v_y^2 + v_z^2}.$$

In 3D there is no simple equivalent to the slope. The direction of a 3D vector is often given in terms of its azimuth and elevation. But, for our purposes it will be best understood by its corresponding unit vector, which we will describe after first defining some key algebraic vector operations.

A.1 SCALING A VECTOR

Multiplication of a vector by a real number scalar leaves the vector's direction unchanged, but scales its magnitude. Algebraically, we multiply each term of the vector by the scalar. For example

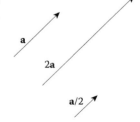

$$2\mathbf{a} = 2 \begin{bmatrix} a_x \\ a_y \end{bmatrix} = \begin{bmatrix} 2a_x \\ 2a_y \end{bmatrix}.$$

Division by a scalar is the same as multiplication by the reciprocal of the scalar:

$$\mathbf{a}/2 = \begin{bmatrix} a_x/2 \\ a_y/2 \end{bmatrix}.$$

A.2   UNIT OR DIRECTION VECTORS

The direction of a vector is most easily described by a *unit vector*, also called a *direction vector*. A unit vector, for a particular vector, is parallel to that vector but of unit length. Therefore, it retains the direction, but not the norm of the parent vector. Throughout this book the notation $\hat{\mathbf{v}}$ will be used to indicate a unit vector in the direction of parent vector $\mathbf{v}$. For example, the unit or direction vector corresponding with the 2D vector $\mathbf{a}$ would be

$$\hat{\mathbf{a}} = \begin{bmatrix} a_x/\|\mathbf{a}\| \\ a_y/\|\mathbf{a}\| \end{bmatrix} = \begin{bmatrix} \hat{a}_x \\ \hat{a}_y \end{bmatrix}.$$

A.3   VECTOR ADDITION

Addition of vectors can be expressed by a diagram. Placing the vectors end to end, the vector from the start of the first vector to the end of the second vector is the sum of the vectors. One way to think of this is that we start at the beginning of the first vector, travel along that vector to its end, and then travel from the start of the second vector to its end. An arrow constructed

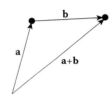

between the starting and ending points defines a new vector, which is the sum of the original vectors. Algebraically, this is equivalent to adding corresponding terms of the two vectors:

$$\mathbf{a} + \mathbf{b} = \begin{bmatrix} a_x \\ a_y \end{bmatrix} + \begin{bmatrix} b_x \\ b_y \end{bmatrix} = \begin{bmatrix} a_x + b_x \\ a_y + b_y \end{bmatrix}.$$

We can think of this as again making a trip from the start of the first vector to the end of the second vector, but this time traveling first horizontally the distance $a_x + b_x$ and then vertically the distance $a_y + b_y$.

A.4   VECTOR SUBTRACTION

Subtraction of vectors can be shown in diagram form by placing the starting points of the two vectors together, and then constructing an arrow from the head of the second vector in the subtraction to the head of the first vector. Algebraically, we subtract corresponding terms:

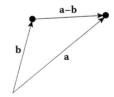

$$\mathbf{a} - \mathbf{b} = \begin{bmatrix} a_x \\ a_y \end{bmatrix} - \begin{bmatrix} b_x \\ b_y \end{bmatrix} = \begin{bmatrix} a_x - b_x \\ a_y - b_y \end{bmatrix}.$$

A.5   POINTS AND VECTORS

This leads us to the idea that points and vectors can be interchanged—almost. While vectors have no position in space, a point is always defined relative to the origin, O. Thus, we can say that a point, $p = (x, y)$, is defined by the origin, $O = (0,0)$ and a vector, $\mathbf{p} = \begin{bmatrix} x \\ y \end{bmatrix}$, i.e.,

$$p = O + \mathbf{p}.$$

Because the origin is assumed to be the point $(0,0)$, points and vectors can be represented the same way, e.g., the point $(2,3)$ can be represented as the vector $\begin{bmatrix} 2 \\ 3 \end{bmatrix}$. This interchangeability can be very convenient in many cases, but can also lead to confusion. It is a good idea to make sure that when storing data, you clearly indicate which values are points, and which are vectors. As will be seen below, the homogeneous coordinates used to define transformations can help with this.

Equivalent to the above, we can write, $\mathbf{p} = p - O$, i.e., a vector defines the measure from the origin to a particular point in space. More generally, a vector can always be defined by the difference between any two points, p and q. The vector $\mathbf{v} = p - q$ represents the direction and distance from point q to point p. Conversely, the point q and the vector $\mathbf{v}$ define the point, $p = q + \mathbf{v}$, which is translated from q by the components of $\mathbf{v}$.

A.6   PARAMETRIC DEFINITION OF LINES AND RAYS

This leads us to a compact definition of a line in space, written in terms of a unit vector and a point. Let $\mathbf{p}$ be a known point (expressed in vector form) on the line being defined, and let $\hat{\mathbf{a}}$ be a unit vector whose direction is parallel to the desired line. Then, the locus of points on the line is the set of all points $\mathbf{x}$, satisfying

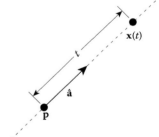

$$\mathbf{x}(t) = \mathbf{p} + t\hat{\mathbf{a}}.$$

The variable t is a real number, and is known as the line parameter. It measures the distance from the point $\mathbf{p}$ to the point $\mathbf{x}(t)$. If t is positive, the point $\mathbf{x}$ lies in the direction of the unit vector from point $\mathbf{p}$, and if t is negative, the point lies in the direction opposite to the unit vector.

The definition of a ray is identical to the definition of a line, except that the parameter t of a ray is limited to the positive real numbers. Thus, a ray can be interpreted as starting from the point $\mathbf{p}$, and traveling in the direction of $\hat{\mathbf{a}}$ a distance corresponding to t, as t goes from 0 to increasingly large positive values. On a ray, the point $\mathbf{p}$ is called the ray origin, $\hat{\mathbf{a}}$ the ray direction, and t the distance along the ray.

A.7 DOT OR INNER PRODUCT

Vector-vector multiplication is not as easily defined as addition, subtraction, and scalar multiplication. There are actually several vector products that can be defined. First, we will look at the *dot product* of two vectors, which is often called their *inner product*.

Defined algebraically, the dot product of two vectors is given by

$$\mathbf{a} \cdot \mathbf{b} = \begin{bmatrix} a_x \\ a_y \end{bmatrix} \cdot \begin{bmatrix} b_x \\ b_y \end{bmatrix} = a_x b_x + a_y b_y.$$

We multiply corresponding terms and add the result. The result *is not a vector*, but is in fact a scalar. This turns out to have many ramifications. The dot product is a *mighty* operation and has many uses in graphics!

A.7.1 Trigonometric Interpretation of Dot Product

The dot product can be written in trigonometric form as

$$\mathbf{a} \cdot \mathbf{b} = \|\mathbf{a}\| \|\mathbf{b}\| \cos \theta,$$

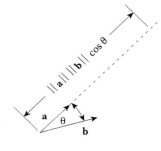

where θ is the smallest angle between the two vectors. Note, that this definition of θ applies in both 2D and 3D. Two nonparallel vectors always define a plane, and the angle θ is the angle between the vectors measured in that plane. Note that if both $\mathbf{a}$ and $\mathbf{b}$ are unit vectors, then $\|\mathbf{a}\| \|\mathbf{b}\| = 1$, and $\mathbf{a} \cdot \mathbf{b} = \cos \theta$. So, in general if you want to find the cosine of the angle between two vectors $\mathbf{a}$ and $\mathbf{b}$, first compute the unit vectors $\hat{\mathbf{a}}$ and $\hat{\mathbf{b}}$ in the directions of $\mathbf{a}$ and $\mathbf{b}$ then

$$\cos \theta = \hat{\mathbf{a}} \cdot \hat{\mathbf{b}}.$$

Other things to note about the trigonometric representation of dot product that follow directly from the cosine relationship are that

1. The dot product of *orthogonal* (perpendicular) vectors is zero, so if $\mathbf{a} \cdot \mathbf{b} = 0$, for vectors $\mathbf{a}$ and $\mathbf{b}$ with non-zero norms, we know that the vectors must be orthogonal.

2. The dot product of two vectors is positive if the magnitude of the smallest angle between the vectors is less than $90°$, and negative if the magnitude of this angle exceeds $90°$.

A.7.2 Geometric Interpretation of Dot Product

Another very useful interpretation of the dot product is that it can be used to compute the component of one vector in the direction parallel to another vector. For example, let $\hat{\mathbf{a}}$ be a unit vector in the direction of vector $\mathbf{a}$. Then the length of the projection of another vector $\mathbf{b}$ in the direction of vector $\mathbf{a}$ is $\hat{\mathbf{a}} \cdot \mathbf{b}$. You can think of this as the length of the shadow of vector $\mathbf{b}$ on vector $\mathbf{a}$. Therefore, the vector component of $\mathbf{b}$ in the direction of $\mathbf{a}$ is

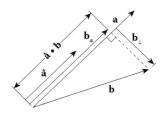

$$\mathbf{b}_a = (\hat{\mathbf{a}} \cdot \mathbf{b})\hat{\mathbf{a}}.$$

So, $\mathbf{b}_a$ is parallel to $\mathbf{a}$ and has length equal to the projection of $\mathbf{b}$ onto $\mathbf{a}$. Note also that $\mathbf{b}_\perp = \mathbf{b} - \mathbf{b}_a$ will be the component of $\mathbf{b}$ perpendicular to vector $\mathbf{a}$.

The dot product has many uses in graphics that the following two examples will serve to illustrate.

A.7.3 Dot Product Example: The Distance from a Point to a Line

Let us look at how dot product can be used to compute an important geometric quantity: the distance from a point to a line. We will use the parametric definition of a line, described above, specified by point $\mathbf{p}$ and a direction vector $\hat{\mathbf{a}}$. To compute the distance of an arbitrary point $\mathbf{x}$ from this line, first compute the vector $\mathbf{b} = \mathbf{x} - \mathbf{p}$, from the point $\mathbf{p}$ on the line to the point $\mathbf{x}$. The component of $\mathbf{b}$ in the direction of vector $\hat{\mathbf{a}}$ is

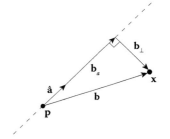

$$\mathbf{b}_a = (\hat{\mathbf{a}} \cdot \mathbf{b})\hat{\mathbf{a}}.$$

The component of $\mathbf{b}$ perpendicular to $\mathbf{a}$ is

$$\mathbf{b}_\perp = \mathbf{b} - \mathbf{b}_a,$$

and the distance of point $\mathbf{x}$ from the line is simply $\|\mathbf{b}_\perp\|$.

A.7.4 Dot Product Example: Mirror Reflection

Another very useful example of the use of dot product in geometric calculations is the computation of the mirror reflection from a surface. Assume that we have a flat mirror surface, whose *surface normal* is the unit vector $\hat{\mathbf{n}}$. The surface normal is defined to be a direction vector perpendicular to the surface. Since there are two such vectors at

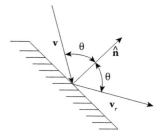

any point on a surface, the convention is to take the direction of the surface normal to be pointing in the "up" direction of the surface. For example, on a sphere it would point out of the sphere, and on a plane it would point in the direction considered to be the top of the plane. Now, we shine a light ray with direction $\mathbf{v}$ at the surface. The direction of the reflected ray will be given by $\mathbf{v}_r$. What must be true is that the angle θ between the normal $\hat{\mathbf{n}}$ and the light ray $\mathbf{v}$ should be the same as the angle between the reflected ray and the normal, and all three vectors $\mathbf{v}$, $\hat{\mathbf{n}}$, and $\mathbf{v}_r$ must lie in the same plane. Given these constraints, below is one way to calculate the light reflection ray $\mathbf{v}_r$.

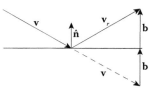

To make the figure to the right, first rotate the scene so everything is in a convenient orientation, with the surface normal $\hat{\mathbf{n}}$ pointing vertically, and the surface horizontal. Now, move vector $\mathbf{v}$ so that its tail is at the reflection point, as shown by the vector drawn with a dashed line in the figure. If $\mathbf{b}$ is the vector parallel to $\hat{\mathbf{n}}$ from the head of $\mathbf{v}$ to the surface, then by vector addition we have

$$\mathbf{v}_r = \mathbf{v} + 2\mathbf{b}.$$

Now the vector $\mathbf{b}$ is just the negative of the component of $\mathbf{v}$ in the direction of $\hat{\mathbf{n}}$. So,

$$\mathbf{b} = -(\hat{\mathbf{n}} \cdot \mathbf{v})\hat{\mathbf{n}}.$$

Thus,

$$\mathbf{v}_r = \mathbf{v} - 2(\hat{\mathbf{n}} \cdot \mathbf{v})\hat{\mathbf{n}}.$$

A.8 CROSS-PRODUCT

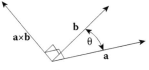

The cross-product $\mathbf{a} \times \mathbf{b}$ between two vectors $\mathbf{a}$ and $\mathbf{b}$ is a new vector perpendicular to the plane defined by the original two vectors. In other words, the cross product of two vectors is a vector that is perpendicular to both of the original vectors. The figure to the right illustrates the construction.

This notion of cross-product does not make sense in 2D space, since it is not possible for a third 2D vector to be perpendicular to two (nonparallel) 2D vectors. Thus, the notion of cross-product is reserved for working in 3D space.

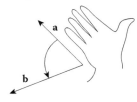

Since there are two directions perpendicular to the plane formed by two vectors, we must have a convention to determine which of these two directions to use. In graphics, it is most common to use the *right-hand rule*, and we use this convention throughout this text. The right-hand rule works as follows. Hold your right hand out flat, with the thumb out, aligning the fingers so they point in the direction of $\mathbf{a}$.

Now, rotate your hand so you can curl your fingers in the direction from vector **a** to vector **b**. Your thumb will point in the direction of $\mathbf{a} \times \mathbf{b}$. If you reverse this, and first align your fingers with **b** and then curl them toward **a** you will see that you have to turn your hand upside down, reversing the direction in which your thumb is pointing. From this it should be apparent that $\mathbf{b} \times \mathbf{a} = -(\mathbf{a} \times \mathbf{b})$. In other words, the order of the operands in the cross-product changes the polarity of the resulting cross-product vector. The result is still perpendicular to both of the original vectors, but the direction is flipped.

A.8.1 Trigonometric Interpretation of Cross-Product

The magnitude of the cross-product is given by

$$\|\mathbf{a} \times \mathbf{b}\| = \|\mathbf{a}\|\|\mathbf{b}\||\sin\theta|,$$

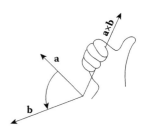

where θ is the small angle between vectors **a** and **b**. Thus, if **a** and **b** are unit vectors, the magnitude of the cross-product is the magnitude of $\sin\theta$.

Note, that the cross-product of two parallel vectors will be the zero vector **0**. This is consistent with the geometric notion that the cross-product produces a vector orthogonal to the original two vectors. If the original vectors are parallel, then there is no unique direction perpendicular to both vectors (i.e., there are infinitely many orthogonal vectors, all parallel to any plane perpendicular to either vector).

Algebraically, the cross-product is defined as follows. If two vectors are defined

$$\mathbf{a} = \begin{bmatrix} a_x \\ a_y \\ a_z \end{bmatrix}, \text{ and } \mathbf{b} = \begin{bmatrix} b_x \\ b_y \\ b_z \end{bmatrix},$$

then

$$\mathbf{a} \times \mathbf{b} = \begin{bmatrix} a_y b_z - a_z b_y \\ a_z b_x - a_x b_z \\ a_x b_y - a_y b_x \end{bmatrix}.$$

The cross-product has many uses in graphics, which the following two examples will serve to illustrate.

A.8.2 Cross-Product Example: Finding Surface Normals

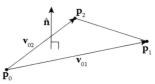

Suppose we have triangle $(\mathbf{p}_0, \mathbf{p}_1, \mathbf{p}_2)$, and we want to find the triangle's surface normal. We can do this easily by use of a cross-product operation. First, define vectors along two of the triangle edges: $\mathbf{v}_{01} = \mathbf{p}_1 - \mathbf{p}_0$, and $\mathbf{v}_{02} = \mathbf{p}_2 - \mathbf{p}_0$. Then the cross-product $\mathbf{v}_{01} \times \mathbf{v}_{02}$ is a vector perpendicular to both $\mathbf{v}_{01}$

and $\mathbf{v}_{02}$, and therefore perpendicular to the plane of the triangle. Scaling this vector to a unit vector yields the surface normal vector

$$\hat{\mathbf{n}} = (\mathbf{v}_{01} \times \mathbf{v}_{02})/\|\mathbf{v}_{01} \times \mathbf{v}_{02}\|.$$

A.8.3 Cross-Product Example: Computing the Area of a Triangle

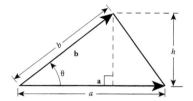

Another application of cross-product to triangles uses the trigonometric definition of the magnitude of the cross-product. Suppose we have a triangle, like the one shown to the right. If we know the lengths of sides a and b, and we know the angle θ between these sides, the area computation is straightforward. Relative to side a, the height of the triangle is given by $h = b \sin \theta$, and we know that the area of the triangle is $A = 1/2ah$, so we have $A = 1/2ab \sin \theta$. If we represent the sides of the triangle by vectors $\mathbf{a}$ and $\mathbf{b}$, $a = \|\mathbf{a}\|$ and $b = \|\mathbf{b}\|$. Since the magnitude of the cross-product $\|\mathbf{a} \times \mathbf{b}\| = \|\mathbf{a}\|\|\mathbf{b}\||\sin \theta|$, it follows that

$$A = 1/2\|\mathbf{a} \times \mathbf{b}\|.$$

Matrix Algebra

$\mathbf{A}$ LTHOUGH IT IS THE INTENT OF THIS BOOK to be reasonably self-contained, the subject of matrices and matrix algebra is a complex topic, subsumed under the field of linear algebra. What we are attempting in this section is to give a simple, and practical overview of some of the basic principles of matrix algebra that will be essential to the introductory study of physically based animation. The student who wishes to go on in computer graphics is strongly encouraged to make a thorough study of linear algebra, since it furnishes many of the key mathematical tools necessary to understand advanced texts and research papers in the field.

B.1 MATRIX DEFINITIONS

A single real number is called a *scalar*. If we have a column of scalars, we have a *vector*. A set of vectors, each with the same number of entries and arranged in a rectangular array is called a *matrix*.[*] This construction can be continued to higher dimensions, collecting a set of matrices together to form a *tensor*. Abstractly, all of these objects are considered to be tensors of various orders: a scalar is an order 0 tensor, a vector an order 1 tensor, and a matrix an order 2 tensor.

The individual scalars making up a matrix are called its *elements*. An arrangement of n horizontal rows, and m vertical columns is called an $n \times m$ matrix. An example would be the matrix

$$M = \begin{bmatrix} a & b & c \\ d & e & f \\ g & h & i \end{bmatrix}.$$

M's elements are the scalars a through i, whose values are real numbers. M is a 3×3 matrix, consisting of the three rows:

$$\begin{bmatrix} a & b & c \end{bmatrix}, \begin{bmatrix} d & e & f \end{bmatrix}, \begin{bmatrix} g & h & i \end{bmatrix};$$

---

[*]Please note the construction of the plural: one matrix, two matrices.

and the three columns:

$$\begin{bmatrix} a \\ d \\ g \end{bmatrix}, \begin{bmatrix} b \\ e \\ h \end{bmatrix}, \begin{bmatrix} c \\ f \\ i \end{bmatrix}.$$

Because M has the same number of rows as columns, it is called a *square matrix*. Since the columns of a matrix, taken individually, are really vectors, they are called *column vectors*. Similarly, the rows of a matrix, taken individually, are called *row vectors*. The sequence of elements of a square matrix forming the diagonal from the upper left to the lower right corner is called the *diagonal* of the matrix. All other elements of the matrix are called the *off diagonal* elements. Our example matrix M has the diagonal $\begin{bmatrix} a & e & i \end{bmatrix}$.

The *transpose* of a matrix is constructed by interchanging its rows and columns. Thus, the transpose of an $m \times n$ matrix will be an $n \times m$ matrix. Returning to our example, the transpose of matrix M is

$$M^T = \begin{bmatrix} a & d & g \\ b & e & h \\ c & f & i \end{bmatrix}.$$

Note, that the row vectors of the original matrix are now the column vectors of the transpose. Likewise, the column vectors are now the row vectors of the transpose.

We can unify the notions of vector and matrix if we consider a column vector of n elements to be an $n \times 1$ matrix. Similarly, a row vector of n elements can be considered to be a $1 \times n$ matrix. If we think of a vector in this way, we can take its transpose, turning a column vector into a row vector. If $\mathbf{v} = \begin{bmatrix} v_x \\ v_y \end{bmatrix}$, then $\mathbf{v}^T = \begin{bmatrix} v_x & v_y \end{bmatrix}$.

The *determinant* of a matrix is a scalar value, written $|M|$. The determinant is defined only for square matrices. For small matrices it is defined as follows:

$$2 \times 2\text{: } M = \begin{bmatrix} a & b \\ c & d \end{bmatrix}, \quad |M| = ad - bc,$$

$$3 \times 3\text{: } M = \begin{bmatrix} a & b & c \\ d & e & f \\ g & h & i \end{bmatrix}, \quad |M| = aei + bfg + cdh - (ceg + bdi + afh).$$

For larger matrices, the definition of the determinant becomes more complex, and the reader is referred to a more advanced text.

Matrix multiplication is defined between matrices of compatible dimensions. An $a \times b$ matrix multiplied by a $b \times c$ matrix yields an $a \times c$ matrix. For example, multiplying a 3×3 matrix by another 3×3 matrix gives you another 3×3 matrix, and multiplying a 2×2 matrix by a 2×1 vector yields another 2×1 vector.

To understand how matrix multiplication works, let us first consider the multiplication of a matrix by a vector, $M\mathbf{v}$. One way to understand this operation is to treat the rows of the matrix as row vectors. The elements of the result vector are formed by taking the dot product of each row by the vector. Using, as our example, the matrix $M = \begin{bmatrix} a & b \\ c & d \end{bmatrix}$ and the vector $\mathbf{v} = \begin{bmatrix} v_x \\ v_y \end{bmatrix}$, the resulting vector is given by

$$M\mathbf{v} = \begin{bmatrix} \begin{bmatrix} a \\ b \end{bmatrix} \cdot \begin{bmatrix} v_x \\ v_y \end{bmatrix} \\ \begin{bmatrix} c \\ d \end{bmatrix} \cdot \begin{bmatrix} v_x \\ v_y \end{bmatrix} \end{bmatrix} = \begin{bmatrix} av_x + bv_y \\ cv_x + dv_y \end{bmatrix}.$$

Another way to understand this operation is to think of the elements of the vector as scaling the corresponding column vector of the matrix, and adding the resulting vectors together:

$$M\mathbf{v} = v_x \begin{bmatrix} a \\ c \end{bmatrix} + v_y \begin{bmatrix} b \\ d \end{bmatrix} = \begin{bmatrix} av_x + bv_y \\ cv_x + dv_y \end{bmatrix}.$$

Matrix-matrix multiplication works like matrix-vector multiplication, treating each column of the second matrix as a vector being multiplied by the first matrix, and returning a new column. For example,

$$\begin{bmatrix} a & b \\ c & d \end{bmatrix} \begin{bmatrix} e & f \\ g & h \end{bmatrix} = \begin{bmatrix} \begin{bmatrix} a \\ b \end{bmatrix} \cdot \begin{bmatrix} e \\ g \end{bmatrix} & \begin{bmatrix} a \\ b \end{bmatrix} \cdot \begin{bmatrix} f \\ h \end{bmatrix} \\ \begin{bmatrix} c \\ d \end{bmatrix} \cdot \begin{bmatrix} e \\ g \end{bmatrix} & \begin{bmatrix} c \\ d \end{bmatrix} \cdot \begin{bmatrix} f \\ h \end{bmatrix} \end{bmatrix} = \begin{bmatrix} ae + bg & af + bh \\ ce + dg & cf + dh \end{bmatrix}.$$

The multiplication operator requires an identity element and an inverse to complete its definition. The identity element for matrix-matrix or matrix-vector multiplication is the identity matrix I, whose diagonal elements are all 1's and whose off diagonal elements are all 0's. The 2D and 3D identity matrices are

$$I_{2\times2} = \begin{bmatrix} 1 & 0 \\ 0 & 1 \end{bmatrix}, \quad \text{and} \quad I_{3\times3} = \begin{bmatrix} 1 & 0 & 0 \\ 0 & 1 & 0 \\ 0 & 0 & 1 \end{bmatrix}.$$

Now, we can define the inverse of a matrix M^{-1}, as that matrix, which when multiplied by the original matrix M, yields the identity matrix I, or

$$MM^{-1} = M^{-1}M = I.$$

For a 2×2 matrix, the inverse is given by

$$M = \begin{bmatrix} a & b \\ c & d \end{bmatrix},$$

$$M^{-1} = \frac{1}{|M|} \begin{bmatrix} d & -b \\ -c & a \end{bmatrix}.$$

For a 3×3 matrix, the inverse is given by

$$M = \begin{bmatrix} a & b & c \\ d & e & f \\ g & h & i \end{bmatrix},$$

$$M^{-1} = \frac{1}{|M|} \begin{bmatrix} ei - fh & ch - bi & bf - ce \\ fg - di & ai - cg & cd - af \\ dh - eg & bg - ah & ae - bd \end{bmatrix}.$$

For larger matrices, the reader is again referred to a more advanced text.

A word of caution is necessary with regard to matrix inverse. First, a matrix that is non-square has no inverse. Second, as we can see from the equations above, computing the inverse of a matrix involves dividing by the determinant of the matrix. If this determinant is 0, the matrix inverse is indeterminate.

B.2 SYSTEMS OF LINEAR EQUATIONS

Matrices arose in an attempt to develop a compact algebra to describe the solution of sets of simultaneous linear equations. Suppose we have two variables x and y, and we want to find the solutions for x and y satisfying the equations

$$ax + by = u$$
$$cx + dy = v$$

One way to solve these equations would be to begin by solving the first equation for $x = (u - by)/a$, and then substitute this expression for x into the second equation, leaving a single equation with only the variable y, which has the solution $y = (av - cu)/(ad - cb)$. Inserting the solution for y into the equation for x gives us $x = (du - bv)/(ad - cb)$.

In linear algebra, the original pair of equations would be written in the form of a matrix and two vectors:

$$\begin{bmatrix} a & b \\ c & d \end{bmatrix} \begin{bmatrix} x \\ y \end{bmatrix} = \begin{bmatrix} u \\ v \end{bmatrix},$$

or more abstractly,

$$M\mathbf{x} = \mathbf{u},$$

where M, $\mathbf{x}$, and $\mathbf{u}$ have the obvious definitions from the original expanded form of the equation. Notationally, we have gone from the more cumbersome original pair of linear equations to a more compact algebraic expression.

We now have the machinery to solve a linear system of equations written in matrix form:

$$Mx = u,$$
$$M^{-1}Mx = M^{-1}u,$$
$$Ix = M^{-1}u,$$
$$x = M^{-1}u.$$

Applying this logic to our two equation example from the start of this section, we have

$$x = M^{-1}u = \frac{1}{ad - bc}\begin{bmatrix} d & -b \\ -c & a \end{bmatrix}\begin{bmatrix} u \\ v \end{bmatrix} = \begin{bmatrix} (du - bv)/(ad - bc) \\ (av - cu)/(ad - bc) \end{bmatrix} = \begin{bmatrix} x \\ y \end{bmatrix},$$

which matches the solutions for x and y obtained by the original substitution process.

Note that there are cases where a system of linear equations will not yield a unique solution. These correspond exactly with cases where the determinant of the system's matrix is 0. For example, suppose we had the following two word-problems regarding a collection of apples and bananas. In both problems, let a be the number of apples, and b be the number of bananas.

1. There are twice as many apples as bananas. The total number of pieces of fruit is 30.

$$a - 2b = 0, \quad a + b = 30$$

$$Mx = u, \text{ with } M = \begin{bmatrix} 1 & -2 \\ 1 & 1 \end{bmatrix}, \quad x = \begin{bmatrix} a \\ b \end{bmatrix}, \quad u = \begin{bmatrix} 0 \\ 30 \end{bmatrix}$$

$$x = M^{-1}u, \text{ with } |M| = 1/3, \quad M^{-1} = \begin{bmatrix} 1 & 2/3 \\ -1/3 & 1/3 \end{bmatrix}$$

$$x = \begin{bmatrix} 20 \\ 10 \end{bmatrix}$$

2. There are twice as many apples as bananas. There are half as many bananas as apples.

$$a - 2b = 0, \quad -1/2a + b = 0$$

$$Mx = u, \text{ with } M = \begin{bmatrix} 1 & -2 \\ -1/2 & 1 \end{bmatrix}, \quad x = \begin{bmatrix} a \\ b \end{bmatrix}, \quad u = \begin{bmatrix} 0 \\ 0 \end{bmatrix}$$

$$x = M^{-1}u, \text{ with } |M| = 0, \text{ so } M^{-1} \text{ is indeterminate}$$

One can easily see why there is no unique solution to the second problem. It is because the second condition, "There are half as many bananas as apples," adds no new information to the problem. We already know that there are twice as many apples as bananas. The consequence, in the formation of matrix M, is that the second row of the matrix is just a scalar multiple $(-1/2)$ of the first row.

In general, a matrix that has a row that is a linear combination (i.e., a weighted sum) of one or more of the other rows will have a determinant of 0, and thus no inverse. Such a matrix is called degenerate, and indicates that the original problem does not have enough information to yield a unique solution.

Affine Transformations

C.1   THE NEED FOR GEOMETRIC TRANSFORMATIONS

O NE COULD IMAGINE A COMPUTER GRAPHICS SYSTEM that requires the user to construct everything directly into a single scene. But, one can also immediately see that this would be an extremely limiting approach. In the real world, things come from various places and are arranged together to create a scene. Further, many of these things are themselves collections of smaller parts that are assembled together. We may wish to define one object relative to another—for example, we may want to place a hand at the end of an arm. Also, it is often the case that parts of an object are similar, like the tires on a car. And, even things that are built on scene, like a house for example, are designed elsewhere, at a scale that is usually many times smaller than the house as it is built. Even more to the point, we will often want to animate the objects in a scene, requiring the ability to move them around relative to each other. For animation we will want to be able to move not only the objects but also the camera, as we render a sequence of images as time advances to create an illusion of motion. We need good mechanisms within a computer graphics system to provide the flexibility implied by all of the issues raised above.

The figure below shows an example of what we mean. On the left, a cylinder has been built in a convenient place, and to a convenient size. Because of the

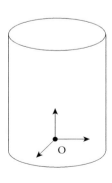

Original cylinder
model

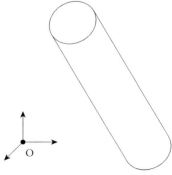

Transformed cylinder. It has
been scaled, rotated, and translated

requirements of a scene, it is first scaled to be longer and thinner than its original design, rotated to a desired orientation in space, and then moved to a desired position (i.e., translated). The set of operations providing for all such transformations, are known as the *affine transforms*. The affines include translations and all linear transformations, such as scale, rotate, and shear.

C.2   2D AFFINE TRANSFORMATIONS

Let us first examine the affine transforms in 2D space, where it is easy to illustrate them with diagrams, then later we will look at the affines in 3D.

Consider a point $\mathbf{x} = (x, y)$. Affine transformations of $\mathbf{x}$ are all transforms that can be written

$$\mathbf{x}' = \begin{bmatrix} ax + by + c \\ dx + ey + f \end{bmatrix},$$

where a through f are scalars.

For example, if $a, e = 1$, and $b, d = 0$, then we have a pure translation

$$\mathbf{x}' = \begin{bmatrix} x + c \\ y + f \end{bmatrix}.$$

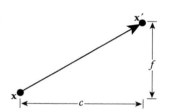

If $b, d = 0$ and $c, f = 0$ then we have a pure scale.

$$\mathbf{x}' = \begin{bmatrix} ax \\ ey \end{bmatrix}$$

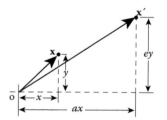

And, if $a, e = \cos\theta$, $b = -\sin\theta$, $d = \sin\theta$, and $c, f = 0$, then we have a pure rotation about the origin

$$\mathbf{x}' = \begin{bmatrix} x\cos\theta - y\sin\theta \\ x\sin\theta + y\cos\theta \end{bmatrix}.$$

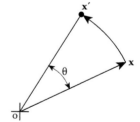

Finally if $a, e = 1$, and $c, f = 0$ we have the shear transforms

$$\mathbf{x}' = \begin{bmatrix} x + by \\ y + dx \end{bmatrix}.$$

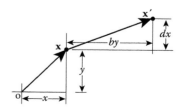

In summary, we have the four basic affine transformations shown in the figure below:

- Translate moves a set of points a fixed distance in x and y.

- Scale scales a set of points up or down in the x and y directions.

- Rotate rotates a set of points about the origin.

- Shear offsets a set of points a distance proportional to their x and y coordinates.

Note that only shear and scale change the shape determined by a set of points.

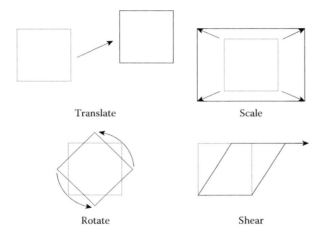

| Translate | Scale |
| Rotate | Shear |

C.3 MATRIX REPRESENTATION OF THE LINEAR TRANSFORMATIONS

The affine transforms scale, rotate, and shear are actually linear transforms and can be represented by a matrix multiplication of a point represented as a vector,

$$\begin{bmatrix} x' \\ y' \end{bmatrix} = \begin{bmatrix} ax + by \\ dx + ey \end{bmatrix} = \begin{bmatrix} a & b \\ d & e \end{bmatrix} \begin{bmatrix} x \\ y \end{bmatrix},$$

or $\mathbf{x}' = M\mathbf{x}$, where M is the matrix.

One very nice feature of the matrix representation is that we can use it to factor a complex transform into a set of simpler transforms. For example, suppose we want to scale an object up to a new size, shear the object to a new shape, and finally rotate the object. Let S be the scale matrix, H be the shear matrix and R be the rotation matrix. Then

$$\mathbf{x}' = R(H(S\mathbf{x}))$$

defines a sequence of three transforms: first-scale, second-shear, third-rotate. Because matrix multiplication is associative, we can remove the parentheses and multiply the three matrices together, giving a new matrix $M = RHS$. Now we can rewrite our transform

$$\mathbf{x}' = (RHS)\mathbf{x} = M\mathbf{x}$$

If we have to transform thousands of points on a complex model, it is clearly easier to do one matrix multiplication, rather than three, each time we want to transform a point. Thus, matrices are a very powerful way to encapsulate a complex transform and to store it in a compact and convenient form.

In matrix form, we can catalog the linear transforms as

$$\text{Scale: } \begin{bmatrix} s_x & 0 \\ 0 & s_y \end{bmatrix}, \text{ Rotate: } \begin{bmatrix} \cos\theta & -\sin\theta \\ \sin\theta & \cos\theta \end{bmatrix}, \text{ Shear: } \begin{bmatrix} 1 & h_x \\ h_y & 1 \end{bmatrix},$$

where s_x and s_y scale the x and y coordinates of a point, θ is an angle of counterclockwise rotation around the origin, h_x is a horizontal shear factor, and h_y is a vertical shear factor.

C.4   HOMOGENEOUS COORDINATES

Since the matrix form is so handy for building up complex transforms from simpler ones, it would be very useful to be able to represent all of the affine transforms by matrices. The problem is that translation is not a linear transform. The way out of this dilemma is to turn the 2D problem into a 3D problem, but in *homogeneous coordinates.*

We first take all of our points $\mathbf{x} = (x, y)$, express them as 2D vectors $\begin{bmatrix} x \\ y \end{bmatrix}$ and make these into 3D vectors with identical (thus the term *homogeneous*) third coordinates set to 1:

$$\begin{bmatrix} x \\ y \end{bmatrix} \Longrightarrow \begin{bmatrix} x \\ y \\ 1 \end{bmatrix}.$$

By convention, we call this third coordinate the w coordinate, to distinguish it from the usual 3D z coordinate. We also extend our 2D matrices to 3D homogeneous form by appending an extra row and column, giving

$$\text{Scale: } \begin{bmatrix} s_x & 0 & 0 \\ 0 & s_y & 0 \\ 0 & 0 & 1 \end{bmatrix}, \text{ Rotate: } \begin{bmatrix} \cos\theta & -\sin\theta & 0 \\ \sin\theta & \cos\theta & 0 \\ 0 & 0 & 1 \end{bmatrix}, \text{ Shear: } \begin{bmatrix} 1 & h_x & 0 \\ h_y & 1 & 0 \\ 0 & 0 & 1 \end{bmatrix}.$$

Note what happens when we multiply our 3D homogeneous matrices by 3D homogeneous vectors:

$$\begin{bmatrix} a & b & 0 \\ d & e & 0 \\ 0 & 0 & 1 \end{bmatrix} \begin{bmatrix} x \\ y \\ 1 \end{bmatrix} = \begin{bmatrix} ax + by \\ dx + ey \\ 1 \end{bmatrix}.$$

This is the same result as in 2D, with the exception of the extra w coordinate, which remains 1. All we have really done is to place all of our 2D points on the plane $w = 1$ in 3D space, and now we do all the operations on this plane. Really, the operations are still 2D operations.

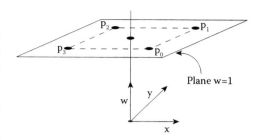

But, the magic happens when we place the translation parameters c and f in the matrix in the third column:

$$\begin{bmatrix} a & b & c \\ d & e & f \\ 0 & 0 & 1 \end{bmatrix} \begin{bmatrix} x \\ y \\ 1 \end{bmatrix} = \begin{bmatrix} ax + by + c \\ dx + ey + f \\ 1 \end{bmatrix}$$

We can now do translations as linear operations in homogeneous coordinates! So, we can add a final matrix to our catalog:

$$\text{Translate:} \begin{bmatrix} 1 & 0 & \triangle x \\ 0 & 1 & \triangle y \\ 0 & 0 & 1 \end{bmatrix},$$

where $\triangle x$ is the translation in the x direction and $\triangle y$ is the translation in the y direction. The astute reader will see the trick behind the magic—2D translation is now being expressed as a shear in 3D space.

Now, suppose we have a 2×2 square centered at the origin and we want to first rotate the square by $45°$ about its center and then move the square so its center is at $(3, 2)$. We can do this in two steps, as shown in the diagram to the right.

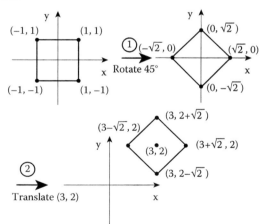

In matrix form:

$$M = T_{(3,2)} R_{45°} = \begin{bmatrix} 1 & 0 & 3 \\ 0 & 1 & 2 \\ 0 & 0 & 1 \end{bmatrix} \begin{bmatrix} \cos 45° & -\sin 45° & 0 \\ \sin 45° & \cos 45° & 0 \\ 0 & 0 & 1 \end{bmatrix}$$

$$= \begin{bmatrix} \cos 45° & -\sin 45° & 3 \\ \sin 45° & \cos 45° & 2 \\ 0 & 0 & 1 \end{bmatrix}$$

$$= \begin{bmatrix} \sqrt{2}/2 & -\sqrt{2}/2 & 3 \\ \sqrt{2}/2 & \sqrt{2}/2 & 2 \\ 0 & 0 & 1 \end{bmatrix}.$$

Note that

$$M \begin{bmatrix} 1 \\ 1 \\ 1 \end{bmatrix} = \begin{bmatrix} 3 \\ 2 + \sqrt{2} \\ 1 \end{bmatrix}, \text{and } M \begin{bmatrix} -1 \\ 1 \\ 1 \end{bmatrix} = \begin{bmatrix} 3 - \sqrt{2} \\ 2 \\ 1 \end{bmatrix},$$

verifying that we get the same result shown in the figure.

C.5 3D FORM OF THE AFFINE TRANSFORMATIONS

Now, we can extend all of these ideas to 3D in the following way:

1. Convert all 3D points to homogeneous coordinates

$$\begin{bmatrix} x \\ y \\ z \end{bmatrix} \Longrightarrow \begin{bmatrix} x \\ y \\ z \\ 1 \end{bmatrix}.$$

The extra (fourth) coordinate is again called the w coordinate.

2. Use matrices to represent the 3D affine transforms in homogeneous form.

The following matrices constitute the basic affine transforms in 3D, expressed in homogeneous form:

$$\text{Translate: } \begin{bmatrix} 1 & 0 & 0 & \triangle x \\ 0 & 1 & 0 & \triangle y \\ 0 & 0 & 1 & \triangle z \\ 0 & 0 & 0 & 1 \end{bmatrix}, \text{ Scale: } \begin{bmatrix} s_x & 0 & 0 & 0 \\ 0 & s_y & 0 & 0 \\ 0 & 0 & s_z & 0 \\ 0 & 0 & 0 & 1 \end{bmatrix},$$

and

$$\text{Shear: } \begin{bmatrix} 1 & h_{xy} & h_{xz} & 0 \\ h_{yx} & 1 & h_{yz} & 0 \\ h_{zx} & h_{zy} & 1 & 0 \\ 0 & 0 & 0 & 1 \end{bmatrix}.$$

In addition, there are three basic rotations in 3D,

$$\text{Rotation about the } x \text{ axis: } \begin{bmatrix} 1 & 0 & 0 & 0 \\ 0 & \cos\theta_x & -\sin\theta_x & 0 \\ 0 & \sin\theta_x & \cos\theta_x & 0 \\ 0 & 0 & 0 & 1 \end{bmatrix},$$

$$\text{Rotation about the } y \text{ axis: } \begin{bmatrix} \cos\theta_y & 0 & \sin\theta_y & 0 \\ 0 & 1 & 0 & 0 \\ -\sin\theta_y & 0 & \cos\theta_y & 0 \\ 0 & 0 & 0 & 1 \end{bmatrix},$$

and

$$\text{Rotation about the } z \text{ axis: } \begin{bmatrix} \cos\theta_z & -\sin\theta_z & 0 & 0 \\ \sin\theta_z & \cos\theta_z & 0 & 0 \\ 0 & 0 & 1 & 0 \\ 0 & 0 & 0 & 1 \end{bmatrix}.$$

The rotations, specified in this way, determine an amount of rotation about each of the individual axes of the coordinate system. The angles θ_x, θ_y, and θ_z of rotation about the three axes are called the Euler angles. They can be used to describe an off-axis rotation, by combining Euler angle rotations via matrix multiplication. Note, however, that the order of rotation affects the end result, so besides specifying Euler angles, an order of rotation must be specified. In general, affine transformations are associative but are not commutative, so the order in which operations are done is highly important. One can see this for rotations by computing the product $R_{\theta_x} R_{\theta_y} R_{\theta_z}$, and comparing with the result obtained by the product $R_{\theta_z} R_{\theta_y} R_{\theta_x}$. Please see Appendix D for a more powerful and general look at rotation.

Coordinate Systems

THE IDEA OF A *coordinate system*, or *coordinate frame* is pervasive in computer graphics. For example, it is usual to build a model in its own *modeling frame*, and later place this model into a scene in the *world coordinate frame*. We often refer to the modeling frame as the *object frame*, and the world coordinate frame as the *scene frame*. The figure below shows a cylinder that has been built in modeling frame **M**. To place the cylinder into the world frame **O**, the modeling frame has first been rotated about its own center, then translated to the position **x** in the world frame. Such a transformation can be encoded in a transformation matrix from the model frame to world frame,

$$M_{mw} = T_{mw} R_{mw},$$

where T_{mw} encodes the translation and R_{mw} encodes the rotation.

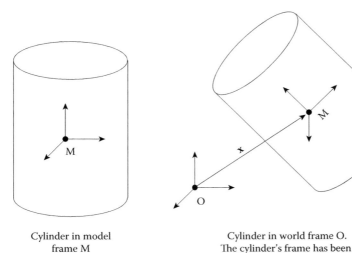

Cylinder in model
frame M

Cylinder in world frame O.
The cylinder's frame has been
rotated and then translated by **x**

D.1 LEFT- AND RIGHT-HANDED COORDINATE FRAMES

Let us develop the idea of a coordinate frame and how we can construct them for use in computer graphics. A 3D coordinate frame might be drawn as shown in the below diagram. The three axes are understood to be at right angles (orthogonal) to each other. In the figure, x denotes the horizontal axis, y the vertical axis, and z the depth axis (coming out of the page). This is the usual *right-handed* coordinate system seen in Computer Graphics.

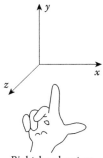

Right-hand system

The coordinate system shown above is called right handed, since if you place your thumb, index finger and the middle finger of the right hand at right angles to each other, as demonstrated in the figure, they look like coordinate axes. The thumb represents the x axis, the index finger represents the y axis, and the middle finger represents the z axis. A left-handed coordinate system is shown in the figure to the right. In a left-handed system, the z axis is reversed, measuring depth into the page, if we keep the x axis going to the right. Some older Computer Graphics texts used this convention so it is good to be aware that it exists, and what the difference is between the two conventions.

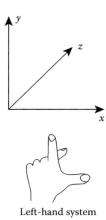

Left-hand system

D.2 COORDINATE FRAME EXPRESSED AS A POINT AND ORTHOGONAL UNIT VECTORS

In any coordinate system, the position where the coordinate axes cross is called the *origin*, and by definition has the coordinates $\mathbf{O} = (0,0,0)$ in that coordinate system. In order to work with coordinate frames in the algebraic language of vectors and matrices, we can re-label the axes of the coordinate system with unit vectors directed along the coordinate directions, as shown

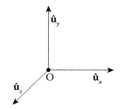

in the diagram. We use the notation $\hat{\mathbf{u}}_x$ to represent a unit vector in the x direction, $\hat{\mathbf{u}}_y$ in the y direction, and $\hat{\mathbf{u}}_z$ in the z direction. With this notation, a 3D point $\mathbf{p} = (p_x, p_y, p_z)$ in this coordinate frame can be rewritten

$$\mathbf{p} = \mathbf{O} + p_x \hat{\mathbf{u}}_x + p_y \hat{\mathbf{u}}_y + p_z \hat{\mathbf{u}}_z.$$

Now, if we wish to rotate our coordinate frame we can apply a rotation matrix to the vectors $\hat{\mathbf{u}}_x$, $\hat{\mathbf{u}}_y$, and $\hat{\mathbf{u}}_z$, and if we wish to translate the frame we can apply a translation matrix to $\mathbf{O}$.

D.3 A NOTATIONAL SCHEME FOR POINTS AND VECTORS

There is a convenient notational trick that can be used to discriminate between vectors and points represented in homogeneous coordinates. We represent 3D vectors on the 4D hyperplane $w = 0$ and 3D points on the hyperplane $w = 1$. For example, a surface normal vector might be written $\hat{\mathbf{n}} = \begin{bmatrix} \hat{n}_x \\ \hat{n}_y \\ \hat{n}_z \\ 0 \end{bmatrix}$, while a point might be written $\mathbf{p} = \begin{bmatrix} p_x \\ p_y \\ p_z \\ 1 \end{bmatrix}$. If we are consistent with this notation, then a rotation matrix will affect both points and vectors, but a translation matrix will affect only points. For example,

$$\begin{bmatrix} 1 & 0 & 0 & \triangle x \\ 0 & 1 & 0 & \triangle y \\ 0 & 0 & 1 & \triangle z \\ 0 & 0 & 0 & 1 \end{bmatrix} \begin{bmatrix} \hat{n}_x \\ \hat{n}_y \\ \hat{n}_z \\ 0 \end{bmatrix} = \begin{bmatrix} \hat{n}_x \\ \hat{n}_y \\ \hat{n}_z \\ 0 \end{bmatrix},$$

but

$$\begin{bmatrix} 1 & 0 & 0 & \triangle x \\ 0 & 1 & 0 & \triangle y \\ 0 & 0 & 1 & \triangle z \\ 0 & 0 & 0 & 1 \end{bmatrix} \begin{bmatrix} p_x \\ p_y \\ p_z \\ 1 \end{bmatrix} = \begin{bmatrix} p_x + \triangle x \\ p_y + \triangle y \\ p_z + \triangle z \\ 1 \end{bmatrix}.$$

A transformation matrix that first rotates and then translates will then work perfectly for transforming both vectors and points in one frame to another frame.

A final note is that to transform geometry from one frame to another frame we have a choice. We can either transform the coordinate frame itself, representing this transformation by a matrix, and leave all of the points and normals in the original coordinate frame. Or, we can transform all the points and normals from the original frame to the new frame. The latter approach is referred to as *baking* the transformation. Baking is usually reserved for cases in which we have applied a set of transformations and wish to preserve the transformed shape as the new base geometry. This technique is frequently used during the modeling process, but rarely used during animation. In an animation it is preferable to keep the geometry in its original frame, and simply update the transformation matrix as the animation proceeds. If, instead, we iteratively bake the transformed geometry, we stand the risk that over many iterations numerical errors will build up causing our geometry to deform from its original shape.

D.4 CREATING COORDINATE FRAMES

If we have two nonparallel 3D vectors and a 3D point we can
use them to conveniently construct a unique 3D coordinate
frame (i.e., three orthogonal directions in space, together
with an origin). Let us say that we have the vectors **a** and
b, and an origin point **p**. To describe our new coordinate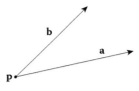
frame, we would like to create three mutually perpendicular unit vectors $\hat{\mathbf{u}}_x, \hat{\mathbf{u}}_y$,
and $\hat{\mathbf{u}}_z$, aligned with the three coordinate axes of the space.

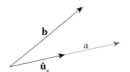

We can arbitrarily pick the x axis direction to be aligned
with **a**, so

$$\hat{\mathbf{u}}_x = \mathbf{a}/\|\mathbf{a}\|.$$

We know that the cross-product between **a** and **b** will be
perpendicular to both vectors, so let us say that this aligns
with the z axis, giving

$$\hat{\mathbf{u}}_z = (\mathbf{a} \times \mathbf{b})/\|\mathbf{a} \times \mathbf{b}\|.$$

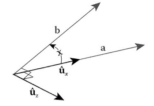

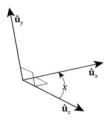

The third, or y axis must be perpendicular to both $\hat{\mathbf{u}}_x$ and
$\hat{\mathbf{u}}_z$, so

$$\hat{\mathbf{u}}_y = \hat{\mathbf{u}}_z \times \hat{\mathbf{u}}_x.$$

Note that $\hat{\mathbf{u}}_y$ is guaranteed to be a unit vector since both $\hat{\mathbf{u}}_x$
and $\hat{\mathbf{u}}_z$ are unit vectors, and the angle between them is 90° (i.e.,
$\sin 90° = 1$).

Providing the origin point **p** completes the construction of the
coordinate frame. In this new coordinate frame the directions of
the vectors $\hat{\mathbf{u}}_x, \hat{\mathbf{u}}_y$, and $\hat{\mathbf{u}}_z$ are the directions of the frame's x, y,
and z coordinate axes, and the origin of the frame is at **p**.

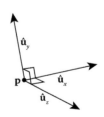

D.5 TRANSFORMING BETWEEN COORDINATE FRAMES

Once we have the three unit vectors and the origin point describing the new coordinate frame, it is easy to turn these into a matrix that transforms from the current
frame to this new frame. Treating the current frame as the modeling frame m, and
the new frame as the world frame w, we construct the rotation matrix

$$R_{mw} = \begin{bmatrix} \hat{\mathbf{u}}_x & \hat{\mathbf{u}}_y & \hat{\mathbf{u}}_z \end{bmatrix},$$

that rotates from the model to the world frame. The columns of this matrix are the three direction vectors of the world frame, expressed in model frame coordinates. You can demonstrate to yourself that this matrix works, since it rotates the three model frame coordinate axes into these new vectors:

$$R_{mw} \begin{bmatrix} 1 \\ 0 \\ 0 \end{bmatrix} = \hat{\mathbf{u}}_x, \quad R_{mw} \begin{bmatrix} 0 \\ 1 \\ 0 \end{bmatrix} = \hat{\mathbf{u}}_y, \quad \text{and} \quad R_{mw} \begin{bmatrix} 0 \\ 0 \\ 1 \end{bmatrix} = \hat{\mathbf{u}}_z.$$

We know that this matrix can do only a pure rotation since it is an *orthogonal matrix*, i.e., its column vectors are mutually orthogonal unit vectors. This is exactly the condition that must hold for a matrix to describe a pure rotation, so an orthogonal matrix is often called a *rotation matrix*. Note that unlike rotations around the three coordinate axes, this form of rotation matrix rotates around an arbitrary rotation axis.

To complete the description of the transform from the current frame to the new frame, we also need to provide a translation from the old origin to the new origin. In going from the model frame to the world frame, the origin of the model frame must be moved to the new origin at point **p**. The translation matrix in homogeneous form

$$T_{mw} = \begin{bmatrix} 1 & 0 & 0 & p_x \\ 0 & 1 & 0 & p_y \\ 0 & 0 & 1 & p_z \\ 0 & 0 & 0 & 1 \end{bmatrix},$$

will do this. Converting the rotation matrix R_{mw} into homogeneous form, and multiplying the translation matrix into the rotation matrix on the left forms the complete transform from the model to world frame,

$$M_{mw} = T_{mw} R_{mw}.$$

Note that this first rotates the coordinate axes into the new orientation and then translates to the new origin.

The matrix to convert back from the world frame to the model frame is simply the inverse of M_{mw}, and may be denoted M_{wm}. By application of the principles of matrix algebra, we can compute this without having to take a matrix inverse. The inverse of the product of two matrices is the product of the inverses of these matrices, but taken in the reverse order, so

$$M_{wm} = M_{mw}^{-1} = (T_{mw} R_{mw})^{-1} = R_{mw}^{-1} T_{mw}^{-1}.$$

Since R_{mw} is a rotation matrix, $R_{mw}^{-1} = R_{mw}^T$. You can demonstrate this to yourself by multiplying R_{mw}^T by R_{mw}. Because the column vectors of R_{mw} are mutually orthogonal unit vectors, the row-column dot products done in computing the elements of the product matrix will yield 0 except on the diagonal where they will yield 1. Therefore,

$$R_{wm} = R_{mw}^T = \begin{bmatrix} \hat{\mathbf{u}}_x^T \\ \hat{\mathbf{u}}_y^T \\ \hat{\mathbf{u}}_z^T \end{bmatrix},$$

i.e., the matrix whose rows are the three direction vectors transposed. The inverse of a translation is simply an equivalent translation but in the opposite direction, so

$$T_{wm} = T_{mw}^{-1} = \begin{bmatrix} 1 & 0 & 0 & -p_x \\ 0 & 1 & 0 & -p_y \\ 0 & 0 & 1 & -p_z \\ 0 & 0 & 0 & 1 \end{bmatrix}.$$

Finally, we have the combined matrix from world space back to model space

$$M_{wm} = R_{wm} T_{wm}.$$

Note that unlike the transform from model to world space, we first translate everything back relative to the origin of the model space and then rotate back to the model space orientation.

D.6   MATRIX-FREE TRANSFORMATIONS

Sometimes we know the origin $\mathbf{p}$ of the new coordinate frame, along with an axis of rotation $\hat{\mathbf{u}}$ and a rotation angle θ. In this case, it may be advantageous to be able to directly rotate points about this axis and then translate, rather than constructing a new coordinate frame and associated transformation matrix. To do this we can first rotate a point $\mathbf{r}$ using Rodrigues' rotation formula [Murray et al., 1994], to obtain

$$\mathbf{r}' = \mathbf{r}\cos\theta + (\hat{\mathbf{u}} \times \mathbf{r})\sin\theta + (\hat{\mathbf{u}} \cdot \mathbf{r})\hat{\mathbf{u}}(1 - \cos\theta),$$

and then translate by $\mathbf{p}$ to obtain the transformed point in the new coordinate frame

$$\mathbf{r}'' = \mathbf{r}' + \mathbf{p}.$$

Quaternions

I N THIS APPENDIX, we explore an alternate representation of rotations, known as *quaternions*. Appendices C and D have described how rotation matrices are used for both representing affine transformations of the geometry of objects and for transforming the coordinate frames of objects. Quaternions provide an equivalent representation of rotations, in that there is a bijective correspondence between the rotation matrices and the rotation quaternions, i.e., any rotation matrix can be directly transformed into a unique equivalent quaternion and any rotation quaternion can be directly transformed into a unique equivalent rotation matrix. In addition, given a rotation matrix R and its equivalent rotation quaternion $\mathbf{q}$, there is a multiplication operation defined between quaternions and any 3D vector $\mathbf{v}$ such that $R\mathbf{v} = \mathbf{q}\mathbf{v}\mathbf{q}^{-1}$. Therefore, quaternions provide a rotation mechanism that can be used as a substitute for rotation matrices or in conjunction with matrices.

There are several benefits to the use of quaternions in place of rotation matrices in physically based animation. First, quaternions contain an explicit representation of the rotation axis and angle, and so can be easily used to specify a rotation around any axis. This is in contrast to rotation matrices, which only have simple representations for rotations around the three major coordinate axes. Second, a quaternion is a four-element object, in contrast to a rotation matrix, which contains nine elements. Finally, in any operations involving interpolation, quaternions are superior to rotation matrices, since interpolating the elements of a rotation matrix does not guarantee that the rows and columns of the matrix will remain orthonormal. If the orthonormal property is lost, instead of providing a pure rotation, the matrix can start to shear or nonuniformly scale an object whose vertices are being transformed by the matrix. This means that rotation matrices should not be part of any system element that is meant to be interpolated or numerically integrated. Quaternions, on the other hand, can be interpolated, and thus integrated without losing their inherent rotational property. We will see that any error induced by interpolation can result only in a uniform scale, which can be corrected by a simple rescaling operation on the quaternion.

E.1   COMPLEX NUMBER ANALOGY

Before introducing the mathematics of quaternions, it will be helpful to take a quick look at the properties of complex numbers. A useful analogy can be made between the algebra of complex numbers and that of quaternions. In particular, both provide a simple encoding of rotation. But, whereas complex numbers describe rotations on a 2D plane, quaternions can describe full 3D rotations.

A complex number

$$c = a + ib,$$

consists of real scalar part a, and imaginary scalar part b, with the imaginary unit i defined implicitly by

$$i^2 = -1.$$

Since an imaginary number has two components, it can be plotted in a 2D coordinate frame, where the Re axis represents the real part of the number and the orthogonal Im axis, the imaginary part. The figure to the right shows this representation, which is very similar to that of a 2D vector. Represented in this way, it can be easily seen that any imaginary number has an alternate representation in polar coordinates

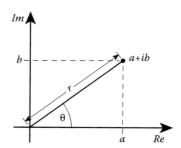

$$c = a + ib = r(\cos\theta + i\sin\theta),$$

where

$$r = \sqrt{a^2 + b^2}$$

is the magnitude of the complex number, and the angle

$$\theta = \tan^{-1} b/a$$

is known as its *phase angle*.

The product of two complex numbers c_1 and c_2 in Cartesian coordinates is

$$c_1 c_2 = (a_1 + ib_1)(a_2 + ib_2) = (a_1 a_2 - b_1 b_2) + i(a_1 b_2 + b_1 a_2),$$

while the product in polar coordinates is

$$c_1 c_2 = r_1(\cos\theta_1 + i\sin\theta_1)r_2(\cos\theta_2 + i\sin\theta_2)$$

or

$$c_1 c_2 = r_1 r_2[(\cos\theta_1 \cos\theta_2 - \sin\theta_1 \sin\theta_2) + i(\sin\theta_1 \cos\theta_2 + \cos\theta_1 \sin\theta_2)],$$

which, by well-known trigonometric identities, can be simplified to

$$c_1 c_2 = r_1 r_2[\cos(\theta_1 + \theta_2) + i\sin(\theta_1 + \theta_2)].$$

Therefore, we see that the product of complex number c_1 by complex number c_2 induces a rotation by θ_2, as well as a scale by r_2. If we assure that c_2 is a unit complex number, i.e., $r_2 = 1$, then the multiplication induces a pure rotation by the angle θ_2. Scaling c_2 to make it a complex number of unit length simply requires division by

$$r_2 = \sqrt{a_2^2 + b_2^2}.$$

E.2   QUATERNION STRUCTURE

Following this discussion of complex numbers, a quaternion is defined as

$$\mathbf{q} = a + ib + jc + kd,$$

consisting of a real scalar part a and three mutually orthogonal scalar imaginary parts b, c, and d. The three corresponding imaginary units i, j, and k are defined implicitly by the relations

$$i^2 = -1, \quad j^2 = -1, \quad k^2 = -1,$$
$$ij = k, \quad jk = i, \quad ki = j, \quad \text{and}$$
$$ji = -k, \quad kj = -i, \quad ik = -j.$$

Following this definition, the product of two quaternions $\mathbf{q}_1$ and $\mathbf{q}_2$ is

$$\begin{aligned}
\mathbf{q}_1\mathbf{q}_2 = {} & a_1 a_2 - (b_1 b_2 + c_1 c_2 + d_1 d_2) \\
& + i(a_1 b_2 + b_1 a_2 + c_1 d_2 - d_1 c_2) \\
& + j(a_1 c_2 + c_1 a_2 + d_1 b_2 - b_1 d_2) \\
& + k(a_1 d_2 + d_1 a_2 + b_1 c_2 - c_1 b_2).
\end{aligned}$$

A more compact alternate representation of the quaternion is

$$\mathbf{q} = (s, \mathbf{u}),$$

where $s = a$ is the real part of the quaternion, and the 3D vector $\mathbf{u} = \begin{bmatrix} b & c & d \end{bmatrix}^T$ encodes the three imaginary parts. With this representation, the product is defined as

$$\mathbf{q}_1\mathbf{q}_2 = (s_1, \mathbf{u}_1)(s_2, \mathbf{u}_2) = (s_1 s_2 - \mathbf{u}_1 \cdot \mathbf{u}_2, \; s_1\mathbf{u}_2 + s_2\mathbf{u}_1 + \mathbf{u}_1 \times \mathbf{u}_2).$$

The reader is invited to carry out the operations in this definition to verify that this product rule for the scalar-vector form of the quaternion produces a result that is identical to the product obtained in the real-imaginary form.

By factoring out the magnitude of the quaternion we can arrive at a polar form, similar to the polar form of the complex numbers. This is

$$\mathbf{q} = r(\cos\theta, \hat{\mathbf{u}}\sin\theta),$$

where

$$r = \sqrt{a^2 + b^2 + c^2 + d^2} = \sqrt{s^2 + \mathbf{u}^2}$$

is the quaternion magnitude,[*]

$$\hat{\mathbf{u}} = \mathbf{u}/\|\mathbf{u}\|$$

is the unit vector in the direction of the quaternion's vector of imaginary components, and

$$\theta = \tan^{-1} \frac{\|\mathbf{u}\|}{s}$$

is the angle between the quaternion's real axis and this vector.

To verify that this works, notice that by trigonometric definition, $\sin\theta = \frac{s}{\sqrt{s^2+\mathbf{u}^2}}$ and $\cos\theta = \frac{\|\mathbf{u}\|}{\sqrt{s^2+\mathbf{u}^2}}$, and so

$$\begin{aligned}
\mathbf{q} &= r(\cos\theta, \hat{\mathbf{u}}\sin\theta) \\
&= \sqrt{s^2 + \mathbf{u}^2}\left(\frac{s}{\sqrt{s^2+\mathbf{u}^2}}, \hat{\mathbf{u}}\frac{\|\mathbf{u}\|}{\sqrt{s^2+\mathbf{u}^2}}\right) \\
&= (s, \hat{\mathbf{u}}\|\mathbf{u}\|) \\
&= (s, \mathbf{u}).
\end{aligned}$$

In polar form, the product of two quaternions $\mathbf{q}_1 = r_1(\cos\theta_1, \hat{\mathbf{u}}_1\sin\theta_1)$ and $\mathbf{q}_2 = r_2(\cos\theta_2, \hat{\mathbf{u}}_2\sin\theta_2)$ is

$$\begin{aligned}
\mathbf{q}_1\mathbf{q}_2 = r_1 r_2 \big(&\cos\theta_1\cos\theta_2 + \hat{\mathbf{u}}_1\cdot\hat{\mathbf{u}}_2\sin\theta_1\sin\theta_2, \\
&\hat{\mathbf{u}}_1\sin\theta_1\cos\theta_2 + \hat{\mathbf{u}}_2\cos\theta_1\sin\theta_2 + (\hat{\mathbf{u}}_1\times\hat{\mathbf{u}}_2)\sin\theta_1\sin\theta_2\big).
\end{aligned}$$

---

[*]Note that the Pythagorean Theorem can be extended to spaces of any number of dimensions. This is an example of its extension to four dimensions, since $\hat{\mathbf{u}}^2 = \hat{\mathbf{u}}\cdot\hat{\mathbf{u}} = u_x^2 + u_y^2 + u_x^2$.

This result is much more complex than the result we obtained when showing that multiplication of complex numbers encodes a rotation. However, this complexity goes away in the special case when $\hat{\mathbf{u}}_1$ and $\hat{\mathbf{u}}_2$ are parallel. In this case, $\hat{\mathbf{u}}_1 = \hat{\mathbf{u}}_2$, $\hat{\mathbf{u}}_1 \cdot \hat{\mathbf{u}}_2 = 1$, and $\hat{\mathbf{u}}_1 \times \hat{\mathbf{u}}_2 = \mathbf{0}$, so the quaternion product reduces to

$$\mathbf{q}_1\mathbf{q}_2 = r_1 r_2 \big((\cos\theta_1 \cos\theta_2 + \sin\theta_1 \sin\theta_2), \ \hat{\mathbf{u}}_1 (\sin\theta_1 \cos\theta_2 + \cos\theta_1 \sin\theta_2) \big),$$

which by trigonometric identities reduces to

$$\mathbf{q}_1\mathbf{q}_2 = r_1 r_2 \big(\cos(\theta_1 + \theta_2), \ \hat{\mathbf{u}}_1 (\sin\theta_1 + \theta_2) \big).$$

This result is analogous to the result obtained when multiplying two complex numbers in trigonometric form, and proves that for this special case quaternion multiplication induces rotation of the first quaternion by the angle of the second. Below, we will prove that this is true in general.

By inspection, we see that the identity element for multiplication is $(1, \mathbf{0})$, i.e., $r = 1$ and $\theta = 0$. So, we can implicitly define the inverse of a quaternion by

$$\mathbf{q}\mathbf{q}^{-1} = (1, \mathbf{0}),$$

which can be solved to yield

$$\mathbf{q}^{-1} = \frac{(\cos\theta, -\hat{\mathbf{u}}\sin\theta)}{r}.$$

If the quaternion is a unit quaternion (i.e., $r = 1$), then we have

$$\mathbf{q} = (\cos\theta, \hat{\mathbf{u}}\sin\theta), \quad \text{and} \quad \mathbf{q}^{-1} = (\cos\theta, -\hat{\mathbf{u}}\sin\theta).$$

Note that the inverse of a unit quaternion is identical to the quaternion, but with its direction vector reversed, or, since $\sin -\theta = -\sin\theta$, with identical direction vectors but with its angle negated. Any quaternion can be scaled to produce a unit quaternion by simply dividing the quaternion by its magnitude r.

E.3 ROTATION VIA QUATERNIONS

Given the polar form of the quaternion, we can go directly to the definition of a rotation quaternion. A quaternion that will rotate a vector through angle θ about an axis $\hat{\mathbf{u}}$ is a unit quaternion defined by

$$\mathbf{q} = (\cos\theta/2, \hat{\mathbf{u}}\sin\theta/2).$$

Note that the cosine and sine of the half angle $\theta/2$, not the full angle, are used to scale the real and vector parts of the quaternion. Also note that since for any angle α, $\cos^2\alpha + \sin^2\alpha = 1$, $\mathbf{q}$ defined in this way will always be a unit quaternion.

Proof that $\mathbf{qrq}^{-1}$ provides a correct vector rotation. We would like to prove that quaternion rotation of a vector $\mathbf{r}$ by angle θ about axis $\hat{\mathbf{u}}$ is given by

$$\mathbf{r}' = \mathbf{qr\,q}^{-1}, \quad \text{where} \quad \mathbf{q} = (s, \mathbf{v}), \quad \text{and} \quad \mathbf{q}^{-1} = (s, -\mathbf{v}),$$

and where

$$s = \cos\theta/2, \quad \text{and} \quad \mathbf{v} = \hat{\mathbf{u}}\sin\theta/2.$$

Converting $\mathbf{r}$ to a quaternion and carrying out the multiplication yields

$$\begin{aligned}
\mathbf{qrq}^{-1} &= (s, \ \mathbf{v})(0, \ \mathbf{r})(s, \ -\mathbf{v}) \\
&= (-\mathbf{v}\cdot\mathbf{r}, \ s\mathbf{r} + \mathbf{v}\times\mathbf{r})(s, \ -\mathbf{v}) \\
&= \left(0, \ \mathbf{r}s^2 + (\mathbf{v}\cdot\mathbf{r})\mathbf{v} + 2(\mathbf{v}\times\mathbf{r})s + \mathbf{v}\times(\mathbf{v}\times\mathbf{r})\right).
\end{aligned}$$

If we expand s and $\mathbf{v}$ to their trigonometric form, and apply double angle trigonometric identities, the terms in the above multiplication become

$$\mathbf{r}s^2 = \mathbf{r}\cos^2\theta/2 = \mathbf{r}\left(\frac{1+\cos\theta}{2}\right)$$

$$(\mathbf{v}\cdot\mathbf{r})\mathbf{v} = (\hat{\mathbf{u}}\cdot\mathbf{r})\hat{\mathbf{u}}\sin^2\theta/2 = (\hat{\mathbf{u}}\cdot\mathbf{r})\hat{\mathbf{u}}\left(\frac{1-\cos\theta}{2}\right)$$

$$2(\mathbf{v}\times\mathbf{r})s = (\hat{\mathbf{u}}\times\mathbf{r})2\sin\theta/2\cos\theta/2 = (\hat{\mathbf{u}}\times\mathbf{r})\sin\theta$$

$$\mathbf{v}\times(\mathbf{v}\times\mathbf{r}) = \hat{\mathbf{u}}\times(\hat{\mathbf{u}}\times\mathbf{r})\sin^2\theta/2 = \hat{\mathbf{u}}\times(\hat{\mathbf{u}}\times\mathbf{r})\left(\frac{1-\cos\theta}{2}\right)$$

By applying these identities, and arranging terms with common trigonometric factors, the quaternion vector multiplication can be written

$$\mathbf{qrq}^{-1} = \left(0, \ \frac{1}{2}[\mathbf{r} + (\hat{\mathbf{u}}\cdot\mathbf{r})\hat{\mathbf{u}} + \hat{\mathbf{u}}\times(\hat{\mathbf{u}}\times\mathbf{r})] + \frac{1}{2}[\mathbf{r} - (\hat{\mathbf{u}}\cdot\mathbf{r})\hat{\mathbf{u}} - \hat{\mathbf{u}}\times(\hat{\mathbf{u}}\times\mathbf{r})]\cos\theta + (\hat{\mathbf{u}}\times\mathbf{r})\sin\theta\right).$$

The diagram to the right can be used to show that the component of vector $\mathbf{r}$ in the direction of $\hat{\mathbf{u}}$ is $(\hat{\mathbf{u}}\cdot\mathbf{r})\hat{\mathbf{u}}$, so its component perpendicular to $\hat{\mathbf{u}}$ is

$$\mathbf{a} = \mathbf{r} - (\hat{\mathbf{u}}\cdot\mathbf{r})\hat{\mathbf{u}}.$$

Since the magnitude of $\mathbf{a}$ is $\|\mathbf{r}\|\sin\phi$, where ϕ is the angle between $\mathbf{r}$ and $\hat{\mathbf{u}}$, it can be easily demonstrated that

$$\mathbf{a} = -\hat{\mathbf{u}}\times(\hat{\mathbf{u}}\times\mathbf{r}).$$

By applying these identities, the quaternion vector multiplication can be rewritten

$$\mathbf{qrq}^{-1} = \left(0, \ \frac{1}{2}[\mathbf{r} + (-\mathbf{a}+\mathbf{r}) - \mathbf{a}] + \frac{1}{2}(\mathbf{a}+\mathbf{a})\cos\theta + (\hat{\mathbf{u}}\times\mathbf{r})\sin\theta\right),$$

which can finally be reduced to

$$\mathbf{qrq}^{-1} = \mathbf{r}\cos\theta + (\hat{\mathbf{u}}\times\mathbf{r})\sin\theta + (\hat{\mathbf{u}}\cdot\mathbf{r})\hat{\mathbf{u}}(1-\cos\theta).$$

This formula is identical to the Rodrigues formula for vector rotation given in Appendix D, Section D.6, and completes the proof.

The rotation of a vector $\mathbf{r}$ by a rotation quaternion $\mathbf{q}$ to produce the vector $\mathbf{r}'$ is accomplished by the product

$$(0, \mathbf{r}') = \mathbf{q}\,(0, \mathbf{r})\,\mathbf{q}^{-1}.$$

A proof that this provides a rotation of angle θ about the quaternion's axis $\hat{\mathbf{u}}$ is given above. Note that the vector is converted to a quaternion whose real part is 0 in order to perform the quaternion multiplication, and that the rotated vector must be extracted from the result quaternion, whose real part is also 0. Notice that the vector $\mathbf{r}$ could represent the position of a point relative to the origin. Thus, quaternion rotation can be applied to a point, and the rotation will be about the origin.

As a notational convenience, quaternion rotation of a vector is usually simply written

$$\mathbf{r}' = \mathbf{q}\mathbf{r}\,\mathbf{q}^{-1},$$

where the expansion of $\mathbf{r}$ to a quaternion, and the extraction of $\mathbf{r}'$ from the product quaternion are understood.

It follows immediately from this representation of quaternion rotation that a series of rotations can be stored as a product of quaternions. Let us say that a rotation given by $\mathbf{q}_1$ is done first, followed by a second rotation given by $\mathbf{q}_2$. This can be written

$$\mathbf{r}' = \mathbf{q}_2(\mathbf{q}_1\mathbf{r}\,\mathbf{q}_1^{-1})\mathbf{q}_2^{-1}.$$

But, since quaternion multiplication is associative, this can be rewritten

$$\mathbf{r}' = (\mathbf{q}_2\mathbf{q}_1)\mathbf{r}\,(\mathbf{q}_1^{-1}\mathbf{q}_2^{-1}),$$

demonstrating that the quaternion product $\mathbf{q}_2\mathbf{q}_1$ encodes consecutive rotations, first by rotation $\mathbf{q}_1$, followed by rotation $\mathbf{q}_2$.

E.4   QUATERNIONS AND ROTATION MATRICES

Rotation matrices and rotation quaternions are equivalent, so it follows that there should be a conversion between the two forms.

A rotation quaternion $\mathbf{q} = (s, \mathbf{u})$, where $s = \cos\theta/2$ and $\mathbf{u} = \hat{\mathbf{u}}\sin\theta/2$, can be converted to a 3×3 rotation matrix via the formula

$$R(\mathbf{q}) = \begin{bmatrix} 1 - 2u_y^2 - 2u_z^2 & 2u_x u_y - 2su_z & 2u_x u_z + 2su_y \\ 2u_x u_y + 2su_z & 1 - 2u_x^2 - 2u_z^2 & 2u_y u_z - 2su_x \\ 2u_x u_z - 2su_y & 2u_y u_z + 2su_x & 1 - 2u_x^2 - 2u_y^2 \end{bmatrix}.$$

Converting from a rotation matrix to a unit quaternion must be done as a set of cases, based upon the diagonal elements of the rotation matrix. We show this in algorithmic form below.

Quaternion `Matrix2Quaternion`(Matrix3x3 M)
The matrix M must be a rotation matrix, meaning that its rows and columns must be mutually orthogonal unit vectors
begin

Quaternion q;
float r;

float $t = M[0][0] + M[1][1] + M[2][2]$ // *the trace of the matrix;*

if $t \geq 0$ **then**
  $r = \mathbf{sqrt}(t+1)$;
  $q.s = r/2$;
  $q.u_x = (M[2][1] - M[1][2])/(2r)$;
  $q.u_y = (M[0][2] - M[2][0])/(2r)$;
  $q.u_z = (M[1][0] - M[0][1])/(2r)$;
else if $M[0][0] > M[1][1]$ **and** $M[0][0] > M[2][2]$ **then**
  $r = \mathbf{sqrt}(M[0][0] - (M[1][1] + M[2][2]) + 1)$;
  $q.u_x = r/2$;
  $q.u_y = (M[0][1] - M[1][0])/(2r)$;
  $q.u_z = (M[2][0] - M[0][2])/(2r)$;
  $q.s = (M[2][1] - M[1][2])/(2r)$;
else if $M[1][1] > M[0][0]$ **and** $M[1][1] > M[2][2]$ **then**
  $r = \mathbf{sqrt}(M[1][1] - (M[2][2] + M[0][0]) + 1)$;
  $q.u_y = r/2$;
  $q.u_z = (M[1][2] - M[2][1])/(2r)$;
  $q.u_x = (M[0][1] - M[1][0])/(2r)$;
  $q.s = (M[0][2] - M[2][0])/(2r)$;
else
  $r = \mathbf{sqrt}(M[2][2] - (M[0][0] + M[1][1]) + 1)$;
  $q.u_z = r/2$;
  $q.u_x = (M[2][0] - M[0][2])/(2r)$;
  $q.u_y = (M[1][2] - M[2][1])/(2r)$;
  $q.s = (M[1][0] - M[0][1])/(2r)$;
end

return q;
end

Barycentric Coordinates

F OR MANY CALCULATIONS OVER TRIANGLES AND TETRAHEDRA, a metric representation called *barycentric coordinates* is very convenient. Barycentric coordinates provide a measuring system that positions a point relative to the vertices of the triangle or tetrahedron, with a very simple scheme for converting from regular 3D spatial coordinates to barycentric coordinates, and from barycentric to 3D spatial coordinates. This provides a convenient way of detecting whether or not a point is inside or outside of a triangle or tetrahedron. They also provide a set of weights that can be used to interpolate 3D position or other values, for example color, stored at a triangle or tetrahedron's vertices.

F.1   TRIANGULAR BARYCENTRIC COORDINATES

Considering the diagram to the right, the point $\mathbf{x}$ is internal to the triangle $\mathbf{p}_0, \mathbf{p}_1, \mathbf{p}_2$, whose area is $A = A_u + A_v + A_w$. The barycentric coordinates of $\mathbf{x}$ are named u, v, and w and are defined as follows:

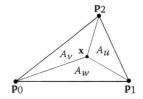

$$u = A_u/A,$$
$$v = A_v/A,$$
$$w = A_w/A = 1 - u - v.$$

For example:

- If $\mathbf{x} = \mathbf{p}_0$, $u = 1, v = 0, w = 0$,

- If $\mathbf{x} = \mathbf{p}_1$, $u = 0, v = 1, w = 0$,

- If $\mathbf{x} = \mathbf{p}_2$, $u = 0, v = 0, w = 1$,

- If $\mathbf{x}$ is on the $\mathbf{p}_1, \mathbf{p}_2$ edge, $u = 0$,

- If $\mathbf{x}$ is on the $\mathbf{p}_2, \mathbf{p}_0$ edge, $v = 0$,

- If $\mathbf{x}$ is on the $\mathbf{p}_0, \mathbf{p}_1$ edge, $w = 0$.

The areas can be found by the trigonometric relation:

$$A = 1/2ab\sin\theta,$$

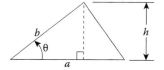

where a and b are two sides of a triangle and θ is the angle between them. Note that $\sin\theta = h/b$, so $h = b\sin\theta$. Therefore, $A = 1/2ah = 1/2ab\sin\theta$. We know that the magnitude of the cross product $\|\mathbf{a}\times\mathbf{b}\| = \|\mathbf{a}\|\|\mathbf{b}\|\sin\theta$, so we can use the cross-product to determine areas.

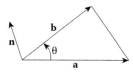

We can do even better if we note that

$$\frac{\mathbf{a}\times\mathbf{b}}{\|\mathbf{a}\times\mathbf{b}\|} = \hat{\mathbf{n}},$$

where $\hat{\mathbf{n}}$ is the normal to the plane defined by $\mathbf{a}, \mathbf{b}$ and a common vertex.

Now, referring to the diagram to the right, let

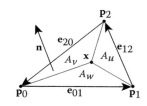

$$\mathbf{e}_{01} = \mathbf{p}_1 - \mathbf{p}_0,$$
$$\mathbf{e}_{12} = \mathbf{p}_2 - \mathbf{p}_1,$$
$$\mathbf{e}_{20} = \mathbf{p}_0 - \mathbf{p}_2,$$
$$\hat{\mathbf{n}} = (\mathbf{e}_{01}\times\mathbf{e}_{12})/\|\mathbf{e}_{01}\times\mathbf{e}_{12}\|.$$

We see that

$$A = \frac{1}{2}(\mathbf{e}_{01}\times\mathbf{e}_{12})\cdot\hat{\mathbf{n}},$$
$$A_u = \frac{1}{2}[\mathbf{e}_{12}\times(\mathbf{x}-\mathbf{p}_1)]\cdot\hat{\mathbf{n}},$$
$$A_v = \frac{1}{2}[\mathbf{e}_{20}\times(\mathbf{x}-\mathbf{p}_2)]\cdot\hat{\mathbf{n}}.$$

And finally,

$$u = A_u/A, \quad v = A_v/A, \quad w = 1 - u - v.$$

Note that computation with dot product instead of vector magnitude gives us a *signed area*. This means that if $\mathbf{x}$ is outside of a triangle, at least one of the u, v, w coordinates will be negative, as demonstrated in the following figures:

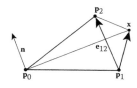

here $[\mathbf{e}_{12}\times(\mathbf{x}-\mathbf{p}_1)]\cdot\hat{\mathbf{n}} < 0$ so $u < 0$,

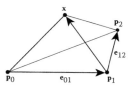

here $A_u + A_w > A$, so $u + w > 1$, thus $v < 0$.

So, given triangle $\mathbf{p}_0, \mathbf{p}_1, \mathbf{p}_2$, a compact way to calculate the barycentric coordinates of 3D point $\mathbf{x}$ with respect to this triangle consists of the following steps:

$$\mathbf{v_n} = (\mathbf{p}_1 - \mathbf{p}_0) \times (\mathbf{p}_2 - \mathbf{p}_1),$$
$$2A = \|\mathbf{v_n}\|,$$
$$\hat{\mathbf{n}} = \mathbf{v_n}/(2A),$$
$$u = [(\mathbf{p}_2 - \mathbf{p}_1) \times (\mathbf{x} - \mathbf{p}_1)] \cdot \hat{\mathbf{n}}/(2A),$$
$$v = [(\mathbf{p}_0 - \mathbf{p}_2) \times (\mathbf{x} - \mathbf{p}_2)] \cdot \hat{\mathbf{n}}/(2A),$$
$$w = 1 - u - v.$$

F.2   USES FOR BARYCENTRIC COORDINATES

Given barycentric coordinates (u, v, w) defined over a triangle, passing the test

$$u \geq 0, \quad v \geq 0, \quad u + v \leq 1,$$

assures that a given point is inside the triangle, and failing the test means that it is outside.

Given barycentric coordinates and vertices $\mathbf{p}_0, \mathbf{p}_1, \mathbf{p}_2$ for a triangle, we can convert back to 3D coordinates by

$$\mathbf{x} = \mathbf{p}_2 + u(\mathbf{p}_0 - \mathbf{p}_2) + v(\mathbf{p}_1 - \mathbf{p}_2).$$

Another way to see this is that u, v, and w weight vertices to give the position of $\mathbf{x}$. By rearranging the equation above, we have

$$\mathbf{x} = u\mathbf{p}_0 + v\mathbf{p}_1 + (1 - u - v)\mathbf{p}_2 = u\mathbf{p}_0 + v\mathbf{p}_1 + w\mathbf{p}_2.$$

This follows directly if we see the u and v coordinates as measuring distance from an edge to a parallel line passing through the opposite vertex as shown in the diagram to the right. We see that u measures the fraction of the full distance from edge $\mathbf{p}_1, \mathbf{p}_2$ to a parallel line through $\mathbf{p}_0$. Defined this way, u is a per unit measure, so $u = 0$ on $\mathbf{p}_1, \mathbf{p}_2$, $u = 1$ on the parallel line containing $\mathbf{p}_0$. The 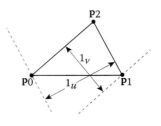 v coordinate is similar, measuring distance from the edge $\mathbf{p}_0, \mathbf{p}_2$ to $\mathbf{p}_1$, and w measures distance from $\mathbf{p}_0, \mathbf{p}_1$ to $\mathbf{p}_2$.

Finally, we can interpolate any quantity defined on the vertices of the triangle, just like we interpolate the vertex positions to get the position in space from the barycentric coordinates. Let us say that we have a color c_i defined at each vertex i. Then, the color $c(u, v, w)$ interpolated from the vertices to the position indicated by the barycentric coordinates will be

$$c(u, v, w) = uc_0 + vc_1 + wc_2.$$

F.3   BARYCENTRIC COORDINATES OVER TETRAHEDRA

Barycentric coordinates can also be defined over tetrahedra in 3D, and in fact over simplices[*] in any dimensional space. Tetrahedra are of particular interest in graphics and animation, since just as triangles are a preferred way of tiling a surface, tetrahedra are a preferred way of tiling a solid.

The extension to tetrahedra is straightforward. Given vertices $\mathbf{p}_0$, $\mathbf{p}_1$, $\mathbf{p}_2$, and $\mathbf{p}_3$, we will have barycentric coordinates u, v, w, and $1 - u - v - w$. The tetrahedron inside-outside test is

$$u \geq 0, v \geq 0, w \geq 0, u + v + w \leq 1,$$

and the corresponding 3D position for a point $\mathbf{x}$ is

$$\mathbf{x} = u\mathbf{p}_0 + v\mathbf{p}_1 + w\mathbf{p}_2 + (1 - u - v - w)\mathbf{p}_3.$$

Just as we could define barycentric coordinates in 2D by a ratio of triangle area to overall triangle area, we could compute the barycentric coordinates for a point in 3D by considering ratios of tetrahedral volumes (e.g., for $\mathbf{x}$, $\mathbf{p}_1$, $\mathbf{p}_2$, and $\mathbf{p}_3$) to the volume of the overall tetrahedron (i.e., points $\mathbf{p}_0$, $\mathbf{p}_1$, $\mathbf{p}_2$, and $\mathbf{p}_3$). But, a different way of computing barycentric values is more general.

Let us first reexamine our derivation of barycentric coordinates for a triangle in 2D space. The problem could have been formulated as a linear system, in which we propose that any point lying inside a triangle is the weighted sum of its three vertices, with weights u, v, and w, subject to the *convexity condition* $u + v + w = 1$. If the point position is $\mathbf{x}$, and the triangle vertices are $\mathbf{p}_0$, $\mathbf{p}_1$, and $\mathbf{p}_2$, we have the linear relationship

$$\mathbf{x} = u\mathbf{p}_0 + v\mathbf{p}_1 + w\mathbf{p}_2,$$

or after applying the constraint $w = 1 - u - v$ and rearranging,

$$u(\mathbf{p}_0 - \mathbf{p}_2) + v(\mathbf{p}_1 - \mathbf{p}_2) = \mathbf{x} - \mathbf{p}_2.$$

Rewriting this in matrix-vector form, we have

$$M\mathbf{u} = \mathbf{x} - \mathbf{p}_2,$$

where

$$\mathbf{u} = \begin{bmatrix} u \\ v \end{bmatrix}, \quad \text{and} \quad M = \begin{bmatrix} x_0 - x_2 & x_1 - x_2 \\ y_0 - y_2 & y_1 - y_2 \end{bmatrix}.$$

---

[*]The 2D simplex is the triangle and the 3D simplex is the tetrahedron. Just like a triangle is an object in 2 space formed by connecting $2 + 1 = 3$ non-colinear points by $2 - 1 = 1$-dimensional line segments, a simplex in an arbitrary D dimensional space is an object formed by connecting D+1 points by truncated D-1 dimensional surfaces, such that the truncated surfaces form the convex hull containing all of the points. For example, the tetrahedron is defined by $3 + 1 = 4$ vertices, every 3 of which define a triangular face embedded in a $3 - 1 = 2$-dimensional plane.

The reader can confirm that inverting matrix M and multiplying by the right-hand side of this equation yields the same barycentric coordinate calculation obtained using the area and cross-product approach outlined above.

This linear-system approach to defining barycentric triangle coordinates can be applied to the problem of defining tetrahedral coordinates. We can let u, v, and w be the coordinates to be determined, along with a fourth coordinate whose value is $1 - u - v - w$, and let $\mathbf{p}_0$, $\mathbf{p}_1$, $\mathbf{p}_2$, and $\mathbf{p}_3$ be the four vertices of the tetrahedron. The barycentric coordinates are then determined by the equation

$$M\mathbf{u} = \mathbf{x} - \mathbf{p}_3,$$

where

$$\mathbf{u} = \begin{bmatrix} u \\ v \\ w \end{bmatrix}, \quad \text{and} \quad M = \begin{bmatrix} x_0 - x_3 & x_1 - x_3 & x_2 - x_3 \\ y_0 - y_3 & y_1 - y_3 & y_2 - y_3 \\ z_0 - z_3 & z_1 - z_3 & z_2 - z_3 \end{bmatrix},$$

so that barycentric coordinates are obtained from 3D position $\mathbf{x}$ by

$$\mathbf{u} = M^{-1}(\mathbf{x} - \mathbf{p}_3).$$

Bibliography

Alicat Scientific (2015). Engineer's handbook. Available at http://www.alicat.com/documents/conversion/Gas_VDC_25C.pdf, accessed May 2015.

Anton Parr (2015). Viscopedia—A free encyclopedia for viscosity. Available at http://www.viscopedia.com, accessed May 2015.

Appel, A. (1985). An efficient program for many-body simulation. *SIAM J. Sci. Stat. Comput.*, 6(1):669–686.

Avallone, E. A. and Baumeister, T. (1996). *Mark's Handbook for Mechanical Engineers, 10th Edition*. McGraw-Hill, New York.

Baraff, D. (1992). Dynamic Simulation of Non-Penetrating Rigid Bodies. PhD thesis, Cornell University, New York.

Baraff, D. and Witkin, A. (1998). Large steps in cloth simulation. *SIGGRAPH '98 Proceedings of the 21st Annual Conference on Computer Graphics and Interactive Techniques*, pages 43–54.

Bargteil, A. W., Goktekin, T. G., O'Brien, J. F., and Strain, J. A. (2006). A semi-Lagrangian contouring method for fluid simulation. *ACM Trans. Graph.*, 25(1):19–38.

Bhat, K. S., Twigg, C. D., Hodgins, J. K., Khosla, P. K., Popović, Z., and Seitz, S. M. (2003). Estimating cloth simulation parameters from video. In *ACM SIGGRAPH/Eurographics Symposium on Computer Animation*, pages 37–51.

Bhatia, H., Norgard, G., Pascucci, V., and Bremer, P.-T. (2012). The Helmholtz-Hodge decomposition; a survey. *IEEE Trans. Vis. Comput. Graph.*, 19(8):1386–1404.

Brackbill, J. and Ruppel, H. (1986). FLIP: A method for adaptively zoned, particle-in-cell calculations of fluid flows in two dimensions. *J. Comput. Phys.*, 65(2):314–343.

Breen, D., House, D., and Getto, P. (1992). A physically-based particle model of woven cloth. *Visual Comput.*, 8(5–6):264–277.

Breen, D., House, D., and Wozny, M. (1994). Predicting the drape of woven cloth using interacting particles. *SIGGRAPH '94 Proceedings of the 21st Annual Conference on Computer Graphics and Interactive Techniques*, pages 365–372.

Bridson, R. (2008). *Fluid Simulation for Computer Graphics*. CRC Press, Taylor & Francis Group, Boca Raton, FL.

Carrier, J., Greengard, L., and Rokhlin, V. (1988). A fast adaptive multipole algorithm for particle simulations. *SIAM J. Sci. Stat. Comput.*, 9(4):669–686.

Courant, R., Friedrichs, K., and Lewy, H. (1967). On the partial difference equations of mathematical physics (reprint of original 1928 Mathematische Annalen article in German). *IBM J. Res. Dev.*, 11(2):215–234.

cplusplus.com (2014). Standard library—miscellaneous headers. Available at http://www.cplusplus.com/reference/std/, accessed August 2014.

Desbrun, M. and Gascuel, M.-P. (1996). Smoothed particles: A new paradigm for animating highly deformable bodies. In Boulic, R. and Hégron, G., editors, *Computer Animation and Simulation '96*, Eurographics, pages 61–76. Springer, Vienna.

Eberly, D. (2003). Polyhedral mass properties (revisited). Available at www.geometrictools.com/Documentation/PolyhedralMassProperties.pdf.

Eberly, D. (2015). Geometric tools. Available at http://www.geometrictools.com, accessed July 2015.

Featherstone, R. (1983). The calculation of robot dynamics using articulated-body inertias. *Int. J. Robot. Res.*, 2(1):13–30.

Fedkiw, R., Stam, J., and Jensen, H. W. (2001). Visual simulation of smoke. In *Proceedings of the 28th Annual Conference on Computer Graphics and Interactive Techniques*, SIGGRAPH '01, pages 15–22, ACM, New York.

FIBA Central Board (2014). *2014 Official Basketball Rules: Basketball Rules & Basketball Equipment*. FIBA—International Basketball Federation, Switzerland.

Foster, N. and Fedkiw, R. (2001). Practical animation of liquids. In *Proceedings of the 28th Annual Conference on Computer Graphics and Interactive Techniques*, SIGGRAPH '01, pages 23–30, ACM, New York.

Foster, N. and Metaxas, D. (1996). Realistic animation of liquids. *Graph. Model. Im. Proc.*, 58(5):471–483.

Goldenthal, R., Harmon, D., Fattal, R., Bercovier, M., and Grinspun, E. (2007). Efficient simulation of inextensible cloth. *ACM Trans. Graph.*, 26(3), Article No. 49.

Goodman, J. E. and O'Rourke, J. (2004). *The Handbook of Discrete and Computational Geometry*, second edition. Chapman & Hall/CRC, Boca Raton, FL.

Guendelman, E., Bridson, R., and Fedkiw, R. (2003). Nonconvex rigid bodies with stacking. *ACM Trans. Graph.*, 22(3):871–878.

Harper, D. (2016). Online etymology dictionary. Available at http://www.dictionary.com/browse/animation, accessed March 18, 2016.

Hart, J. C. (1993). Ray tracing implicit surfaces. In *Siggraph 93 Course Notes: Modeling, Visualizing, and Animating Implicit Surfaces, Course 25*, pages 1–16. ACM, New York.

Haumann, D. and Parent, R. (1988). The behavioral testbed: Obtaining complex behavior from simple rules. *Visual Comput.*, 4:332–347.

Hinckley, M. E. (1998). Toon physics and the automation of computer animation. M.S. Thesis, Texas A&M University, College Station, TX.

House, D., DeVaul, R., and Breen, D. (1996). Towards simulating cloth dynamics using interacting particles. *Int. J. Cloth. Sci. Tech.*, 8(3):75–94.

Inria (2015). Eigen. Available at http://eigen.tuxfamily.org, accessed June 2015.

ITF Technical Centre (2014). *ITF Approved Tennis Balls, Classified Surfaces & Recognised Courts 2014—A guide to products and test methods.* International Tennis Federation, London.

Kagan, D. and Atkinson, D. (2004). The coefficient of restiution of baseballs as a function of relative humidity. *Phys. Teach.*, 42:89–92.

Kawabata, S. (1980). *The Standardization and Analysis of Hand Evaluation.* The Textile Machinery Society of Japan, Osaka.

Kokkevis, V. (2004). Practical physics for articulated characters. In *Game Developers Conference*, San Jose. Available at http://www.gdcvault.com/free/gdc-04#page-3.

Lin, M. C. and Canny, J. F. (1991). A fast algorithm for incremental distance calculation. In *Robotics and Automation, 1991. Proceedings of the 1991 IEEE International Conference on*, pages 1008–1014. IEEE.

Lorensen, W. E. and Cline, H. E. (1987). Marching cubes: A high resolution 3d surface construction algorithm. In *Proceedings of the 14th Annual Conference on Computer Graphics and Interactive Techniques*, SIGGRAPH '87, pages 163–169, ACM, New York.

Mirtich, B. (1996a). Fast and accurate computation of polyhedral mass properties. *J. Graph. Tools*, 1(2):31–50.

Mirtich, B. (1996b). *Impulse-Based Dynamic Simulation of Rigid Body Systems.* PhD thesis, University of California, Berkeley.

Monaghan, J. J. (1992). Smoothed particle hydrodynamics. *Annu. Rev. Astron. Astrophys.*, 30:543–574.

Müller, M. (2008). Hierarchical position based dynamics. In Faure, F. and Teschner, M., editors, *Workshop in Virtual Reality Interactions and Physical Simulation (VRIPHYS 2008)*. The Eurographics Association, Geneva.

Müller, M., Charypar, D., and Gross, M. (2003). Particle-based fluid simulation for interactive applications. In *Proceedings of the 2003 ACM SIGGRAPH/Eurographics Symposium on Computer Animation*, SCA '03, pages 154–159, Eurographics Association, Aire-la-Ville, Switzerland.

Murray, R., Li, Z., and Sastry, S. (1994). *A Mathematical Introduction to Robotic Manipulation.* CRC Press, Boca Raton, FL.

Ozgen, O. and Kallmann, M. (2011). Directional constraint enforcement for fast cloth simulation. In *Proceedings of The Fourth International Conference on Motion in Games (MIG), 2011*, pages 424–435. Springer, Berlin, Heidelberg.

Pabst, S., Krzywinski, S., Schenk, A., and Thomaszewski, B. (2008). Seams and bending in cloth simulation. In *Workshop in Virtual Reality Interactions and Physical Simulation, VRIPHYS 2008*, Geneva.

Press, W. H., Teukolsky, S. A., Vetterling, W. T., and Flannery, B. P. (2007). *Numerical Recipes: The Art of Scientific Computing*, third edition. Cambridge University Press, Cambridge, UK.

Provot, X. (1995). Deformation constraints in a mass-spring model to describe rigid cloth behavior. In *Proc. of Graphics Interface '95*, pages 147–155.

Reeves, W. T. (1983). Particle systems—A technique for modeling a class of fuzzy objects. *ACM Trans. Graph.*, 2(2):91–108.

Research Equipment (London) Limited (2015). Viscometers and viscosity solutions. Available at www.research-equipment.com/research-equipment.html, follow Viscosity Chart link, accessed May 2015.

Reynolds, C. (1987). Flocks, herds, and schools: A distributed behavioral model. *Comput. Graph. Proc. SIGGRAPH 87*, 21(4):25–34.

Ritter, J. (1990). An efficient bounding sphere. In Glassner, A., editor, *Graphics Gems I*, pages 301–303. Academic Press, New York.

Sederberg, T. and Parry, S. (1986). Free-form deformation of solid geometric models. *Comput. Graph. Proc. SIGGRAPH 86*, 20(4):151–160.

Sims, K. (1990). Particle animation and rendering using data parallel computation. *Comput. Graph. Proc. SIGGRAPH 90*, 24(4):405–413.

Solenthaler, B. and Pajarola, R. (2009). Predictive-corrective incompressible sph. *ACM Trans. Graph.*, 28(3):40:1–40:6.

Stam, J. (1999). Stable fluids. In *Proceedings of the 26th Annual Conference on Computer Graphics and Interactive Techniques*, SIGGRAPH '99, pages 121–128, ACM Press/Addison-Wesley, New York.

Stam, J. and Fiume, E. (1995). Depicting fire and other gaseous phenomena using diffusion processes. In *Proceedings of the 22Nd Annual Conference on Computer Graphics and Interactive Techniques*, SIGGRAPH '95, pages 129–136, ACM, New York.

Strang, G. (2009). *Introduction to Linear Algebra*, fourth edition. Wellesley-Cambridge Press, Wellesley, MA.

The Engineering Toolbox (2016). Friction and coefficients of friction. Available at http://www.engineeringtoolbox.com, accessed February 2016.

Watt, A. and Watt, M. (1992). *Advanced Animation and Rendering Techniques: Theory and Practice*. Addison-Wesley, Boston.

Wedge, C. (1987). Balloon guy. Available at https://www.youtube.com/watch?v=InC92AfGAk4, accessed July 2015.

Wejchert, J. and Haumann, D. (1991). Animation aerodynamics. *Comput. Graph. Proc. SIGGRAPH 91*, 25(4):19–22.

Witkin, A. and Baraff, D. (2001). Physically based modeling: Principles and practice. *SIGGRAPH 2001 Course Notes*, page 28.

Yu, J. and Turk, G. (2013). Reconstructing surfaces of particle-based fluids using anisotropic kernels. *ACM Trans. Graph.*, 32(1):5:1–5:12.

Zhu, Y. and Bridson, R. (2005). Animating sand as a fluid. *ACM Trans. Graph.*, 24(3):965–972.

Zwicker, M., Pfister, H., van Baar, J., and Gross, M. (2001). Surface splatting. In *Proceedings of the 28th Annual Conference on Computer Graphics and Interactive Techniques*, SIGGRAPH '01, pages 371–378, ACM, New York.

Index

9780367658205